Current Progress in Multimedia

Volume II

Current Progress in Multimedia Volume II

Edited by **Alicia Witte**

CLANRYE
INTERNATIONAL

New Jersey

Published by Clanrye International,
55 Van Reypen Street,
Jersey City, NJ 07306, USA
www.clanryeinternational.com

Current Progress in Multimedia: Volume II
Edited by Alicia Witte

International Standard Book Number: 978-1-63240-129-8 (Hardback)

Printed in the United States of America.

Contents

Preface

Multimedia refers to content that uses a combination of different content forms. It is concerned with the electronically controlled integration of graphics, text, drawings, video, animation, audio, and any other media where every type of information can be represented, stored, transmitted and processed digitally. This is in contrast with media that use only basic computer displays such as traditional forms of printed or hand-produced material. Multimedia combines a huge plethora of media forms that deal with interactivity like text, audio, still images, animation and video, as previously said. Multimedia as a field can be broadly divided into two categories- linear and non-linear. Linear active content is multimedia that usually advances mostly without any directional control for the viewer such as a cinema presentation. On the other hand non-linear multimedia uses interaction to monitor progress as with a self-paced computer based training or video game. Hypermedia is another example of non-linear content. Multimedia can be usually recorded and played, displayed, or accessed by information content processing devices, such as computerized and electronic devices, but can also be part of a live performance. Such a multiplicity of interactions and avenues for advancements that better our lives makes the field of multimedia crucial to human development.

I am grateful to those who put their hard work, effort and expertise into these research projects as well as those who were supportive in this endeavour.

Editor

Real-Time QoS-Aware Video Streaming: A Comparative and Experimental Study

Basem Al-Madani, Anas Al-Roubaiey, and Zubair A. Baig

Department of Computer Engineering, King Fahd University of Petroleum & Minerals, Eastern Province, Dhahran 31261, Saudi Arabia

Correspondence should be addressed to Anas Al-Roubaiey; roubaiey@kfupm.edu.sa

Academic Editor: Costas Kotropoulos

Due to its flexibility, scalability, real-time, and rich QoS features, Data Distribution Service (DDS) middleware provides seamless integration with high-performance, real-time, and mission-critical networks. Unlike traditional client-server communication models, DDS is based on the publish/subscribe communication model. DDS improves video streaming quality through its efficient and high-performance data delivery mechanism. This paper studies and investigates how DDS is suitable for streaming real-time full-motion video over a communication network. Experimental studies are conducted to compare video streaming using a the VLC player with the DDS overlay. Our results depict the superiority of DDS in provisioning quality video streams at the cost of low network bandwidth. The results also show that DDS is more scalable and flexible and is a promised technology for video distribution over IP networks where it uses much less bandwidth while maintaining high quality video stream delivery.

1. Introduction

Video streaming applications are experiencing fast growth and demand for diverse business needs. Applications of video streaming include, for example, commercial applications such as e-learning, video conferencing, stored-video streaming; and military applications such as video surveillance of targeted field or specific objects. Video traffic is resource intensive and consumes a lot of network bandwidth; therefore it is challenging issue to stream video over limited-bandwidth networks, for example, WSN or Bluetooth. In many cases, bandwidth usage implies direct cost on end-users. In this work, we try to enhance the end-user experience both in terms of quality and cost, through the deployment of the DDS middleware.

1.1. DDS Overview and Video QoS Polices. DDS stands for Data Distribution Service. It is a set of specifications standardized by the Object Management Group (OMG). The DDS middleware is a known standard with built-in data-structures and attributes specified by meta-information called topics. Every topic describes a set of associated data-samples with the same data-property and data-structure. For

example, a topic named "temperature" can be used to store samples of temperature monitored by a distributed set of sensors [1].

The entities that write and read the data-samples using a DDS-based middleware are the publishers and the subscribers. A publisher consists of a set of data writer modules, each of which is used to write information on a particular topic. On the other hand, a subscriber reads the data samples of topics by using its data reader modules. A topic is qualified by a wide set of Quality of Service (QoS) parameters that manage a number of aspects of the distribution of linked data-samples.

For instance, the "lifespan" QoS parameter computes the maximum time a data-sample can stay within the system from time of inception of writing. The "history" QoS specifies the maximum number of data-samples that can be stored in the middleware; if this maximum number is reached, then the newest data-sample substitutes the oldest one. When an application requires data-samples on a particular topic, it simply feeds the DDS interface with the name of the topic. The DDS middleware does the setup of the underlying networking resources for data delivery.

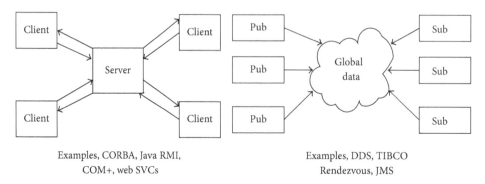

Examples, CORBA, Java RMI,   Examples, DDS, TIBCO
COM+, web SVCs   Rendezvous, JMS

FIGURE 1: Publish subscribe versus client server architecture.

This buffering function of History QoS is beneficial for video streaming where the late joining participants can still view previously delivered video. It is also worth mentioning that an application can determine a filtering-condition correlated to the content of data-samples, for example, temperature measurement less than 20 degrees. In this case, the DDS transfers only data-samples complying with the filtering condition. This filtering is very useful in many video transmission scenarios; for example, for safe web browsing, we may use content based filters to delete undesired frames. Another important QoS is the RELIABILITY QoS, which has two main values RELIABLE and BEST_EFFORT. For real-time applications such as video transmission, RELIABILITY QoS is set to BEST_EFFORT specially in case of real-time video streaming where retransmission significantly affects the video playback. DDS also supports reliable QoS for data sensitive applications such as FTP through the RELIABLE. In video streaming, presumably new values for the samples are generated often enough that it is not necessary to resend or acknowledge any samples [2].

There are two approaches for establishing communication between heterogeneous systems. The first one, *publish/subscribe*, is a messaging pattern where senders of messages, called publishers, do not program the messages to be sent directly to specific receivers, called subscribers. Instead, published messages are classified into several topics with unique identifications, without knowledge of what, if any, subscribers there are. Similarly, subscribers express interest in one or more classes (topics) and only receive messages that are of interest, without knowledge of what, if any, publishers there are; see Figure 1. Due to its loosely coupled property, *publish/subscribe* architecture is more flexible and scalable for distributed systems; in our work, this architecture is represented by DDS standard.

The second approach is the traditional *client/server* pattern, which is a tightly coupled pattern where the programmer here should specify the clients and servers addresses and they have to work at the same time. That makes it less scalable than publish/subscribe pattern. In brief, Corsro [3] summarizes the advantages of publish/subscribe over client/server architecture as publish/subscribe is plug and play, loosely coupled, fault resilient, and inherently many-to-many architecture, whereas client/server architecture is complex in development, tight coupling, fragile to fault, and

inherently one-to-one architecture. The client-server pattern is represented in this paper using VLC player.

1.2. Contributions. The main contribution of this paper is to examine the behavior of real-time video streaming over both publish subscribe and client server architectures using the DDS middleware and the VLC player. To the best of our knowledge, this is the first attempt to examine and contrast these scenarios where we concentrate on examining the total bandwidth consumed and video quality of video traffic by evaluating network throughput, packet loss, and jitter with different network load, number of subscribers. Furthermore we demonstrate the most important quality of service performance parameters of DDS and describe how these can be configured to improve video transmission quality over networks.

Our results prove that DDS is very much applicable and a promising technology for video streaming. Its key features such as platform independent, reliability, and scalability help it significantly improve the quality of stored video streaming over heterogeneous platforms. In addition, we also discuss the utilization of DDS QoS to maximize application performance.

1.3. Paper Organization. The paper is organized as follows. Section 2 presents the literature review. Section 3 gives a background on DDS QoS and VLC and describes how DDS QoS can be used to improve networked video streaming. In Section 4, we demonstrate the experimental work and conduct a results analysis. Finally, conclusions and future work are discussed in Section 5.

2. Literature Review

In this section, we summarize the previous work in the literature for enhancing video streaming over wireless networks.

Detti et al. [1] evaluated and demonstrated a technique for streaming H.264 SVC video over a DDS middleware. The structure of the DDS data unit designed by them was able to carry H.264 SVC [4] video-units. Also they designed a receiver-driven rate-control mechanism based on the DDS data unit, which exploited specific DDS functionality. Finally, they implemented and showed the effectiveness of their mechanism in an 802.11 wireless scenario, comparing their proposal with other solutions.

Clavijo et al. proposed that a CORBA middleware implementation can be used to offer real-time video streaming [5]. Furthermore, in [6], Kaff et al. introduced a CORBA based platform to respond to changing resource requirements in video applications using video streaming service. CORBA is a very complete technology that introduces a big number of interfaces for almost any type of required middleware functionality; however, it is a complex architecture that introduces implementation overheads, particularly when compared with other lighter weight technologies such as ICE (Internet Communications Engine) [7], DDS (Data Distribution Service for real-time systems) [2], or some specific real-time Java based solutions [8]. Therefore, existing approaches can be improved to facilitate real-time video transmission with guaranteed QoS. In addition, using new standard middleware introduces flexibility for video transmission in two ways. First, compared to direct implementation over the network level, the utilization of a middleware is already more flexible. Second, utilizing middleware solutions provides QoS management to appropriately initiate real-time and QoS-aware support for video transmission.

Vora and Brown [9] studied DDS deployment for the newer 802.11n standard. Their performance metrics were throughput, delay, and jitter when video streaming is brought in a network carrying merely data traffic. They also studied the approximate number of users streaming high rate videos that can be supported over various network configurations. In [10], the authors analyzed and evaluated the performance of H.264-based video streaming over multihop wireless local area networks (WLANs). Guidance was provided on how to achieve the optimal balance for a given scenario, which is important when deploying end-to-end video streaming services with quality of service guarantees. For WLANs, we have conducted a previous study to examine DDS over WLANs [11], but the video that we used was very low motion video and the codec bit-rate was 128 kbps which is much less than what is used in this paper. That adjustment was done to meet the limited WLAN bandwidth; the results showed that consumed bandwidth was nearly twice less than that in the proposed work.

Chen and Zakhor proposed several TFRC connections as an end-to-end rate control solution for wireless video streaming. They showed that this approach not only avoids modifications to the network infrastructure or network protocols, but also results in full utilization of the wireless channel [12]. Stockhammer et al. proposed that the separation between a delay jitter buffer and a decoder buffer is in general suboptimal for video transmitted over VBR channels [13]. They specified the minimum initial delay and the minimum required buffer for a given video stream and a deterministic VBR channel.

In [14], Nasser proposes QoS adaptive multimedia service models for controlling the traffic in multimedia wireless networks (MWN) for cellular networks. The suggested framework is designed to take advantage of the adaptive bandwidth allocation (ABA) algorithm with new calls in order to improve the system usage and blocking probability

of new calls. Simulation results showed that the QoS adaptive multimedia service framework outperforms the existing framework in terms of new call blocking probability, handoff call dropping probability, and bandwidth utilization.

Li and Pan [15], through their study in a WDS-based multihop wireless environment, found out that it is likely for multihop wireless networks to increase coverage and sustain improved video streaming performance at the same time. When they analyzed the throughput of IEEE 802.11 multihop wireless networks, they proposed a complete two-dimensional Markov-chain model in their paper. The model considered the retry bound and post-back off step into account to better capture the performance of IEEE 802.11 MAC protocols in a non-ideal channel and with non-persistent traffic. The throughput analysis is validated by network simulation with extended lower and upper-layer simulation modules. The achievable throughput gives an upper bound of the video streaming performance, which is further validated by our H.264-based video streaming simulation with application-layer performance metrics (provided in subsequent sections). The results correspond to the observation they had on the multihop test bed. Another study [16] highlights that since the advent of ad hoc networks, it has been viewed as a potential multiapplication technology. This paper presents a comparative study of multicasting of video and video-like data using two different ad hoc routing protocols, namely, OLSR and PUMA. Their NS2 simulations show that OLSR produces higher throughput and lower latency.

A cross-layer solution for video streaming QoS support has been proposed recently in [17]. This work focused on low bandwidth networks. The authors evaluated the feasibility of transmitting streaming video flows by using the Contention Free Period (CFP), considering the necessary coordination between the CFP period of the IEEE 802.15.4 MAC standard and the real features of the wireless medium as well as the limitations of the sensor electronics and their power-consumption. This coordination is performed through two steps. (1) The first one is the generation of safety time gaps in the MAC frame. These gaps are created for ensuring that delayed frames arrive at the sink on time and avoiding collisions with other frames; (2) The second one is the design of a distributed protocol, developed at the application layer, that allows to measure and calculate several metrics (QoS parameters) such as frames or images delay, video throughput, and the subjective impression perceived by the users when they receive the video sequence. The subjective perception is measured by the Peak Signal-to-Noise Ratio (PSNR) and Mean Opinion Score (MOS) values. From the analysis of these metrics, the proposed protocol controls the optimum MAC gap sizes, the available video transmission rate, and the minimum power consumption of the WPAN network nodes. This protocol is denoted as Cross-Layer Multimedia Guaranteed Time Slot (CL-MGTS), since it uses application-level QoS parameters to tune the MAC and physical layers. However, their solution is tightly coupled to the IEEE 802.15.4 MAC layer protocol which makes it importable; DDS has a resource management QoS that could be used to control such types of networks.

One of the latest proposals on enhancing QoS support for video transmission is by Huang et al. [18]. They improved the quality of video transmission by proposing a multipath technique that extends the Datagram Congestion Control Protocol (DCCP), which is an unreliable transport layer protocol with a congestion control mechanism used for multimedia streaming. In order to use multiple network interfaces to transmit streaming data smoothly, a Multi-Path Datagram Congestion Control Protocol (MP-DCCP) is proposed and presented in this work. Video streaming transmission through multipath faces three problems: (1) out-of-ordering packets at the receiver side, (2) conditions of paths that are changed anytime, and (3) the importance of frames/packets that is different. The first problem may let video streaming data be delivered to the application layer too late, especially for the live streaming data. The second and third problems may let a packet be scheduled to an unsuitable path for transmission. Since the importance of video streaming frames/packets is different, it should consider how to schedule the transmission of frames/packets properly. For example, an important frame/packet should be transmitted through the more reliable path. In order to resolve these three problems, a QoS-aware Order Prediction Scheduling (QOPS) scheme for MP-DCCP is also proposed. QOPS estimates packets' arrival orders at the receiver side through these multiple paths before packets are scheduled into the transmission at the sender side. From simulation results, the authors show that the out-of-ordering problem of packets in MPDCCP can be countered using the proposed QOPS scheme.

Another recently proposed technique to improve video transmission quality using tightly coupled solutions is found in [19]. The authors proposed a new multirate H.264 scalable video multicast in lossy networks using network coding. They first prioritize video layers based on its effect on the end-to-end video quality. Each video layer is routed via the path obtained from the optimization framework under the constraints on QoS guarantees. Different destinations may receive different number of video layers that depended on their max flows. The bottleneck in the network is resolved by using network coding to ensure that all destinations receive the rate equaling their max flows. The network coding is only applied within the same layer. Simulation and numerical results under randomly generated networks show the advantage of the proposed scheme in terms of objective and subject qualities of the end-to-end video.

Although most of the previous research focused on the video streaming QoS in terms of delay, throughput, and quality, DDS in addition to taking delay and performance in consideration because it is originally for real-time distributed systems also adds more QoS mechanisms that were not existent in previous approaches, such as content-based filter, time-based filter, and resource management; see Section 3. Furthermore, allowing each participant to tune his QoS parameters independently adds significant improvement to the application and makes it more flexible and portable. Subsequent sections of this paper focus on merging these capabilities and how they affect the video streaming performance.

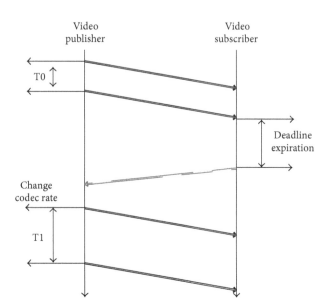

FIGURE 2: Deadline QoS and congestion control.

3. QoS Architecture of Video Streaming

In this section we review and discuss the QoS of DDS that can be adapted to improve video streaming and reduce the effect of network congestion. Also, we provided an analysis on the use of DDS with the VLC video streaming application.

3.1. DDS QoS Polices for Video Streaming Support. Many QoS policies are used by DDS middleware to support smooth video transmission over networks and also to minimize the required bandwidth, this is very important for many companies and institutions that have to pay for bandwidth usage. A proof of concept study from Granada University [20] is performed to proof the suitability of video streaming over DDS; they stated some of the QoS policies that affect video streaming. In this section, we investigate these polices and show how they can be used to support video streaming applications.

  (i) *Deadline and congestion control*, network congestion occurs when a link or node is overloaded and as a consequence it results in packet loss, increased delays, and at times blocking of connections. A lot of research has been done for mitigating network congestion. In the middleware layer, a deadline QoS policy can be used for congestion detection and control, as illustrated in Figure 2. If the subscriber waiting time for the next packet exceeds a certain predefined deadline, it sends a notification to the publisher who will start minimizing the codec rate to avoid congestion on the subsequent streams. When the congestion is overcome, the previous status is recovered.

 (ii) *Time-Based Filtering* is the minimum separation time between two successive packets received at the subscriber side. This QoS policy used in video applications is to reduce application load (receiving rate) at

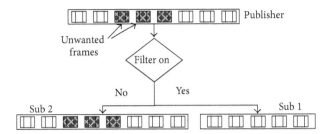

FIGURE 3: Content-filtered topic.

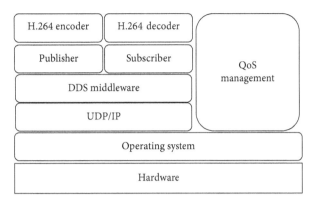

FIGURE 4: Architecture of video streaming over DDS.

the subscriber side. For instance, suppose that the publisher is a server and subscribers are different devices that have different capabilities, for example, laptop, PDA, cell phones, or even sensors in WSNs, each one of them has to adapt the receiving rate based on its available resources using such policy. Note that because the deadline is the maximum wait time for data update on the subscriber side, the time-based filter value must be less than the deadline value.

(iii) *Lifespan* avoids delivering stale data, where each packet has its expiration date that will be examined on the subscriber side before playing it back. In video transmission, it can be used to drop the stale received packets because video application is only interested in data with short delays; this QoS is very useful on live video streaming to keep a consistent playback.

(iv) *Best Effort and Presentation* are related to each other; the presentation QoS is used to assert that subscribers will receive data in the order in which it was sent by the publisher, where video samples should be retrieved in the same order. In the best effort QoS, the video frames are delivered with minimum delay; thus it is useful in real-time video transmission where time is more sensitive than packet loss; this QoS policy uses the presentation QoS to assert ordered packet delivery.

(v) *Content-Filtered Topic* is a very useful feature if you want to filter data received by the subscriber. It also helps to control network and CPU usage on the subscriber's side because only data that is of interest to the subscriber is sent. In video transmission, this feature can be used to filter the received video such that each subscriber will just receive only relevant data. Figure 3 depicts the behavior of this QoS policy.

3.2. H.264 in DDS. In order to keep this paper self-contained, we describe briefly the H.264/AVC video compression codec used by DDS. For more detailed information about H.264/AVC, the reader is referred to the standard [21] or corresponding overview papers [22–25].

For video coding, DDS video streaming tool has been integrated with the H.264/AVC (advanced video coding) standard [21]. H.264/AVC is the latest video coding standard of the ITU-T Video Coding Experts Group and the ISO/IEC Moving Picture Experts Group. The main goals of

the H.264/AVC standardization effort have been enhanced compression performance and provision of a "network-friendly" video representation addressing "conversational" (video telephony) and "nonconversational" (storage, broadcast, or streaming) applications. H.264/AVC has achieved a significant improvement in rate distortion efficiency relative to existing standards. However, one of the open research issues is to improve this tool by using H.264/SVC (Scalable Video Coding) [4]. SVC enables the transmission and decoding of partial bit streams to provide video services with lower temporal or spatial resolutions or reduced fidelity while retaining a reconstruction quality that is high relative to the rate of the partial bit streams. Hence, SVC provides functionalities such as graceful degradation in lossy transmission environments as well as bit-rate, format, and power adaptation.

An H.264 stream is a sequence of NALUs (network adaptive layer units). A NALU is formed by a header and a payload carrying the actual encoded video frame. The NALU header contains information about the NALU type and its relevance in the decoding process. From the information reported in the NALU header, we are specifically interested in the three parameters called dependency id (DID), temporal id (TID), and quality id (QID). Each parameter determines a specific scalability facility. DID allows coarse grain scalability, TID allows Temporal Scalability and QID allows Medium Grain Scalability.

The NALUs are represented by DDS using NALU-topic which used to deliver NALUs containing video frames. The structure of the data-sample of the NALU-Topic contains: a H.264 NALU, the ssid and a marker-bit. Both ssid and marker-bit are used for rate-control purpose [1]. The video-publisher is the sender of the video: it executes the software logic interacting with the DDS facility and hosts the data writers. The video-publisher is fed by H.264 NALUs coming from the encoder and, by parsing entering NALUs, builds data-samples and sends them to data writers (DWs). Figure 4 shows the architecture that we have used in this work. The video-subscriber is the module used to receive the video, executes the software logic interacting with the DDS facility, and hosts the Data Readers (DRs).

3.3. VideoLAN VLC Media Player. VLC stands for Video LAN Client, but since VLC is no longer a simple client, this abbreviation is not applicable. VLC is a highly portable free and open source media player and streaming media server written by the VideoLAN project [26]. Video streaming on VLC is based on the client server architecture and thus is an ideal streamed player for our evaluation. VideoLAN is a group of people, who produce and distribute free and open source software for video and multimedia purposes, released under Open Source licenses. It started as a student project at the French École Centrale Paris but is now a worldwide project with developers from everywhere and dozens of millions of people using VideoLAN's software.

Taking these QoS parameters and architectures into consideration, the next section focuses on examining the performance and QoS effect of DDS on video streaming and compares it with the VLC video player.

4. Experimental Work

In this section, we experimentally evaluated the performance of stored video streaming over LAN using both DDS middleware and VLC player.

4.1. Hardware and Software Specifications. The experiment was carried using hardware and software tools; the measurement and monitoring tools and hardware platform specifications that were used are described in Tables 1 and 2, respectively.

4.2. Experimental Setup and Performance Metrics. As shown in Figure 5, the experiment test-bed was composed of three HP computers that are connected using speed-touch hub with 100 Mbps speed; those computers are provided with measurement and monitoring tools that are shown in Table 1. The two technologies, DDS and VLC, are examined by transmitting a full motion video clip of 72 seconds of length, 640×480 resolution, and 600 codec bit-rate at 25 fps for each, using H.264 decoder. This video clip was taken from the RTI DDS video streaming tool that we used in our experimental evaluation, for vehicle traffic that shows high motion of cars, making the comparison more accurate.

The QoS parameters are adjusted to meet the existing network link specification; for example, the deadline is adjusted to infinite, lifespan is also infinite, and reliability is the best effort. These parameters are suitable for dedicated and fast networks such as Ethernet LAN because they are congestion free, fast, and reliable. One computer represents a publisher and the others represent the subscribers. In our experiment, we examined the network with different numbers of subscribers (3, 6, 9, 12, 15); however, the effect was not clear in the visual frames; therefore, we used the background traffic (generated by Jperf) to make the comparison of DDS and VLC more visible. Since it was very difficult to examine the technology scalability by increasing number of subscribers or clients, we used Jperf to generate background traffic to make our experiments more realistic. The background traffic was 75% of the available bandwidth which is nearly 98 Mbps

TABLE 1: Tools and programs.

Tool	Version	Purpose
VLC player	1.0.6	Video streaming
RTI DDS	4.5	Video streaming
Wire-shark	1.2.7	Measure BW, PKT loss, Jitter
Jperf	2.0.2	Generate background traffic
RTI Analyzer	4.5	QoS monitoring and network debugging

(measured by wire-shark). This percentage of background traffic is specified after performing intensive experiments until we observed the effect of traffic on the video quality.

The consumed bandwidth is a very important metric for performance evaluation because consumers have to pay for used bandwidth; also reducing the used bandwidth increases the network performance in terms of delay, jitter, and packet loss. Thus, our performance metrics concentrate onbandwidth and in addition we also study packet loss, and jitter (Packet Delay Variation). Besides these objective measurements, we added a subjective measurement [27] which makes it easier for human eye evaluation of screen shoots during simulations.

4.3. Results and Analysis. The results were collected after repeating the experiments several times and then averaging out. Figure 6 shows the effect of background traffic on video traffic from both DDS and VLC. The frames have been taken during playback at the subscriber side in three cases, with 3, 9, and 15 subscribers. And for those cases where there was some distortion in the frames, we selected those frames where the damage was visible. We start examining the effect of background traffic from 25% and 50%, but no effect was visible, then we adjusted it to 75% and then the effect began to appear from the case with 9 subscribers in VLC and from the case with 15 subscribers in the DDS setup. In general, the figure shows that DDS outperforms VLC, where in the case of 15 clients in VLC, the system was unstable and the picture was very choppy, whereas in DDS, the picture started behaving intermittently for case of 15 subscribers, and it was quite choppy. This indicates the effectiveness and scalability of DDS video streaming over VLC.

In Figure 7, the consumed bandwidth is considered as the comparison performance metric, measured without adding the background traffic. From this figure, you can see that the consumed bandwidth is almost the same for the same technology both with background traffic and without it since the video traffic is the same in both cases. The slight increase in VLC is due to the increase of control packets to mitigate the overloaded network. Intuitively larger number of subscribers lead to more bandwidth consumption; but it is clear that VLC increases its rate at a higher rate than DDS where the slope of the line is less and more stable (linear). The figure shows that DDS clearly consumes much less bandwidth than VLC and moreover the difference is even more evident with increasing number of subscribers, where it was nearly 2 Mbps in case of 3 subscribers and it reaches about 5 Mbps in case of

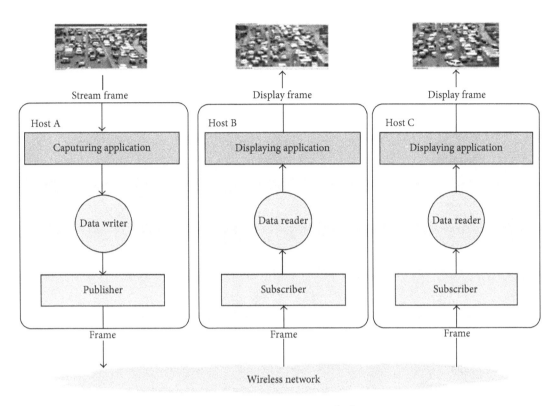

FIGURE 5: Experiment test-bed.

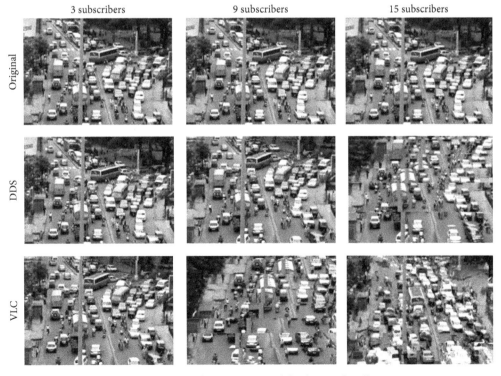

FIGURE 6: Visual comparison with background traffic.

TABLE 2: Platform specifications.

	Publisher	Subscriber A	Subscriber B
CPU	Intel(R) Core(TM) i5 2.40 GHZ	Intel Core (TM) i5 2.40 GHZ	Intel(R) Core(TM) i5 2.40 GHZ
Memory	1.8 GiB	1.8 GiB	1.8 GiB
OS	Ubuntu (lucid) Release 10.04 LTS Kernel Linux 2.6.32-37-generic GNOME 2.30.2	Ubuntu (lucid) Release 10.04 LTS Kernel Linux 2.6.32-37-generic GNOME 2.30.2	Ubuntu (lucid) Release 10.04 LTS Kernel Linux 2.6.32-37-generic GNOME 2.30.2
Network connection	Ethernet 100 Mbps	Ethernet 100 Mbps	Ethernet 100 Mbps

TABLE 3: BW consumption by video streams using DDS and VLC.

No. of sub.	Without BG traffic		With BG traffic	
	DDS	VLC	DDS	VLC
3	1.5%	2.8%	1.4%	2.6%
6	3%	4.4%	2.7%	4.6%
9	4.4%	7%	4.1%	7.2%
12	5.6%	10.8%	5.4%	10.7%
15	7.1%	11.5%	6.1%	12%

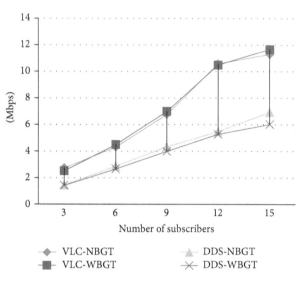

FIGURE 7: Consumed bandwidth with and without background traffic.

15 subscribers. Table 3 shows exactly how much bandwidth percentage is consumed for both technologies.

In contrast to Figure 7, Figure 8 illustrates that VLC and DDS had similar number of dropped packets both with and without background traffic. This is because the packet dropping of DDS in case of no background traffic is very different than when background traffic is present, whereas, for bandwidth, the background traffic has a significant effect. In case of no background traffic, both mechanisms had acceptable performance. As can be seen in the figure, the worst case result was with 15 subscribers and 5000 VLC packets, which represent less than 3% of the total packets sent, thus nullifying the effect of background traffic. The packet loss effect was clear on the other cases with background traffic, where it was very visible especially in case of VLC that the frames were very choppy and even the color was variable, with high failure of certain clients during the video streaming process.

Figure 9 shows the jitter, that is, packet delay variation, both with and without background traffic for DDS and VLC. It is clear that DDS outperforms VLC, where the difference is about 40 ms. The stream is mostly affected by the packet loss factor, because jitter is unaffected by this loss, whereas, for delays greater than 100 ms, the jitter effect is more visible.

In Figure 10, we examine the content-based filter QoS; we use a scenario of tracking an object location by the publisher and sending the coordinates to the subscribers who show interest in a specific region. Each subscriber can specify in his contract a subarea of interest to avoid bothering itself with irrelevant data. As can be seen from the figure, the filter size of the y axis ranges from 25 to 100%. The filter size illustrates the area percentage covered by a given publisher. As the filter size narrows, the throughput at the subscriber's side decreases nonlinearly (because of the object movement

randomization). Therefore, the figure shows that in case of 25%, the throughput almost halves as in case of 100%. Likewise, time-based filter QoS can also be used to control the receiving rate of the published data, for example, to avoid overwhelming the limited resource devices at the subscriber side.

Figure 11 also examines two main QoS parameters used in DDS, both being presented at the transport layer by TCP and UDP protocols. However, because DDS uses UDP in the transport layer, it supports reliable transmission by adding reliable and best effort QoS to the application layer (middleware layer). Reliable and best effort QoS are examined using data readings (nonheavy traffic) in Figure 11. The consumed bandwidth appears to be quite low with respect to video traffic. As can be seen from the figure, the reliable scenario uses more bandwidth as the number of subscribers increase. Similar to TCP, DDS also uses acknowledgment packets to assure reliability over UDP; intuitively, these extra packets increase as number of subscribers increase.

In Figure 12, we compare the data readings traffic and video camera traffic. The video camera traffic is derived indoors, and thus very low traffic (surveillance with almost no movement) is observed. Thereby, we examine the DDS middleware with three types of traffic; data readings, low

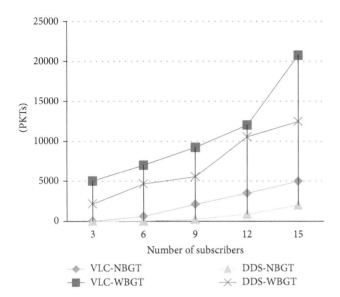

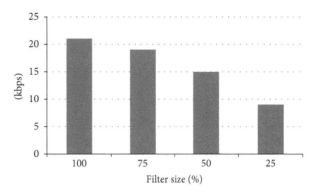

FIGURE 10: Impact of filter size in content-based filter QoS on DDS middleware traffic.

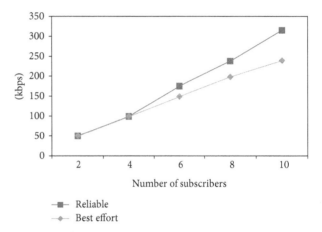

FIGURE 8: Dropped packets with and without background traffic.

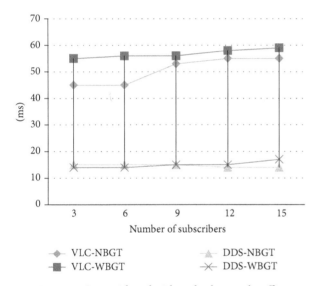

FIGURE 11: Reliable and best effort QoSs comparison in terms of consumed bandwidth.

FIGURE 9: Jitter with and without background traffic.

traffic video surveillance, and high traffic video streaming. In video camera traffic, the throughput reaches almost 1.8 Mbps in case of 10 subscribers which makes it suitable as a low price choice for video surveillance applications. Moreover, Figure 13 illustrates the impact of interference on DDS performance (in WLAN); it shows that the consumed bandwidth increases due to control packets used for mitigating packet dropping and congestions; reaching 4 Mbps in case of 10 subscribers.

5. Conclusions and Future Work

This paper introduced a performance evaluation for video transmission over LAN using Data Distributed Service (DDS). To the best of our knowledge, this is the first study examining the real effect of video distribution using DDS on

the network bandwidth and jitter, while comparing it with VLC video streaming player. From our results we conclude that this technology is a promising technology for distributing video over networks, since it consumes low bandwidth, has low jitter, and causes lesser packet loss. Furthermore, it gives more control on video streaming through the use of a rich set of QoS polices that are provided by the DDS middleware.

DDS is designed for large-scale distributed systems; however, in our experiments, we considered only 1 publisher and 15 subscribers, whereas, in real-life distributed applications, this number is quite small. This limitation was because of the lack of DDS simulators and limited number of machines that we used in our experiments. Also, the examination of DDS implementation over indoor dedicated WLAN makes the implementation easier because no mechanisms are built to adapt the video streaming to the time-varying bandwidth of the error-prone wireless channels. Thus, this implementation still lakes mechanisms that leverage the DDS QoS support for adaptively streaming the video frames according to the available time-varying network bandwidth. Practically, DDS-based solution, however, is still applicable because it is compared with VLC video streaming tool which is a practical and well-known player in current market.

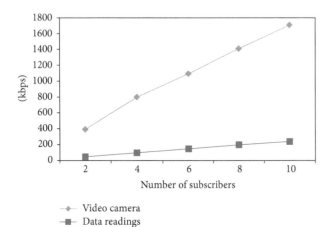

FIGURE 12: Video surveillance versus data readings traffic.

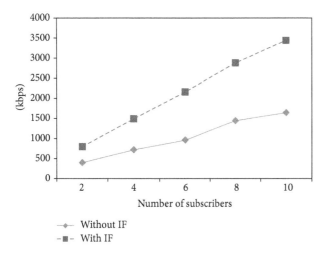

FIGURE 13: Impact of interference on video traffic over DDS.

As future work, we intend to do this study on more restricted networks such as Bluetooth personal area networks, and examine the QoS parameters to come up with the best configuration for specific conditions. The QoS parameters, also, can be used to solve perennial network problems such as network congestion. Furthermore, scalable video streaming over DDS QoS policies is to be proposed. This mechanism adaptively is supporting video streaming over time-varying bandwidth and error-prone networks.

Conflict of Interests

The authors declare that there is no conflict of interests regarding the publication of this paper.

Acknowledgments

The authors would like to acknowledge RTI Ltd. Also, they would like to thank King Fahd University of Petroleum & Minerals for their support for conducting this research work.

References

[1] A. Detti, P. Loreti, N. Blefari-Melazzi, and F. Fedi, "Streaming H.264 scalable video over data distribution service in a wireless environment," in *Proceedings of the IEEE International Symposium on A World of Wireless, Mobile and Multimedia Networks (WoWMoM '10)*, June 2010.

[2] OMG, "Data Distribution Service for Real-time systems," Object Management Group, 1. 2 formal/07-01-01 edition, January 2007.

[3] A. Corsro, *The OMG Data Distribution Service for Real-Time Systems*, Opensplice DDS, PrismTech, 2008.

[4] H. Schwarz, D. Marpe, and T. Wiegand, "Overview of the scalable video coding extension of the H.264/AVC standard," *IEEE Transactions on Circuits and Systems for Video Technology*, vol. 17, no. 9, pp. 1103–1120, 2007.

[5] J. A. Clavijo, M. J. Segarra, C. Baeza et al., "Real-time video for distributed control systems," *Control Engineering Practice*, vol. 9, no. 4, pp. 459–466, 2001.

[6] D. A. Kaff, C. Rodrigues, Y. Krishnamurthy, I. Pyarali, and D. C. Schmidt, "Application of the QuO quality-of-service framework to a distributed video application," in *Proceedings of the 3rd International Symposium on Distributed Objects and Applications (DOA '01)*, pp. 299–308, 2001.

[7] ZeroC, "Distributed Programming with ICE," Zero Company, version 3. 3. 1., March 2009.

[8] P. B. Val, M. García-Valls, and I. Estévez-Ayres, "Simple asynchronous remote invocations for distributed real-time java," *IEEE Transactions on Industrial Informatics*, vol. 5, no. 3, pp. 289–298, 2009.

[9] V. Vora and T. Brown, "High rate video streaming over 802. 11nin dense Wi-Fi environments," in *Proceedings of the 5th IEEE Workshop on Network Measurements (WNM '10)*, Denver, Colo, USA, 2010.

[10] D. Li and J. Pan, "Performance analysis and evaluation of H.264 video streaming over multi-hop wireless networks," in *Proceedings of the IEEE Global Telecommunications Conference (GLOBECOM '08)*, pp. 5003–5007, December 2008.

[11] B. Al-madani, A. Al-Roubaiey, and T. Al-shehari, "Wireless video streaming over data distribution service middleware," in *Proceedings of the IEEE 3rd International Conference on Software Engineering and Service Science (ICSESS '12)*, pp. 263–266, June 2012.

[12] M. Chen and A. Zakhor, "Rate control for streaming video over wireless," in *Proceedings of the 23th Annual Joint Conference of the IEEE Computer and Communications Societies (INFOCOM '04)*, pp. 1181–1190, March 2004.

[13] T. Stockhammer, H. Jenkač, and G. Kuhn, "Streaming video over variable bit-rate wireless channels," *IEEE Transactions on Multimedia*, vol. 6, no. 2, pp. 268–277, 2004.

[14] N. Nasser, "Service adaptability in multimedia wireless networks," *IEEE Transactions on Multimedia*, vol. 11, no. 4, pp. 786–792, 2009.

[15] D. Li and J. Pan, "Performance evaluation of video streaming over multi-hop wireless local area networks," *IEEE Transactions on Wireless Communications*, vol. 9, no. 1, pp. 338–347, 2010.

[16] P. Manjul, V. Balasubramanian, Y. Li, and J. Xu, "Real-time video streaming over multi-hop ad-hoc networks," in *Proceedings of the 2nd International Conference on Networking and Distributed Computing*, vol. 4, pp. 7695–4427, 2011.

[17] A.-J. Garcia-Sanchez, F. Garcia-Sanchez, J. Garcia-Haro, and F. Losilla, "A cross-layer solution for enabling real-time video

transmission over IEEE 802.15.4 networks," *Multimedia Tools and Applications*, vol. 51, no. 3, pp. 1069–1104, 2011.

[18] C.-M. Huang, Y.-C. Chen, and S.-Y. Lin, "The QoS-Aware Order Prediction Scheduling (QOPS) Scheme for Video Streaming Using the Multi-path Datagram Congestion Control Protocol (MP-DCCP)," in *Proceedings of the 15th International Conference on Network-Based Information Systems (NBiS '12)*, pp. 276–283, September 2012.

[19] S. Jina, S. Tarnoi, and W. Kumwilaisak, "QoS-aware multi-rate H. 264 scalable video multicast with network coding in lossy networks," in *Proceedings of the 9th International Conference on Electrical Engineering/Electronics, Computer, Telecommunications and Information Technology (ECTI-CON '12)*, pp. 1–4, May 2012.

[20] J. M. Lopez-Vega, J. Sanchez-Monedero, J. Povedano-Molina, and J. M. Lopez-Soler, "QoS policies for audio/video distribution over DDS middleware," in *Proceedings of the Real-time and Embedded Systems Workshop*, 2008.

[21] ITU-T and ISO/IEC JTC 1, "Advanced video coding for generic audiovisual services," *ITU-T Recommendation H. 264 and ISO/IEC, 14496-10 (MPEG-4 AVC)*, Version 8 (including SVC extension): Consented in July 2007.

[22] T. Wiegand, G. J. Sullivan, G. Bjøntegaard, and A. Luthra, "Overview of the H.264/AVC video coding standard," *IEEE Transactions on Circuits and Systems for Video Technology*, vol. 13, no. 7, pp. 560–576, 2003.

[23] G. J. Sullivan and T. Wiegand, "Video compression-from concepts to the H.264/AVC standard," *Proceedings of the IEEE*, vol. 93, no. 1, pp. 18–31, 2005.

[24] D. Marpe, T. Wiegand, and G. J. Sullivan, "The H.264/MPEG4 advanced video coding standard and its applications," *IEEE Communications Magazine*, vol. 44, no. 8, pp. 134–142, 2006.

[25] G. J. Sullivan, H. Yu, S.-I. Sekiguchi et al., "New standardized extensions of MPEG4-AVC/H.264 for professional-quality video applications," in *Proceedings of the 14th IEEE International Conference on Image Processing (ICIP '07)*, pp. I13–I16, San Antonio, Tex, USA, September 2007.

[26] J.-B. Kempf, VideoLAN project, http://www.videolan.org/.

[27] J.-S. Lee, F. De Simone, T. Ebrahimi, N. Ramzan, and E. Izquierdo, "Quality assessment of multidimensional video scalability," *IEEE Communications Magazine*, vol. 50, no. 4, pp. 38–46, 2012.

A New One-Dimensional Chaotic Map and Its Use in a Novel Real-Time Image Encryption Scheme

Radu Boriga,[1] **Ana Cristina Dăscălescu,**[1] **and Adrian-Viorel Diaconu**[2]

[1] *Faculty of Computer Science, Titu Maiorescu University, 040051 Bucharest, Romania*
[2] *IT & C Department, University of South-East Europe Lumina, 021187 Bucharest, Romania*

Correspondence should be addressed to Radu Boriga; radu.boriga@prof.utm.ro

Academic Editor: Stefanos Kollias

We present a new one-dimensional chaotic map, suitable for real-time image encryption. Its theoretical analysis, performed using some specific tools from the chaos theory, shows that the proposed map has a chaotic regime and proves its ergodicity, for a large space of values of the control parameter. In addition, to argue for the good cryptographic properties of the proposed map, we have tested the randomness of the values generated by its orbit using NIST statistical suite. Moreover, we present a new image encryption scheme with a classic bimodular architecture, in which the confusion and the diffusion are assured by means of two maps of the previously proposed type. The very good cryptographic performances of the proposed scheme are proved by an extensive analysis, which was performed regarding the latest methodology in this field.

1. Introduction

Image encryption schemes have been increasingly studied in order to ensure real-time secure images transmission through the Internet or through the communication networks. To meet this challenge, many new encryption schemes based on classical algorithms (e.g., Blowfish, AES, DES, etc.) have been proposed in the last years [1–5]. Starting from 1989, when Robert Matthews proposed the first chaos-based cryptosystem, in which he used the logistic map, chaotic maps have become a new direction to develop image encryption schemes which have, in many aspects, similar properties to the conventional ones [6–10]. Recently, many researchers have proposed different encryption schemes based on chaotic maps, being encouraged by the chaotic properties of dynamical systems such as high sensitivity to the initial conditions, ergodicity, and topological transitivity [11–17].

It is well known that a good encryption algorithm should be sensitive to the secret key, and the key space should be large enough to make brute-force attacks infeasible [18, 19]. In-based encryption schemes, the secret key space is defined by the control parameters and/or the initial conditions of the maps underling chaos. For some of the proposed chaos-based

encryption schemes it was proved that an incorrect selection of the initial condition or the use of chaotic maps which have a small range of the control parameters or an uneven values distribution leads to a weak security [19–25].

In this sense, we proposed in [26] a new chaotic map with large interval of parameters values for which the chaos is fulfilled, obtained by compounding a periodic real map with a bounded real map. Using specific mathematical and numerical tools from chaos theory and statistics, we proved that the proposed map has very good cryptographic properties. Then, the proposed map was used to design a new PRNG/PRBG model, based on a well-known binary operation [26]. In this paper, we have extended our work by studying not only theoretically but also only numerically the behavior of another map designed in the same manner. Thus, we used the topological conjugacy mechanism with logistic map, in order to study the behavior of the proposed map. Also, we have calculated the analytic form of Lyapunov exponent, which allows us to prove theoretically that the proposed map is chaotic for a large interval of parameters values. Moreover, the proposed chaotic map is used in a new real-time image encryption scheme, in which the confusion property is ensured by a new algorithm for generating random permutations, while the diffusion property is achieved using a new efficiently XOR-scheme.

The paper is organized as follows: in Section 2 we present the design of the newly proposed chaotic map, including its chaotic behavior assessment. Section 3 showcases the detailed and comprehensive randomness' testing process of sequences generated by the orbit of the new chaotic map. Section 4 presents a new image encryption scheme based on the map proposed in Section 2. Section 5 presents the performance analysis of the proposed image encryption scheme. Finally, Section 6 concludes the work carried out so far.

2. The Proposed Chaotic Map

In any encryption system, the basic issue is the selection process of the secret keys. According to the principle postulated by Menezes et al. [18], the security of the cryptosystem must depend only on the secret key. Even if an encryption algorithm is well designed, if the secret key is incorrectly chosen or the key space size is small, the security is endangered. Chaotic-based cryptosystems proposed so far have not defined a clear set of rules to be followed in the selection process of the secret key [27]. In many cases, the idea that the secret key is constituted by the control parameters and/or the initial condition of the map for which this is chaotic and ergodic was implicitly admitted. Most used maps in chaos-based encryption schemes proposed so far, respectively, the logistic map, tent map, and Hénon map, have small ranges of the parameters' values, for which the two requirements are achieved, that is, intervals (3.999, 4], (0.999, 1), and [1.1, 1.4]. Due to the discretization (i.e., implementation of the real numbers is realized with a finite precision in computers), the key space size of a cryptosystem based on chaotic map will actually collapse to a finite and a small set of numbers [6, 19, 24, 25, 28, 29].

The new chaotic map proposed in this paper uses (1) as model. Here, whilst g represents a periodic real map (selected so as to ensure a large phase space), h represents a bounded real map (which, by an appropriate selection, restricts the phase space to a closed interval in which the map has good chaotic properties):

$$x_{n+1} = h\left(g\left(x_n\right)\right). \tag{1}$$

Therefore, the proposed one-dimensional chaotic map, which is defined with respect to (1), is given by

$$x_{n+1} = f\left(x_n\right),$$

$$f : [-1, 1] \longrightarrow [-1, 1], \qquad f(x) = \frac{2}{\pi}\arcsin\left(\sin\left(\pi x\right)\right). \tag{2}$$

The behavior of a map can be easily studied using the mechanism of topological conjugacy with a map whose behavior is already known; thus it established an equivalent relationship between their dynamics [30, 31]. So, we have determined the topological conjugacy between the proposed

map f and the logistic map, whose properties are already well-known.

Proposition 1. *The* $f : [-1, 1] \longrightarrow [-1, 1]$ *map given by relation* (2) *and the logistic map g extended on the interval* $[-1, 1]$ *given by*

$$g : [-1, 1] \longrightarrow [-1, 1],$$

$$g(x) = \begin{cases} 4x(1+x), & x \in [-1, 0), \\ 4x(1-x), & x \in [0, 1], \end{cases} \tag{3}$$

are topologically conjugated through the homeomorphism

$$h : [-1, 1] \longrightarrow [-1, 1], h(x)$$

$$= \begin{cases} -\dfrac{1}{\pi}\arccos\left(1 + 2x\right), & x \in [-1, 0) \\ \dfrac{1}{\pi}\arccos\left(1 - 2x\right), & x \in [0, 1]. \end{cases} \tag{4}$$

Once the conjugation map h (between maps f and g) is determined, the study of the evolution in time of an orbit $\{x_0, f(x_0), f^2(x_0), \ldots, f^k(x_0)\}$, of period k and belonging to f map, can be realized through the analysis of the behavior of an orbit $\{x_0, g(x_0), g^2(x_0), \ldots, g^k(x_0)\}$, of period k, of and belonging to g map, using the bijection h.

Proof. To prove that the f_N and f_L maps are topologically conjugated through the homeomorphism h, we check that the following condition is satisfied:

$$\left(f_N \circ h\right)(x) = \left(h \circ f_L\right)(x). \tag{5}$$

For $x \in [-1, 0]$ the left term from (5) becomes

$$\left(f_N \circ h\right)(x) = \frac{2}{\pi}\arcsin\left(\sin\left(-\arccos\left(1 + 2x\right)\right)\right)$$

$$= -\frac{2}{\pi}\arcsin\left(\sqrt{1 - (1 + 2x)^2}\right). \tag{6}$$

For $x \in [-1, 0]$ the right term from (6) becomes

$$\left(h \circ f_l\right)(x) = -\frac{2}{\pi}\arccos\left(1 - 4x(1 + x)\right). \tag{7}$$

Substituting the relations (6) and (7) in (5), we obtain

$$-\frac{2}{\pi}\arcsin\left(\sqrt{1 - (1 + 2x)^2}\right) = -\frac{2}{\pi}\arccos\left(1 - 4x(1 + x)\right) \tag{8}$$

which is equivalent with

$$1 - \sin^2\left(\arcsin\left(\sqrt{1 - (1 + 2x)^2}\right)\right) = 1 - 4x(1 + x) \tag{9}$$

and hence

$$1 + 8x + 8x^2 = 1 + 8x + 8x^2. \tag{10}$$

Summing up, condition (5) is satisfied.

In a similar manner, condition (5) was proven for $x \in [0, 1]$, which concludes the proof of the proposition. $\square$

Theorem 2. *The f map, given by relation (2), has chaotic orbits on the interval* $[-1, 1]$.

Proof. In order to study the asymptotic behavior of an orbit $\{x_0, x_1, \ldots, x_k\}$ of the chaotic map f, in the phase space, which starts from an initial point $x_0 \in [-1, 1]$, we will use a strong instrument from the chaos theory, such as the Lyapunov exponent λ_f [31], given by the relation

$$\lambda_f = \lim_{k \to \infty} \frac{1}{k} \sum_{i=1}^{k} \ln \left| f'(x_i) \right|. \tag{11}$$

The maps f and g are topologically conjugated through the conjugation map h given by relation (4); thus, after applying the derivation rule of the continue maps, we obtain

$$f'(h(x)) \cdot h'(x) = h'(g(x)) \cdot g'(x) \tag{12}$$

from which it results that

$$g'(x) = \frac{f'(h(x)) \cdot h'(x)}{h'(g(x))}. \tag{13}$$

Therefore, we obtain the relation

$$\begin{aligned}
&\ln \left| g'(x_1) g'(x_2) \cdots g'(x_k) \right| \\
&= \sum_{i=1}^{k} \ln \left| \frac{f'(h(x_i)) \cdot h'(x_i)}{h'(x_{i+1})} \right| \\
&= \sum_{i=1}^{k} \ln \left| \frac{h'(x_i)}{h'(x_{i+1})} \cdot f'(h(x_i)) \right| \\
&= \ln \left| h'(x_1) \right| - \ln \left| h'(x_{k+1}) \right| + \sum_{i=1}^{k} \ln \left| f'(h(x_i)) \right|.
\end{aligned} \tag{14}$$

Dividing the last relation by k, we obtain

$$\begin{aligned}
&\frac{1}{k} \sum_{i=1}^{k} \ln \left| g'(x_i) \right| \\
&= \frac{1}{k} \left[\ln \left| h'(x_1) \right| - \ln \left| h'(x_{k+1}) \right| + \sum_{i=1}^{k} \ln \left| f'(h(x_i)) \right| \right].
\end{aligned} \tag{15}$$

Appling the limit after k in the last relation, we obtain the following relation:

$$\lim_{k \to \infty} \frac{1}{k} \sum_{i=1}^{k} \ln \left| g'(x_i) \right| = \lim_{k \to \infty} \frac{1}{k} \sum_{i=1}^{k} \ln \left| f'(h(x_i)) \right|. \tag{16}$$

The Lyapunov exponent of the logistic map is given by the relation [31]

$$\lambda_g = \lim_{k \to \infty} \frac{1}{k} \sum_{i=1}^{k} \ln \left| g'(x_i) \right| = \ln 2. \tag{17}$$

Relation (16) shows that the Lyapunov exponent of the orbits corresponding to the f map is identical with the g map one, so we obtain

$$\lambda_f = \ln 2. \tag{18}$$

Due to the fact that the Lyapunov exponent is positive, the asymptotic behavior of any orbit of the f map is chaotic [30, 32, 33].

The next objective is to determine a statistical image of the f map dynamics, in the phase space, using the same mechanism of topologic conjugation, through theoretical results postulated by Grossman and Thomae in [30]. □

Proposition 3. *The f map given by relation (2)* conserves an *absolute invariant density function that is continuous on the interval* $[-1, 1]$ *and is equal to 1.*

Proof. Let ρ_f and ρ_g be the probability densities of the maps f and g. Because these maps are topologically conjugated through conjugation map h, applying the Grossman-Thomae theorem [30], we obtain the relation

$$\rho_f = \rho_g \left(h^{-1}(x) \right) \left| \frac{dh^{-1}(x)}{dx} \right|. \tag{19}$$

For $x \in [0, 1]$, conjugation map h is given by the relation

$$h(x) = \frac{1}{\pi} \arccos(1 - 2x). \tag{20}$$

Thus, we obtain that

$$h^{-1}(x) = \frac{1 - \cos \pi x}{2}. \tag{21}$$

The invariant density function of the logistic map has the following analytical expression [33]:

$$\rho = \frac{1}{\pi \sqrt{x(1-x)}}. \tag{22}$$

So, relation (19) becomes

$$\begin{aligned}
\rho_f &= \rho_g \left(\frac{1 - \cos \pi x}{2} \right) \left| \pi \sin \pi x \right| \\
&= \frac{\pi \sin \pi x}{2\pi \sqrt{((1 - \cos \pi x)/2)((1 + \cos \pi x)/2)}} = 1.
\end{aligned} \tag{23}$$

From (23) we conclude that the density function of probability of the f map is equal to 1, for any $x \in [0, 1]$. In the same manner, we can prove that the probability density function of the f map is equal to 1, for any $x \in [-1, 0]$, which concludes the proof of the statement. □

2.1. The Parameterization of the Proposed Dynamic System. From the theoretical results, that is, the ones presented above, we can conclude that the map f has a chaotic behavior and an invariant probability measure on the interval $[-1, 1]$.

The chaotic maps used as base of cryptosystems are defined in a parametric way; for example, their dynamics depend on one or several control parameters. Moreover, those chaotic systems show a chaotic behavior for certain values of the associated control parameters. Therefore, the design of a cryptosystem based on any of those dynamical systems must be done by guaranteeing the use of a set of values for the control parameters leading to chaos.

Following the method described by Fridrich in [34], we parameterized f map, as follows:

$$x_{n+1} = f_r(x_n)$$
$$f_r : [-1,1] \longrightarrow [-1,1],$$
$$f_r(x) = \frac{2}{\pi} \arcsin(\sin(\pi r x)),$$
(24)

where $r > 0$ is the control parameter of the map.

The behavior, in time, of the discreet system $x_{n+1} = f_r(x_n)$, depends both on the control parameter r and on the initial condition x_0.

First, we analyze the stability of the fixed points in order to determine the sensitivity level of the system to the initial conditions. The map f_r has the following fixed points:

$$x_k^1 = \frac{4k}{2r-1}, \qquad x_k^2 = \frac{2(2k+1)}{2r+1}, \qquad k \in \mathbb{Z}. \quad (25)$$

According to the theorem of fixed points [31], the points x_1 and x_2 are attractors if the following condition is fulfilled:

$$\left| f_r'(x_i) \right| < 1, \quad i = \overline{1,2} \quad (26)$$

which implies that the control parameter r must fulfill the condition

$$r < \frac{1}{2}. \quad (27)$$

The map f_r is defined on the interval $[-1,1]$; therefore, from condition (24), it results that the fixed point $x_k^2 \notin [-1,1]$ for any $k \in \mathbb{Z}$ and the fixed point $x_k^1 \in [-1,1]$ only for $k = 0$. So, for values of the parameter $r < 1/2$, any trajectory which starts from any initial point $x_0 \in [-1,1]$ converges in time to the attractor point $x_0^1 = 0$. After the value of the parameter r exceeds the value $1/2$, the fixed point x_0^1 loses its stability and another instable fixed point $x_0^2 = 2/(2r+1)$ appears. The trajectory with the initial condition x_0 converges, at the beginning, in the neighborhood of x_0^2, and then leaves it, entering into a chaotic regime. The stability of the fixed points of the map f_r is also emphasized through the bifurcation diagram presented in Figure 1.

It can be observed that for a value of the parameter $r > 1/2$ the f_r map has an instable behavior and for the parameter $r > 1$ the map enters in a complete chaotic regime.

The road to chaos of the f_r map with parameter $r > 1/2$ is not achieved through the doubling process of the period, specific to some chaotic maps [31], but is induced by the existence of a dense set of periodic orbits of any period in the interval $[-1,1]$.

The sensitivity of the f_r map to infinitesimal changes of the initial conditions is illustrated in Figures 2 and 3.

In Figure 2, two orbits of the map f_r with fixed control parameter $r = 5$ starting from two very close initial points in phase space are plotted, while in Figure 3 two orbits generated by two maps which start from the same initial point x_o whose control parameters differ by 10^{-6} are plotted. It can be noticed, in both figures, that, after some iterations, the orbits have a completely different behavior, becoming divergent by an exponential law in time.

Next, using the Lyapunov exponent we proved that the orbits of the map f_r have a chaotic behavior on the interval $(-1,1)$ for values of the control parameter $r > 1/2$.

Theorem 4. *The orbits of the map f_r given by relation (24) have a chaotic behavior on the interval $(-1,1)$ for values of the control parameter $r > 1/2$.*

Proof. The sensitivity level to the initial conditions of a periodic orbit $\{x_1, x_2, \ldots, x_k\}$ generated by f_r map is determined using the Lyapunov exponent:

$$\lambda_f = \lim_{k \to \infty} \frac{1}{k} \sum_{i=1}^{k} \ln \left| f_r'(x_i) \right|$$
$$= \lim_{k \to \infty} \frac{1}{k} \sum_{i=1}^{k} \ln \left| 2r \frac{\cos \pi r x_i}{|\cos \pi r x_i|} \right| = \ln 2r. \quad (28)$$

The orbit $\{x_1, x_2, \ldots, x_k\}$ is chaotic if the Lyapunov exponent λ_f is positive, so we obtain the relation $\ln 2r > 0$, which is equivalent to $r > 1/2$. □

Figure 4 represented the Lyapunov exponent, numerically calculated using Wolf's algorithm [35], according to the control parameter $r \in [0,10]$. It can be observed that for values of the parameter $r > 1/2$ the orbits of the map f_r are chaotic.

Following on, the analysis of the shape of a dynamical system attractor can provide information about its behavior in time for certain values of its parameters. The attractor of a dynamical system with a periodic behavior has a regular shape, while the one corresponding to chaotic dynamical system has a complex structure, of fractal type, and it is called strange attractor. The attractor of the f_r map for $r = 7$ is represented in Figure 5.

The fractal structure of an attractor is indicated by a fractional value of its fractal dimension, which is a ratio providing a statistical index of complexity comparing how details in a pattern change with the scale at which they are. Several types of fractal dimension can be estimated theoretically and empirically, such as box-counting dimension, Hausdorff dimension, Minkowski-Bouligand dimension, information dimension, and correlation dimension [36–38]. Using the plots from Figure 6, we established that the attractor of the f_r map has a box-counting dimension $D_b = 0.97863$ and a correlation dimension $D_c = 0.97064$.

The fractional values of both estimated fractal dimensions allow us to conclude that the proposed map f_r has a strange attractor, which indicates a chaotic behavior.

In the next stage of our analyses we tested the ergodicity property. The ergodic property is a basic requirement for

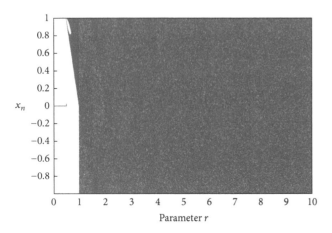

FIGURE 1: The bifurcation diagram of the f_r map for $r \in [0, 10]$.

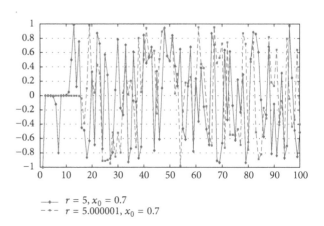

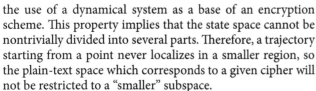

FIGURE 3: The sensibility of the f_r map to changes of the control parameter r.

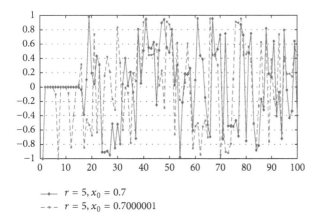

FIGURE 2: The sensibility of the f_r map to changes of the initial point x_0.

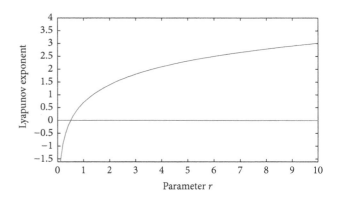

FIGURE 4: The Lyapunov exponent of the f_r map for $r \in [0, 10]$.

the use of a dynamical system as a base of an encryption scheme. This property implies that the state space cannot be nontrivially divided into several parts. Therefore, a trajectory starting from a point never localizes in a smaller region, so the plain-text space which corresponds to a given cipher will not be restricted to a "smaller" subspace.

Indeed, if a dynamical system is ergodic, the long-term behavior of its orbits is independent of the initial condition and can be studied using statistical analysis. Using Birkhoff's theorem [30, 31] in conjunction with Kolmogorov-Smirnov test [39] we proved that the dynamical system f_r is ergodic for $r > 1$. The Kolmogorov-Smirnov test is applied on two series of experimental independent data $(x_1, x_2, \ldots, x_n)$ and $(y_1, y_2, \ldots, y_n)$, corresponding to the measurements of two random variables X and Y. The random variable X is obtained iterating for n times the f_r map using a fixed parameter $r > 1$ and an initial condition $x_0 \in [-1, 1]$. The second random variable Y is obtained by selecting the values extracted from n distinct orbits of the f_r map at a moment k, orbits that start from n initial points of the interval $[-1, 1]$, using the same fixed parameter. The moment $k = 100$ is chosen from the stationary zone of f_r, previously established using Kolmogorov-Smirnov test described in [39, 40].

Due to the fact that the random variables X and Y correspond to time average of f_r after time n and space average, respectively,, the purpose of the test is to establish if the two experimental sets of data derive from populations with the same distribution or not, in respect to Birkhoff's theorem. The analysis is based on the experimental distribution functions Fe_X and Fe_Y of the two random variables X and Y.

The hypotheses of the Kolmogorov-Smirnov test are as follows:

(i) H_0: both variables X and Y have the same probability law;

(ii) H_1: both variables X and Y have different probability laws.

The Kolmogorov-Smirnov test is applied as follows.

(1) The δ test value is calculated; that is, the maximum absolute difference between the two experimental distribution functions is

$$\delta = \max_u \left| Fe_X(u) - Fe_Y(u) \right|. \tag{29}$$

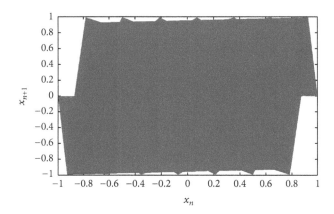

FIGURE 5: The attractor of the f_r map for $r = 7$.

TABLE 1: The results of ergodicity property testing for f_r map.

Number	Parameter value	KS-Test value	Result
1	5.429208420782631	0.958	SUCCESS
2	9.119643904063768	0.944	SUCCESS
3	9.982798857377562	0.958	SUCCESS
4	6.478547914065082	0.952	SUCCESS
5	8.101080150367013	0.954	SUCCESS
6	4.183180696373615	0.948	SUCCESS
7	7.066962832367738	0.968	SUCCESS
8	4.985348171318265	0.934	SUCCESS
9	5.068908118426080	0.942	SUCCESS
10	3.072806838451141	0.958	SUCCESS

(2) For a chosen α significance level, Δ_α is calculated, where α is the quantile of the probability law of the random value Δ; that is, $P(\Delta > \Delta_\alpha) = \alpha$,

$$\Delta_\alpha \cong \sqrt{\frac{n+m}{nm}} \sqrt{\frac{1}{2} \ln \frac{2}{\alpha}}. \tag{30}$$

(3) If $\delta \leq \Delta_\alpha$, the hypothesis H_0 is accepted. In other words, if the absolute maximum distance between the two experimental distribution functions is lower than a certain accepted value Δ_α, then it will be decided if the random variables X and Y have the same probability law. Otherwise, if $\delta > \Delta_\alpha$, the test rejects the H_0 hypotheses for the chosen level; that is, the two sets of experimental data come from random variables with different probability laws [40].

The Kolmogorov-Smirnov test was performed for a sample of $n = m = 100000$ and a significance level $\alpha = 0.05$. The decision regarding the ergodicity can be based on a Monte Carlo analysis, which evaluates the ability of the Kolmogorov-Smirnov test to accept bad data as good data. For example, the above experiment can be repeated 500 times, finally recording the acceptance proportion of the hypothesis H_0, which is [0.93, 097].

The overall results are summarized in Table 1. One can observe that, in case of all values selected for r parameter, with $r \in (1, 10]$, the acceptance proportion of H_0 hypothesis lies within the confidence interval. Thus, ergodicity of the proposed chaotic map is confirmed over the entire interval of interest of the parameter r.

Based on the results numerically obtained, using instruments from the chaos theory, it can be concluded that the f_r map has a chaotic behavior, without intermittent scenarios, for values of the control parameters $r > 1$. Therefore, the dynamical system can be successfully used to build strong cryptographic applications, because of the very large space of the keys that ensures a high level of security and also due to the ergodicity property which ensures the efficiency of the diffusion process.

According to Theorem 4, the map f_r is sensitive to the initial conditions on interval $[-1, 1]$, for values of the parameter $r > 1/2$, and it becomes chaotic and ergodic for $r > 1$.

Because the control parameter of a chaotic map defines the corresponding cryptosystem's key space, the fact that map f_r can be used for the construction of robust encryption scheme is confirmed.

3. Randomness Analysis

Evaluation process in terms of cryptographic properties of a dynamical system must include, in addition to the study of the chaotic behavior, a statistical analysis of the randomness of the values generated, in order to determine the security level of the system against some statistics cryptanalytic attacks. There are several options available for analyzing the randomness of a new developed pseudorandom bit generator. The most popular suites of statistical tests for randomness are NIST [41] and DIEHARD [42].

Chaotic cryptography deals with real numbers; thus, in order to use the NIST statistical suite, we firstly apply a computationally method to transform a chaotic sequence of real number into a bitstream. The used discretization method has consisted of the extraction of the first 15 digits from the fractional part of the real numbers generated by the chaotic f_r map. For the numerical experimentations we have generated $m = 2000$ different binary sequences from 500 randomly chosen orbits, each sequence having a length of $n = 1000000$ bits, and computed the P value corresponding to each sequence for all the 15 tests of the NIST suite.

The significance level of each test in NIST is set to 1%, which means that 99% of test samples pass the tests if the random numbers are truly random. The acceptance region of the passing ratio is given by $[p - 3\sqrt{(p(1-p))/m}, p + 3\sqrt{(p(1-p))/m}]$, where m represents the number of samples tested and $p = 1 - \alpha$ is the probability of passing each test. For $m = 2000$ and the probability $p = 0.99$ (corresponding to the significance level $\alpha = 0.01$), we obtained the confidence interval $[0.983, 0.996]$. In the second column of Table 2 we have summarized the results obtained after applying nonparameterized and parameterized tests of the NIST suite on the binary sequences produced by the discrete orbit of the proposed map. The computed proportion for each test lies inside the confidence interval. Hence, the tested binary sequences are random according to all tests of NIST suite [41].

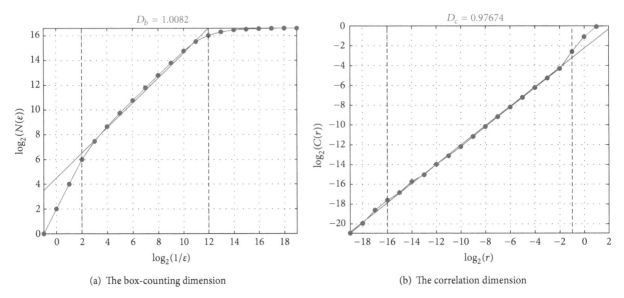

(a) The box-counting dimension

(b) The correlation dimension

FIGURE 6: The fractal dimensions of the attractor of the f_r map.

TABLE 2: The results of the NIST tests.

Test name	Passing ratio of the test	Uniformity P value	Result
Frequency	0.992	0.602803	SUCCESS
Block frequency	0.990	0.748891	SUCCESS
Cumulative sums	0.991	0.090388	SUCCESS
Runs	0.990	0.939005	SUCCESS
Longest run	0.989	0.592443	SUCCESS
Rank	0.991	0.840367	SUCCESS
FFT	0.989	0.242363	SUCCESS
Nonoverlapping template	0.983	0.761719	SUCCESS
Overlapping template	0.983	0.230755	SUCCESS
Universal	0.987	0.050629	SUCCESS
Approximate entropy	0.988	0.959347	SUCCESS
Random excursions	0.987	0.614382	SUCCESS
Random excursions variant	0.984	0.830939	SUCCESS
Serial	0.986	0.209392	SUCCESS
Linear complexity	0.989	0.764655	SUCCESS

If the tested sequences are truly random, then P values would be uniformly distributed in the interval $[0, 1)$. NIST recommends to apply a χ^2-test in which the interval $[0, 1)$ is divided into 10 subintervals. Defining F_i as number of occurrences of P value in ith interval, then the χ^2 statistic is $\chi^2 = \sum_{i=1}^{10} (F_i - (m/10))^2/(m/10)$. NIST recommends to set its significance level to 0.01%, so the acceptance region

of statistics is $\chi^2 \leq 33.72$. The P value corresponding to the uniformity of the P values is calculated as igamc $(9/2, \chi^2/2)$, so it must be greater than 0.0001 to ensure that the P values could be considered uniformly distributed. The results from the third column of Table 2 lead us to the conclusion that the P values for each statistical test are uniformly distributed.

The calculating method of the total test passing ratio of total test and the uniformity P value of total test samples follows the same methodology described above. In this case, we considered the number of samples $m = 30000$, so the acceptance region is $[0.988, 0.992]$. For the passing ratio of the total test we obtained the value 0.988 and the P value corresponding to the uniformity of the P values from the total test was 0.294808. Thus, the pseudorandom bit sequences obtained by discretization of the f_r orbits passed the total test.

4. Description of the Proposed Cryptosystem

The proposed cryptosystem is a symmetric one and has a bimodular architecture, in which one of the modules performs the diffusion process using a random permutation generated by a chaotic map f_1 of type (24), while the second one performs the confusion process by modifying pixel values using a deterministic algorithm which implies another map f_2 of type (24).

Assuming that the pixels of a RGB image with size $n = W \times H$ pixels are numbered on rows, from top to down and from left to right on each row, we denote the plain image by $P = \{p_0, p_1, \ldots, p_{n-1}\}$ and the corresponding encrypted one by $C = \{c_0, c_1, \ldots, c_{n-1}\}$, both of the same size n. Also, both in the encryption and in decryption process, we will use an auxiliary image of size n, too, denoted by $A = \{a_0, a_1, \ldots, a_{n-1}\}$.

Next, we will describe in detail the implementation and functionality of each module of the proposed cryptosystem.

4.1. The Secret Key. The secret key of the proposed cryptosystem, shared by the emitter and the receiver, consists of

(i) two real numbers r_1 and r_2 representing the parameters of the maps f_1 and f_2 chosen so that both maps might be in a chaotic and ergodic regime (i.e., $r_1, r_2 > 1$);

(ii) two real numbers x_0^1 and x_0^2 representing the initial conditions of the maps f_1 and f_2, chosen from the interval $[-1, 1]$;

(iii) two unsigned integers m_1 and m_2 representing the preiterations numbers of the maps f_1 and f_2, required to assure a chaotic and ergodic behavior (we recommend to choose $m_1, m_2 \geq 100$);

(iv) an unsigned integer iv, representing the initial value used to encrypt/decrypt the first pixel of the plain/encrypted image.

4.2. The Encryption Process

4.2.1. The Diffusion Process. In a bimodular image encryption/decryption scheme, the diffusion process consists of the pixels permutation from the plain image, so that the default redundancy of the image might be distributed throughout the encrypted image [34]. In [43], we proposed a fast algorithm for generating random permutations with a high shift factor, suitable for image scrambling.

The algorithm combines the use of random values, generated by a chaotic map, with the use of nonrandom ones, determined algorithmically. Practically, a permutation $q = (q_1, q_2, \ldots, q_n)$ of degree n is constructed element by element, as follows: a random value between 1 and n, obtained by discretization of a real value generated by the f_1 map, is assigned to the current element and then it is checked if the value was previously used; if not, the maximum unused value is assigned to it. In this way, it is clear that a part of the elements from the beginning of the permutation will have large values and a part of the elements from the end of the permutation will have small ones, so the shift factor of the permutation will be high.

Using the chaotic map f_1 and the recurrence $x_{k+1}^1 = f_1(x_k^1)$, where $x_0^1 \in [-1, 1]$, firstly we discard the preiterated values $\{x_1^1, \ldots, x_{m_1}^1\}$ and we construct an orbit $\{x_{m_1+1}^1, \ldots, x_{m_1+n}^1\} \subset \mathbb{R}$ of length n. Next, we construct a discretized sequence $\{d_1, d_2, \ldots, d_n\}$ of unsigned integers by extracting the first 15 digits from the fractional part of each real number from the orbit $\{x_{m_1+1}^1, \ldots, x_{m_1+n}^1\}$, that is, $d_i = \text{floor}(10^{15} \times x_{i+m_1}^1)$ for any $i \in \{1, 2, \ldots, n\}$.

The proposed algorithm for generating a random permutation $q = (q_1, q_2, \ldots, q_n)$ of degree n, starting from the sequence $\{d_1, d_2, \ldots, d_n\}$ and using a labeling array L of dimension n (i.e., $L[i]$ is equal to 1 if a value $i \in \{1, 2, \ldots, n\}$

is used in permutation q; else $L[i]$ is equal to 0), is as follows [43].

Input. Unsigned integers are $n, d_1, d_2, \ldots, d_n$.

Output. Random permutation is $q = (q_1, q_2, \ldots, q_n)$.

(1) For i from 1 to n do the following.

    (1.1) Set $L[i] \leftarrow 0$.

(2) Set max $\leftarrow n + 1$ (variable max stores the maximum unused value between 1 and n in permutation q).

(3) For i from 1 to n do the following.

    (1) Set $q[i] \leftarrow 1 + d[i] \bmod n$.
    (2) If $L[q[i]] = 1$, then go to step 3, else go to step 7.
    (3) Set $k \leftarrow \text{max} - 1$.
    (4) If $L[k] = 1$, then go to step 5; else go to step 6.
    (5) Set $k \leftarrow k - 1$ and go to step 4.
    (6) Set $q[i] \leftarrow k$ and max $\leftarrow k$.
    (7) Set $L[q[i]] \leftarrow 1$.

(4) Return (q).

In [43] we proved that the proposed algorithm has an almost linear complexity if the used map is chaotic and ergodic, condition satisfied by the f_1 map.

In the encryption process, the pixels from the plain image P are shuffled using the following algorithm, based on the permutation $q = (q_1, q_2, \ldots, q_n)$.

Input. This includes plain image $P = \{p_0, p_1, \ldots, p_{n-1}\}$ and the permutation q of degree n.

Output. Shuffled image is $A = \{a_0, a_1, \ldots, a_{n-1}\}$.

(1) For i from 0 to $n - 1$ do the following.

    (1.1) Set $a_{q_{i+1}-1} \leftarrow p_i$.

(2) Return (A).

4.2.2. The Confusion Process. In an image encryption/decryption scheme, the confusion process tries to hide the correlations between the plain image, the encrypted image, and encryption key, usually by substitutions of the values of all pixels in a deterministic way [34].

As we mentioned above, the confusion process is based on one chaotic map f_2 of type (24), used in conjunction with the recurrence $x_{k+1}^2 = f_2(x_k^2)$, where $x_0^2 \in [-1, 1]$. The preiterated values $\{x_1^2, \ldots, x_{m_2}^2\}$ are discarded and we construct an orbit $\{x_{m_2+1}^2, \ldots, x_{m_2+n}^2\} \subset \mathbb{R}$ of length n. Next, we construct the keystream as a discretized sequence $\{k_0, k_1, \ldots, k_{n-1}\}$ of unsigned integers by extracting the first 15 digits from the fractional part of each real number from the orbit $\{x_{m_2+1}^2, \ldots, x_{m_2+n}^2\}$, that is, $k_i = \text{floor}(10^{15} \times x_{i+m_2+1}^2)$ for any $i \in \{0, 1, \ldots, n - 1\}$ (function floor(x) returns the nearest integer less than or equal to x).

To ensure a high level of security against differential attacks, we alter the value of a pixel a_i from the shuffled image $A = \{a_0, a_1, \ldots, a_{n-1}\}$, before XOR-ing it with the keystream and the value of the previously encrypted pixel, by the sum s_i of the three values corresponding to the color channels RGB of the pixels previously encrypted. Assuming that a pixel c_i from the encrypted image is a triplet $c_i = (c_i^R, c_i^G, c_i^B)$, then we define s_i as

$$s_i = \sum_{j=0}^{i-1} \left(c_j^R + c_j^G + c_j^B \right) \qquad (31)$$

for any $i \in \{1, \ldots, n-1\}$ and $s_0 = 0$.

Thus, the values of the pixels from the encrypted image are obtained according to the following formula:

$$c_0 = a_0 \oplus iv \oplus k_0$$
$$c_i = ((a_i + s_i) \bmod 256) \oplus c_{i-1} \oplus k_i, \quad 1 \le i \le n-1. \qquad (32)$$

4.3. The Decryption Process. Due to the fact that the proposed cryptosystem is a symmetric one, in the decryption process the same secret key is used, which leads to the same keystream $\{k_0, k_1, \ldots, k_{n-1}\}$. The decryption process consists of next two steps.

Step 1. On the pixels of the encrypted image $C = \{c_0, c_1, \ldots, c_{n-1}\}$, we apply the inverse transformation of (24), obtaining the auxiliary image $A = \{a_0, a_1, \ldots, a_{n-1}\}$:

$$a_0 = c_0 \oplus iv \oplus k_0,$$
$$a_i = (c_i \oplus c_{i-1} \oplus k_i + 256 - s_i) \bmod 256, \quad 1 \le i \le n-1, \qquad (33)$$

where s_i is defined by (23).

Step 2. On the pixels of the auxiliary image $A = \{a_0, a_1, \ldots, a_{n-1}\}$, we apply the inverse q^{-1} of the permutation q, obtaining the plain image $P = \{p_0, p_1, \ldots, p_{n-1}\}$.

5. Performances of the Proposed Cryptosystem

5.1. Security Analysis of the Proposed Cryptosystem. A strong encryption scheme should resist against known cryptanalytic attacks, such as known-plain-text attack, cipher-text only attack, statistical attack, differential attack, and various brute-force attacks. For the proposed image encryption system we performed standard security analysis, such as key space analysis, statistical analysis, and differential analysis. Thus, several specific statistical tests were performed, such as image pixels distribution, the correlation between adjacent pixels of the image encrypted, entropy, the correlation between original image and the encrypted one, NPCR, and UACI. The performances of the proposed cryptosystem were evaluated using 10 various standard test images from USC-SIPI Image Database [44], Kodak Digital Camera Sample Pictures [45], personal photos, and so forth. All the pictures used were 24 bit-color bitmaps, with different dimensions varying from 256 × 256 to 3000 × 4000 pixels. All tests were performed for each of the three color channels (red, green, and blue) in order to achieve a rigorous and detailed analysis of proposed cryptosystem performance.

5.2. Key Space Analysis. A secure image encryption algorithm should have enough large key space to resist against brute-force attacks.

The secret key of the proposed cryptosystem contains 4 real numbers and 3 unsigned integers. The real numbers must be stored and transmitted using a real data type with high precision to prevent them from negative effects caused by the discretization. If the implementation of the cryptosystem is done using a programming language that complies with *IEEE Standard 754-2008*, then it is recommended to use the double data type, which stores real numbers on 8 bytes, with an accurate 15 decimal places. In this case, the secret key length will be 352 bits, which means that the size of the secret key space will be equal to $2^{352} \approx 9.17 \times 10^{105}$, a value large enough to prevent guessing the secret key in a reasonable time, using exhaustive search.

5.3. Key Sensitivity Analysis. A secure image cryptosystem should be sensitive to any small change in the secret key, so the use of two secret keys which are very small different one from another leads to two completely different encrypted images. In Figure 7, 2 images are shown obtained by encrypting Lena image using 2 secret keys which has only a double data type component different by 10^{-12}, along with the difference image.

In our key sensitivity analysis, we considered 10 plain images and 10 corresponding secret keys. Each plain image was encrypted using 7 secret keys, which differ from the initial one by 10^{-12} on components of double data type or by one bit on components of unsigned integer data type, and the 7 encrypted images obtained were compared with the image obtained by encrypting the plain image using the initial secret key. In all the 70 cases, we obtained a correlation coefficient very close to 0, which confirms that the encrypted images are completely different.

Furthermore, the sensitivity to any small change in the secret key must be present in the decryption process, too. So, the use of a secret key which is different in very few respects from the original one must lead to a decrypted image completely different from the initial plain one. Figure 8 shows an image obtained by decrypting the encrypted Lena image using a secret key which has only one double data type component different by 10^{-12} from the original secret key. Note that the image is totally different from the plain-image Lena and, moreover, the decrypted image seems to be a noise.

In this step of our key sensitivity analysis, we considered 10 plain images and 10 corresponding secret keys, too. Each plain image was encrypted using the corresponding secret key and the encrypted image obtained was decrypted using 7 secret keys, which differ from the initial one by 10^{-12} on components of double data type or by one bit on components of unsigned integer data type, and all the 7 decrypted images obtained were compared to the initial plain image. In all 70

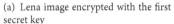

(a) Lena image encrypted with the first secret key

(b) Lena image encrypted with the second secret key

(c) The difference image of the two encrypted images

FIGURE 7: Images that resulted from encrypting the Lena image using two secret keys which differ by 10^{-12} on a single double data type component.

(a) Decrypted using the original secret key

(b) Decrypted using an altered secret key

FIGURE 8: Images that resulted from decrypting the encrypted Lena image.

cases, we obtained a correlation coefficient very close to 0, which confirms that the decrypted images are completely different from the initial plain images.

So, we can conclude that the proposed encryption algorithm is very sensitive to the key, because a small change in the secret key will generate a completely different decrypted image and cannot obtain the correct plain image.

5.4. Statistical Analysis. In his most famous work, "*Communication Theory of Secrecy Systems*" [46], Shannon said that "*It is possible to solve many kinds of ciphers by statistical analysis.*" In this sense, he suggested two methods of diffusion and confusion in order to crack the attacks based on statistical analysis.

In order to prove that the proposed image encryption system has a superior confusion and diffusion properties, we performed tests on the histograms and entropies of the encrypted images, along with a statistical test on the correlations between adjacent pixels in the encrypted image.

5.4.1. Histogram of the Encrypted Images. A cryptosystem with high security level needs to produce encrypted images with a uniform distribution of pixels in each color channel, in order to hide the uneven distribution from the plain image.

The most often used visual analysis tool to study the distribution of a color image of pixel values is the *color histogram*, in which the pixel values frequencies are plotted separately for each color channel. Figure 9 contains a pair of plain image, encrypted image, along with the associated color histograms.

Note that, after the encryption of Lena image, which has a strong color uneven distribution (Figure 9(a)), we obtained an image with a uniform distribution of pixel values (Figure 9(d)) for each color channel, so an attacker cannot extract statistical information about the plain image or about the encryption key used.

To analyze the distribution of pixel values for a large number of encrypted images, we used the χ^2 test [47].

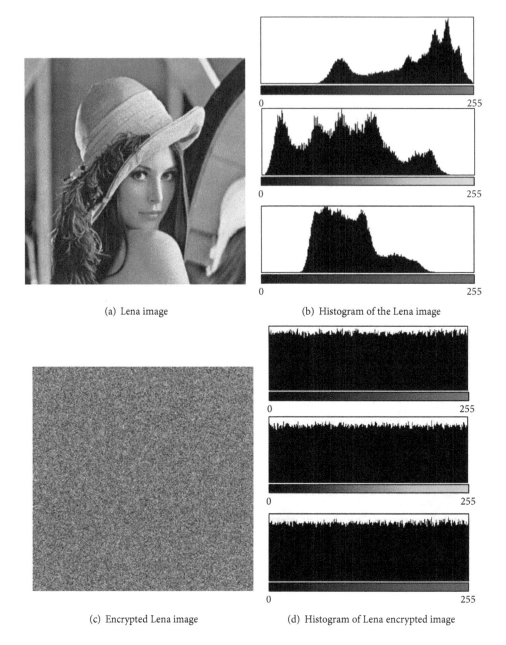

(a) Lena image

(b) Histogram of the Lena image

(c) Encrypted Lena image

(d) Histogram of Lena encrypted image

FIGURE 9: Analysis of the standard image Lena.

The value of the χ^2 test for an encrypted image of dimension $m \times n$ is given by the following formula:

$$\chi^2 = \sum_{i=0}^{255} \frac{(v_i - v_0)^2}{v_0}, \tag{34}$$

where v_i is the observed frequency of a pixel value i ($0 \le i \le 255$) and v_0 is the expected frequency of a pixel value i, so $v_0 = (m \times n)/256$.

The results obtained by applying the χ^2 test on 10 encrypted images can be summarized as follows: for 9 images the values of the χ^2 test obtained were lower than the critical value $\chi^2_{255,0.05} = 293.25$ and for one image the value obtained was 294.68, which is very close to the critical value

$\chi^2_{255,0.05} = 293.25$. Thus, we conclude that the distribution of pixel values is uniform in the encrypted image, which demonstrates that the proposed cryptosystem is able to resist against statistical attacks.

5.4.2. Entropy. Considering the pixel values as a quantification of the information contained in an image, we can estimate the uncertainty of its content through the notion of *entropy*, defined by Shannon [46]. The entropy $H(S)$ of an image source S can be calculated as

$$H(S) = -\sum_{i=0}^{255} P(i) \log_2 P(i), \tag{35}$$

where $P(i)$ represents the probability of a pixel value i ($0 \leq i \leq 255$) from a color channel RGB of an image and the entropy is expressed in bits.

The 10 plain images used in the testing process had entropy values between 5.762235 and 7.752217. Through the encryption process images with entropies between 7.999330 and 7.99986 were obtained, being very close to the maximal theoretical value of 8, so that the information leakage in the encryption process is negligible and the encryption system is secure upon the entropy attack.

5.4.3. Correlation of Adjacent Pixels. In an ordinary image, each pixel is usually highly correlated with its adjacent pixels either in horizontal, vertical, or diagonal directions [9, 48, 49] which is indicated by a value of Pearson's correlation coefficient very close to 1 [47].

In order to analyze the encryption quality of the proposed algorithm, the correlation coefficient was used to evaluate the correlations between adjacent pixels of the plain/encrypted images. Firstly, we randomly selected 1000 pairs of two adjacent pixels from plain/encrypted image, and, using the values from each color channel RGB, we constructed two series of data $X = \{x_1, x_2, \ldots, x_{1000}\}$ and $Y = \{y_1, y_2, \ldots, y_{1000}\}$. Then, we calculated the correlation coefficient between X and Y using the following formula:

$$\rho_C(X, Y) = \frac{\text{cov}(X, Y)}{\sqrt{D(X)}\sqrt{D(Y)}}, \qquad (36)$$

where C is the color channel, $D(\cdot)$ denotes the variance of a random variable, and $\text{cov}(\cdot, \cdot)$ denotes the covariance of two random variables [47].

In Figure 10(a) we plotted the value of the pixel at the position (x, y) versus the value of the pixel at the position $(x+1, y)$ from the Lena image, while in Figure 10(b) we plotted them from the encrypted Lena image. We repeated the same plotting for vertically adjacent pixels (Figures 10(c) and 10(d)), respectively, for diagonally adjacent pixels (Figures 10(e) and 10(f)).

For all the 10 pairs of plain/encrypted test we obtained average values of the correlation coefficient from the interval $[-0.00915, 0.010345]$, very close to 0, which confirms that the encryption process eliminates the inherent strong correlation existing between the pixels of the plain image. This fact proves, once again, that the proposed system will resist against cryptanalytic attacks of statistical type.

5.5. Differential Attacks Analysis. Testing the security of a cryptosystem against differential attacks is necessary to evaluate how a minor change in the plain image is reflected upon the encrypted image. For this purpose, we consider two plain images $P_1 = \{p_0^{(1)}, p_1^{(1)}, \ldots, p_{n-1}^{(1)}\}$ and $P_2 = \{p_0^{(2)}, p_1^{(2)}, \ldots, p_{n-1}^{(2)}\}$ which differ by the value of a single pixel in a RGB color channel and their corresponding encrypted images $C_1 = \{c_0^{(1)}, c_1^{(1)}, \ldots, c_{n-1}^{(1)}\}$ and $C_2 = \{c_0^{(2)}, c_1^{(2)}, \ldots, c_{n-1}^{(2)}\}$.

To test the influence of one-pixel change in the plain image on the whole encrypted image using the proposed encryption scheme, two common measures are used: *number of pixels change rate* (NPCR) and *unified average changing intensity* (UACI) [49].

The NPCR indicator measures the percentage of different pixel numbers between the encrypted images C_1 and C_2 and it is defined as follows:

$$\text{NPCR} = \left(\frac{1}{n} \sum_{i=0}^{n-1} d_i \right) \times 100\%, \qquad (37)$$

where $d_i = 0$ if $c_i^{(1)} = c_i^{(2)}$ and $d_i = 1$ if $c_i^{(1)} \neq c_i^{(2)}$ for any $i \in \{0, 1, \ldots, n-1\}$.

The UACI indicator measures the average intensity of differences between the encrypted images C_1 and C_2 and it is defined as follows:

$$\text{UACI} = \left(\frac{1}{n} \sum_{i=0}^{n-1} \frac{\left| c_i^{(1)} - c_i^{(2)} \right|}{255} \right) \times 100\%. \qquad (38)$$

Considering two random images, the maximum expected value of NPCR is found to be 99.609375%, while the maximum expected value of UACI is 33.463541% [49]. Using the proposed cryptosystem, 10 tests were performed, achieving values of the NPCR indicator between 98.78% and 99.16% and between 32.77% and 33.14% for the UACI indicator, which confirms that the proposed cryptosystem will withstand to the differential attacks.

5.6. Quality of the Decryption Process. Within the cryptosystem performances evaluation, the quality of the decryption process should be also checked. Basically, this consists in testing that the image obtained after decryption process coincides with the plain one.

In this sense, we evaluated the *mean squared error* (MSE) between a plain image $P = \{p_0, p_1, \ldots, p_{n-1}\}$ and the corresponding decrypted one $D = \{d_0, d_1, \ldots, d_{n-1}\}$, on each RGB color channel, using the following formula [47]:

$$\text{MSE}(P, D) = \frac{1}{n} \sum_{i=0}^{n-1} (p_i - d_i)^2. \qquad (39)$$

A value close to 0 of MSE indicates a good quality of the decryption process, while other values indicate the occurrence of errors in this process.

In all 10 tests performed, the value of MSE was 0 for each RGB color channel, which indicates that decryption is carried out without any loss of information.

5.7. Speed Performance. Another important factor to consider when analyzing the efficiency of a cryptosystem is its speed. In this sense, we run the proposed algorithm implemented in C language (MinGW compiler) under Windows 7, using a PC with Intel(R) Core (TM) i3 @2.53 GHz CPU and 3 GB RAM. We used 10 standard test bitmaps (256×256) with sizes of 256×256, 512×512, 720×576, 1024×1024, and 3000×4000 [44, 45]. The mean speeds obtained are summarized in Table 3.

Analyzing the mean speeds from Table 3, we can conclude that the proposed algorithm is faster than the ones presented in [50–52], having a mean encryption/decryption speed about 4 MB/s, being suitable for real-time image encryption.

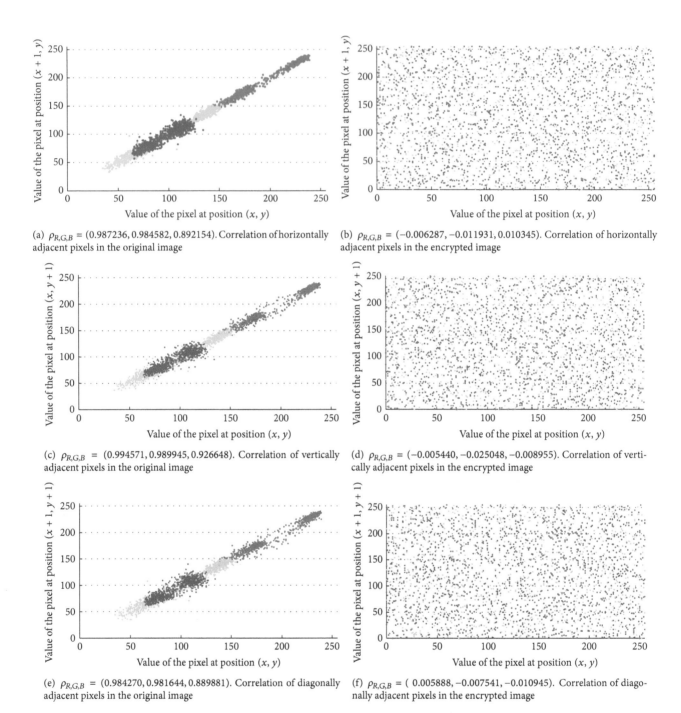

(a) $\rho_{R,G,B}$ = (0.987236, 0.984582, 0.892154). Correlation of horizontally adjacent pixels in the original image

(b) $\rho_{R,G,B}$ = (−0.006287, −0.011931, 0.010345). Correlation of horizontally adjacent pixels in the encrypted image

(c) $\rho_{R,G,B}$ = (0.994571, 0.989945, 0.926648). Correlation of vertically adjacent pixels in the original image

(d) $\rho_{R,G,B}$ = (−0.005440, −0.025048, −0.008955). Correlation of vertically adjacent pixels in the encrypted image

(e) $\rho_{R,G,B}$ = (0.984270, 0.981644, 0.889881). Correlation of diagonally adjacent pixels in the original image

(f) $\rho_{R,G,B}$ = (0.005888, −0.007541, −0.010945). Correlation of diagonally adjacent pixels in the encrypted image

FIGURE 10: Correlation of adjacent pixels from Lena plain/encrypted image.

5.8. Performances' Comparison with Other Image Encryption Schemes. Furthermore, we present below the results obtained by comparing the performances of the proposed system to other new similar encryption schemes [50–52]. Table 4 shows a summary of the mean values obtained for correlation coefficient of adjacent pixels (CCAP), NPCR, UACI, and speed.

Taking into account the results from Table 4, it can be seen that the proposed image encryption scheme has similar results regarding the level of security with other

recent proposed schemes [50–52], but our scheme is much faster than all of them, so it is suitable for real-time image encryption.

6. Conclusions

Development of new chaotic maps which meet the current demands of security is an actual research direction in the field of chaotic cryptography. The main objective was to obtain a large key space, induced by the control parameter

TABLE 3: Speed performance of the proposed cryptosystem (encryption/decryption).

Image size (pixels)	Image size (MB)	Mean time (s)	Mean speed (MB/s)
256×256	0.19	0.05	3.80
512×512	0.75	0.17	4.41
720×576	1.19	0.28	4.25
1024×1024	3.00	0.75	4.00
3000×4000	34.30	8.85	3.88

TABLE 4: Performances' comparison.

Indicator	Stoyanov and Kordov [50]	Pareek et al. [51]	Ghebleh et al. [52]	Our scheme
NPCR	99.61	99.46	99.61	99.16
UACI	33.45	N/A	33.72	33.14
CCAP				
Horizontal	−0.0006	0.0083	−0.0043	−0.0058
Vertical	0.0008	−0.0162	0.0049	−0.0046
Diagonal	0.0013	0.0078	0.0057	0.0029
Speed (MB/s)	1.11	0.37	2.4	4

and/or initial conditions, for which the map is chaotic and ergodic. In this respect, in this paper we have developed a new one-dimensional map that meets these requirements. Using specific mathematical tools from chaos theory and the mechanism of topological conjugation, we proved, by Propositions 1 and 3 and Theorems 2 and 4, the very good cryptographic properties of the proposed map. In addition, to argue for the good cryptographic properties of the proposed map, we tested the randomness of the values generated by its orbit, using the NIST statistical suite. Using the proposed map we designed a new image encryption scheme. The confusion property is ensured by an algorithm that generates a random permutation for shuffling the pixels of plain image and the diffusion property is ensured by a new XOR-scheme. Through the experimental tests performed, we demonstrated that the new image encryption scheme is fast and has a high level of security, being suitable for real-time image encryption.

Conflict of Interests

The authors declare that there is no conflict of interests regarding the publication of this paper.

References

[1] A. Cheddad, J. Condell, K. Curran, and P. McKevitt, "A hash-based image encryption algorithm," *Optics Communications*, vol. 283, no. 6, pp. 879–893, 2010.

[2] F. Riaz, S. Hameed, I. Shafi, R. Kausar, and A. Ahmed, "Enhanced image encryption techniques using modified advanced encryption standard," *Communications in Computer and Information Science*, vol. 281, pp. 385–396, 2012.

[3] S. Dey, "SD-AEI: an advanced encryption technique for images: an advanced combined encryption technique for encrypting images using randomized byte manipulation," in *Proceedings of the 2nd International Conference on Digital Information Processing and Communications (ICDIPC '12)*, pp. 68–73, Klaipeda, Lithuania, July 2012.

[4] S. M. Seyedzade, R. E. Atani, and S. Mirzakuchaki, "A novel image encryption algorithm based on hash function," in *Proceedings of the 6th International Conference on Machine Vision and Image Processing (MVIP '10)*, pp. 1–6, Isfahan, Iran, October 2010.

[5] V. M. Silva-García, R. Flores-Carapia, and C. Rentería-Márquez, "Triple-DES block of 96 bits: an application to colour image encryption," *Applied Mathematical Sciences*, vol. 7, no. 21-24, pp. 1143–1155, 2013.

[6] N. K. Pareek, V. Patidar, and K. K. Sud, "Image encryption using chaotic logistic map," *Image and Vision Computing*, vol. 24, no. 9, pp. 926–934, 2006.

[7] K.-W. Wong, B. S.-H. Kwok, and W.-S. Law, "A fast image encryption scheme based on chaotic standard map," *Physics Letters A*, vol. 372, no. 15, pp. 2645–2652, 2008.

[8] H. Yang, X. Liao, K.-W. Wong, W. Zhang, and P. Wei, "A new cryptosystem based on chaotic map and operations algebraic," *Chaos, Solitons and Fractals*, vol. 40, no. 5, pp. 2520–2531, 2009.

[9] G. Chen, Y. Mao, and C. K. Chui, "A symmetric image encryption scheme based on 3D chaotic cat maps," *Chaos, Solitons and Fractals*, vol. 21, no. 3, pp. 749–761, 2004.

[10] T. Gao and Z. Chen, "A new image encryption algorithm based on hyper-chaos," *Physics Letters A*, vol. 372, no. 4, pp. 394–400, 2008.

[11] A.-V. Diaconu and K. Loukhaoukha, "An improved secure image encryption algorithm based on rubik's cube principle and digital chaotic cipher," *Mathematical Problems in Engineering*, vol. 2013, Article ID 848392, 10 pages, 2013.

[12] O. Mirzaei, M. Yaghoobi, and H. Irani, "A new image encryption method: parallel sub-image encryption with hyper chaos," *Nonlinear Dynamics*, vol. 67, no. 1, pp. 557–566, 2012.

[13] C. K. Huang, C. W. Liao, S. L. Hsu, and Y. C. Jeng, "Implementation of gray image encryption with pixel shuffling and gray-level encryption by single chaotic system," *Telecommunication Systems*, vol. 52, no. 2, pp. 563–571, 2013.

[14] G. Ye and K.-W. Wong, "An efficient chaotic image encryption algorithm based on a generalized arnold map," *Nonlinear Dynamics*, vol. 69, no. 4, pp. 2079–2087, 2012.

[15] G. Ye and K.-W. Wong, "An image encryption scheme based on time-delay and hyperchaotic system," *Nonlinear Dynamics*, vol. 71, no. 1-2, pp. 259–267, 2013.

[16] X. Tong and M. Cui, "Feedback image encryption algorithm with compound chaotic stream cipher based on perturbation," *Science in China F: Information Sciences*, vol. 53, no. 1, pp. 191–202, 2010.

[17] Z.-X. Zhang and T. Cao, "A chaos-based image encryption scheme with confusion-diffusion architecture," *Communications in Computer and Information Science*, vol. 152, no. 1, pp. 258–263, 2011.

[18] A. J. Menezes, P. C. Oorschot, and S. A. Vanstone, *Handbook of Applied Cryptography*, CRC Press, 1997.

[19] D. Arroyo, G. Alvarez, S. Li, C. Li, and J. Nunez, "Cryptanalysis of a discrete-time synchronous chaotic encryption system," *Physics Letters A*, vol. 372, no. 7, pp. 1034–1039, 2008.

[20] C. Li, L. Y. Zhang, R. Ou, K.-W. Wong, and S. Shu, "Breaking a novel colour image encryption algorithm based on chaos," *Nonlinear Dynamics*, vol. 70, no. 4, pp. 2383–2388, 2012.

[21] F. Huang and Y. Feng, "Security analysis of image encryption based on twodimensional chaotic maps and improved algorithm," *Frontiers of Electrical and Electronic Engineering in China*, vol. 4, no. 1, pp. 5–9, 2009.

[22] J. Wang, G. Jiang, and B. Lin, "Cryptanalysis of an image encryption scheme with a pseudorandom permutation and its improved version," *Journal of Electronics*, vol. 29, no. 1-2, pp. 82–93, 2012.

[23] R. Rhouma and S. Belghith, "Cryptanalysis of a new image encryption algorithm based on hyper-chaos," *Physics Letters A: General, Atomic and Solid State Physics*, vol. 372, no. 38, pp. 5973–5978, 2008.

[24] G. Álvarez, F. Montoya, M. Romera, and G. Pastor, "Cryptanalysis of an ergodic chaotic cipher," *Physics Letters A: General, Atomic and Solid State Physics*, vol. 311, no. 2-3, pp. 172–179, 2003.

[25] D. Arroyo, J. M. Amigoy, S. Li, and G. Alvarez, "On the inadequacy of unimodal maps for cryptographic applications," in *XI Reunion Espanola sobre Criptologia y Seguridad de la Informacion (XI RECSI)*, pp. 37–42, Universitat Rovira i Virgili, Tarragona, Spain, 2010.

[26] A. C. Dăscălescu, R. E. Boriga, and A. V. Diaconu, "Study of a new chaotic dynamical system and its usage in a novel pseudorandom bit generator," *Mathematical Problems in Engineering*, vol. 2013, Article ID 769108, 10 pages, 2013.

[27] C. Li, S. Li, G. Alvarez, G. Chen, and K.-T. Lo, "Cryptanalysis of two chaotic encryption schemes based on circular bit shift and XOR operations," *Physics Letters A: General, Atomic and Solid State Physics*, vol. 369, no. 1-2, pp. 23–30, 2007.

[28] V. Patidar, K. K. Sud, and N. K. Pareek, "A pseudo random bit generator based on chaotic logistic map and its statistical testing," *Informatica*, vol. 33, no. 4, pp. 441–452, 2009.

[29] M. Hénon, "A two-dimensional mapping with a strange attractor," *Communications in Mathematical Physics*, vol. 50, no. 1, pp. 69–77, 1976.

[30] S. Grossmann and S. Thomae, "Invariant distributions and stationary correlation functions of one-dimensional discrete processes," *Zeitschrift fur Naturforschung*, vol. 32, pp. 1353–1363, 1977.

[31] K. T. Alligood, T. D. Sauer, and J. A. Yorke, *Chaos: An Introduction to Dynamical Systems*, Springer, 1st edition, 1996.

[32] M. T. Rosenstein, J. J. Collins, and C. J. De Luca, "A practical method for calculating largest Lyapunov exponents from small data sets," *Physica D: Nonlinear Phenomena*, vol. 65, no. 1-2, pp. 117–134, 1993.

[33] H. G. Schuster, *Deterministic Chaos: An Introduction*, Wiley-VCH, 3rd edition, 1995.

[34] J. Fridrich, "Symmetric ciphers based on two-dimensional chaotic maps," *International Journal of Bifurcation and Chaos in Applied Sciences and Engineering*, vol. 8, no. 6, pp. 1259–1284, 1998.

[35] A. Wolf, J. B. Swift, H. L. Swinney, and J. A. Vastano, "Determining Lyapunov exponents from a time series," *Physica D: Nonlinear Phenomena*, vol. 16, no. 3, pp. 285–317, 1985.

[36] P. Grassberger and I. Procaccia, "Measuring the strangeness of strange attractors," *Physica D: Nonlinear Phenomena*, vol. 9, no. 1-2, pp. 189–208, 1983.

[37] J. D. Farmer, E. Ott, and J. A. Yorke, "The dimension of chaotic attractors," *Physica D: Nonlinear Phenomena*, vol. 7, no. 1-3, pp. 153–180, 1983.

[38] J. Theiler, "Estimating fractal dimension," *Journal of the Optical Society of America A*, no. 7, pp. 1055–1079, 1990.

[39] L. I. Shujun, G. Chen, and X. Mou, "On the dynamical degradation of digital piecewise linear chaotic maps," *International Journal of Bifurcation and Chaos in Applied Sciences and Engineering*, vol. 15, no. 10, pp. 3119–3151, 2005.

[40] A. Luca, A. Vlad, B. Badea, and M. Frunzete, "A study on statistical independence in the tent map," in *Proceedings of the International Symposium on Signals, Circuits and Systems (ISSCS '09)*, pp. 1–4, Iaşi, Romania, July 2009.

[41] A. Rukhin, J. Soto, J. Nechvatal et al., "A statistical test suite for the validation of random number generators and pseudo random number generators for cryptographic applications," NIST Special Publication 800-22, 2010.

[42] http://www.stat.fsu.edu/pub/diehard/.

[43] A. C. Dăscălescu and R. E. Boriga, "A novel fast chaos-based algorithm for generating random permutations with high shift factor suitable for image scrambling," *Nonlinear Dynamics*, vol. 74, no. 1-2, pp. 307–318, 2013.

[44] USC-SIPI Image Database, University of South California, Signal and Image Processing Institute, http://sipi.usc.edu/database/database.php.

[45] Kodak Digital Camera Sample Pictures, Kodak, http://www.kodak.com/digitalImages/samples/samples.shtml.

[46] C. E. Shannon, "Communication theory of secrecy systems," *The Bell System Technical Journal*, vol. 28, no. 4, pp. 656–715, 1949.

[47] D. R. Cox and C. A. Donnelly, *Principles of Applied Statistics*, Cambridge University Press, 2011.

[48] H. Gao, Y. Zhang, S. Liang, and D. Li, "A new chaotic algorithm for image encryption," *Chaos, Solitons and Fractals*, vol. 29, no. 2, pp. 393–399, 2006.

[49] H. S. Kwok and W. K. S. Tang, "A fast image encryption system based on chaotic maps with finite precision representation," *Chaos, Solitons and Fractals*, vol. 32, no. 4, pp. 1518–1529, 2007.

[50] B. Stoyanov and K. Kordov, "Novel image encryption scheme based on Chebyshev polynomial and Duffing map," *The Scientific World Journal*, vol. 2014, Article ID 283639, 11 pages, 2014.

[51] N. K. Pareek, V. Patidar, and K. K. Sud, "Substitution-diffusion based Image Cipher," *International Journal of Network Security and Its Applications (IJNSA)*, vol. 3, no. 2, pp. 149–160, 2011.

[52] M. Ghebleh, A. Kanso, and H. Noura, "An image encryption scheme based on irregularly decimated chaotic maps," *Signal Processing: Image Communication*, vol. 29, no. 5, pp. 618–627, 2014.

3

A IEEE 802.11e HCCA Scheduler with a Reclaiming Mechanism for Multimedia Applications

Anna Lina Ruscelli and Gabriele Cecchetti

TeCIP Institute, Scuola Superiore Sant'Anna, 56124 Pisa, Italy

Correspondence should be addressed to Anna Lina Ruscelli; a.ruscelli@sssup.it

Academic Editor: Mei-Ling Shyu

The QoS offered by the IEEE 802.11e reference scheduler is satisfactory in the case of Constant Bit Rate traffic streams, but not yet in the case of Variable Bit Rate traffic streams, whose variations stress its scheduling behavior. Despite the numerous proposed alternative schedulers with QoS, multimedia applications are looking for refined methods suitable to ensure service differentiation and dynamic update of protocol parameters. In this paper a scheduling algorithm, *Unused Time Shifting Scheduler* (UTSS), is deeply analyzed. It is designed to cooperate with a HCCA centralized real-time scheduler through the integration of a bandwidth reclaiming scheme, suitable to recover nonexhausted transmission time and assign that to the next polled stations. UTSS dynamically computes with an $O(1)$ complexity transmission time providing an instantaneous resource overprovisioning. The theoretical analysis and the simulation results highlight that this injection of resources does not affect the admission control nor the centralized scheduler but is suitable to improve the performance of the centralized scheduler in terms of mean access delay, transmission queues length, bursts of traffic management, and packets drop rate. These positive effects are more relevant for highly variable bit rate traffic.

1. Introduction

Service differentiation tailored to the type of applications and stations requirements is a key issue of *Quality of Service* (QoS) provided by a network. The focus of the research on this topic is motivated by the spreading diffusion of multimedia applications that users ask the network to conveniently support. Indeed, applications like *Voice over IP* (VoIP), video streaming, video conference, and *High Digital TV* (HDTV) have different features and must be appropriately handled.

IEEE 802.11e *Medium Access Control* (MAC) *Hybrid Coordination Channel Access Function* (HCCA) [1], based on a centralized polling mechanism, has been proposed in order to introduce QoS support by means of differentiation and negotiation of stations service parameters. In particular, a new protocol parameter, *Transmission Opportunity* (TXOP), has been introduced in order to guarantee a maximum transmission time for each station, whereas the polling period is managed by the *Service Interval* (SI) parameter. The purpose of the other 802.11e MAC function, *Enhanced*

Distributed Channel Access (EDCA), is the same but based on *Carrier Sense Multiple Access/Collision Avoidance* mechanism and on differentiation of contention parameters.

However, since these parameters are set by the *reference scheduler* as fixed values in time and for the different stations, the network shows poor performances and the QoS management is not yet satisfactory for applications with variable bandwidth, data rate, packet size, and so forth [2–5]. Indeed, in the case of *Constant Bit Rate* (CBR) traffic, the network is yet suitable to guarantee the required service, whereas, as far as *Variable Bit Rate* (VBR) applications are concerned, it is not able to conveniently follow the traffic changes. Therefore, in order to meet the QoS applications requirements, the MAC scheduling of stations and resources must be refined by means of more specific differentiation mechanisms. The differentiation of service, in the case of IEEE 802.11e HCCA, can be based on diverse approaches, such as (1) modifying the scheduling engine to provide variable TXOP and SI; (2) adopting a simple overprovisioning method (for instance, considering worst case conditions parameters values); (3) integrating/introducing mechanisms to tune the MAC parameters accordingly to the changing traffic profile. An example of the latter solution is the instantaneous dynamic computation of resource assignment respecting the admission control that deals with the capacity allocation constrained by the thresholds of available resources. Otherwise bandwidth reclaiming methods can be adopted: they simply recover the exceeding allocated resources, not used by some stations, and assign that to other stations, without any impact on the resource allocation performed by the admission control, but like a "legal" form of overprovisioning.

In this paper a recently proposed scheduling algorithm, *Unused Time Shifting Scheduler* (UTSS) [6], based on a simple reclaiming mechanism, is deeply analyzed. It is inspired by the consideration that in HCCA standard reference scheduler when a station has finished to transmit but it has not exhausted its assigned transmission time, that is, its TXOP, this residue of time is simply lost and the right to transmit is transferred to the next polled station. Furthermore, the resource allocation is based on the TXOP computation performed during the admission control, when the considered station asked to be associated to the *QoS Access Point* (QAP). In general, this computation takes into account mean traffic conditions, in order to have enough chances to meet stations requirements but, at the same time, avoiding expensive overprovisioning. Consequently, in the case of VBR traffic, when data rate decreases, the accorded TXOP can exceed the actually used transmission time but, if no reclaiming mechanisms are implemented, the exceeding capacity is lost. Otherwise, if it were possible to keep memory of this not spent transmission time and use that for stations with strict QoS requirements, a more efficient resources management would be possible, without affecting the overall admission control computation.

UTSS has been conceived as a cooperative centralized scheduler that can be integrated in any preexistent HCCA centralized scheduler. It simply recovers the nonexhausted portion of TXOP and allocates that to the next polled station. Thus, if this *Qos STAtion* (QSTA) experiences an instantaneous increase of data rate not satisfied with its TXOP, the recovered portion of transmission time can absorb the burst of traffic, without violating the QoS of other admitted stations and without eroding their accorded capacity. The behavior of UTSS will be analyzed both from the analytical and the simulation points of view; considering that, since UTSS is a supplementary mechanism that collaborates with a preexistent algorithm, each effect has to be evaluated with respect to the centralized scheduler that biases the behavior of the global scheduler. In particular, both theoretical and simulative results highlight that it does not impact on admission control and on the scheduling engine of the centralized scheduler, but that it allows a considerable improvement of network performances of the centralized scheduler in terms of access delay, throughput, packets drop rate, and transmission queues length. The analysis has been performed considering CBR and VBR traffic with increasing data rate (VoIP, video conference, video streaming, and bursty traffic) in order to reflect real world multimedia traffic and the

impact on the related TXOPs computation is investigated. In particular, the choice of VBR scenarios composed by different TSs with increasing data rate stresses UTSS just where most of the QoS schedulers proposed in literature show poor performance; moreover it highlights how and where the contribution with UTSS can be beneficial. Theoretical analysis and simulations will show that UTSS is outperforming in the case of highly variable VBR TSs whereas, in the case of CBR traffic or of traffic with low variable bite rate, its contribution is limited because the centralized QoS scheduler is suitable to efficiently serve the considered traffic streams allocating the required resource. Indeed, UTSS simply operates as a greedy algorithm that recovers unexhausted resources avoiding their waste and allocates that to the next polled station, without verifying through monitoring or statistical studies if this station really needs that. This is its flaw but also its strength since it is suitable to improve network performance without impacting on the system overhead due to $O(1)$ computational complexity, as it will be analytically shown. Thus, even when its action in not needed, it does not overload the scheduler computation.

Furthermore, with the aim to provide a deep insight on the cooperation of UTSS with a centralized scheduler, choosing as example *Wireless Capacity-Based Scheduler* (WCBS), the obtained global scheduler has been compared with two other advanced peer methods well known in literature, *Fair HCF* (FHCF) [7] and *Real-Time HCCA* (RTH) [8].

The rest of the paper is organized as follows. In Section 2 the IEEE 802.11e HCCA protocol along with its reference scheduler are described. In Section 3 the state of arts about some scheduling algorithms with QoS, proposed as alternative to the reference one, are summarized highlighting their pros and cons, whereas in Section 4 UTSS is illustrated. Then, in Section 5 UTSS is analyzed from the theoretical point of view considering its impact on admission control and on the real-time behavior of the global scheduler; furthermore TXOP computation and management of VBR traffic like VoIP, video conference, video streaming, and bursty traffic are investigated. Section 6 reports the simulations results that confirm the analytical considerations and are corroborated by them and provides a comparison of the global scheduler against two QoS advanced methods. Finally, Section 7 draws some conclusions.

2. IEEE 802.11e Standard

The IEEE 802.11e standard amends the previous IEEE 802.11b with two further MAC functions, suitable to provide QoS support and coordinated by the *Hybrid Coordination Function* (HCF): the *Enhanced Distributed Channel Access* (EDCA) distributed mode and the *HCF Controlled Channel Access* (HCCA) centralized scheme.

EDCA is the evolution of the basic IEEE 802.11b *Distributed Channel Access* (DCF), where stations contend the access to the medium. EDCA adds a prioritization of service based on QoS requirements of the QSTAs that can choose between four different Access Categories. HCCA updates the centralized polling scheme of IEEE 802.11b *Point Coordination Function* (PCF) to introduce QoS negotiation. The standard establishes EDCA and HCCA as totally compliant with the original DCF and PCF functions, ensuring compatibility whit legacy devices.

Since HCCA is object of the presented study, it will be deeply analyzed in the following.

2.1. HCCA Function. HCCA function is managed by A QoS-aware *Hybrid Coordinator* (HC), located in the QAP, that takes action during the *Controlled Access Phase* (CAP), and that uses a polling mechanism to allocate guaranteed channel access to traffic streams, based on their QoS requirements. This scheme allows a station to transmit only if required by the QAP that sends the CF-Poll frame. In order to be included in the polling list of HC, a QSTA sends it a QoS reservation request by means of the *Add Traffic Stream* (ADDTS) QoS management frame, which collects stream information (mean data rate, mean packet size, MAC service data unit size, maximum tolerable delay, etc.). In order to implement service differentiation up to eight traffic classes, the *Traffic Streams* (TSs), with different QoS levels, are supported.

TSs parameters are collected in the *Traffic Specification* (TSPEC), whose values are negotiated between QSTA and QAP and used by the resource scheduler enabling a parameterized QoS.

2.2. HCCA Reference Scheduler. The IEEE 802.11e standard draws some guidelines for a nonmandatory HCCA *reference* scheduler suitable to take into account QoS requirements of QSTAs and used as reference for the design of any other HCCA scheduling algorithm. This reference scheduler deals with the computation of the main protocol parameters used to manage the access to the medium. It computes SI and TXOP as fixed values. SI is calculated as a unique value for all admitted QSTAs with the aim to globally meet their temporal service expectations. In particular, in order to ensure that each QSTA is polled at least once during the beacon interval, the scheduler establishes that SI has to be less than the beacon interval itself. Moreover, to guarantee that the polling period constraints of all traffic streams are respected, it has to be less than the minimum *Maximum Service Interval* (MSI).

Adopting a conservative approach TXOP is computed as the maximum time to transmit, at the minimum physical rate Γ_i, the total amount of bits enqueued during SI:

$$N_i = \left\lceil \frac{\text{SI} \cdot R_i}{L_i} \right\rceil, \qquad \text{TXOP}_i = \max\left(\frac{N_i \cdot L_i}{\Gamma_i}, \frac{M_i}{\Gamma_i} \right) + O, \tag{1}$$

where M_i is the maximum *MAC Service Data Unit* (MSDU) size, that is, 2304 bytes, L_i is the nominal MSDU size, R_i is the mean data rate, and O is the transmission overhead due to interframe spaces, ACK, and CF-Poll.

As previously mentioned, the computation of TXOP and SI is necessary to distribute the available resources taking into account the QoS requirements of each station that asks to transmit. Furthermore, due to resource constraints, only

the stations that can be served with the available resources taking into account more stringent QoS needs are selected to transmit. The HCCA reference admission control test for deciding whether to admit a new stream is the following:

$$\frac{\text{TXOP}_{k+1}}{\text{SI}} + \sum_{i=0}^{k} \frac{\text{TXOP}_i}{\text{SI}} \leq \frac{T - T_{\text{CP}}}{T} \leq 1, \tag{2}$$

where k is the number of yet admitted streams, $k + 1$ indexes the newly admitted stream, T is the beacon interval, and T_{CP} is the duration of the *Contention Period*, managed by EDCA.

After the admission control phase SI and TXOP are recomputed only if a new traffic stream arrives to the station. Since their values are based on *worst case* conditions the admission control test results to be too stringent and the resource management is not optimal. Moreover, since SI is the same for all admitted QSTASs and TXOP is globally assigned to all the streams of a QSTA, all different TSs of a station are polled with the same period and are served with the same computation time. Therefore, as highlighted by numerous studies and evaluations [2–5], the reference scheduler is suitable to serve CBR traffic but unable to efficiently adapt the resource management to VBR TSs.

3. HCCA Scheduling Algorithms

Due to the limitations of the reference scheduler on QoS provisioning, illustrated above, many alternative scheduling algorithms have been proposed to improve the resource management [3, 9–11] and few of them are focused on the real-time support [12], that is, on temporal guarantees. In the following, to the best of our knowledge, some significant QoS schedulers are summarized. They range over different methods used to mix together efficient resource management and QoS guarantees, including queue length models, feedback-based schemes, deadlines management, integration of additional schedulers, exploitation of EDCA resources by means of the IEEE 802.11e *HCCA-EDCA Mixed Mode* (HEMM) mode that allows to jointly use both the HCCA and the EDCA MAC mechanisms, and bandwidth reclaiming methods. Moreover, for each of them we try to highlight pros and cons going deep inside into their features and performance.

The need of a variable TXOP, due to VBR traffic streams, was perceived also before the establishment of IEEE 802.11e amendment.

Predictive-HCCA (P-HCCA) [13] yet provided a rough mechanism to predict the mean data rate during the next polling phase and to assign a variable transmission time tailored to VBR traffic. Despite this, it does not consider the effect of this computation on the admission control feasibility test.

An example of use of traffic queues model is *Fair HCF* (FHCF) [7]. It mathematically models the uplink traffic streams queues length to estimate the global packets delay and to compute variable TXOPs with the aims to improve the fairness of both CBR and VBR traffic and the delay performances. FHCF provides a deep insight on the delay components and on queues length, modeling the queues at the beginning of the polling phase in order to have an evaluation of the actual queues length. In particular, the packets queuing delay, influenced by the variations in packet size and data rate, is distinguished from the waiting time delay between the packet arrival time and the QSTA polling time. The investigation in the case of both CBR and VBR traffic is functional to distinguish where the reference scheduler performs well, and queues are empty since the scheduler allocated the required resources, and the case where more capacity could be needed. Being composed by two schedulers, one located at the QAP and one local to the node, FHCF is able to refine the TXOP computation. Indeed, whereas the QAP scheduler takes into account estimated and ideal queues length, the node scheduler, using its exact value, is able to recompute the needed time and redistribute the additional resources between the different TSs. Even if this complex structure impacts on system overhead and efficiency, a variable TXOP, useful in the case of VBR traffic, improves access delay.

The closed loop feedback control of *Feedback Based Dynamic Scheduler* (FBDS) [14] tries to ensure a tailored delivery of enqueued packets, limiting the maximum delay. A discrete time model of queues length at the beginning of the CAP, where HCCA is used, corrected by the actual queues length information sent by each QSTA, is used to dynamically compute TXOPs through a simple proportional controller. In particular, TXOP is assigned a value suitable to dispatch at the average depletion rate the amount of packets that can be enqueued during a CAP, whereas SIs have fixed values, as calculated during the admission control. Unfortunately the queues model and the setting of TXOP consider mean rates and MSDU size and assume the contribution of EDCA in the emptying queues, without any deeper analysis. As far as the admission control is concerned, the authors distinguish when there is network overload and when new TSs ask to be admitted to transmit. In the first case they propose to decrease all TXOPs of an amount proportional to the corresponding data rate. This solution aims not penalize stations with low data rate but does not take into account any type of QoS requirement. In the second case a new admission test is proposed that includes different TXOP values and CAP duration in the place of SI; this results in admitting a less number of streams with respect to the reference scheduler.

Instead of queues length estimation, in *Explicit Traffic Aware scheduling with Explicit Queue length Notification* (ETA-EQN) [15] QAP computes the current TXOP considering the exact queues length notification sent by the stations to the QAP at the end of their transmissions through EDCA function, (to avoid using HCCA resources). Furthermore the *TXOPLimit* standard parameter, that sets the maximum accorded TXOP considered during the admission control, is increased in order to provide instantaneous longer transmission time and to avoid excessive reduction of SI that can increase the system overhead. This is obtained by setting some unused bits of TSPEC without modifying the structure of *TXOPLimit* fields. This simple dynamic TXOP computation is suitable to increase network throughput and to reduce mean delay and packets loss rate. However, being based on simple notifications, the proposed algorithm is agnostic of every traffic profile.

Arora et al. [16] proposed a mechanism to provide an adaptive TXOP, applicable to existing schedulers and based on the concept of link adaptation, addressed by few schedulers, to consider channel conditions. Assuming the TXOP computation provided by the centralized scheduler, the introduced algorithm takes into account the channel state and degrades the TXOP of stations with bad channel conditions until a minimum, distributing the exceeding time to the stations into good channel conditions and returning the stations to their normal TXOP when the channel state becomes good again. This allows for maximizing the overall throughput taking into account the current physical rate of nodes. Moreover, in order to ensure long-term and short-term temporal fairness, a lead-lag counter is used for accounting the transmissions state of each station with respect to the corresponding error-free service model as provided by a general centralized scheduler. Finally, two counters are used to memorize the received and the returned transmission time.

As far as the use of both HCCA and EDCA modes is concerned, if the purpose is to improve and extend in time the QoS service when HCCA has exhausted its accorded duration, a possible shortcut is trying to use EDCA to continue delivery of TSs packets. Few studies have investigated both these access functions and their behavior with different types of traffic. The Markov channel model in [17] shows that incrementing the HCCA duration increases the medium utilization of large WLAN in saturation conditions and the channel control determinism. Instead, large EDCA networks are affected by growing collisions that degrade their performance.

In [18] the economic model used to efficiently manage elastic traffic over EDCA and HCCA highlights that CSMA/CA method, *Request To Send/Clear To Send* (RTS/CTS) scheme, and the setting of CW_{min} parameter impact channel congestion and throughput. Moreover, the optimal HCCA-EDCA ratio is deduced through optimization techniques.

The *Adaptively Tuned HCF* (AT-HCF) algorithm [19] dynamically adapts the HCCA and the EDCA durations to the different types of traffic (VBR and CBR), until they converge to the optimal values to improve the delay and the throughput of the overall system. It is based on a two-step algorithm that adjusts the value of the CapLimit standard parameter that sets the maximum HCCA duration, without impacting on the different used schedulers but simply modifying the relative duration of the two MAC functions.

The *Overboost* local node scheduler [20] exploits EDCA bandwidth to integrate HCCA with the aim to limit the delay experienced by the traffic streams waiting for the next HCCA polling time and improve the network performance. Before the Contention Period begins, Overboost moves the TSs traffic exceeding the assigned HCCA TXOPs from the HCCA queues to the higher priority Access Category EDCA queue, providing the best QoS as available through the contention access. This scheduler can be integrated with any type of centralized HCCA scheduling algorithm that continues to manage admission control, scheduling parameters, and polling list. Moreover it does not require any modification in the standard protocol parameters used to manage EDCA and HCCA, neither does it affect the scheduling of stations during HCCA and their accorded QoS but simply exploits EDCA to continue transmitting QoS TSs. Since EDCA is a distributed scheme, that is, without a central entity, Overboost is located in each node, allowing each QSTA to operate according to the contention rules and accessing to EDCA queues mechanism. Simulation and analytical results show that Overboost positively impacts on efficient resource management and on queues length and access delay. Indeed, the cooperation with Overboost has performance comparable with those of overprovisioning, admitting the same number of TSs with a better QoS or admitting more TSs with the same QoS, but without impacting on the admission control. From a different point of view, it allows same results than underprovisioning, saving resources but maintaining the negotiated QoS.

As example of first reclaiming mechanisms, in [21] a bandwidth reclaiming scheme for the PCF function with *Weighted Round Robin* (WRR) scheduling policy is proposed. It determines when the unused transmission time can be either used to advance the next polling opportunity or assigned to the Contention Period. Moreover, the WRR polling list is modified in order to put the stations with higher probability of generating unused time at the end of the list. This rearrangement aims to reduce the number of reclaimed stations but it makes the solution not extensible to HCCA function, where the polling order is strictly related to real-time guarantees.

In [22] an HCCA bandwidth reclaiming mechanism is presented and open-loop strategies, based on the use of TSPEC, and closed-loop strategies, that use the transmission queues information sent by stations to the QAP, are compared. Two different *max-min fairness* algorithms are proposed to reduce the HCCA delay in the case of VBR traffic by recovering spare resources through a proportional controller. A weighted proportional function assigns an additional amount of resources proportionally to the traffic class and to the buffer length. *MaxMin Fair-Adaptive* (MMF-A) assumes fixed SI, whereas *MaxMin Fair-Adaptive with Rescheduling* (MMF-AR) considers dynamic SI values. The nonlinearities that can affect the abovementioned work are overcome by [23] with an optimal controller, based on Model Predictive Control [24], that dynamically assigns resources in order to empty buffers of the stations and reduce packets loss.

Moreover, in [25] both cited proportional controller and optimal controller algorithms are applied to multiclass traffic with different priorities and to heterogenous traffic in order to find the resource assignment tailored to maximize the throughput, reducing the packet loss experienced by the different types of traffic.

Immediate Dynamic TXOP HCCA [26] scheduler introduces a bandwidth reclaiming scheme that tunes the assigned transmission time considering the transmission duration of previous polling of the considered station, in order to avoid providing further capacity when it is not needed.

However, since it is suitable to provide only short-term fairness in allocating recovered resources, same authors proposed *Dynamic TXOP HCCA* [27] algorithm that refines TXOP computation integrating a mechanism suitable to estimate the required transmission time at the current polling by the use of time series forecasting applied to previous polling phases selected by a Moving Average. This provides a more accurate estimation of needed transmission time and a long-term fairness by means of a traffic monitoring window with tunable length.

The concept of deadlines is suitable to report timing constraints and to meet temporal requirements. The *Scheduling Estimated Transmission Time-Earliest Due Date* (SETT-EDD) [28] algorithm uses a token bucket of time units, or TXOP timer, to vary TXOP over time according to the node requirements. Indeed, considering the minimum and the maximum TXOP durations instead of using the mean value of TXOP, the authors propose to increase its value of a constant rate equal to the total fraction of time a QSTA can transmit during polling with respect to its minimum SI. This allows to adapt the transmission interval to VBR TSs. SI of each node is computed taking into account its traffic profile, varying from its minimum value (minimum SI) and the maximum one (maximum SI), which corresponds to its deadline. This solution, one of the first proposed for HCCA, allows for making TXOP and SI variable just exploiting the protocol parameters that set their minimum and the maximum values. Finally Delay-EDD [29], that computes deadlines considering delay bounds, determines the polling order. Variable TXOP and SI enhance the scheduler flexibility and lead to significant reduction in average transmission delay and packet loss ratio.

Instead the timer-based scheduler presented in [30] aims at providing variable and different SIs. SI of each station is computed as the smallest between the downlink and uplink deadlines that are calculated considering the different delay bounds of stations, in order to introduce a service differentiation tailored for CBR and VBR TSs. Then, traffic streams are scheduled according to *Earliest Deadline First* (EDF) [31] algorithm. This solution, even not exhaustive in terms of QoS since does not take into account the need of different TXOPs, is suitable to reduce the delay, the jitter, and the packets loss experienced by diverse types of traffic (voice and video) as well as increase the network capacity serving more video streams with respect to the reference scheduler, assuming the same packet loss.

Real-Time HCCA (RTH) [8] scheduler aims at ensuring each QSTA a fixed transmission time with a fixed period. In order to lighten the online scheduling, RTH has two components, the offline and the online activities. The first one performs the more complex work, executing admission control, computing transmission parameters, and scheduling timetable, where the TSPEC parameters are converted in capacity and period. Instead the online activity schedules traffic streams transmissions, simply applying the results of the first one (enforcement procedure); thus its computational complexity is $O(1)$. Since an EDF-based algorithm schedules TSs transmissions that introduce a prioritization of streams, RTH manages TXOP as critical section, which cannot be interrupted by higher priority flows, by using *Stack Resource Policy* (SRP) algorithm [32]. This implies the inclusion of critical sections in the admission control schedulability test and increases the computational load. However, in the case of a new TS asking to be admitted, RTH states that the QAP can simply positively or negatively answer and postpone the transmission of the new TS in order to take the time to perform the heavy computation. Despite its complexity, RTH is suitable to improve the system efficiency, with respect to reference scheduler, admitting more TSs and living more capacity to EDCA, while ensuring the same QoS.

Adaptive Resource Reservation over WLANs (ARROW) [33] dynamically computes TXOPs by taking into account the actual buffered TSs data at the beginning of the polling. In particular, it simply uses the standard protocol *Queue Size* field of *QoS Data* frame to feedback the queue length at the beginning of transmission and that will be used to compute the duration of the subsequent TXOP as the sum the of maximum duration of each TSs. This allows for adapting the transmission interval to traffic profile that is useful especially in the case of VBR and bursty streams, as discussed in the previous sections. Moreover, a strict upper bound is set for MSI in order to ensure no deadline miss and delay requirements. Despite increased system overhead due to the augmented number of polling and the consequent increase of delay, the higher frequency of TXOP recomputation improves the system throughput in terms of number of served TSs, fraction of used TXOP, packets loss, and channel occupancy. Finally *Earliest Due Date* (EDD) [34] deadlines scheduling manages the QSTAs polling list.

The *Application-Aware Adaptive HCCA Scheduler* [35], derived from ARROW, distinguishes uplink and downlink schedulers, while EDF defines the QSTAs polling order taking into account the stations deadlines. The uplink scheduler assigns each QSTA a minimum and a maximum SI that imposes the respect of traffic period and delay bound, tailored to application (CBR and VBR) and network conditions and to the buffered traffic. Thus QAP continuously monitors transmission beginning and ending time plus new transmission requests and actual size of packets for each TS, and then compares these variables with the corresponding in TSPEC. In the case of downlink scheduler this computation exploits QAP buffered traffic and PHY rate. Even if this structure implies a precise signaling of this overall information and a cross-layer coordination between QSTAs and QAP, it allows improvements in terms of overall throughput, packets loss, and delay.

Since in what follows of this study *Wireless Capacity Based Scheduler* (WCBS) [36] will be used for the implementation of UTSS as example of centralized scheduler suitable to provide variable TXOP and polling order and different SI, it will be deeply analyzed in the subsequent subsection.

(1) Wireless Capacity Based Schedule. WCBS [36] is a deadlines-based centralized scheduler that aims at introducing a dynamic mechanism for allocating-recharging capacity taking into account used transmission time and temporal requirements. First of all, being focused on real-time expectations of TSs, it dynamically updates the polling list of TSs by means of EDF. The order of increasing deadlines allows reordering the original first-in first-out list to poll

first the stations with TSs with more strict temporal needs. Then the resource allocation and the access to the medium are managed by means of static and dynamic parameters, assigned differently to each QSTA to adapt the transmissions scheduling to its TSs characteristics. In particular, during the admission control, a pair of static parameters, unchanged until there are modifications in the service negotiation, for instance due to the association of new stations with more strict QoS requirements, are assigned to each TS_i taking into account its $TSPEC_i$: the budget Q_i, that is equivalent to $TXOP_i$, and the polling period P_i, that is, the service interval SI_i. Their ratio $U_i = Q_i/P_i$ is the utilization factor of the stream, that is, its bandwidth that is considered in the admission control feasibility test. These two parameters set the transmission time allocation for the considered station and the general polling time limitation. In particular P_i is computed as the maximum SI for the considered TS. Instead Q_i is obtained by a weighted function of the minimum time Q_{min} and the maximum time Q_{max}. Q_{min} is the time interval needed to transmit, during a period P_i, and at the mean data rate R_i a MSDU of nominal size L_i, whereas Q_{max} is the time needed to send at peak data rate Π_i, a MSDU of maximum size M_i:

$$Q_{min} = \left\lceil \frac{R_i P_i}{L_i} \right\rceil \cdot t_n, \qquad Q_{max} = \left\lceil \frac{\Pi_i P_i}{M_i} \right\rceil \cdot t_n, \qquad (3)$$

where t_n is the nominal transmission time during a polling, computed as $t_n = t_{DATA} + t_{SIFS} + t_{ACK} + t_{SIFS}$.

Different from the reference scheduler, the polling periods can be different for the diverse QSTAs, in dependency of their TSs. Therefore the admission control test expressed by (2) begins as follows, where now different value of SIs are considered:

$$\frac{TXOP_{k+1}}{SI_{k+1}} + \sum_{i=0}^{k} \frac{TXOP_i}{SI_i} \leq \frac{T - T_{CP}}{T} \leq 1. \qquad (4)$$

Instead, the dynamic parameters characterize the scheduling phase of each TS_i and its evolution. At each polling WCBS assigns a station its allocated resources, taking into account its Q_i. However, since during a transmission, especially in the case of VBR TSs, a station cannot exhaust its Q_i, WCBS, already using a recovery mechanism, does not waste the remaining transmission time but takes memory of that through the dynamic parameter c_i, the remaining time of the transmission just finished and that will be assigned to TS_i during its next polling. Different from the previously mentioned reclaiming mechanisms, WCBS preserves the saved resources only for the station that has not used that. Thus it acts like an accordion mechanism that does not waste resource but, at the same time, it is not able to follow traffic profile and add additional resources when needed. As far as the polling action is concerned a further dynamic parameter, the absolute deadline d_i, is used. It sets the absolute time within Q_i has to be exhausted, that is, it is related to the maximum delay bound that can be tolerated. Moreover it is used to determine the next polling time p_i that is updated when, during the current polling, there are no more data to transfer or $TXOP_i$ is exhausted. Finally the stream *state* defines its condition during the evolution of the scheduling: the state is *idle* if there are no data to send for the considered traffic stream, *polling* if this TS is in the polling list, *active* if it has been extracted from the polling queue and inserted in the EDF transmission queue, and *transmitting* if the it is during its sending time.

Consequently, after these definitions, the scheduling engine is as follows.

(i) During the admission control each TS_i is assigned the static parameters Q_i and P_i.

(ii) At the beginning $c_i = Q_i$ and $p_i = d_i$. TSs with *active* state are inserted in the EDF-ordered polling list considering their deadlines d_i.

(iii) WCBS extracts the first TS from the polling queue and sets $TXOP_i = c_i$, changes its state into *transmitting*, and allows the corresponding station to transmit until there is sufficient capacity.

(iv) When $TXOP_i$ is exhausted, WCBS recharges the capacity $c_i = Q_i$, and the next polling time as $p_i = d_i$ or postponing deadline, if the current time $t_c > d_i$, as $d_i = t_c + P_i$. The state becomes *polling*.

(v) When $p_i \leq t_c TS_i$ will be polled again.

(vi) If a transmission ends without exhausting the assigned budget, the remaining capacity will be simply preserved for the next polling.

4. Unused Time Shifting Scheduler

4.1. Motivation. Satisfactory QoS performance of HCCA networks for VBR traffic with real-time guarantees, typical of multimedia applications, has not yet been completely achieved and the HCCA reference polling mechanism shows some inefficiencies in the case of VBR traffic. Moreover, despite many QoS scheduling algorithms proposed as alternative to the reference one, some of them mentioned in Section 3, this type of traffic stresses the behavior of the different families of schedulers. Thus it is pressing to provide tailored and more efficient scheduling policies. For instance, EDF-based algorithms are well performing in the case of CBR traffic streams, whereas they are not able to follow the variations of the VBR ones [12]. Indeed, even if the postponing deadlines mechanism allows a more flexible scheduling in dependency of the actual resource needs, it hinders the respect of delay bounds requirements.

Furthermore, the waste of resources due to data rate variations affects the schedulers that do not implement any recovery policy. In particular, when the instant data rate drops down, a polled QSTA transmits data for an amount of time shorter than its assigned TXOP, easily dispatching the arriving traffic and the eventual enqueued packets. Then, as stated by the reference scheduler, the QoS Access Point, listening the idle channel for a time longer than a *Short Interframe Space* SIFS, assumes the control of the medium and polls the next station. Therefore the unused portion of TXOP is lost. On the other hand, when the instant data rate

goes up, the assigned TXOP, computed considering mean data rate, is not sufficient to deliver the incoming traffic and the station queue length increases. This has the side effect to increase the end-to-end delay and the number of discarded packets, due to the expiration of their validity time. A more flexible scheduling scheme could offer advantages in terms of end-to-end delay and amount of dropped packets in the case of high and variable data rate traffic.

4.2. UTSS Description. Unused Time Shifting Scheduler (UTSS) [6] aims at facing off the problem of not efficient resource management, especially in the case of VBR traffic, by reclaiming the unused transmission time. It provides a shortcut to have an instantaneous dynamic TXOP, without modifying the admission control (see Section 5). The basic idea is to remove from stations the unspent transmission time and to make that available to the next polled stations, especially for those requiring a longer transmission interval. In order to do that UTSS, that is, at its turn, a centralized mechanism, that is, it is located in the QAP, simply introduces a supplementary resource scheduling rule that just handles the recovery of the unused time, without effects on the centralized scheduling scheme. This is a valid alternative to the overprovisioning mechanism that affects admission control and efficient resource provisioning. The UTSS approach is greedy since it does not make differentiations between applications and stations but assigns the recovered resources to the next polled station, which can use this additional transmission capacity without impacting on the admission control threshold, as it will be shown in Section 5.

To illustrate its feature, as example of application of UTSS with a centralized QAP scheduler, the cooperation of UTSS with WCBS, that has been described in Section 3, is considered. Since WCBS is an EDF-based scheduler, whose limits have been explained above, it can be a meaningful case study suitable to show how UTSS works and its advantages.

UTSS integrates the action of the centralized HCCA scheduler by keeping the same admission control and scheduling algorithm. This is due to the fact that the admission control, that computes the basic protocol parameters (TXOP and SI) used during the following polling phases, is performed at the association of the stations to the QAP (it is reiterated only if a new QSTA asks to be admitted to transmit) and precedes the subsequent CAPs. It has no knowledge about the instantaneous unspent time of future transmissions and its computation is based on mean value of QoS parameters, as negotiated with the corresponding QSTAs. These considerations are valid for all centralized schedulers that do not use any type of traffic prediction mechanism.

Figure 1 summarizes the admission control activities of a centralized scheduler, like WCBS, that tests the feasibility condition and, then, computes the static parameters, the initial values of the dynamic ones, and the enqueuing of newly admitted TSs in the polling list, EDF-ordered for WCBS.

UTSS adds its further scheduling rule during the subsequent CAPs, in particular during the updating of the dynamic parameters and immediately before the polling

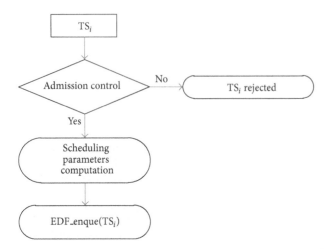

FIGURE 1: Admission control test and activity of a centralized scheduler.

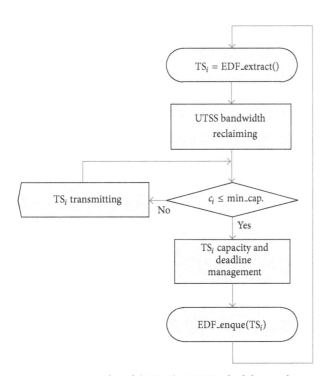

FIGURE 2: EDF-based (WCBS) + UTSS scheduling cycle.

of the considered station, by modifying the related TXOP computed during the admission control, if some unused time is available.

Figure 2 describes the interaction between the EDF-based WCBS and UTSS. The global scheduler based on their cooperation, after the extraction of the next TS_i from the polling queue, performs the UTSS bandwidth reclaiming that affects the currently assigned $TXOP_i$. Then, if there is enough capacity to transmit, TS_i is scheduled for transmission. Otherwise, in the considered example, WCBS operates according to its scheduling rules replenishing the capacity and, if necessary, postponing the deadline. Therefore, while WCBS uses a constant TXOP assigned during the admission

control phase, UTSS can make this parameter variable each time a TS is scheduled for transmission. In particular, each time a QSTA does not use its full allocated TXOP, UTSS assigns this unused time to the next scheduled TS extracted from the EDF queue during the current CAP. In order to illustrate this bandwidth reclaiming scheme the following notation is adopted:

t_{end}: ending time of the transmission $t_{end} = t_p + TXOP$, when TXOP is completely exhausted (t_p is the polling time);

T_{spare}: spare time of TXOP, computed as the difference $t_{end} - t_{effective\text{-}end}$, where $t_{effective\text{-}end}$ is the time when QSTA has actually finished its transmission.

T_{spare} is the variable used by UTSS and it is computed every time QAP polls a QSTA. In particular, $T_{spare} > 0$ if

(i) a station ends its transmission before t_{end} and it does not have enqueued traffic;

(ii) a station ends its transmission before t_{end}, dispatching the incoming traffic and emptying its transmission queue before the ending of TXOP.

Then the current T_{spare} is added to the assigned $TXOP_i$ of the next polled station $QSTA_i$ that will receive a new $TXOP'_i$ computed as follows:

$$TXOP'_i = \begin{cases} TXOP_i, & \text{if } T_{spare} = 0, \\ TXOP_i + T_{spare}, & \text{if } T_{spare} > 0. \end{cases} \quad (5)$$

Figure 3 better details UTSS and its interaction with the centralized scheduler, here WCBS. After the extraction from the EDF queue of the next TS to transmit, UTSS verifies if some spare time from previous transmissions is available. In such case, it adds T_{spare} to the TXOP computed by WCBS ($TXOP_i = c_i - t_p$), (in general, to the TXOP computed by the centralized scheduler). Then the scheduler updates the estimated transmission ending time.

Hence next scheduled traffic streams can be transmitted not only exploiting the correspondent TXOP assigned during the admission control phase, (or the remaining capacity, if they have been already served, in the case of WCBS), but also by using the surplus T_{spare}.

Figure 4 shows a simplified scheduling example where a centralized scheduler and the centralized scheduler plus UTSS are compared. In the case of the centralized algorithm alone the unused bandwidth of TS_2 is wasted whereas, with the help of UTSS, TS_3 transmits its data during also the unused time of previously polled TSs, here of TS_2.

In this way it is possible to reclaim all unused TXOP portions. The total amount of T_{spare} can contribute to satisfy the temporal requirements of a highly variable traffic with a temporary load greater than the mean value used to calculate TXOP during the admission control. Hence T_{spare} can be useful to absorb traffic peaks which characterize highly variable bit rate applications, improving the obtained performance.

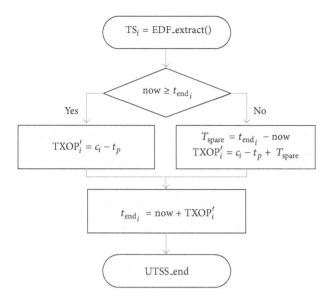

FIGURE 3: UTSS mechanism integrated with the centralized scheduler.

5. UTSS Scheduling Analysis

This section analyzes the UTSS algorithm in order to highlight its effects on the performance of a centralized HCCA scheduler. First of all the general properties of UTSS are studied focusing on its computational complexity, its impact on the system overhead, and its ability to preserve the temporal isolation, that is, to ensure a not interruptible transmission time. Then its strictly related real-time features are investigated. The purpose is to assess whether UTSS changes the admission control feasibility condition. Moreover, it is checked if the backlog mechanism of T_{spare} from previous transmissions can rise or not a deadline miss, jeopardizing the real-time behavior of the global scheduler, and an upper bound of the maximum acceptable T_{spare} is computed. This allows also for reducing the starvation eventually experienced by subsequent stations due to the greedy nature of UTSS.

Furthermore a deep study of the impact of UTSS on the instantaneous TXOP assigned to each station during the current polling has been performed considering different types of traffic: the aim is to highlight whether the integration of UTSS benefits the management of VBR traffic, improving flexibility and efficiency of QoS provisioning. This investigation is particularly meaningful since UTSS has been introduced to overcome the limit of some centralized HCCA schedulers when they, dealing with multimedia applications with highly variable bit rate, are not able to follow traffic variations. Different classes of data streams are considered, from CBR TSs to increasing VBR ones (from video conference to video streaming and to bursty traffic).

Finally, the impact of UTSS on transmission queues length is considered.

5.1. General Properties. First of all the computational complexity of UTSS is analyzed in order to evaluate if the integration of UTSS with a centralized scheduler has some disadvantages with regard to the computational complexity of the global scheduling engine.

Proposition 1. *The computational complexity of UTSS is $O(1)$.*

Proof. Since UTSS simply computes $T_{\text{spare}} = t_{\text{end}} - t_{\text{effective-end}}$ and it does not perform further operations like reordering and so forth, the computational complexity of the alone UTSS is $O(1)$. Thus the complexity of the global scheduler, obtained integrating UTSS, is equal to that of the centralized scheduler. The simplicity of UTSS is its basic strength and it makes UTSS a lightweight solution to improve the network performance without changing the centralized scheduler and without adverse effects from the point of view of the computational complexity. □

Proposition 2. *UTSS does not increase the system overhead.*

Proof. As deducible by the description of UTSS in Section 4, at the end of a polling this algorithm simply updates T_{spare}, whose value is used by the centralized scheduler to compute the next instantaneous TXOP. No exchange of additional information is required, nor the sending of special frames that can delay messages handshake. Thus it is possible to conclude that UTSS does not affect the centralized scheduler overhead. This deduction along with the previous Proposition 1 show that UTSS is not impacting on the basic scheduling features of the centralized scheduler. □

Proposition 3. *UTSS preserves the temporal isolation provided by the centralized scheduler.*

Proof. As temporal isolation is intended the not overlapping of transmissions of different QSTAs and the not interruption of a transmission. IEEE 802.11e guarantees the temporal isolation of the transmission of each station by introducing the concept of Transmission Opportunity. Indeed, as stated by the standard, TXOP assigned to a station cannot be consumed by other QSTAs and allows to perform a bandwidth reservation and assigns a station a maximum transmission duration, computed taking into account its QoS requirements. Moreover TXOP avoids execution overruns, due to stations aiming at transmitting more time than the negotiated one and that can jeopardize the service provided to other QSTAs.

When UTSS is scheduled in combination with a centralized scheduler, is the temporal isolation maintained? The answer is positive since UTSS preserves the TXOP set during the admission control and simply assigns an additional portion of sending time. Also this additional interval is not interruptible and it is not subtracted to other stations, jeopardizing their received service, but recovered from QSTAs that did not need that. □

These first propositions highlight how the adding of UTSS does not affect the basic scheduling features of the centralized scheduler. This makes the choice of integrating UTSS a low-cost solution to refine network performance.

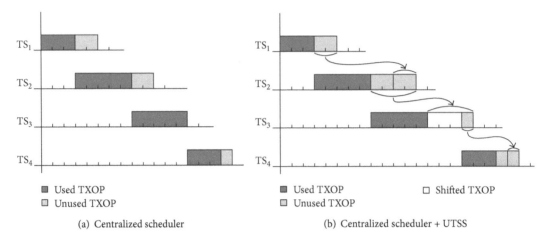

(a) Centralized scheduler   (b) Centralized scheduler + UTSS

FIGURE 4: Scheduling example.

5.2. Real-Time Analysis. Since the introduction of UTSS aims at improving the real-time behavior of the centralized HCCA scheduler, some main real-time properties of the global scheduler are analyzed in the following. First of all the impact of UTSS on the admission control feasibility test is studied. Then, as diagnosis of deteriorated real-time performance, the presence of a deadline miss is investigated in the case of UTSS. Indeed, if an algorithm is not suitable to respect a temporal requirement, a deadline, intended as the time until the considered transmission has to be finished, is missed.

Theorem 4. *UTSS does not affect the admission control feasibility test.*

Proof. Equation (4) can be written as follows:

$$T_{\text{CAP}} + T_{\text{CP}} = \sum_{i=0}^{K} T_i + T_{\text{CP}} \leq H, \tag{6}$$

where H is the hyperperiod duration, T_{CAP} is the portion of H assigned to HCCA, whereas T_{CP} is the one assigned to EDCA, K is number of admitted HCCA stations, and T_i is TXOP$_i$ of QSTA$_i$.

Without loss of generality if it is assumed that, for instance, QSTA$_1$ does not use its whole assigned TXOP$_1$, then $T_{\text{spare}_1} > 0$. Therefore, when UTSS reclaims unspent time and assigns T_{spare_1}, the following relationship holds:

$$
\begin{aligned}
\sum_{i=0}^{K} T_i' &= T_0 + T_{\text{eff}_1} + T_2' + \cdots + T_K \\
&= T_0 + T_{\text{eff}_1} + T_2 + T_{\text{spare}_1} + \cdots + T_K \\
&= T_0 + T_{\text{eff}_1} + T_2 + T_1 - T_{\text{eff}_1} + \cdots + T_K \\
&= \sum_{i=0}^{K} T_i \leq H - T_{\text{CP}},
\end{aligned}
\tag{7}
$$

where T_i' is the new T_i computed taking into account T_{spare}, and T_{eff_1} is the used portion of TXOP$_1$. This relationship shows as UTSS simply rearranges the assignment of the transmission intervals, without using more resources than the allocated ones. □

In Section 6 the analysis of null rate, polling interval, and throughput will confirm that UTSS does not affect the centralized scheduler policy.

Theorem 5. *The UTSS mechanism of T_{spare} assignment does not raise deadline miss.*

Proof. We distinguish two cases: (1) assignment of T_{spare} during a CAP, that is, the T_{spare} propagation is limited to the considered CAP and (2) assignment of T_{spare} during a CAP derived from the last polled QSTA of the previous CAP, that is, T_{spare} residue of a CAP can be transferred to the next one.

Case 1. During a CAP, the assignment of T_{spare} does not miss the deadlines of polled QSTAs. Indeed, the HCCA scheduling algorithms manage the temporal sequence of QSTAs access to the medium by the use of fixed interframe space intervals (*SIFS* and *PCF InterFrame Space PIFS*) specified by the reference scheduler. They set, respectively, the time interval between sending consecutive frames during a transmission and the waiting time between the end of a station transmission and the polling of the subsequent QSTA listed in the polling queue. These strict rules avoid the presence of idle blocking time between polled stations transmissions, as in general it could happen in real-time systems. Indeed, in general, in real-time systems an idle time can elapse between the processing of two consecutive tasks in dependency of their activation time, and the addition of a further slot of transmission time could jeopardize the real-time behavior of the next process to execute, raising a deadline miss. Instead, due to the mentioned IEEE 802.11e MAC scheduling rules, when $T_{\text{spare}} \neq 0$, there is only an advance of the transmission of next polled QSTA, without impacting its behavior, as shown in Figure 4.

Case 2. When T_{spare} is derived from the last polled QSTA during a CAP (see Figure 5(a)) two additional cases exist. If T_{spare} recovered from the transmission of the last QSTA in the

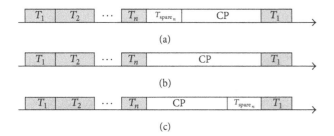

FIGURE 5: Example of T_{spare} propagation.

current CAP is shifted to the subsequent Contention Period, the beginning of the following CAP is not affected since, in this case, there is only a redistribution of time portions between *Contention Free Period* (CFP) and CP of the same hyperperiod; see Figure 5(b). Instead, if T_{spare} is propagated to the next CAP, by assigning the unused transmission time of the last polled QSTA to the first QSTA at the beginning of the next CAP, there is only an early polling of this QSTA of the same time interval; see Figure 5(c), whereas all other QSTAs are polled by respecting their delay bounds, thus without deadline miss. Moreover this choice increases the algorithm fairness by handling all QSTAs, includeing the first one of the new CAP, in the same way. □

The greedy nature of UTSS, due to the assignment of the whole T_{spare} to the next polled station, can cause starvation for the following QSTAs, especially when T_{spare}, derived from different CAPs, is large. This can result in deadline miss and reduce the global fairness. Moreover, a longer waiting time experienced by subsequent stations can imply the need of bigger buffers to collect the incoming traffic and can increase the packets drop rate. Thus, in order to avoid an unpredictable growing of T_{spare}, especially due to accumulation of a large number of unused portions of TXOPs when the T_{spare} propagation across consecutive CAPs is enabled, an upper bound Θ is set, suitable to meet the deadlines. Furthermore this upper bound fairly mitigates the greedy nature of UTSS.

Proposition 6. *The upper bound of T_{spare}, suitable to avoid deadline miss, is equal to $\Theta = d_i - t_{\text{end}_i} + \delta$.*

Proof. In the case of one-hope propagation, that is, in the case of propagation of T_{spare_i} only to the following QSTA$_i$:

$$T_i \leq T_i' \leq T_i + T_{i-1},\qquad(8)$$

where

$$T_i' = T_i + T_{\text{spare}_i}.\qquad(9)$$

Instead, if all previous QSTAs of the current and, eventually, of the previous CAPs do not use their TXOPs,

$$0 \leq T_{\text{spare}_i} \leq \sum_{j=1}^{i-1} T_j.\qquad(10)$$

Precisely, in this case T_{spare} is made available for the next polling after the currently polled QSTA has informed QAP

that it has no data to send by responding to CF-Poll frame with a CF-Null frame. This handshake requires a time interval equal to $\tau = \text{SIFS} + t_{\text{NULL}} + \text{SIFS}$, where t_{NULL} is the time to send a CF-Null frame. Thus the general expression holds:

$$0 \leq T_{\text{spare}_i}$$

$$\leq \sum_{j=1}^{i-1} \left(T_j - \tau\right)\qquad(11)$$

$$\leq \sum_{j=1}^{i-1} \left(T_j\right) - (i-1)\,\tau.$$

This shows as T_{spare} can grow jeopardizing the respect of deadlines.

Finally, in order to avoid deadline miss, we can assume to accept T_{spare_i} if and only if it respects the upper bound Θ:

$$0 \leq T_{\text{spare}_i} \leq d_i - t_{\text{end}_i} + \delta = \Theta,\qquad(12)$$

where d_i is the absolute deadline of the polled QSTA$_i$ and δ is a safety offset. □

The previous analysis demonstrates that, also about real-time properties, UTSS does not modify the related features of the centralized scheduler. Indeed its action is limited to the TXOP assignment, as shown in the following.

5.3. Transmission Opportunity and T_{spare} Analysis. Since UTSS acts on the transmission time assigned at each polling of a QSTA, it is interesting to evaluate how it impacts on the transmission time duration of different types of traffic and, in particular, on the service provided to QSTAs with VBR applications. Indeed, as previously remarked, TXOPs, computed during the admission control considering mean value parameters, may not be sufficient to follow the variations of VBR traffic, deteriorating network performance.

As mentioned in Section 2, during the admission control TXOP is computed by (1) as stated by the HCCA reference scheduler guidelines. Thus, in order to investigate the UTSS behavior with different types of traffic, VoIP, video conference, video streaming, and bursty traffic, that show increasing data rate variations, are considered. It is analyzed how the centralized scheduler computes the corresponding TXOPs and if these are suitable to provide the required service. Then, for each considered class of applications, the new expression of TXOP, modified by the introduction of UTSS, is analyzed and compared with the previous one in order to highlight any changes.

(1) VoIP Traffic. Since VoIP streams are characterized by ON periods, where the source generates CBR packets, and OFF periods, where no packets are sent, this type of traffic is an interesting example of how UTSS interacts with the management of CBR traffic.

Proposition 7. *UTSS does not interfere in the CBR traffic management, like the VoIP one, provided by the centralized scheduler.*

Proof. The talkspurt (ON) period of VoIP traffic is distributed according to the Weibull distribution [37] that models a one-to-one conversation. Thus the *probability density function* (p.d.f.) of its length T_{ON} is

$$p_{T_{\text{ON}}}(x; \lambda, k) = \begin{cases} \dfrac{k}{\lambda} \cdot \left(\dfrac{x}{\lambda}\right)^{k-1} \cdot e^{(-x/\lambda)^k}, & x \geq 0, \\ 0, & x < 0, \end{cases} \quad (13)$$

where k is the *shape* parameter and λ is the *scale* parameter depending on the streams.

The expected value of T_{ON} is $E[T_{\text{ON}}] = \lambda \cdot \Gamma(1 + 1/k)$, where $\Gamma(z) = \int_0^\infty t^{z-1} \cdot e^{-t} dt$ is the *Gamma* function.

If during the admission control the protocol parameters are computed considering

$$\text{SI} = T_{\text{ON}} + T_{\text{OFF}},$$

$$R = R_{\text{ON}} \cdot \frac{T}{(T_{\text{ON}} + T_{\text{OFF}})}, \quad (14)$$

where T_{OFF} is the OFF period duration, $R_{\text{ON}} = 1/T_{\text{ON}}$ is the mean data rate during the ON period, and T is the CBR traffic period, the protocol parameters reflect the traffic profile and the centralized scheduler is suitable to efficiently manage the incoming streams and to dispatch the enqueued ones. Thus, even without overprovisioning, the centralized scheduler is able to provide the needed resources and T_{spare}, if present, is not used. □

In Section 6 the analysis of queues length, mean delay, and dropped packets will confirm as, in the case of CBR traffic, the scheduler parameters and the offered service are untouched by the introduction of T_{spare}, whereas in the case of low VBR its contribution is limited. This is due to the fact that the centralized QoS scheduler is already suitable to serve the considered traffic streams allocating the required resource. Consequently, in this case the capacity added by UTSS is not necessary. Indeed, UTSS does not perform any traffic monitoring and/or prediction; thus it is not able to adapt its behavior to a different traffic profile. It simply operates as a greedy algorithm that recovers unexhausted resources avoiding their waste and allocates that to the next polled station, without verifying through monitoring or statistical studies if this station has shown a traffic behavior that can be benefited by these further resources. This is its flaw but also its strength since using a simple mechanism is suitable to improve network performance without impacting on the system overhead due to $O(1)$ computational complexity, as shown in Proposition 1. Thus, even when its action is not needed, it is running without overloading the scheduler computation.

(2) Video Traffic. The analysis of video traffic is useful to verify how VBR TSs are managed by the centralized scheduler when it collaborates with UTSS. The study has been performed considering low variable (video conference) and high variable (video streaming) applications.

(a) Video Conference Traffic

Proposition 8. *UTSS positively impacts on video conference traffic management.*

Proof. The literature has shown that video conference traffic has a stochastic behavior and already first studies provided some analytical models of these traffic sources. In particular, we are interested in "quantify" and modeling the traffic fluctuations. For instance, already in [38, 39] it is shown that, using a Discrete Autoregressive Model, for video conference traffic over ATM networks the number of cells (packets) per frames is a stationary stochastic process distributed accordingly with the negative binomial distribution:

$$f_{k,r,p} = \binom{k + r - 1}{k} p^r q^k, \quad k = 0, 1, \dots, \quad (15)$$

where k is the number of successes, $0 < p < 1$ is the failure probability, $q = 1 - p$ is the success probability, and $r > 0$ is the number of failures. Its mean value and variance are equal to

$$m = \frac{r(1-p)}{p}, \qquad v = \frac{r(1-p)}{p^2}. \quad (16)$$

In the same works it has been shown that also the number of cells per frame and the bit data rate can be modeled by the Gamma distribution. This distribution has a mean value $m = s/\lambda$ and a variance $v = s/\lambda^2$, both depending on the values of shape s and scale λ parameters. In both cases, considering the reference scheduler computation of TXOP based on mean value parameters, (1) begins as follows:

$$\text{TXOP}_{i_{\text{videoconf}}} = \max\left(\frac{N_i \cdot \mu \cdot m_{ci}}{m_{ri}}, \frac{M_i}{m_{ri}}\right) + O, \quad (17)$$

where m_{ci} is the mean value of number of cells per frame, μ is the mean dimension of cells, and m_{ri} is the mean data rate, whose expressions can be derived by the cited distributions. Even if video conference traffic is characterized by low variable bit rate, it is affected by fluctuations around its mean value, expressed by the variance v. Thus, even without taking into account deeper statistical analysis about the distribution of cells per I, B or, P frames, the computation of TXOP and SI using mean values parameters does not reflect traffic variations and underestimates the instantaneous resource needs, harming the supported QoS.

These considerations are independent from the used codec but reflect the traffic and data rate profile. Thus this type of application can benefit from the use of UTSS. □

(b) Video Streaming Traffic

Proposition 9. *The service provided to video streaming traffic may benefit from the cooperation with UTSS.*

Proof. Video streaming traffic is characterized by highly variable bit rate. Adopting the same approach as in the case of video conference, its basic features about data rate and frame size distributions are analyzed. VBR MPEG4 traffic is composed by *Groups of Pictures* (GoP) that consist of twelve I, P, and B frames, following the pattern IBBPBBPBBPBB, each of them differently coded and with different lengths. Moreover, some correlations exist between GoPs and it is shown that the related probability density and autocorrelation functions are characterized by both *Short Range Dependence* (SRD) and *Long Range Dependence* (LRD), [40]. Thus, due to its complexity, the study of video streaming traffic is challenging and numerous models have been proposed in the literature [40–42], most of them derived from the basic works on *AutoRegressive Moving Average* model [43]. Furthermore an increasing attention has been recently addressed to traffic dynamic prediction, [44]. The huge effort in modeling this type of traffic trying to reflect its variations implies that, also and especially in this case, the use of mean value parameters in the TXOP computation, as stated by the reference scheduler, is really far from being able to follow VBR variations, independently from the used model. Hence, also in this case, it is possible to deduce that provide additional resources by means of UTSS can help absorb traffic variations. □

In Section 6, the analysis through simulations of queues length, mean delay, and dropped packets will show the positive impact of UTSS on video conference and video streaming traffic scheduling.

5.4. Bursty Traffic. Finally, analyzing the effects of UTSS on the service provided to traffic with increasing VBR, its impact on bursty traffic, that has highly variable packets interarrival time, is studied.

Theorem 10. *When UTSS is used, the resulting global scheduler is able to manage greater bursts of traffic, with a burstiness factor $B_i' < B_i$.*

Proof. At the polling time of a station $QSTA_i$ its new $TXOP_i'$, computed by UTSS considering (1), is

$$TXOP_i' = \max\left(\frac{N_i \cdot L_i}{R_i}, \frac{M_i}{R_i}\right) + O + T_{spare_i}. \qquad (18)$$

A metric useful to characterize the burstiness of traffic with high rate variability is the *burstiness factor* (B), defined as the *ratio between mean data rate R during a long time interval and peak data rate Π during the activity interval*. Its value ranges from 1, in the case of CBR traffic, to 0, as the peak rate increases. Introducing B the expression of $TXOP_i'$ becomes as follows:

$$TXOP_{i_{burst}}' = \max\left(\frac{N_i \cdot L_i}{B_i \cdot \Pi_i}, \frac{M_i}{B_i \cdot \Pi_i}\right) + O + T_{spare_i}, \qquad (19)$$

where R_i and Π_i are, respectively, mean data rate and peak data rate of $QSTA_i$. When $T_{spare_i} > 0$, $TXOP_i' > TXOP_i$. In this case, if T_{spare_i} is incorporated in the first term of the previous equation, since N_i, M_i, Π_i, and L_i do not change being related to the considered TS, then the only element that

can vary is B_i. Consequently, since $TXOP_i' > TXOP_i$, then $B_i' < B_i$, and $TXOP_i'$ can be expressed as follows:

$$TXOP_{i_{burst}}' = \max\left(\frac{N_i \cdot L_i}{B_i' \cdot \Pi_i}, \frac{M_i}{B_i' \cdot \Pi_i}\right) + O. \qquad (20)$$

This implies that UTSS is able to manage greater bursts of traffic through an overprovisioning of resources, due to T_{spare}, local to the current polling and without any effect on the admission control, as previously demonstrated. □

(1) Analysis of Burstiness Admissible by the System. The previous theorem suggests that the burstiness admissible by the system can increase when UTSS is used. In the following this effect is deeply investigated, trying to quantify this increase and its impact on the provided service.

Theorem 11. *UTSS is suitable to increase the maximum tolerable burstiness, locally at the current polling, and raise the service rate r.*

Proof. Assume to adopt a token bucket model for the enqueued traffic of a QSTA and for the network service. If a centralized HCCA scheduler, like WCBS, is considered the state of the traffic incoming and outcoming is illustrated in Figure 6, where the x axis is the time and the y axis is the packets.

In this case the maximum admissible burstiness is represented by the *bucket dept b* parameter, whereas the mean data rate R is equivalent to the mean service rate r, represented by the slope of the service curve. Furthermore the total delivered packets during the current polling are represented by the parameter ψ that takes into account the token bucket depth and the service rate. All these parameters are evaluated during the current polling, that is, during the time interval ranging from the polling time t_{p_i} to the transmission ending time t_{end_i} of $QSTA_i$, that is, where UTSS takes action.

If UTSS is integrated with the centralized scheduler, when $QSTA_i$ is polled and $T_{spare} \neq 0$, the station can transmit its ψ bytes plus the φ bytes sent during T_{spare}. The new situation is shown in Figure 7.

Since UTSS makes available T_{spare} at the polling time t_{p_i}, if it is assumed that the service rate r is constant, this situation is equivalent to have a greater token bucket dept $b' = b + \varphi$. This deduction confirms Theorem 10.

Figure 7 allows a further consideration: if it is assumed that the burstiness is constant, providing T_{spare} is equivalent to have a service curve with a higher slope, that is, to increase the service rate r'. This implies an overprovisioning local to the current polling, not obtained by rerunning the admission control, and yet confirms, from a different point of view, Theorem 10. These results are valid for any type of TS and corroborate the considerations about VBR applications.

Such overprovisioning can positively influence network performance expressed in terms of end-to-end delay and can reduce the packets waiting time in the queues, the packets drop, and the queues length. This conclusion will be confirmed by delay, packets drop rate, and queue length analysis illustrated in Section 6. The risks of starvation and

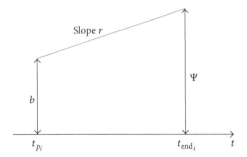

FIGURE 6: Service model of a HCCA centralized scheduler.

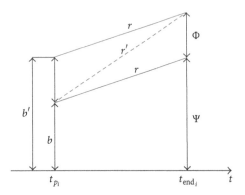

FIGURE 7: Service model of a HCCA centralized scheduler + UTSS.

increase of buffering amount and of exceeding the admission control threshold are avoided by taking advantage of UTSS features that do not impact on the admission control feasibility test (see Theorem 4) and improves the system fairness; see Proposition 6. □

In the following the maximum burstiness tolerable by the network will be computed.

Theorem 12. *With UTSS the maximum traffic burstiness tolerable by the system is increased and the corresponding burstiness factor $B_{\max}$ is equal to*

$$
\begin{aligned}
B_{\max} &= \frac{t_{\mathrm{end}_i} - t_{p_i}}{T_{\mathrm{spare}_{\max}} + t_{\mathrm{end}_i} - t_{p_i}} \\
&= \frac{t_{\mathrm{end}_i} - t_{p_i}}{\Theta + t_{\mathrm{end}_i} - t_{p_i}} \leq B,
\end{aligned} \tag{21}
$$

where B is the burstiness factor without UTSS and Θ is the upper bound of T_{spare}; see Proposition 6.

Proof. As shown by the previous results, $T_{\mathrm{spare}} \neq 0$ allows for dispatching more enqueued traffic, especially in the case of VBR traffic, and improving the capacity of absorbing traffic streams peaks. Thus, with regard to the assigned TXOP, UTSS has the same effect of instantaneously increasing the delivery rate. When a $QSTA_i$ does not use its whole T_i, then

$$
\tau \leq t_{\mathrm{end}_i} - t_{p_i} = T_{\mathrm{eff}_i} \leq T_i, \tag{22}
$$

where $\tau = \mathrm{SIFS} + t_{\mathrm{NULL}} + \mathrm{SIFS}$, is the minimum transmission time used by a station when it has no data to send, and r' is equal to

$$
r'_i = \frac{\varphi_i + r \cdot (t_{\mathrm{end}_i} - t_{p_i})}{t_{\mathrm{end}_i} - t_{p_i}} = \frac{r \cdot (T_{\mathrm{spare}} + t_{\mathrm{end}_i} - t_{p_i})}{t_{\mathrm{end}_i} - t_{p_i}}, \tag{23}
$$

where φ_i is the bytes sent using T_{spare}. Thus the maximum burstiness $B_{\max}$ tolerable by the system, taking advantage by the use of UTSS, is

$$
B_{\max} = \frac{t_{\mathrm{end}_i} - t_{p_i}}{T_{\mathrm{spare}_{\max}} + t_{\mathrm{end}_i} - t_{p_i}} \leq B, \tag{24}
$$

and, if we consider Θ, the upper bound of T_{spare}, the following equation holds:

$$
B_{\max} = \frac{t_{\mathrm{end}_i} - t_{p_i}}{\Theta + t_{\mathrm{end}_i} - t_{p_i}} \leq B. \tag{25}
$$

□

5.5. Transmission Queues Length Analysis. The previous analyses about the impact of UTSS on the TXOP duration suggest a deeper investigation on its effect on the stations queues length.

Theorem 13. *When UTSS is ON $T_{\mathrm{spare}} \neq 0$ allows increasing the portion of dispatched traffic during a polling phase and reducing the transmission queues length.*

Proof. In order to evaluate the impact of T_{spare} on the transmission queues length, it is considered, as worst case, a station $QSTA_i$ with backlogged traffic: in this case the station can exhaust its $TXOP_i$ and may need more time to dispatch the incoming traffic. In general, the traffic that can be delivered during a polling of a ith station, which is assigned its $TXOP_i$, is equal to

$$
\lambda_i = TXOP_i \cdot r, \tag{26}
$$

where r is the mean transmission rate. When $T_{\mathrm{spare}} \neq 0$ a longer transmission time is available and the delivered traffic begins as follows:

$$
\lambda'_i = (TXOP_i + T_{\mathrm{spare}_i}) \cdot r. \tag{27}
$$

Since an upper bound of T_{spare_i}, Θ_i, is set in order to avoid deadline miss, it limits also the maximum dispatched traffic:

$$
\lambda'_{i_{\max}} = (TXOP_i + \Theta_i) \cdot r \geq \lambda_i. \tag{28}
$$

Thus the expression of the maximum time gain $g_{(t_i)\max}$ for $QSTA_i$, obtained with UTSS during the current polling and intended as the percentage of increase of transmission time duration, is

$$
\begin{aligned}
g_{t_i} &= \frac{r \cdot (TXOP_i + T_{\mathrm{spare}_i})}{r \cdot TXOP_i} = \frac{TXOP_i + T_{\mathrm{spare}_i}}{TXOP_i} \\
&\leq g_{(t_i)\max} = \frac{TXOP_i + \Theta_i}{TXOP_i}.
\end{aligned} \tag{29}
$$

The enqueued traffic of QSTA$_i$ during the jth polling can be expressed as

$$Q_{i_j} = Q_{i_{j-1}} + \pi_i - \lambda_i = Q_{i_{j-1}} + \text{TXOP}_i \cdot R_i - \text{TXOP}_i \cdot r, \tag{30}$$

where $Q_{i_{j-1}}$ is the enqueued traffic residue from the previous $(j-1)$th polling phase, π_i is the incoming traffic during the current jth polling, and R_i is the mean data rate. When $T_{\text{spare}} \neq 0$ the enqueued traffic Q'_{i_j} is bounded by $Q'_{i_j \, \min}$ and it is such that

$$\begin{aligned} Q'_{i_j \, \min} &= Q_{i_{j-1}} + \text{TXOP}_i \cdot R_i - (\text{TXOP}_i + \Theta_i) \cdot r \\ &\leq Q'_{i_j} = Q_{i_{j-1}} + \text{TXOP}_i \cdot R_i - (\text{TXOP}_i + T_{\text{spare}_i}) \cdot r \\ &\leq Q_i. \end{aligned} \tag{31}$$

$\square$

In Section 6 the simulations results about queues length will confirm these analytical deductions.

6. Performance Analysis

In this section the performance of the proposed UTSS scheduling algorithm integrated with WCBS versus WCBS, FHCF, RTH, and reference schedulers are evaluated through extensive simulation results. The reference scheduler is the usual benchmark when analysing the behavior of alternative scheduling algorithms. Instead WCBS has been considered a right candidate to evaluate the effect of UTSS integration on the real-time behavior of a global scheduler since, being an EDF-based algorithm, its real-time performance is not optimal for VBR TSs [12]. Furthermore, even if its capacity recharging mechanism does not waste the accorded budget and efficiently assigns resources trying to follow traffic needs, it can be further improved through the UTSS recovery mechanism. The performances of WCBS are the starting point where UTSS takes action, like in the case of any other centralized scheduler, and, consequently, they affect the behavior of the final global scheduler. Indeed UTSS has been conceived as a cooperative scheduling algorithm. Thus, since the final performances are affected by the original scheduler, each effect has to be evaluated against the centralized one (WCBS) and, consequently, the comparison between WCBS and its integration with UTSS is an example suitable to highlight how UTSS influences and changes the scheduler behavior. As far as FHCF and RTH are concerned, their selection is based on similar goals and/or scheduling schemes. Indeed, since the aim of this section is to analyze the benefits introduced by UTSS with respect to a centralized scheduler alone, we decided to focus the comparison on algorithms showing some common features with WCBS, instead of considering algorithms belonging to different families that can show different performance. In particular, we have chosen FHCF first of all since it is a famous benchmark in the evaluation of HCCA schedulers alternative to the reference one, and, then, since it provides variable TXOPs such as WCBS. Instead

TABLE 1: MAC/PHY simulation parameters.

Parameter	Value
SIFS (μs)	10
DIFS (μs)	28
PIFS (μs)	19
Slot time (μs)	9
PLCP header (b)	24
Preamble (b)	72
Data rate (Mbit/s)	54
Basic rate (Mbit/s)	1

RTH has been selected since, even if its resource assignment is different from WCBS, it is based on a similar EDF-based polling scheduling.

In particular, the analysis takes into account the utilization efficiency of the network, the mean access delay, the discarding rate of enqueued packets with expired delay bound, and the transmission queues length. A description of the simulation tools, their settings, the traffic models, and the considered scenario precedes the simulation results analysis.

6.1. Simulation Settings and Traffic Model. Performance is evaluated through simulation using *ns-2* network simulator [45]. It is assumed that QSTAs communicate directly without hidden node problem; RTS/CTS mechanism, MAC level fragmentation, and multirate support are disabled. The physical layer is specified in the IEEE 802.11g standard where OFDM (*Orthogonal Frequency-Division Multiplexing*) is the mandatory modulation scheme; its parameters are listed in Table 1.

The presented results have been obtained simulating independent replications of 700 s with a warm-up time of 100 s until the 95% confidence interval is reached for each measure.

The network scenario chosen for simulations is composed by seven QSTAs and one QAP. Each QSTA transmits *one* uplink TS which is received by the QAP. Each TS has a different TSPEC. In particular, one station sends G.729A VoIP traffic, one station a video conference, and five stations video streaming applications. Finally, one station transmits data traffic with SDU of 1500 bytes through legacy Distributed Coordination Function and operates in asymptotic condition; that is, it is always backlogged in order to saturate the channel. The VoIP traffic parameters are shown in Table 2.

Video streaming traffic has been generated using preencoded high quality MPEG4 trace files of 60 minutes each from the Internet archive of traces [46]. Such traces are as follows: *Jurassic Park* (VS1), *Silence of the lambs* (VS2), *Mr. Bean* (VS3), *Die hard III* (VS4), and *Robin Hood* (VS5). The video conference (VC) session has been represented by the preencoded *LectureHQ-Reisslein* trace file. The video streaming and video conference parameters are summarized in Table 3.

6.2. Efficiency Analysis. In this paragraph the efficiency of the resource management performed by UTSS integrated with

TABLE 2: G.729A VoIP traffic stream parameters.

Parameter	Value
Frame size (B)	10
Frame per packet	2
Period (s)	0.02
Data rate (kb/s)	24
Payload size (B)	20
IP/UDP/RTP	
Header size (B)	40
SDU size (B)	60

TABLE 3: Video streaming and video conference parameters.

Parameter	VC	VS1	VS2
Mean frame size (B)	600	3800	2900
Maximum frame size (B)	11386	16745	22239
Period (s)	0.033	0.040	0.040
Mean data rate (kb/s)	158	770	580
Maximum data rate (kb/s)	2733	3300	4400
Parameter	VS3	VS4	VS5
Mean frame size (B)	2900	3500	4600
Maximum frame size (B)	15251	16960	16550
Period (s)	0.040	0.040	0.040
Mean data rate (kb/s)	580	700	910
Maximum data rate (kb/s)	3100	3400	3300

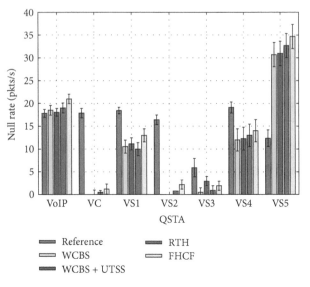

FIGURE 8: Null rate.

WCBS (labeled as UTSS + WCBS) is evaluated and compared with that of the mentioned schedulers used as benchmark (FHCF and RTH).

The first efficiency parameter is the *null rate* defined as the number of CF-Null packets sent by a QSTA as answer to a CF-Poll, when it has no traffic to transmit. A high value of null rate highlights a polling period more frequent than necessary for the considered application and can increase the system overhead due to unnecessary polling phases that occupy a minimum time interval.

In Figure 8 UTSS + WCBS and WCBS alone have similar values of null rate for each traffic stream: this is because they use the same polling interval, since UTSS does not affect this action. Often their null rate and that of RTH are better than that of the reference scheduler since they poll the stations using different SI for each TS: such feature lets these schedulers perform a zero null rate with some TSs (e.g., VC and VS2), or, however, small values. As expected FHCF shows a null rate less than the reference scheduler but, in most cases, higher than that of WCBS, WCBS + UTSS, and RTH since, even if it does not provide SIs different from the reference, it is more aggressive in emptying transmission queues. Also, in the case of VoIP traffic, it shows the greater null rate. For the same reason, for some video streams UTSS + WCBS, WCBS, and RTH have a null rate greater than that

of the reference: since they provide tailored TXOPs they are able to dispatch more packets and the QAP can poll the stations finding empty queues; the integration of UTSS can exalt this phenomenon. In particular, this evaluation suggests a distinction: considering the reference scheduler the high values of null rate are due to the fact that it polls all TSs with the same SI, less than the minimum MSI, with the risk of polling some QSTAs more frequently than needed. Instead, focusing on the improved schedulers, a sporadic greater null rate (see FHCF) is due to the efficient computation of TXOP, tailored to the type of traffic. This is the same reason of the null rate of UTSS + WCBS greater than that of WCBS and, sometimes of RTH, in the case of some video streaming (VS1, VS3, VS4, and VS5), in particular that with high variability in the data rate. In this scenario the UTSS reclaiming mechanism adds the capacity needed to dispatch more enqueued traffic, having the same effect of a dynamic computation of TXOP tailored to the different TSs.

Finally, in the case of WCBS + UTSS, even if the polling instant can be advanced, the polling interval variation is negligible and it does not affect the average null rate. This confirms that UTSS does not affect the polling timing of the centralized scheduler.

To go deep inside this deduction Figure 9 displays the polling interval used by the schedulers with each TS. The reference scheduler and FHCF use a unique value of the polling interval for all TSs, as reported in Section 3, which is less than the minimum MSI of all admitted TSs. Instead, WCBS, WCBS + UTSS, and RTH poll each TS_i using its SI_i. In particular, WCBS and RTH show similar values since they use EDF to sort the next polling time, taking into account the deadline of each stream, whereas WCBS + UTSS has the same values than WCBS since UTSS does not care about the polling scheduling that continues to be managed by the centralized scheduler, in this case WCBS. This confirms that the integration of UTSS with WCBS does not touch its polling policy, as stated in Section 4.

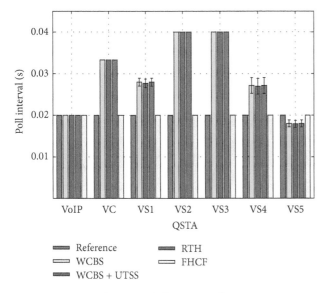

FIGURE 9: Polling interval.

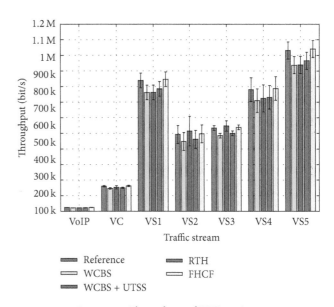

FIGURE 10: Throughput of VBR stations.

Finally, Figure 10 shows that UTSS does not significantly affect the global throughput; thus global network utilization is roughly the same. However, more specifically, UTSS can produce a throughput greater than that of WCBS, using more efficiently the allocated resources and improving the behavior of the global scheduler: since it takes action especially in the case of high variable data rate, its positive effect is more relevant for high VBR TSs, like VS2 and VS3, where WCBS + UTSS is able to outperform also RTH and FHCF, unlike WCBS. In the remaining cases, where the contribution of UTSS is less meaningful, WCBS + UTSS performs better but its behavior is biased by WCBS.

As proof that UTSS is effectively suitable to recover not exhausted transmission time, in Figure 11 an example of dynamic evolution of T_{spare} is displayed. The x axis reports the scheduler tick since T_{spare} is sampled when the scheduler takes action. This Figure illustrates as, in dependency of the different type of traffic streams, T_{spare} shows extended variations, reaching some significant values around 5-6 ms. This could happen in the case of low VBR TSs, when the data rate drops down allowing the recovery of a considerable portion of transmission time.

6.3. Delay Analysis. In this paragraph the analysis is focused on the real-time behavior of the considered schedulers, intended as temporal performance expressed in terms of access delay. The access delay is defined as the time elapsed from when the frame reached the MAC layer until when the frame is successfully acknowledged.

Figure 12 highlights that the mean value of access delay of WCBS + UTSS is improved with respect to WCBS, RTH, and FHCF, in particular for traffic streams with higher VBR, (VS2 and VS3). This confirms the analytical results about deadline miss (see Theorem 5). Compared to the reference scheduler, WCBS and, consequently, WCBS + UTSS and RTH perform worse when serving TSs with less variable bit rate.

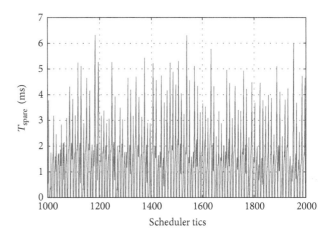

FIGURE 11: Example of dynamic evolution of T_{spare}.

In particular, WCBS is always underperforming due to its postponing deadlines and capacity recharging mechanisms that provide a variable TXOP but not tailored to the type of traffic. This result points out to the mentioned drawback of EDF-based schemes [12], since their postponing deadline mechanism improves the scheduling responsiveness but can increase the experienced delay. This is confirmed by the RTH behavior in comparison to the reference scheduler.

The previous considerations about the resource efficiency and the scheduling profile of WCBS + UTSS are not surprising since the behavior of the global scheduler is affected by that of the centralized one; thus, if this is underperforming in terms of access delay, like WCBS, this aspect can be propagated also in the global scheduler. However the cooperation with UTSS can improve the global performance in terms of the access delay with respect to WCBS, as shown in the case of all the analyzed TSs. Indeed, even if the access delay of WCBS + UTSS continues to be biased by the performance of WCBS, as previously motivated, in the case of highly VBR TSs

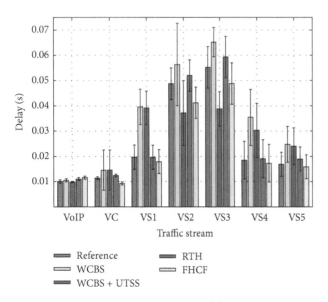

FIGURE 12: Mean access delay.

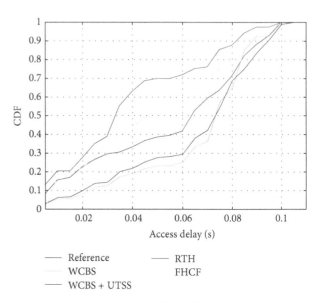

FIGURE 13: Access delay CDF of VS3 traffic stream.

(see VS3 and VS4), where WCBS fails against the other alternative algorithms, when UTSS is added, the global scheduler is able to outperforms also RTH and FHCF. This corroborates the validity of the UTSS scheme that results in being suitable to meaningfully improve the performances of WCBS in the situations where it performs worse.

This deduction suggests to further investigate the impact of UTSS on high VBR TSs in order to quantify the introduced changes. Looking at the *Cumulative Distribution Function* (CDF) of the access delay in the case of VS3, that has high VBR and showed in the previous Figure 12 an interesting improvement of access delay, Figure 13 displays that, after a time interval of 0.05 s, UTSS + WCBS allows 70% of transmitted packets whereas WCBS is limited to only 30%. This is the most important result that highlights how UTSS is suitable for improving the real-time behavior of WCBS in the case of high VBR traffic. Moreover, it corroborates the theoretical deductions illustrated in Section 5 about the effect of the UTSS integration on the TXOP computation with different types of multimedia applications with an increasing variable bit rate, and in the case of low VBR and CBR TSs (see Proposition 7). Therefore UTSS is outperforming in the case of highly variable VBR TSs, whereas, in the case of CBR or low VBR traffic, its contribution is limited because the centralized scheduler is suitable to efficiently serve the considered streams allocating the required resource. The UTSS simple greedy algorithm has its main strength in improving the network performance without impacting on the system overhead due to $O(1)$ computational complexity, but, as shown, despite its simplicity, its effects are relevant.

6.4. Packets Drop Analysis. In the following the amount of packets dropped from the transmission queues, due to expiration of their delay bound, is evaluated. Such parameter is chosen taking into account the length of the play-out buffer of a typical consumer device and it is tailored to the type of traffic. For this reason the analysis aims to highlight the differences between the schedulers and not the absolute value performed by each single scheduler.

Focusing on dropping rate, Figure 14 illustrates the positive impact of UTSS. Also for this performance parameter, the main consideration is that each effect has to be evaluated in comparison to the centralized scheduler (WCBS). This means that if WCBS is underperforming with respect to RTH and FHCF, this can influence the behavior of the global scheduler. First of all, looking at the considered VBR TSs in order to provide a global evaluation, UTSS is suitable to reduce the number of dropped packets since, adding a further transmission capacity, it can dispatch more traffic and reduce the waiting time in the queues. The phenomenon is more evident with respect to the mean access delay since this one is an aggregated result about all the packets of the considered TSs, whereas in the case of dropping rate, individual performances about the packets are considered. Instead, considering the CBR traffic, since WCBS is suitable to serve these TSs polling the station with the required period, UTSS does not modify the final performance, as expected. Consequently the number of dropped packets is improved by UTSS in particular when the considered TS is highly variable, since, as shown by the simulations about the access delay, UTSS, while recovering the unused time from the previous transmissions, reduces the waiting time of the scheduled TS. In this case UTSS does its best and is suitable to make the global scheduler outperform also RTH and FHCF (see VS3 and VS4). In particular, VS3 TS experiences an improvement up to 60% with respect to WCBS, RTH, and reference schedulers. This result confirms the analytical consideration about the VBR applications (see Section 5.3 and in particular about the burstiness that the network can support, (see Theorem 12) and demonstrates that UTSS is suitable to absorb data rate peaks.

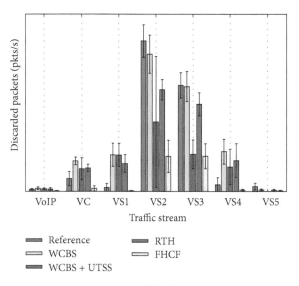

FIGURE 14: Packets drop rate.

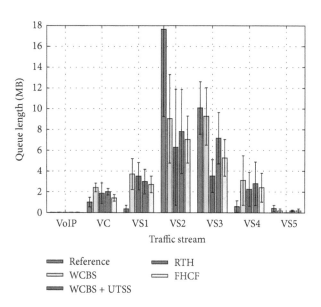

FIGURE 15: 99th percentile of HCCA buffer length.

6.5. Transmission Queues Length Analysis. As studied in Section 5.5, when UTSS collaborates with a centralized scheduler, there is a positive effect also on the transmission queues length. In this section the simulation is focused on the 99th percentile of queues length.

In Figure 15 it is shown that, with the exception of VoIP TS, when high VBR TSs are transmitted, as in case of VS2 and VS3, and the data rate exceeds its mean value the buffers length grows. For these TSs already WCBS, RTH and, FHCF reduce the number of enqueued packets against the performance obtained by the reference scheduler, but UTSS is able to further improve this result since the reclaimed portion of unused bandwidth helps the scheduler to transmit more frames and to shorten the occupied portion of transmission queues.

In order to deeply analyze the previous result, Figure 16 illustrates the CDF of the HCCA buffer length when VS3 traffic stream is transmitted by different schedulers. Also in this case this stream is the right candidate to evaluate the algorithms behavior when stressed by high traffic variations since it has high VBR. The simulations confirm that with high VBR TSs UTSS is able to keep the queues length shorter than the other schedulers. In particular, in the considered scenario, the greater gap between the schedulers is with a buffer length of 3 Megabytes, when UTSS shows a 66% of the probability the queue will be shorter than 3 Megabytes, while the other schedulers require about the double of this length. This is a meaningful result impacting both on the resource scheduling design as well as on the physical devices design.

6.6. Final Considerations. Summarizing, like other schedulers, UTSS does not aim to globally improve network performance. As proved in [12], a unique algorithm suitable to globally outperform all other solutions does not exist since each scheduler, due to its feature and scheduling rules, is tailored to face off some aspects of the complex resource management. Hence a scheduler can be focused to improve,

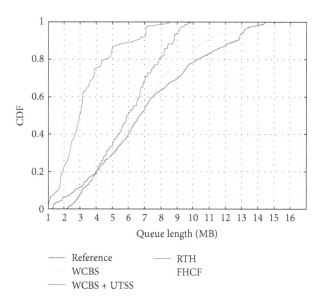

FIGURE 16: CDF of HCCA buffer length in the case of VS3 TS.

for instance, the network delay, whereas a different algorithm is better in terms of fairness or efficiency or system overhead, and so forth. In this context UTSS tries to do its best to fill in the gaps of the underlying centralized schedulers, whose features, however, continues to condition the global algorithm behavior. Indeed, the global scheduler performance suffers the imprinting of the centralized scheduling scheme. UTSS gives its contribution starting from this situation and, since it is conceived as a cooperative scheduling algorithm, the actual improvement can be perceived only comparing the performance of the centralized scheduler along with the global scheduler, obtained from the cooperation with UTSS. In particular some deductions can be made as follows.

(i) Considering the different types of traffic, since the centralized IEEE 802.11e scheduler, reference of alternative, is suitable to serve CBR traffic, in this case the contribution of UTSS is limited but, due to its $O(1)$ computational complexity, it does not impact on the global scheduling complexity and does not overload the system. Instead, UTSS is beneficial in the case of VBR TSs that stress the centralized schedulers.

(ii) Focusing on the efficiency, UTSS does not modify the scheduling policy and timing, but it is able to improve the use of allocated resources by means of its reclaiming mechanism. In particular, it is beneficial especially in the case of highly VBR TSs since, dispatching more packets, it shows a local increase of null rate and throughput.

(iii) Considering the mean access delay and taking into account that the behavior of the global scheduler is affected by that of the centralized one, the simulation results show that the cooperation with UTSS can improve the global performance. Indeed, even if the access delay of WCBS + UTSS continues to be biased by the performance of WCBS, in the case of highly VBR TSs, where WCBS fails with respect to the other alternative schedulers, when UTSS is added, the global scheduler is able to outperform RTH and FHCF.

(iv) Focusing on packets drop rate, UTSS is suitable to reduce the number of dropped packets since, adding a further transmission capacity, it can dispatch more traffic and reduce the waiting time in the queues, especially in the case of highly VBR TSs, where UTSS does its best and is suitable to make the global scheduler outperform also RTH and FHCF.

(v) Finally, in the case of transmission queues, UTSS is able increase their reduction obtained by the alternative schedulers.

7. Conclusions and Future Works

Multimedia applications with VBR traffic are a challenge for the QoS provisioning of IEEE802.11e networks: they require a flexible scheduling policy suitable to follow traffic variations.

In this paper a bandwidth reclaiming scheduling algorithm, *Unused Time Shifting Scheduler* (UTSS), is deeply analyzed. UTSS cooperates with a HCCA centralized scheduler and dynamically computes the transmission time by recovering the exceeding time from previous transmissions, providing an instantaneous resource overprovisioning.

The analytical and simulations results, comprising its comparison against some advanced QoS algorithms, highlight that it does not violate the admission control feasibility test and does not affect the centralized scheduler behavior. By means of its greedy reclaiming mechanism with $O(1)$ computational complexity, it positively impacts on the efficiency of the resource management improving network performance. In particular, being a cooperative mechanism, its positive effects can be appreciated in comparison to the performance

of the centralized scheduler: it is suitable to improve the global scheduler behavior in terms of mean access delay, throughput, transmission queues length, bursts of traffic management, and packets drop rate. These positive effects are more relevant for highly VBR traffic.

Future works include the study of the UTSS behavior using an elastic traffic model, as well as its integration with Overboost algorithm with the aim to investigate how the collaboration of these cooperative mechanisms, each one suitable to improve the provided QoS seamlessly with respect to preexistent HCCA schedulers, may amplify their individual results. Additional object of future investigation is the comparison of UTSS with the recently proposed reclaiming mechanisms IDTH and DTH in terms of short-term and long-term fairness.

Conflict of Interests

The authors declare that there is no conflict of interests regarding the publication of this paper.

References

[1] IEEE802.11, "Wireless LAN medium access control (MAC) and physical layer (PHY) specification," IEEE, Piscataway, NJ, USA, 2007, http://standards.ieee.org/getieee802/download/802.11-2007.pdf.

[2] A. Grilo and M. Nunes, "Performance evaluation of IEEE 802.11E," in *Proceedings of the 13th IEEE International Symposium on Personal, Indoor and Mobile Radio Communications (PIMRC '02)*, vol. 1, pp. 511–517, Lisboa, Portugal, September 2002.

[3] S.-L. Tsao, "Extending earliest-due-date scheduling algorithms for wireless networks with location-dependent errors," in *Proceedings of the 52nd IEEE Vehicular Technology Conference (VTC-Fall '00)*, vol. 1, pp. 223–228, Boston, Mass, USA, September 2000.

[4] S. Mangold, S. Choi, P. May, O. Klein, G. Hiertz, and L. Stibor, "IEEE 802.11e wireless LAN for quality of service," in *Proceedings of the European Wireless*, vol. 1, pp. 32–39, Florence, Italy, February 2002.

[5] J. Cowling and S. Selvakennedy, "A detailed investigation of the IEEE 802.11e HCF reference scheduler for VBR traffic," in *Proceedings of the 13th International Conference on Computer Communications and Networks (ICC '04)*, pp. 453–459, Chicago, Ill, USA, October 2004.

[6] A. L. Ruscelli, G. Cecchetti, G. Lipari, and A. Mastropaolo, "A greedy reclaiming scheduler for IEEE 802.11e HCCA real-time networks," in *Proceedings of the 14th ACM International Conference on Modeling, Analysis, and Simulation of Wireless and Mobile Systems (MSWiM '11)*, pp. 223–230, Miami, Fla, USA, November 2011.

[7] P. Ansel, Q. Ni, and T. Turletti, "FHCF: a simple and efficient scheduling scheme for IEEE 802.11e wireless LAN," *Mobile Networks and Applications*, vol. 11, no. 3, pp. 391–403, 2006.

[8] C. Cicconetti, L. Lenzini, E. Mingozzi, and G. Stea, "Design and performance analysis of the Real-Time HCCA scheduler for IEEE 802.11e WLANs," *Computer Networks*, vol. 51, no. 9, pp. 2311–2325, 2007.

[9] H. Fattah and C. Leung, "An overview of scheduling algorithms in wireless multimedia networks," *IEEE Wireless Communications*, vol. 9, no. 5, pp. 76–83, 2002.

[10] S. Lu, V. Bharghavan, and R. Srikant, "Fair scheduling in wireless packet networks," *IEEE/ACM Transactions on Networking*, vol. 7, no. 4, pp. 473–489, 1999.

[11] A. Grilo, M. Macedo, and M. Nunes, "A service discipline for support of IP QoS in IEEE 802.11 networks," in *Proceedings of the IFIP TC6/WG6.8 Working Conference on Personal Wireless Communications (PWC '01)*, Laapenranta, Finland, August 2001.

[12] G. Cecchetti and A. L. Ruscelli, "Real-time support for HCCA function in IEEE 802.11e networks: a performance evaluation," *Wiley Security and Communication Networks*, vol. 4, no. 3, pp. 299–315, 2011.

[13] L. Yang, "P-HCCA: a new scheme for real-time traffic with QoS in IEEE 802.11e based networks," in *Proceedings of the APAN Network Research Workshop*, Cairns, Australia, July 2004.

[14] G. Boggia, P. Camarda, L. A. Grieco, and S. Mascolo, "Feedback-based control for providing real-time services with the 802.11e MAC," *IEEE/ACM Transactions on Networking*, vol. 15, no. 2, pp. 323–333, 2007.

[15] K. Y. Lee, K. S. Cho, and W. Ryu, "Efficient QoS scheduling algorithm for multimedia services in IEEE 802.11e WLAN," in *Proceedings of the IEEE 74th Vehicular Technology Conference (VTC Fall '11)*, San Francisco, Calif, USA, September 2011.

[16] A. Arora, S.-G. Yoon, Y.-J. Choi, and S. Bahk, "Adaptive TXOP allocation based on channel conditions and traffic requirements in IEEE 802.11e networks," *IEEE Transactions on Vehicular Technology*, vol. 59, no. 3, pp. 1087–1099, 2010.

[17] C. Kuan and K. Dimyati, "Utilization model for HCCA EDCA mixed mode in IEEE 802.11e," *ETRI Journal*, vol. 29, no. 6, pp. 829–831, 2007.

[18] V. A. Siris and C. Courcoubetis, "Resource control for the EDCA mechanism in multi-rate IEEE 802.11e networks," in *Proceedings of the 4th International Symposium on Modeling and Optimization in Mobile, Ad Hoc and Wireless Networks (WiOpt '06)*, pp. 1–6, Boston, Mass, USA, 2006.

[19] W. K. Lai, C.-S. Shieh, and C.-S. Jiang, "Adaptation of HCCA/EDCA ratio in IEEE 802.11e for improved system performance," *International Journal of Innovative Computing, Information and Control*, vol. 5, no. 11, pp. 4177–4188, 2009.

[20] A. L. Ruscelli, G. Cecchetti, A. Alifano, and G. Lipari, "Enhancement of QoS support of HCCA schedulers using EDCA function in IEEE 802.11e networks," *Ad Hoc Networks*, vol. 10, no. 2, pp. 147–161, 2012.

[21] J. Lee, I. Shin, G. Park, W. Song, J. Kim, and J. Hong, "An efficient bandwidth reclaim scheme for the integrated transmission of real-time and non real-time messages on the WLAN," in *Computational Science—ICCS 2007*, vol. 4490 of *Lecture Notes in Computer Science*, pp. 925–932, 2007.

[22] P. Larcheri and R. L. Cigno, "Scheduling in 802.11e: open-loop or closed-loop?" in *Proceedings of the 3rd Annual Conference on Wireless on-demand Network Systems and Services (WONS '06)*, Les Ménuires, France, January 2006.

[23] L. Palopoli, R. Lo Cigno, and A. Colombo, "Control and optimisation of HCCA 802.11e access scheduling," in *Proceedings of the 46th IEEE Conference on Decision and Control (CDC '07)*, pp. 4427–4432, New Orleans, La, USA, December 2007.

[24] C. E. García, D. M. Prett, and M. Morari, "Model predictive control: theory and a survey," *Automatica*, vol. 25, no. 3, pp. 335–348, 1989.

[25] R. Lo Cigno, L. Palopoli, and A. Colombo, "Analysis of different scheduling strategies in 802.11e networks with multi-class traffic," in *Proceedings of the 32nd IEEE Conference on Local Computer Networks (LCN '07)*, pp. 455–462, Dublin, Ireland, October 2007.

[26] G. Cecchetti, A. L. Ruscelli, A. Mastropaolo, and G. Lipari, "Providing variable TXOP for IEEE 802.11e HCCA real-time networks," in *Proceedings of the IEEE Wireless Communications and Networking Conference (WCNC '12)*, Paris, France, April 2012.

[27] G. Cecchetti, A. L. Ruscelli, A. Mastropaolo, and G. Lipari, "Dynamic TXOP HCCA reclaiming scheduler with transmission time estimation for IEEE 802.11e real-time networks," in *Proceedings of the 15th ACM international conference on Modeling, analysis and simulation of wireless and mobile systems (MSWiM '12)*, Paphos, Cyprus, October 2012.

[28] A. Grilo, M. Macedo, and M. Nunes, "A scheduling algorithm for QoS support in IEEE 802.11E networks," *IEEE Wireless Communications*, vol. 10, no. 3, pp. 36–43, 2003.

[29] D. Ferrari and D. C. Verma, "A Scheme for real-time channel establishment in wide-area networks," *IEEE Journal on Selected Areas in Communications*, vol. 8, no. 3, pp. 368–379, 1990.

[30] Y. Fan and C. Huang, "Real-time traffic sheduling algorithm in WLAN," in *Proceedings of the 4th Generation Mobile Forum (GMF '05)*, San Diego, Calif, USA, 2005.

[31] C. L. Liu and J. W. Layland, "Scheduling algorithms for multi-programming in a hard-real-time environment," *Journal of the ACM*, vol. 20, pp. 46–61, 1973.

[32] T. P. Baker, "Stack-based scheduling of realtime processes," *Real-Time Systems*, vol. 3, no. 1, pp. 67–99, 1991.

[33] D. Skyrianoglou, N. Passas, and A. K. Salkintzis, "ARROW: an efficient traffic scheduling algorithm for IEEE 802.11e HCCA," *IEEE Transactions on Wireless Communications*, vol. 5, no. 12, pp. 3558–3567, 2006.

[34] J. R. Jackson, *Scheduling a Production Line to Minimize Maximum Tardiness*, Management Science Research Project, University of California, Los Angeles, Calif, USA, 1955.

[35] C. Inan, F. Keceli, and E. Ayanoglu, "An adaptive multimedia QoS scheduler for 802.11e wireless LANs," in *Proceedings of the IEEE International Conference on Communications (ICC '06)*, pp. 5263–5270, Istanbul, Turkey, July 2006.

[36] G. Cecchetti and A. L. Ruscelli, "Performance evaluation of Real-Time schedulers for HCCA function in IEEE 802.11e wireless networks," in *Proceedings of the 4th ACM International Symposium on QoS and Security for Wireless and Mobile Networks (Q2SWinet '08)*, pp. 1–8, Vancouver, Canada, October 2008.

[37] P. T. Brady, "A model for generating on-off speech pattern in two way conversation," *Bell System Technical Journal*, vol. 48, pp. 2445–2472, 1969.

[38] D. P. Heyman, A. Tabatabai, and T. V. Lakshman, "Statistical analysis and simulation study of video teleconference traffic in ATM networks," *IEEE Transactions on Circuits and Systems for Video Technology*, vol. 2, no. 1, pp. 49–59, 1992.

[39] A. Elwalid, D. Heyman, T. V. Lakshman, D. Mitra, and A. Weiss, "Fundamental bounds and approximations for ATM multiplexers with applications to video teleconferencing," *IEEE Journal on Selected Areas in Communications*, vol. 13, no. 6, pp. 1004–1016, 1995.

[40] P. Wan, Z. Du, and W. Wu, "A simple and efficient mpeg-4 video traffic model for wireless network performance evalautation," in

Proceedings of the IEEE Wireless Communications and Network-
ing Conference (WCNC '04), Atlanta, Ga, USA, March 2004.

[41] A. Adas, "Traffic models in broadband networks," *IEEE Com-*
munications Magazine, vol. 35, no. 7, pp. 82–89, 1997.

[42] Y. Sun and J. N. Daigle, "A source model of video traffic based
on full-length VBR MPEG4 video traces," in *Proceedings of the*
IEEE Global Telecommunications Conference (GLOBECOM '05),
pp. 766–770, St. Louis, Mo, USA, December 2005.

[43] R. Grunenfelder, J. P. Cosmas, S. Manthorpe, and A. Odinma-
Okafor, "Characterization of video codecs as autoregressive
moving average processes and related queueing system performance," *IEEE Journal on Selected Areas in Communications*, vol.
9, no. 3, pp. 284–293, 1991.

[44] D. Jun and L. Jun, "VBR MPEG video traffic dynamic prediction
based on the modeling and forecast of time series," in *Proceed-*
ings of the 5th International Joint Conference on INC, IMS and
IDC (NCM '09), pp. 1752–1756, Seoul, Korea, August 2009.

[45] "Network Simulator 2," 1995, http://www.isi.edu/nsnam/ns/.

[46] 2005, http://trace.eas.asu.edu/.

4

Seamless Integration of RESTful Services into the Web of Data

Markus Lanthaler[1] and Christian Gütl[1,2]

[1] *Institute for Information Systems and Computer Media, Graz University of Technology, 8010 Graz, Austria*
[2] *School of Information Systems, Curtin University of Technology, Perth WA 6102, Australia*

Correspondence should be addressed to Markus Lanthaler, markus.lanthaler@student.tugraz.at

Academic Editor: Nabil Tabbane

We live in an era of ever-increasing abundance of data. To cope with the information overload we suffer from every single day, more sophisticated methods are required to access, manipulate, and analyze these humongous amounts of data. By embracing the heterogeneity, which is unavoidable at such a scale, and accepting the fact that the data quality and meaning are fuzzy, more adaptable, flexible, and extensible systems can be built. RESTful services combined with Semantic Web technologies could prove to be a viable path to achieve that. Their combination allows data integration on an unprecedented scale and solves some of the problems Web developers are continuously struggling with. This paper introduces a novel approach to create machine-readable descriptions for RESTful services as a first step towards this ambitious goal. It also shows how these descriptions along with an algorithm to translate SPARQL queries to HTTP requests can be used to integrate RESTful services into a global read-write Web of Data.

1. Introduction

We live in an era where exabytes of data are produced every single year; never before in human history had we to deal with such an abundance of information. To cope with this information overload, more sophisticated methods are required to access, manipulate, and analyze these humongous amounts of data. Service-oriented architectures (SOAs) built on Web services were a first attempt to address this issue, but the utopian promise of uniform service interface standards, metadata, and universal service registries, in the form of SOAP, WSDL, and UDDI has proven elusive. This and other centralized, registry-based approaches were overwhelmed by the Web's rate of growth and the lack of a universally accepted classification scheme. In consequence, the usage of SOAP-based services is mainly limited to company-internal systems and to the integration of legacy systems. In practice, however, such a clear and crisp definition of data is rare. Today's systems integrate data from many sources. The data quality and meaning are fuzzy and the schema, if present, are likely to vary across the different sources. In very large and loosely coupled systems, such as the Internet, the gained adaptability, flexibility, and extensibility, in a transition away from strict and formal typing to simple name/value pairs or triples, outweighs the resulting loss off "correctness."

Thus, it is not surprising that RESTful services, and there especially the ones using the lightweight JavaScript Object Notation (JSON) [1] as the serialization format, are increasingly popular. According to ProgrammableWeb, 74% of the Web services are now RESTful and 45% of them use JSON as the data format [2], but, in spite of their growing adoption, RESTful services still suffer from some serious shortcomings.

The major problem is that, for RESTful services or *Web APIs*, a recently emerged term to distinguish them from their traditional SOAP-based counterparts, no agreed machine-readable description format exists. All the required information of how to invoke them and how to interpret the various resource representations is communicated out-of-band by human-readable documentations. Since machines have huge problems to understand such documentations, machine-to-machine communication is often based on static knowledge resulting in tightly coupled system. The challenge is thus to bring some of the human Web's adaptivity to the Web of machines to allow the building of loosely coupled, reliable, and scalable systems.

Semantic annotations could prove to be a viable path to achieve that, but, while the vision of a Semantic Web has been around for more than fifteen years, it still has a long way to go before mainstream adoption will be achieved. One of the reasons for that is, in our opinion, the fear of average Web developers to use Semantic Web technologies. They are often overwhelmed by the (perceived) complexity or think they have to be AI experts to make use of the Semantic Web. Others are still waiting for a killer application making it a classical chicken-and-egg problem. A common perception is also that the Semantic Web is a disruptive technology which makes it a showstopper for enterprises needing to evolve their systems and build upon existing infrastructure investments. Obviously, some developers are also just reluctant to use new technologies. Nevertheless, we think most Web developers fear to use Semantic Web technologies for some reason or another; a phenomenon we denoted as *Semaphobia* [3]. To help developers get past this fear, and to show them that they have nothing to fear but fear itself, clear incentives along with simple specifications and guidelines are necessary. Wherever possible, upgrade paths for existing systems should be provided to build upon existing investments.

That is exactly what made the Linked Data movement so successful. It simplified the technology stack and provided clear incentives for annotating data. In consequence, it is not surprising that after being ignored by the majority of the Web developers for a long time, lightweight semantic annotations finally start to gain acceptance across the community. Facebook's Open Graph protocol, for example, was implemented in over 50,000 Web sites within the first week of its launch [4] and the current estimates are that roughly 10% of all Web pages are annotated with it.

It would just seem consequent to combine the strengths of both, REST and the Linked Data principles, but in practice they still remain largely separated. Instead of providing access to Linked Data via a RESTful service interface, current efforts deploy centralistic SPARQL endpoints or simply upload static dumps of RDF data. This also means that most current Semantic Web projects just provide read-only interfaces to the underlying data. This clearly inhibits networking effects and engagement of the crowd.

To address these issues, we developed a novel approach to semantically describe RESTful data services which allows their seamless integration into a Web of Data. We put a strong emphasis on simplicity and on not requiring any changes on the Web service itself. This should lower the entry barrier for future Web developers and provide a viable upgrade path for existing infrastructure. At the same time, the approach is extensible and flexible enough to be applicable in a wide application domain.

The reminder of the paper is organized as follows. In Section 2, we give an overview of related work. Then, in Section 3, we present the requirements and the design of SEREDASj, our approach to semantically describe RESTful services. Section 4 shows how SEREDASj can be used to integrate different RESTful services into the Web of Data, and finally, Section 5 concludes the paper and gives an overview of future work.

2. Related Work

In contrast to traditional SOAP-based services, which have agreed standards in the form of WSDL and SAWSDL [5] to be described, both, syntactically and semantically, no standards exist for RESTful services. In consequence, RESTful services are almost exclusively described by human-readable documentations describing the URLs and the data expected as input and output. There have been made many proposals to solve this issue; SA-REST [6], hRESTS [7], and WADL [8] are probably the best-known ones.

The Web Application Description Language's approach (WADL) [8] is closely related to WSDL in that a developer creates a monolithic XML file containing all the information about the service's interface. Given that WADL was specifically designed for describing RESTful services (or HTTP-based Web applications as they are called in WADL's specification), it models the resources provided by the service and the relationships between them. Each service resource is described as a request containing the used HTTP method and the required inputs as well as zero or more responses describing the expected service response representations and HTTP status codes. The data format of the request and response representations are described by embedded or referenced data format definitions. Even though WADL does not mandate any specific data format definition language, just the use of RelaxNG and XML Schema are described in the specification. The main critique of WADL is that it is complex and thus requires developers that have a certain level of training and tool support to enable the usage of WADL. This complexity contradicts the simplicity of RESTful services. In addition, WADL urges the use of specific resource hierarchies which introduce an obvious coupling between the client and the server. Servers should have the complete freedom to control their own namespace.

hRESTS (HTML for RESTful Services) [7] follows a quite different approach as it tries to exploit the fact that almost all RESTful services already have a textual documentation in the form of Web pages. hRESTS' idea is hence to enrich those, mostly already existent, human-readable documentations with so-called microformats [9] to make them machine-processable. A single HTML document enriched with hRESTS microformats can contain multiple service descriptions and conversely multiple HTML documents can together be used to document a single service (it is a common practice to split service documentations into different HTML documents to make them more digestible). Each service is described by a number of operations, that is, actions a client can perform on that service, with the corresponding URI, HTTP method, the inputs and outputs. While hRESTS offers a relatively straightforward solution to describe the resources and the supported operations, there is some lack of support for describing the used data schemas. Apart from a potential label, hRESTS does not provide any support for further machine-readable information about the inputs and outputs. Extensions like SA-REST [6] and MicroWSMO [10] address this issue.

MicroWSMO is an attempt to adapt the SAWSDL approach for the semantic description of RESTful services. It uses, just as hRESTS, on which it relies, microformats for adding semantic annotations to the HTML service documentation. Similar to SAWSDL, MicroWSMO has three types of annotations: (1) *Model*, which can be used on any hRESTS service property to point to appropriate semantic concepts; (2) *Lifting*, and (3) *Lowering*, which specify the mappings between semantic data and the underlying technical format such as XML. Therefore, MicroWSMO enables the semantic annotation of RESTful services basically in the same way in which SAWSDL supports the annotation of Web services described by WSDL.

Another approach for the semantic description of RESTful services is the before-mentioned SA-REST [6]. It relies on RDFa for marking service properties in an existing HTML service description, similar to hRESTS with MicroWSMO. As a matter of fact, it was the first approach reusing the already existing HTML service documentation to create machine-processable descriptions of RESTful services. The main differences between the two approaches are indeed not the underlying principles but rather the implementation technique. SA-REST offers the following service elements: (1) *Input* and (2) *Output* to facilitate data mediation; (3) *Lifting* and (4) *Lowering schemas* to translate the data structures that represent the inputs and outputs to the data structure of the ontology, the grounding schema; (5) *Action*, which specifies the required HTTP method to invoke the service; (6) *Operation* which defines what the service does; and (7) *Fault* to annotate errors.

In principle, a RESTful service could even be described by using WSDL 2.0 [11] with SAWSDL [5] and an ontology like OWL-S or WSMO-Lite. OWL-S (Web Ontology Language for Web Services) [12] is an upper ontology based on the W3C standard ontology OWL used to semantically annotate Web services. OWL-S consists of the following main upper ontologies: (1) the *Service Profile* for advertising and discovering services; (2) the *Service (Process) Model*, which gives a detailed description of a service's operation and describes the composition (choreography and orchestration) of one or more services; (3) the *Service Grounding*, which provides the needed details about transport protocols to invoke the service (e.g., the binding between the logic-based service description and the service's WSDL description). Generally speaking, the Service Profile provides the information needed for an agent to discover a service, while the Service Model and Service Grounding, taken together, provide enough information for an agent to make use of a service, once found [12]. The main critique of OWL-S is its limited expressiveness of service descriptions in practice. Since it practically corresponds to OWL-DL, it allows only the description of static and deterministic aspects; it does not cover any notion of time and change, nor uncertainty. Besides that, an OWL-S process cannot contain any number of completely unrelated operations [13, 14], in contrast to WSDL.

WSMO-Lite [15] is another ontology to fill SAWSDL's annotations with concrete service semantics. SAWSDL itself does not specify a language for representing the semantic models but just defines how to add semantic annotations to various parts of a WSDL document. WSMO-Lite allows bottom-up modeling of services and adopts, as the name suggests, the WSMO [16] model and makes its semantics lighter. WSMO-Lite describes the following four aspects of a Web service: (1) the *Information Model*, which defines the data model for input, output, and fault messages; (2) the *Functional Semantics*, which define the functionality, which the service offers; (3) the *Behavioral Semantics*, which define how a client has to talk to the service; (4) the *Nonfunctional Descriptions*, which define nonfunctional properties such as quality of service or price. A major advantage of WSMO-Lite is that it is not bound to a particular service description format, for example, WSDL. Consequently, it can be used to integrate approaches like, for example, hRESTS (in conjunction with MicroWSMO) with traditional WSDL-based service descriptions. Therefore, tasks such as discovery, composition, and data mediation could be performed completely independent from the underlying Web service technology.

Even though at a first glance all the above-described ideas seem to be fundamentally different from WSDL, their underlying model is still closely related to WSDL's structure. In consequence, all presented approaches heavily rely on RPC's (Remote Procedure Call) flawed [17] operation-based model ignoring the fundamental architectural properties of REST. Instead of describing the resource representations, and thus allowing a client to understand them, they adhere to the RPC-like model of describing the inputs and outputs as well as the supported operations which result in tight coupling. The obvious consequence is that these approaches do not align well with clear RESTful service design.

One of the approaches avoiding the RPC-orientation, and thus more suitable for RESTful services, is ReLL [18], the Resource Linking Language. It is a language to describe RESTful services with emphasis on the hypermedia characteristics of the REST model. This allows, for example, a crawler to automatically retrieve the data exposed by Web APIs. One of the aims of ReLL is indeed to transform crawled data to RDF in order to harvest those already existing Web resources and to integrate them into the Semantic Web. Nevertheless, ReLL does not support semantic annotations but relies on XSLT for the transformation to RDF. This clearly limits ReLL's expressivity as it is not able to describe the resource representations semantically.

There are many other approaches that allow, just as ReLL, to transform data exposed by Web APIs to RDF. In fact, large parts of the current Web of Data are generated from non-RDF databases by tools such as D2R [19] or Triplify [20] but one of the limitations of the current Semantic Web is that it usually just provides read-only interfaces to the underlying data. So, while several Semantic Web browsers, such as Tabulator [21], Oink [22], or Disco [23], have been developed to display RDF data, the challenge of how to edit, extend, or annotate this data has so far been left largely unaddressed. There exist a few single-graph editors including RDFAuthor [24] and ISAViz [25] but, to our best knowledge, Tabulator Redux [26] is the only editor that allows the editing of graphs derived from multiple sources.

To mitigate this situation, the *pushback project* [27] was initiated in 2009 (it is not clear whether this project is still active) to develop a method to write data back from RDF graphs to non-RDF data sources such as Web APIs. The approach chosen by the pushback project was to extend the RDF wrappers, which transform non-RDF data from Web APIs to RDF data, to additionally support write operations. This is achieved by a process called *fusion* that automatically annotates an existing HTML form with RDFa. The resulting *RDForm* then reports the changed data as RDF back to the pushback controller which in turn relays the changes to the RDF write wrapper that then eventually translates them into an HTTP request understandable to the Web API. One of the major challenges is to create the read-write wrappers as there are, as explained before, no agreed standards for describing RESTful services; neither syntactically nor semantically. Exposing these Web APIs as read-write Linked Data is, therefore, more an art than a science.

3. Semantic Description of RESTful Services

A machine-readable documentation of a service's interface and the data it exposes is a first step towards their (semi-) automatic integration. In this section, we first discuss the requirements for a semantic description language for RESTful services and then present SEREDASj, a novel approach to address this ambitious challenge.

3.1. Requirements. Analyzing the related work and taking into account our experience in creating RESTful services and integrating them into mashups, we derived a set of core requirements for a semantic description language.

Since the description language is targeted towards RESTful services, it clearly has to adhere to REST's architectural constraints [28] which can be summarized as follows: (1) *stateless interaction*, (2) *uniform interface*, (3) *identification of resources*, (4) *manipulation of resources through representations*, (5) *self-descriptive messages*, and (6) *hypermedia as the engine of application state*. Stateless interaction means that all the session state is kept entirely on the client and that each request from the client to the server has to contain all the necessary information for the server to understand the request; this makes interactions with the server independent of each other and decouples the client from the server. All the interactions in a RESTful system are performed via a uniform interface which decouples the implementations from the services they provide. To obtain such a uniform interface, every resource is accessible through a representation (whether the representation is in the same format as the raw source, or is derived from the source, remains hidden behind the interface) and has to have an identifier. All resource representations should be self-descriptive, that is, they are somehow labeled with their type which specifies how they are to be interpreted. Finally, the *hypermedia as the engine of application state* (HATEOAS) constraint refers to the use of hyperlinks in resource representations as a way of navigating the state machine of an application.

To be widely accepted, the approach has to be based on core Web standards. That means it should use Uniform Resource Identifiers (URIs) for identifying resources, the Hypertext Transfer Protocol (HTTP) for accessing and modifying resource representations, and the Resource Description Framework (RDF) as the unified data model for describing resources. To ease tasks such as data integration, a uniform interface to access heterogeneous data sources in a uniform and intuitive way, has to be provided as well. This, in turn, will lead to reusability and flexibility which are important aspects for the adoption of such a new approach. By having semantically annotated data, a developer could also be supported in the data integration and mediation process which is not only important in enterprise scenarios but also for the creation of mashups. All too often the required data mediation code is longer than the actual business logic. By having semantically annotated data, it is possible to integrate it (semi-) automatically with other data sources.

While all of these constraints are important when designing a RESTful service, the most important aspects for a semantic description language are how the resources can be accessed, how they are represented, and how they are interlinked. The description language should be expressive enough to describe how resource representation can be retrieved and manipulated, and what the meaning of those representations is. To integrate the service into the Semantic Web, the description language should also provide means to transform the representations in RDF triples. In order to be able to evolve systems and build upon existing infrastructure, an important requirement is that no (or just minimal) changes on the existing system are required; this implies a requirement to support partial descriptions. Last but not least, the approach should be as simple as possible to lower the entry barrier for developers and to foster its adoption.

3.2. SEREDASj. Considering the requirements described in the previous section, we designed SEREDASj a language to describe *SEmantic REstful DAta Services*. The "j" at the end should highlight that we based the approach on JSON. JSON's popularity in Web APIs is not the only reason for that.

The inherent impedance mismatch (the so-called O/X impedance mismatch) between XML, which is used in traditional SOAP-based Web services, and object-oriented programming constructs often results in severe interoperability problems. The fundamental problem is that the XML Schema language (XSD) has a number of type system constructs which simply do not exist in commonly used object-oriented programming languages such as, for example, Java. This leads in consequence to interoperability problems because each SOAP stack has its own way of mapping the various XSD-type system constructs to objects in the target platform's programming language and vice versa.

In most use cases addressed by Web services, all a developer wants to do is to interchange data—and here we are distinguishing between data interchange and document interchange. JSON was specifically designed for this: it is a lightweight, language-independent data-interchange format which is easy to parse and easy to generate. Furthermore, it

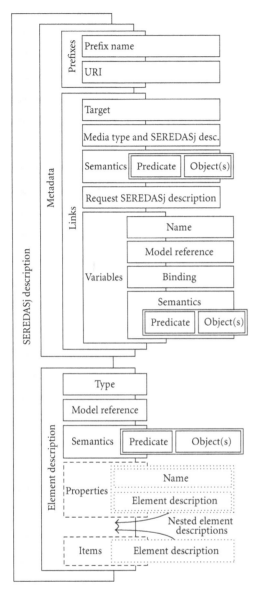

FIGURE 1: The SEREDASj description model.

is much easier for developers to understand and use. JSON's whole specification [1] consists of ten pages (with the actual content being a mere four pages) compared to XML where the XML Core Working group alone [29] lists *XML, XML Namespaces, XML Inclusions, XML Information Set, xml:id, XML Base*, and *Associating Stylesheets with XML* as standards; not even including *XML Schema Part 1* and *XML Schema Part 2*.

Summarized, JSON's simplicity, ease of integration, and raising adoption across the Web community [2] made it the first choice for our description language, but we would like to highlight that the principles of our approach are applicable to any serialization format.

To describe a RESTful service, SEREDASj specifies, similar to schemas, the syntactic structure of a specific JSON representation. Additionally, it allows to reference JSON elements to concepts in a vocabulary or ontology and to

further describe the element itself by semantic annotations. Figure 1 depicts the structure of an SEREDASj description.

A description consists of metadata and a description of the structure of the JSON instance data representations it describes. The metadata contains information about the hyperlinks related to the instance data and prefix definitions to abbreviate long URIs in the semantic annotations to CURIEs [30]. The link descriptions contain all the necessary information for a client to retrieve and manipulate instance data. Additionally to the link's target, its media type and the target's SEREDASj description, link descriptions can contain the needed SEREDASj request description to create requests and semantic annotations to describe the link, for example, its relation to the current representation. The link's target is expressed by link templates where the associated variables can be bound to an element in the instance data and/or linked to a conceptual model, for example, a class or property in an ontology. The link template's variables can be further described by generic semantic annotations in the form of predicate-object pairs. The links' SEREDASj request description allows a client to construct the request bodies used in POST or PUT operations to create or update resources.

The description of the structure of instance representations (denoted as element description in Figure 1) defines the JSON data type(s) as well as links to conceptual models. Furthermore, it may contain semantic annotations to describe an element further and, if the element represents either a JSON object or array, a description of its properties, respectively, items in term of, again, an element description. The structure of the JSON instance arises out of nested element descriptions. To allow reuse, the type of an element description can be set to the URI of another model definition or another part within the current model definition. To address different parts of a model, a slash-delimited fragment resolution is used. In Listing 1, for instance, `event.json#properties/enddate` refers to the end date property defined by the SEREDASj document `event.json`.

In order to better illustrate the approach, a simple example of a JSON representation and its corresponding SEREDASj description are given in Listing 1. The example is a representation of an event and its performers from an imaginary event site's API. Without annotations, the data cannot be understood by a machine and even for a human it is not evident that a performer's ID is in fact a hyperlink to a more detailed representation of that specific performer. SEREDASj solves those problems by describing all the important aspects of such a representation. In consequence, it is not only possible to extract the hyperlinks, but also to create a human-readable documentation of the data format (as shown in [3]) and to translate the JSON representation to an RDF representation.

The SEREDASj description in Listing 1 contains two link definitions. The first one specifies the link to the performers' representations via their ID. It uses a URI template whose variable is bound to `#properties/performers/id`. This link definition also shows how further semantic annotations can be used; this is described in detail in Section 4.1. The second link specifies a search interface and is thus not

```
                              Instance Data
                        http://example.com/event/e48909
{
  "id": "e48909",
  "name": "Dick Clark's New Year's Rockin' Eve",
  "startdate": "2011-12-31",
  "enddate": "2012-01-01",
  "performers": [
    { "id": "p84098", "name": "Lady Gaga",
        "birthdate": "1986-03-28" }
  ]
}
                            SEREDASj Description
                        http://example.com/models/event.json
{
  "meta": {
    "prefixes": {
      "owl": "http://www.w3.org/2002/07/owl#",
      "so": "http://schema.org/",
      "ex": "http://example.com/onto#",
      "iana": "http://www.iana.org/link-relations/"
    },
    "links": {
      "/person/{id}": {
        "mediaType": "application/json",
        "seredasjDescription": "person.json",
        "semantics": {
          "owl:sameAs": "<#properties/performers>"
        },
        "variables": {
          "id": {
            "binding": "#properties/performers/id",
            "model": "[ex:id]"
          }
        },
        "requestDescription": "person-createupdate.json"
      },
      "/events/search{?query}": {
        "mediaType": "application/json",
        "seredasjDescription": "eventlist.json",
        "semantics": {
          "[iana:relation]": "[iana:search]" },
        "variables": {
          "query": { "model": "[so:name]" }
        }
      }
    }
  },
  "type": "object",
  "model": "[so:Event]",
  "properties": {
    "id": {
      "type": "string", "model": "[ex:id]" },
    "name": {
      "type": "string", "model": "[so:name]" },
    "startdate": {
      "type": "string", "model": "[so:startDate]" },
    "enddate": {
      "type": "string", "model": "[so:endDate]" },
```

LISTING 1: Continued.

```
"performers": {
  "type": "array",
  "model": "[so:performers]",
  "items": {
    "type": "object", "model": "[so:Person]",
    "properties": {
      "id": {
        "type": "string", "model": "[ex:id]" },
      "name": {
        "type": "string", "model": "[so:name]" },
      "birthdate": {
        "type": "string", "model": "[so:birthDate]" }
    }
  }
}
}
```

LISTING 1: An exemplary JSON representation and its corresponding SEREDASj description.

bound to any element in the instance data; instead, the variable's model reference is specified. Again, this link is semantically annotated so that an agent will know that this link specifies a search interface. These semantic annotations allow developers to implement smarter clients understanding the relationships of resources and thus following REST's hypermedia as the engine of application state constraint.

The following description of the representation's structure basically maps the structure to the ontology defined by schema.org [31]. The mapping strategy is similar to the table-to-class, column-to-predicate strategy of current relational database-to-RDF approaches [32]; JSON objects are mapped to classes, all the rest to predicates. By reusing schema.org's ontology wherever possible, the developer is able to exploit the already available human-readable descriptions for the various elements and generate completely automatically a human-readable documentation.

SEREDASj descriptions do not have to be complete, that is, they do not need to describe every element in all details. If an unknown element is encountered in an instance representation, it is simply ignored. This way, SEREDASj allows forward compatibility as well as extensibility and diminishes the coupling. In this context, it should also be emphasized that a SEREDASj description does not imply a shared data model between a service and a client. It just provides a description of the service's representations to ease the mapping to the client's data model.

4. Seamless Integration of RESTful Services into a Web of Data

Currently mashup developers have to deal with a plethora of heterogeneous data formats and service interfaces for which little to no tooling support is available. RDF, the preferred data format of the Semantic Web, is one attempt to build a universal applicable data format to ease data integration, but,

unfortunately, current Semantic Web applications mostly provide just read-only interfaces to their underlying data. We believe it should be feasible to standardize and streamline the mashup development process by combining technologies from, both, the world of Web APIs and the Semantic Web. This would, in the first place, result in higher productivity which could subsequently lead to a plethora of new applications. Potentially it could also foster the creation of mashup editors at higher levels of abstraction which could, hopefully, even allow non-technical experts to create mashups fulfilling their situational needs.

Based on SEREDASj which we introduced in the previous section, we would like to propose a new reference model for integrating traditional Web service interfaces into a global read-write graph of data. Figure 2 shows the architecture of our approach.

We broadly distinguish between an application-specific (at the top) and an application-independent layer (at the bottom). The application-independent layer at the bottom is used as a generic data access layer. It separates the application and presentation logic from the common need to manage and manipulate data from a plethora of different data sources. This separation of concerns should result in better reusability and increased development productivity.

Data from JSON-based Web services described by SEREDASj are translated into RDF data and stored along with data from native RDF sources such as SPARQL endpoints, static RDF dumps, or RDF embedded in HTML documents in a local triple store. This unification of the data format is the first step for the integration of these heterogeneous data sources. We use RDF because it reflects the way data is stored and interlinked on the Web, namely, in the form of a graph. The fact that it is schema-free and based on triples makes it the lowest common denominator for heterogeneous data sources, flexible, and easily evolvable. In addition to acting as a data integration layer, this local triple store is also used for caching the

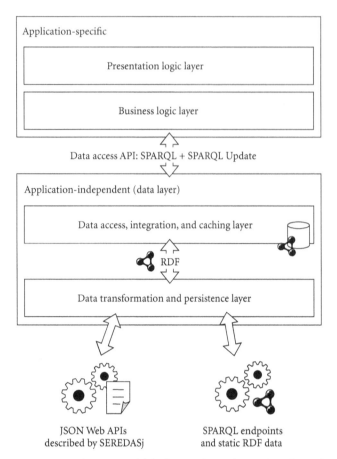

FIGURE 2: A reference model for integrating Web APIs into the Web of Data.

data which is a fundamental requirement in networked applications. Furthermore, centralized processing is much more efficient than federated queries and the like. Just look at, for example, Google's centralized processing compared to federated database queries and please keep in mind that we are not arguing against achievable speed increases by parallelization.

All data modifications are passed through the data access and persistence layer and will eventually be transferred back to the originating data source. The interface connecting the data access layer and the business logic layer has to be aware of which data can be changed and which cannot since some data sources or part of the data representations might be read-only. Depending on the scenario, a developer might choose to include a storage service (either a triple store or a traditional Web API) which allows storing changes even to immutable data. It is then the responsibility of the data integration layer to "replace" or "overwrite" this read-only data with its superseding data. Keeping track of the data's provenance is thus a very important feature.

In order to decouple the application-specific layer from the application-independent data layer, the interface between them has to be standardized. There exist already a standard and a working draft for that, namely, SPARQL [33] and SPARQL Update [34]. We reuse them in order to build our approach upon existing work. Of course, an application

developer is free to add another layer of abstraction on top of that—similar to the common practice of using an O/R mapper (object-relational mapper) to access SQL databases.

While this three-tier architecture is well known and widely used in application development, to our best knowledge it has not been used for integrating Web services into the Semantic Web. Furthermore, this integration approach has not been used to generalize the interface of Web services. Developers are still struggling with highly diverse Web service interfaces.

4.1. Data Format Harmonization. Translating SEREDASj described JSON representations to RDF triples, the first step for integrating them into the Linked Data Cloud, is a straightforward process. The translation starts at the root of the JSON representation and considers all model references of JSON objects and tuple-typed arrays to be RDF classes, while all the other elements' model references are considered to be RDF predicates where the value of that element will be taken as object. If a representation contains nested objects, just as the example in Listing 1, a slash-delimited URI fragment is used to identify the nested object. Semantic annotations in the form of the `semantics` property, as the one shown in the performer's link in Listing 1, contain the predicate and the object. The object might point to a specific element in the SEREDASj description and is eventually translated to a link in the instance data.

The automatic translation of the example from Listing 1 to RDF is shown in Listing 3. The event and its performers are nicely mapped to schema.org ontology. For every array item, a new object URI is created by using a slash-delimited URI fragment. Eventually, those URIs are mapped to the performer's "real" URI by the link's semantic annotation. Please note that the query link is not included in the RDF representation. The reason for this is that the query variable is not bound to any instance element and thus its value is unknown. In consequence, the translator is unable to construct the URI.

4.2. Integration with Other Data Sources. As explained in the previous section, the conversion to RDF is a first step towards integration of data from different sources. To be fully integrated, the data from all sources eventually has to use the same semantic annotations, that is, the same vocabulary and the same identifiers. Traditionally, this homogenization has been done in an imperative way by writing data mediation code. The Semantic Web technology stack on the other hand embraces the inevitable heterogeneity and provides means to address this issue in a declarative way by creating new knowledge in the form of, for example, schema or identifier mappings. By studying the contents of data and the relationships between different data items, it is sometimes possible to infer (semi-) automatically that two seemingly different items are really the same.

It is straightforward to integrate the data from our example in Listing 3 with data about Lady Gaga stored in, for example, DBpedia (a project aiming to extract structured content from the information contained in Wikipedia). All we have to do is to map some of schema.org concepts and

```
1 PREFIX foaf: <http://xmlns.com/foaf/0.1/>
2 PREFIX xsd: <http://www.w3.org/2001/XMLSchema#>
3 PREFIX dbpprop: <http://dbpedia.org/property/>

4 SELECT ?s
5 WHERE {
6   ?s foaf:name ?name;
7      dbpprop:birthDate ?dob.
8   FILTER(str(?name) = "Lady Gaga").
9   FILTER(str(?dob) = "1986-03-28")  }
```

LISTING 2: SPARQL query to find Lady Gaga's identifier in DBpedia.

```
1   @base <http://example.com/event/e48909>.

2   @prefix rdf:
3     <http://www.w3.org/1999/02/22-rdf-syntax-ns#>.

4   @prefix owl: <http://www.w3.org/2002/07/owl#>.
5   @prefix so: <http://schema.org/>.
6   @prefix ex: <http://example.com/onto#>.

7   <#> rdf:type so:Event.
8   <#> ex:id "e48909".
9   <#> so:name "Dick Clark's New Year's Rockin' Eve".
10  <#> so:startDate "2011-12-31".
11  <#> so:endDate "2012-01-01".
12  <#> so:performers <#performers/0>.

13  <#performers/0> rdf:type so:Person.
14  <#performers/0> ex:id "p84098".
15  <#performers/0> so:name "Lady Gaga".
16  <#performers/0> so:birthDate "1986-03-28".

17  <http://example.com/person/p84098> owl:sameAs
18    <#performers/0>.
```

LISTING 3: The example in Listing 1 translated to RDF.

our local identifier to concepts and Lady Gaga's identifier in DBpedia. Schema mappings are already provided by DBpedia (http://mappings.dbpedia.org/) so all we have to do is to find DBpedia's identifier and map it to our local identifier. An inference engine could do this easily by running the query shown in Listing 2 at DBpedia's SPARQL endpoint. The result is the URI we are looking for: `http://dbpedia.org/resource/Lady_Gaga`. After mapping that URI to our local identifier by using OWL's `sameAs` concept, we can easily query all the data about Lady Gaga from DBpedia as it would be part of our Web service;

the data layer in Figure 2 is responsible to take care of all the necessary details.

4.3. Storing Changes Back to the Source. Just as DBpedia, a big part of the current Semantic Web consists of data transformed from Web APIs or relational databases to RDF or by data extracted from Web sites. In consequence, the vast majority of the current Semantic Web is just read-only, that is, changes cannot be stored back to the original source. Thus, in this section, we will show how SEREDASj allows data to be updated and transferred back to the originating

Web service (obviously we are not able to update static Web pages).

For the following description, we assume that all data of interest and the resulting Web of interlinked SEREDASj descriptions have already been retrieved (whether this means crawled or queried specifically is irrelevant for this work). The objective is then to update the harvested data or to add new data by using SPARQL Update.

SPARQL Update manipulates data by either adding or removing triples from a graph. The INSERT DATA and DELETE DATA operations add, respectively, remove a set of triples from a graph by using concrete data (no named variables). In contrast, the INSERT and DELETE operations also accept templates and patterns. SPARQL has no operation to change an existing triple as triples are considered to be binary: the triple either exists or it does not. This is probably the biggest difference to SQL and Web APIs and complicates the translation between an SPARQL query and the equivalent HTTP requests to interact with a Web service.

4.4. Translating Insert Data and Delete Data. In regard to a Web service, an INSERT DATA operation, for example, can either result in the creation of a new resource or in the manipulation of an existing one if a previously unset attribute of an existing resource is set. The same applies for a DELETE DATA operation which could just unset one attribute of a resource or delete a whole resource. A resource will only be deleted if all triples describing that resource are deleted. This mismatch or, better, conceptual gap between triples and resource attributes implies that constraints imposed by the Web service's interface are transferred to SPARQL's semantic layer. In consequence, some operations which are completely valid if applied to a native triple store are invalid when applied to a Web API. If these constraints are documented in the interface description, that is, the SEREDASj document, in the form of semantic annotations, a client is able to construct valid requests, respectively, to detect invalid requests and to give meaningful error messages. If these constraints are not documented, a client has no choice but to try and issue requests to the server and evaluate its response. This is similar to HTML forms with, and without client side form validation in the human Web.

In order to better explain the translation algorithm, and as a proof of concept, we implemented a simple event guide Web service based on the interface described in Listing 1. Its only function is to store events and their respective performers via a RESTful interface. The CRUD operations are mapped to the HTTP verbs POST, GET, PUT, and DELETE and no authentication mechanism is used as we currently do not have an ontology to describe this in an SEREDASj document (this is a limitation that will be addressed in future work).

The event representations can be accessed by /event/{id} URIs while the performers are accessible by /person/{id} URIs. Both can be edited by PUTing an updated JSON representation to the respective URI. New events and performers/persons can be created by POSTing a JSON representation to the collection URI. All this information as well as the mapping to the respective

vocabularies is described machine-readable by SEREDASj documents.

Since SPARQL differentiates between data and template operations, we split the translation algorithm into two parts. Algorithm 1 translates SPARQL DATA operations to HTTP requests interacting with the Web service and Algorithm 2 deals with SPARQL's DELETE/INSERT operations using patterns and templates.

Listing 4 contains an exemplary INSERT DATA operation which we will use to explain Algorithm 1. It creates a new event and a new performer. The event is linked to the newly created performer as well as to an existing one.

To translate the operations in Listing 4 into HTTP requests suitable to interact with the Web service, in the first step (line 2 in Algorithm 1), all potential requests are retrieved. This is done by retrieving all SEREDASj descriptions which contain model references corresponding to classes or predicates used in the SPARQL triples; this step also takes into consideration whether an existing resource should be updated or a new one created. Since Listing 4 does not reference existing resources (pers:p84098 in line 10 is just used as an object), all potential HTTP requests have to create new resources, that is, have to be POST requests. In our trivial example, we get two potential requests, one for the creation of a new event resource and a second for a new person/performer resource. These request templates are then filled with information from the SPARQL triples (line 6) as well as with information stored in the local triple store (line 7). Then, provided a request is valid (line 8), that is, it contains all the mandatory data, it will be submitted (line 9). As shown in Listing 5, the first valid request creates a new event (lines 1–3). Since the ID of the blank node _:bieber is not known yet (it gets created by the server), it is simply ignored. Provided the HTTP request was successful, in the next step the response is parsed and the new triples exposed by the Web service are removed from the SPARQL triples (line 11) and added to the local triple store (line 12). Furthermore, the blank nodes in the remaining SPARQL triples are replaced with concrete terms. In our example, this means that the triples in line 7–10 in Listing 4 are removed and the blank node in the triple in line 11 is replaced by the newly created/event/e51972 URI. Finally, the request is removed from the potential requests list and a flag is set (line 13-14, Algorithm 1) signaling that progress has been made within the current do while iteration. If in one loop iteration, which cycles through all potential requests, no progress has been made, the process is stopped (line 18). In our example, the process is repeated for request to create a person which again results in a POST request (line 6–8, Listing 5). Since there are no more potential requests available, the next iteration of the do while loop begins.

The only remaining triple is the previously updated triple in line 11 (Listing 4), thus, the only potential request this time is a PUT request to update the newly created/event/e51972. As before, the request template is filled with "knowledge" from the local triple store and the remaining SPARQL triples and eventually processed. Since there are no more SPARQL triples to process, the do while loop terminates and a success message is returned

```
1  do
2     requests ← retrievePotentialRequests(triples)
3     progress ← false
4     while requests.hasNext() = true do
5         request ← requests.next()
6         request.setData(triples)
7         request.setData(tripleStore)
8         if isValid(request) = true then
9           if request.submit() = success then
10              resp ← request.parseResponse()
11              triples.update(resp.getTriples())
12              tripleStore.update(resp.getTriples())
13              requests.remove(request)
14              progress ← true
15            end if
16          end if
17     end while
18  while progress = true
19  if triples.empty() = true then
20     success()
21  else
22     error(triples)
23  end if
```

ALGORITHM 1: SPARQL DATA operations to Web API translation algorithm.

```
1 PREFIX owl: <http://www.w3.org/2002/07/owl#>
2 PREFIX foaf: <http://xmlns.com/foaf/0.1/>
3 PREFIX so: <http://schema.org/>
4 PREFIX ex: <http://example.com/onto#>
5 PREFIX pers: <http://example.com/person/>

6 INSERT DATA {
7     _:greatg a so:Event;
8           so:name "Great Gig";
9           so:startDate "2012-08-03";
10          so:performers pers:p84098;
11          so:performers _:bieber.
12    _:bieber a so:Person;
13          so:name "Justin Bieber";
14          so:gender "male";
15          so:birthDate "1994-03-01".
16 }
```

LISTING 4: Examplary INSERT DATA operation.

to the client (line 20, Algorithm 1) as all triples have been successfully processed.

4.5. Translating DELETE/INSERT Operations. In contrast to the DATA-form operations that require concrete data and do not allow the use of named variables, the DELETE/INSERT operations are pattern based using templates to delete or add groups of triples. These operations are processed by first executing the query patterns in the WHERE clause which bind values to a set of named variables. Then, these bindings are used to instantiate the DELETE and the INSERT templates. Finally, the concrete deletes are performed followed by the concrete inserts. The DELETE/INSERT operations are, thus, in fact, transformed to concrete DELETE DATA/INSERT

```
1  →  POST /event/
2        { "name": "Great Gig",
3          "performers": [{ "id": "p84098" }]}
4  ←  201 Created
5      Location: /event/e51972

6  →  POST /person/
7        { "name": "Justin Bieber", "gender": "male",
8          "birthdate": "1994-03-01" }
9  ←  201 Created
10     Location: /person/p92167

11 →  PUT /event/e51972
12       { "name": "Great Gig",
13         "performers": [ { "id": "p84098" },
14                         { "id": "p92167" } ] }
15 ←  200 OK
```

LISTING 5: INSERT DATA operation translated to HTTP requests.

```
1 select ← createSelect(query)
2 bindings ← tripleStore.execute(select)

3 for each binding in bindings do
4    deleteData ← createDeleteData(query, binding)
5    operations.add(deleteData)
6    insertData ← createInsertData(query, binding)
7    operations.add(insertData)
8 end for

9 operations.sort()
10 translateDataOperations(operations)
```

ALGORITHM 2: SPARQL DELETE/INSERT operations to HTTP requests translation algorithm.

```
1 DELETE {
2  ?per so:gender ?gender.
3 }
4 INSERT {
5    ?per so:gender "female".
6 }
7 WHERE {
8    ?per a so:Person;
9       so:name "Lady Gaga";
10      so:birthDate "1986-03-28";
11      so:gender ?gender.
12 }
```

LISTING 6: Examplary DELETE/INSERT operation.

```
1 DELETE DATA {
2    </person/p84098> so:gender "unknown".
3 }
4 INSERT DATA {
5    </person/p84098> so:gender "female".
6 }
```

LISTING 7: DELETE DATA/INSERT DATA operations generated by Algorithm 2 out of Listing 6.

to DELETE DATA/INSERT DATA operations which are then translated by Algorithm 1 into HTTP requests.

Listing 6 contains an exemplary DELETE/INSERT operation which replaces the gender of all persons whose name "Lady Gaga" and whose birth date is March 28, 1986, with "female" regardless of what it was before. This operation is first translated to a DELETE DATA/INSERT DATA operation by Algorithm 2 and then to HTTP requests by Algorithm 1.

DATA operations before execution. We exploit this fact in Algorithm 2 which transforms DELETE/INSERT operations

The first step (line 1, Algorithm 2) is to create a `SELECT` query out of the `WHERE` clause. This query is then executed on the local triple store returning the bindings for the `DELETE` and `INSERT` templates (line 2). This implies that all relevant data has to be included in the local triple store (an assumption made earlier in this work), otherwise, the operation might be executed just partially. For each of the retrieved bindings (line 3), one `DELETE DATA` (line 4) and one `INSERT DATA` (line 6) operation are created. In our example, the result consists of a single binding, namely, `</person/p84098>` for `per` and some unknown value for `gender`. Therefore, only one `DELETE DATA` and one `INSERT DATA` operation are created as shown in Listing 7. Finally, these operations are sorted (line 9) as deletes have to be executed before inserts and eventually translated into HTTP requests (line 10) by Algorithm 1.

In many cases, just as demonstrated in the example, a `DELETE/INSERT` operation will actually represent a replacement of triples. Thus, both, the `DELETE DATA` and the `INSERT DATA` operation are performed locally before issuing the HTTP request. This optimization reduces the number of HTTP requests since attributes do not have to be reset before getting set to the desired value. In our example this consolidates the two PUT requests to one.

5. Conclusions and Future Work

In this paper, we presented SEREDASj, a new approach to describe RESTful data services. In contrast to previous approaches, we put strong emphasis on simplicity to lower the entry barrier. Web developers can use tools and knowledge they are mostly already familiar with. Since SEREDASj does not require any changes on the described Web service, it provides a viable upgrade path for existing infrastructure. We also introduced two algorithms to translate SPARQL Update operations to HTTP requests interacting with an SEREDASj-described Web API. This creates a standardized interface which not only increases the developer's productivity but also improves code reusability.

A limitation of the current proposal is that it is restricted to resources represented in JSON; no other media types are supported at the moment. In future work, support should be extended to other formats such as, for example, XML. Potentially, this could be done by mapping XML representations to JSON as there are already promising approaches such as the JSON Markup Language (JsonML) [15] to do so. This would allow to transparently support XML representations without changing the current approach. Similarly, URI templates could be used to support the popular *application/x-www-form-urlencoded* media type.

In future work, we would also like to create a tool suite for developers to support the creation of SEREDASj descriptions and, if needed, the automatic creation of domain ontologies with techniques similar to the ones used to create domain ontologies from relational databases [32]. Moreover, we would like to research aspects such as service discovery and composition which includes issues like authentication that might require the creation of a lightweight ontology to be described.

References

[1] The application/json Media Type for JavaScript Object Notation (JSON), Request for Comments 4627, Internet Engineering Task Force (IETF), 2006.

[2] T. Vitvar and J. Musser, "ProgrammableWeb.com: statistics, trends, and best practices," in *Proceedings of the 4th International Workshop on Web APIs and Services Mashups*, 2010.

[3] M. Lanthaler and C. Gütl, "A semantic description language for RESTful data services to combat Semaphobia," in *Proceedings of the 5th IEEE International Conference on Digital Ecosystems and Technologies (DEST '11)*, pp. 47–53, IEEE, 2011.

[4] S. L. Huang, "After f8—resources for building the personalized Web," Facebook Developer Blog, 2010, http://developers.facebook.com/blog/post/379.

[5] Semantic Annotations for WSDL and XML Schema (SAWSDL), W3C Recommendation, 2007.

[6] J. Lathem, K. Gomadam, and A. P. Sheth, "SA-REST and (S)mashups: adding semantics to RESTful services," in *Proceedings of the International Conference on Semantic Computing(ICSC '07)*, pp. 469–476, IEEE, September 2007.

[7] J. Kopecký, K. Gomadam, and T. Vitvar, "hRESTS: an HTML microformat for describing RESTful Web services," in *Proceedings of the IEEE/WIC/ACM International Conference on Web Intelligence and Intelligent Agent Technology (WI '08)*, pp. 619–625, 2008.

[8] M.J. Hadley, Web Application Description Language (WADL), 2009.

[9] R. Khare and T. Çelik, "Microformats: a pragmatic path to the semantic web, 2006," Tech. Rep. 06-01, CommerceNet Labs, Palo Alto, CA, USA, http://wiki.commerce.net/wikiima-ges/e/ea/CN-TR-06-01.pdf.

[10] J. Kopecký and T. Vitvar, D38v0.1 MicroWSMO: Semantic Description of RESTful Services, 2008, http://wsmo.org/TR/d38/v0.1/20080219/d38v01_20080219.pdf.

[11] Web Services Description Language (WSDL) Version 2.0, W3C Recommendation, 2007.

[12] OWL S: Semantic Markup for Web Services, W3C Member Submission, 2004, http://www.w3.org/Submission/OWL-S/.

[13] M. Klusch, "Semantic web service description," in *CASCOM: Intelligent Service Coordination in the Semantic Web*, M. Schumacher, H. Schuldt, and H. Helin, Eds., pp. 31–57, Birkhäuser, Basel, Germany, 2008.

[14] R. Lara, D. Roman, A. Polleres, and D. Fensel, "A conceptual comparison of WSMO and OWL-S," in *Proceedings of the European Conference on Web Services (ECOWS '04)*, vol. 3250, pp. 254–269, Erfurt, Germany, 2004.

[15] JSON Markup Language (JsonML), 2011, http://jsonml.org/.

[16] D. Roman, U. Keller, H. Lausen, and J. D. Bruijn, "Web service modeling ontology," *Applied Ontology*, vol. 1, no. 1, pp. 77–106, 2005.

[17] J. Waldo, G. Wyant, A. Wollrath, and S. Kendall, "A note on distributed computing," Tech. Rep., Mountain View, Calif, USA, 1994.

[18] R. Alarcón and E. Wilde, "Linking data from RESTful services," in *Proceedings of the 3rd Workshop on Linked Data on the Web*, 2010.

[19] C. Bizer and R. Cyganiak, "D2R server—publishing relational databases on the Semantic Web," in *proceedings of the 5th International Semantic Web Conference (ISWC '06)*, 2006.

[20] S. Auer, S. Dietzold, J. Lehmann, S. Hellmann, and D. Aumueller, "Triplify—lightweight linked data publication from relational databases," in *Proceedings of the 18th International Conference on World Wide Web (WWW '09)*, pp. 621–630, 2009.

[21] T. Berners-Lee, Y. Chen, L. Chilton et al., "Tabulator: exploring and analyzing linked data on the semantic web," in *3rd International Semantic Web User Interaction Workshop (SWUI '06)*, 2006.

[22] O. Lassila, "Browsing the Semantic Web," in *Proceedings of the 5th International Workshop on Semantic (WebS '06)*, pp. 365–369, 2006.

[23] C. Bizer and T. Gauß, Disco—Hyperdata Browser, http://www4.wiwiss.fu-berlin.de/bizer/ng4j/disco/.

[24] D. Steer, RDFAuthor, http://rdfweb.org/people/damian/RDF-Author/.

[25] E. Pietriga, IsaViz: a visual authoring tool for RDF, http://www.w3.org/2001/11/IsaViz/.

[26] T. Berners-Lee, J. Hollenbach, K. Lu, J. Presbrey, E. Pru d'ommeaux, and M.M. Schraefel, "Tabulator Redux: writing into the semantic web," Tech. Rep. ECSIAM-eprint14773, University of Southampton, Southampton, UK, 2007.

[27] pushback—Write Data Back From RDF to Non-RDF Sources, http://www.w3.org/wiki/PushBackDataToLegacySources.

[28] R.T. Fielding, *Architectural styles and the design of network-based software architectures*, Ph.D. dissertation, Department of Information and Computer Science, University of California, Irvine, Calif, USA, 2000.

[29] XML Core Working Group Public Page—Pubblications, XML Core Working Group, 2011, http://www.w3.org/XML/Core/#Publications.

[30] CURIE syntax 1.0: a syntax for expressing compact URIs, W3C Working Group note. W3C, 2010, http://www.w3.org/TR/curie/.

[31] Google Inc., Yahoo Inc., and Microsoft Corporation., Schema.org, http://www.schema.org/.

[32] F. Cerbah, "Learning highly structured semantic repositories from relational databases: the RDBToOnto tool," in *Proceedings of the 5th European Semantic Web Conference (ESWC '08)*, pp. 777–781, Springer, 2008.

[33] SPARQL Query Language for RDF. W3C Recommendation, 2008, http://www.w3.org/TR/2008/REC-rdf-sparql-query-20080115/.

[34] SPARQL 1.1 Update. W3C Working Draft, 2011, http://www.w3.org/TR/2011/WD-sparql11-update-20110512/.

5

Heritage Multimedia and Children Edutainment: Assessment and Recommendations

Naif A. Haddad

Department of Conservation Science, Queen Rania Institute of Tourism and Heritage, The Hashemite University, Zarqa, Jordan

Correspondence should be addressed to Naif A. Haddad; naifh@hu.edu.jo

Academic Editor: Stefanos Kollias

Despite the rising commodification of heritage sites and practices, children engagement in their own cultures remains incredibly low, greatly endangering the future preservation of nations' unique nonrenewable resource. Considering children's very early engagement with cultural attitudes and identities, it is increasingly critical to develop a deeply rooted culture of responsibility and conservation from the earliest years, ensuring that children naturally feel invested in their surroundings. Unfortunately, heritage education remains largely undervalued, with most efforts relying on in-person experiences in formal cultural institutions. This paper thus aims to explore how heritage education can be redefined, using some of the most innovative virtual imaging and artificial reality technologies to at once expand access and engagement with one's own history. Though there have been introductory applications of this edutainment multimedia technology, it will require a multidisciplinary team to create heritage programming which is as entertaining as it is intellectually challenging for young children. With the rich resources of 3D imaging and interactive programming already at our disposal, we are well-equipped to do so, given a coordinated effort.

1. Introduction

Heritage is associated with the old and museums, history books, lectures. These were its relatives. But as countries construct their own national identities, and as those identities become marketed international brands, heritage has become a vivid lived-in experience. *"On our today's world, heritage is no longer just a memory or a cultural reference, or even a place or an object. Heritage is moving towards broader and wider scenarios, where it becomes often the driven forces for commerce, business, leisure and politics"* [1].

And yet, the youth population is as disengaged as they ever have been from the dust and bones of their birthplace and families. Archeological sites, traditional arts, and ancestral folklore are being relegated to the bin of history, only to be accessed when a parent or teacher forces the issue. But what is the source of this disengagement? How can it be rectified? And why does it matter?

Kailash states that *"there is a problem due to the lack of cultural heritage input in our curriculum both at school level and at the level of college and higher studies"* [2]. As the saying goes, children are like sponges; they absorb everything around them, developing a sense of self based on their environment.

If however their environment does not provide the needed stimulus or access, children naturally develop a disinterest in the matter, in this case knowledge of their own heritage.

One of the major challenges facing heritage education initiatives has been the slow mobilization of new theory into practice [3, Page 103], or rather its geographically limited use. Perhaps the most successful cases are found in European systems, where cultural-historical theory is becoming increasingly influential for informing early educational curricula. Schools are developing initiatives to connect pupils more closely to the world of culture and arts, through organized visits to places of artistic and cultural interest or direct partnerships with artists, musicians and creative directors. In addition, there are several examples of cultural heritage-related festivals, celebrations and competitions where pupils are encouraged to participate. The permanence of these efforts is evidenced by their institutionalization, with a variety of cultural bodies and networks giving roots to the movement [4].

European governments have also been active in creating the appropriate policy environment to promote cultural education. In 2005, the Council of Europe launched a Framework Convention on the value of cultural heritage for the society, which identified the need for European countries to preserve cultural resources, promote cultural identity, respect diversity and encourage intercultural dialogue [5]. Article 13 of the framework acknowledged the important place of cultural heritage within arts education, and also recommended developing linkages between courses in different fields of study [5]. The European Commission also joined the effort, proposing in 2007 a European Agenda for Culture in a Globalizing World, which acknowledges the value of arts education in developing creativity [6]. Furthermore, the EU strategic framework for European cooperation in education and training over the next decade clearly emphasises the importance of transversal key competences, including cultural awareness and creativity.

In 2008 the Council published a "White paper on intercultural dialogue," which offered an intercultural approach to managing cultural diversity. The paper identified educational organizations (including museums, heritage sites, kindergartens and schools) as having the potential to support intercultural exchange, learning and dialogue through arts and cultural activities [7]. In fact 2009 was the European year of creativity and innovation, which further recognized the connection between cultural awareness and creativity.

This attention is of course not maintained worldwide. Indeed, at the culmination of UNESCO's five-year collaboration with its arts education partners in Lisbon, the organization highlighted the need to promote arts education in all societies, as detailed in "*The wow factor: global research compendium on the impact of the arts in education*" [8, 9]. The conference document asserts that providing arts education helps to prepare students for higher education, promote the expression of cultural diversity, and uphold the human right to cultural participation.

In the case of Arab countries, unfortunately significantly less attention has been given to heritage education, resulting from a variety of obstacles including lack of funding and governmental interest (There are many obstacles; Perhaps the largest is that Arab Ministries of Education are generally less interested in early children development programs, which parallels the public's lack of awareness of its importance. Correspondingly there is lack of clear development strategies or policies in government, particularly towards any sort of nonmath or noscience curriculum. In countries where policy does exist, teachers are often ill-equipped to properly deliver more interactive lesson, thus dulling their effectiveness. In addition to the lack of appropriate school buildings and facilities, lack of qualified personnel such as teachers, supervisors, instructors and administrative committees in various fields, lack of teaching aids such as specialized books, publications, games and Toys, and lack of kindergarten curricula that is based on scientific and education basis [10, 11]). Even the limited number of organizations actively funding early education projects in the Middle East, the most notable of which is the Arab Gulf Programme for United Nations Development Organizations (AGFUND) remained unengaged in art education initiatives. (Based on its mission priority, since its establishment in 1980, AGFUND is still funding projects and programs aiming at supporting childhood development in less development countries, that adopted a comprehensive approach in focusing on major aspects which affects child

life and needs especially in the health and education sectors, institutional and capacity building sector, and special nature development programs and projects. AGFUND is implementing these projects in collaboration with Ministries of Education and the UNESCO in 11 different Arab countries [10]).

Given the decreasing engagement with traditional learning methods, and the world's already overstretched educational systems, it becomes critical to explore independent alternatives to arts and cultural education [12]. In their vision for twenty-first century education, Shank and Kozma [13, Pages 253-254] predict a model where schools, homes, the workplace, libraries, museums, and social services integrate education into the fabric of the community, suggesting the need to expand our notions of where education can happen. Such a multisurface approach is perfectly complimented by the advances in multimedia and communication technologies. There is already a trend towards incorporating technological innovations within classes. The new "Classroom 2000" developments, for example, focus attention on the student's experience, bringing students closer to the technology and letting them interact with and add to the captured content (For example, the Living Schoolbook in New York State is working with Video on Demand and demonstration projects for K-12 [14]. Useful publications for a cross-curricula approach of geography and the historic environment, math and science, produced by English Heritage Education Services [15]). Thus, for a field as interacting and expressive as art, one can easily imagine how technology, particularly advances in 2D & 3D animation, gaming and website design, could offer greater access and collaborative potential for children who may otherwise be disinterested.

Heeter stated in 1999 that, "*We have only begun to realize the potential connectivity possible in a networked world. Parents, teachers, scientists, community leaders, friends, reporters—anyone can participate in a learning experience, particularly if it is online.*" Thus the rapidly expanding world of multimedia has enormous potential to engage children in their cultural heritage, providing them with a channel to actively engage in its development.

However, meanwhile animation lends itself perfectly to direct communication without barriers of language or cultural differences [16], actually, we still "*have a long way to go in designing intuitive interfaces and that is what will distinguish the educational applications of tomorrow*" [17]. We are still though at the early stages of using immersive edutainment multimedia (EM) to experience cultural heritage and virtual reality systems.

As the potential of this fusion continues to be discovered, it behooves us to think concretely and practically about its future applications, including its role in developing a genuine appreciation and understanding of heritage. The modern education system must adapt to the changing global conditions, allowing children to feel engaged in societies that are in constant flux. However, without the tools of "Edutainment Multimedia," we cannot hope to create a generation confident or invested enough to carry our society safely into the 21st century.

To explore edutainment multimedia's role in cultural identity building, the following sections aim to define and clarify:

(i) children's current perception of heritage in relation to informal and formal education and edutainment multimedia,

(ii) current approaches in heritage education,

(iii) initial considerations for edutainment multimedia's role in heritage education,

(iv) interactive virtual reality and heritage education.

2. Cultural Heritage from a Child's Perspective

Very few researchers have examined children's understanding of culture, in part because it is difficult to design appropriate measures. Indeed most young children do not grasp the relationships between nations, national origin, and traditions, and do not have a concept of culture. Throughout childhood, they absorb prevailing views and draw conclusions that affect their perceptions and feelings about themselves, their heritage, and other individuals and groups. In essence, cultural patterns of interaction silently guide the developing child, in the same way that adults often do not recognize the source of their beliefs. But these patterns also become the basis for their definitions of self and personal identity, something that they are inherently a part of.

Developmental accomplishments and cultural heritage manifestation are bound together, and, as a consequence, specific behaviors come to be synonymous with specific phases of development itself. Beginning in the early years, attitudes and values can be shaped, while in later grades, development tends to be more action oriented, what children do with the ideas that they have. Thus, by the time children are five years old, they have already learned a great deal. They have reached "developmental competence" and "maturity," meaning that they have achieved the normative learning benchmarks of their community [18, Page 217]. These benchmarks coordinate biological growth and social learning, and under ordinary circumstances children's knowledge and skills match those required in the social and cultural settings in which they live. At ages 6–10 years, however, children shift from relying on visible racial cues and begin to understand cultural aspects of ethnicity such as language, food, ancestry and heritage [19, Page 226]. (However, children who are adopted internationally are at this risk of losing their ethnic heritage, and social workers in the field have a vital role to play in minimizing this risk. Childhood, then, is a critical time for intervention in the schooling of at-risk children if we expect to change outcomes [20, Page 1-2]).

If one is aiming to build a culture of appreciation towards culture and heritage, this education must therefore start at a very young age, such that it is incorporated into their understanding of self. In considering how that knowledge could best be imparted, it is necessary to reflect on children's relationship to learning, and how they process information. Indeed, from a young child's perspective, playing and learning are nearly indistinguishable [18, Pages 217-218]; [21, Pages 623–625], as children learn from all varieties of new stimuli.

Arts and cultural heritage education is a communication process, which is based on an intense engagement with artwork or cultural artifacts as well as cultural values and symbolic systems [12]. Thus, achieving heritage education requires sustained interactive access to these cultural objects [22], with the time for children to play through the new knowledge. Given this need for sustained engagement, the highly entertaining tools of games and virtual realities are particularly important, for they will allow the child to absorb far more than traditionally directed methods. Interesting is the Japanese perception for edutainment; it has considerable importance from the academic point of view. One example is the Institute for Research Edutainment which organizes forums dedicated to its application in schools. It is important to note that the Japanese edutainment is not focused exclusively on the intellectual; in fact, Nintendo has some of the best edutainment games/family as Wario Ware and Mario Party 3-4, which are focused on the playful side [23].

To summarize, teaching future generations, especially in the childhood stage, to be aware of our cultural heritage is in fact the best way to guarantee the endurance of cultural heritage traditions and heritage sites. Meanwhile, children's early experience with heritage can be also an important first step in their own enjoyment creative exploration. Now, perhaps more than ever, we are able to contemplate the past as creative tool for plotting our future [24, Pages 190-191]. Childhood personnel though need to be better prepared in cultural heritage issues to help children for whom school represents a major challenge.

3. Formal and Informal Heritage Education

According to Gruber and Glahn [22], the educational process of arts and cultural heritage education includes the following three components: the artwork or the cultural artifact to which we refer as the object, the recipient person who esteems this object (visitor), and the facilitator or mediator who communicates additional context information to the recipient. The mediator refers to social or technical systems that facilitate the communication to the recipient in terms of direct interaction, and can vary depending on the educational method in use.

The most recently discussed is a direct approach to cultural education, mediated by specific formal cultural institutions such as museums and libraries [4]. These methods are particularly appealing given the potential to redress inequality in terms of access to cultural resources.

With the aforementioned development of advanced multimedia, heritage education could also be media by technology itself. Unlike formal education which uses a cognitive approach to imparting information and skills to problem solving, edutainment multimedia relies on affective and sensory learning, based on experiential and participatory methodologies that help children reconnect awareness and caring in a concrete way.

The re-creation of historic environments for serious education and entertainment is of course not new [25, 26], although the methods for achieving the objectives have evolved considerably over time. Historically, story tellers conjured up visions of events and places, before the days of widespread books and printing, providing their listeners with an impression of realities (often augmented realities) elsewhere in space and time. Alternatively, theatre, fine art, and cinema have added to the richness of the explicit visual experience of interpretations available to the viewer [27, Pages 23-24].

However, research in virtual reality (VR) and archaeology is a relatively young field which has shown considerable growth in recent years, as the development of new interactive technologies has inevitably impacted the more traditional sciences and arts. This is more evident in the case of novel interactive technologies which appeal to a broader public, as has always been the case with virtual reality [28]. Although early virtual heritage works have been criticized for their lack of visual realism [29, Page 22], nowadays advances in computer hardware and sophisticated 3D modeling packages allow creating compelling visualizations of static objects.

Of particular interest in the use of virtual reality displays and computer generated interactive experiences is the fact that they can allow visitors to feel like they are traveling through space and time [25, 27, 30]. The experience is thus immersive experience and interactive, generating a sense of "presence" which encourages collaborative activities amongst multiple remote users.

4. Methodological Considerations

Before engaging in an assessment of the potential role of edutainment multimedia in heritage education, it is important to understand the limited nature of this study. As discussed in the previous section, developing an interest in heritage requires a redefinition of the *recipient* and *mediator* guidelines, taking into consideration the radical changes opened by edutainment multimedia. This reevaluation, as attempted in this paper, requires an initial evaluation of the current conceptions of the terms, in order to understand the present state of cultural education. Based on these findings, one can begin to see the gaps in both content and methodology, leading to recommendations about how to make the experience the most valuable to children in the digital age. Only with this clarity can we imagine the most suitable space for technological interventions. This paper however does not have sufficient space for such a comprehensive review and thus is intended an introduction to the potential relationship between the two, as opposed to a thorough going methodological recommendation.

5. Multimedia in Heritage Education: Current Assets

In order to understand the potential role of multimedia in heritage education it is necessary to assess current efforts, including virtual modeling, electronic games, and TV programs.

5.1. Virtual Reality and Cultural Heritage. Many cultural heritage projects have developed virtual museums depending on their own concepts and policies [17, 23, 25, 31–35]. Although

innovative mobile technologies have been deployed in museums, there is still a lack of research on how novel ubiquitous computing can be developed and deployed to augment the museum educational experience for children [33]. An exception to this is the Virtual Site Museum's authentic database, which together with advanced VR technology contributed positively to both research and experience in the classroom. The following selected cases thus give us an indication of potentiality of cultural heritage virtual reality projects, as well as drawing the limits of our achievements. As Plowman and Stephen [36, Page 160] note "New technologies may lead to new concepts of play and learning/especially as new ways are found of conceptualizing ICT so that the term does not simply denote standard computers."

5.1.1. LIFEPLUS Project. The LIFEPLUS project proposes a new development for the innovative revival of life in ancient frescos paintings in ancient Pompeii and creation of narrative spaces. The revival is based on real scenes captured on live video sequences augmented with real-time autonomous groups of 3D virtual fauna and flora. The metaphor, which inspires the project approach, makes "transportation in fictional and historical spaces," as depicted by frescos paintings as realistic, immersive and interactive as possible. Thus the visitor of the ancient site is presented with an immersive multisensory trip to the past. In the context of cultural heritage sites such as the ancient city of Pompeii, people would be able to observe and understand the behaviours and social patterns of living people from ancient Roman times, superimposed in the natural environment of the city [37, Pages 235–240].

For that purpose, LIFEPLUS aims to position itself between the extremes of real life and virtual reality, in the spectrum of "Mixed Reality" and especially augmented reality (AR), in which views of the real world are combined in some proportion with specific graphic enhancements or augmentations (Apart from virtual heritage, LIFEPLUS addresses the following emerging market needs [37, Page 237]. (a) Tourism and edutainment. Novel operational paradigms (immersive AR virtual life) for edutainment experiences are preconditions for economic viability for all types of future cultural and memory institutions, location-based entertainments and E-visitor attractions. (b) on set visualization and virtual studio: Film studios currently shoot films expecting to add in computer generated (CG) effects such as backgrounds, dinosaurs or CG characters later. Directors would benefit from the ability to see in real time or very soon afterwards an overlay of real and planned CG elements to decide whether the composition is acceptable). Although initially targeted at cultural heritage centers, the paradigm is by no means limited to such subjects, but encompasses all types of future Location-Based Entertainments, E-visitor attractions as well as on-set visualizations for the TV/movie industry [27, Pages 11–16].

5.1.2. Northwest Palace of Ashurnasirpal. The Palace of King Ashurnasirpal II (883–859 BC), located in northeastern Iraq, is a famous Assyrian world heritage archaeological site. Learning Sites, Inc. built the original digital model of the Palace of Ashurnasirpal (Learning Sites, 2003), as an authentic reconstruction of the archaeological site, with VRML interaction, and animation. Easily disseminated by digital media such as CD, DVD, or internet, it runs on a PC platform with VRML viewers. This model of the palace was used as the basis for the Virtual Site Museum. From this base model, optimized 3D models were recreated for the real-time, high-end VR application described by [32]. Learning Sites built links in the model to access data (photos, drawings, and notes) that were used to create the VR model. The full-body immersion and interaction with the king have proved to be effective means to engage the students, providing an understanding of ancient society (Figure 1).

It offers user-oriented interfaces so that a user can navigate the palace and activate prepared information. The user-oriented device interfaces assisted the researchers to expand their knowledge in surroundings displaying integrated information. These human-factored applications will make the Virtual Site Museum a more reliable and productive VR experience for archaeological research and education. Students, however, with an instructor, were able to stop and observe the various iconographic representations of King Ashurnasirpal and his protective deities. They can stand outside the doorways and look into the various rooms of the palace or stop in the doorways and look around, or stand where the king or his courtiers or the representatives of foreign countries may have stood during the various ceremonies associated with the various palace audience halls [32].

Students in this way can learn different aspects of the ancient site. In the class setting in the virtual space at the supercomputer, they can experience the artifacts in their original contexts and at a nearly real scale.

They can access the supporting data first digitally and then, in the conventional classroom, discuss—or look up at home and in the library—data in the traditional publications. Students and scholars also invent projects in the palace over the web on Assyrian art and architecture [32].

5.1.3. The Battle of the Ancient City of Syracuse. This project represents a virtual recreation of the siege by the sea of the ancient city of Syracuse by the Romans in 212 BC. It allows the collaboration of two users. The pilot simulation battle combines the positive aspects of multiuser virtual environments, edutainment VR applications, and new human computer interaction (HCI) interfaces. The educational purpose of this multiplayer setup was the transmission of historical information and presentation of the battle through the great scientific inventions of Archimedes and information about its life. The whole experience is targeted towards users between 9–15 years of age, and uses established video game techniques and metaphors like 3D graphics, cinematic story line, high action based interaction and dramatic closure. The actual educational information passed gives students the opportunity to learn about the ancient city of Syracuse, its prominent position in the ancient world and the historical context of the conflict between Rome and Carthage. Some details about Archimedes and his position in the global intellect are also explained [17].

The audience has the opportunity to experience the information just communicated by Archimedes (his inventions and the usage of war machines and siege ships during the Syracuse siege by the Romans) (Figure 2), as part of a multiplayer game. Two participants compete against each other, controlling the siege machines and ships. After the end of the game sessions, which are considered the climax and most entertaining moments of the application, the ending sequence is presented which again communicates historical information about the actual outcome of the battle and the fate of Archimedes. The project evaluation took place at the facilities of the Foundation of Hellenic World, while the external component and software for the optical motion tracking systems used in project were developed by the researchers of the Center for Research and Technology Hellas/Informatics and Telematics Institute (ITI) within the project "e-interface" [17].

5.1.4. Ancient Rome in Interactive Virtual Reality Project. The work is a reconstruction of ancient Rome in interactive virtual reality, and involves the development of a fully interactive model of ancient Rome that includes both its architecture and the machinery systems (Figure 3). The visitor to the virtual site will be able to wander through a full-scale city and enter most of its large public monuments, in addition to a few residences. The body of source material is directly accessible via the interactive model.

The educational objective is to provide university and secondary school students, and also the public at large, with a vivid illustration of ancient Rome and an example of the ancient urban reality that is not available through traditional archaeological means. For example, a program exhibited is the journey through the ancient city; the audience can choose the path through the city just as in a real tour [26]. They may also "knock" on doors to enter buildings, or fly up high to view the city from above—all this with the use of simple devices such as a joystick (The work produced by the project can be accessed via the website (http://www.unicaen.fr/rome), and via a stereoscopic display at the University of Caen). During an interactive visit, the visitor can use the emperor "*Marcus*" who provides a scale and who walks and runs like a real human, though is subject to the laws of gravity. We can also see the virtual environment with Marcus' eyes [38, Pages 174–178].

5.1.5. Shared Miletus. The archaeological site of Miletus is no longer accessible, as its ruins have sunk into a swamp near the Turkish coast. Thus, the main goal of this project was to give visitors a full-body immersion remotely using high-speed telecommunication. The international Grid (iGrid) was used for networking, and real-time interactions were accomplished in the CAVE with C_ and VR libraries, such as Performer (SGI, 2000), CAVELib, CAVERNsoft, and Ygdrasil [32].

5.1.6. ERATO Project. ERATO is a research project (2003–2006) entitled "Identification, Evaluation and Revival of the Acoustical Heritage of Ancient Theatres and Odea," that was implemented within the Fifth Framework INCO-MED Programme of the European Commission, under the thematic title "Preserving and Using Cultural Heritage." Actually, the ancient theatre in its many aspects has attracted

FIGURE 1: Body proportion (a), skeleton-skin model (b), and animation sequence (based upon an image of an ancient statue in the British Museum, [32, Figure 5, Page 252].

FIGURE 2: Screenshot from the battle simulation. Roman siege ships are attacking the wall. Defensive weapons are already mounted on the wall (a). The animated avatar of Archimedes talking about the siege of Syracuse (b) [17].

a great deal of interest in the recent years. Theatres and Odea served as a cultural centre and stood as a huge multi-functional, social, religious, and political meeting space [39, Page 265-266]. The project was designed to identify virtual restoration and the revival of the acoustical and architectural heritage. One of the objectives of this work was recreation of 3D models of selected archaeological open-air and roofed theatres of the Hellenistic and Roman period, and a creation of the real-time crowd engine in order to animate a virtual audience according to historical sources and surveys. This was generated using a collection of tools, including custom ones developed specifically for this task, in addition to standard 3D modeling applications [40], Figure 4. In order to more intuitively answer the question of what ancient Roman theatres sounded like, auralised sound examples of various theatres can be heard on http://historyoftheancientworld .com/2011/03/how-did-the-ancient-roman-theatres-sound/. An interactive real-time scenario of a virtual audience was created in the ancient Roman Odeon of Aphrodisias. The audience not only reacted to their favorite actors, but they also responded to the play as well: approving, disapproving, laughing out loud, crying, hailing a character, or discussing with a neighbor. This virtual reality approach provides users

with details as small as appearances of the Romans (such as clothes, shoes, hairstyles and bodies) and their distribution by social classes.

5.1.7. ATHENA Project. Theatres Enhancement for New Actualities. In a similar vein, the ATHENA project is also with ancient theatres, which is now being implemented within Euromed Heritage IV, European Commission. The project aims to create a general strategy for dealing with tangible and intangible heritage aspects, developing a methodology for recognizing ancient theatres as part of a cultural cluster while promoting a wider consciousness in local populations (especially in young generations) about cultural clusters. It also strives to improve the overall level of knowledge concerning the sites, in addition to increasing the sites general relevance and popularity [41].

5.1.8. Foundation of the Hellenic World (FHW). The FHW, based in Greece, is a nonprofit cultural heritage institution working to preserve and disseminate Hellenic culture, historical memory and tradition. Through the creative use of state-of-the-art multimedia and technology, they have taken considerable steps in "edutainment VR." The organization's aim is to promote the understanding of the past and to

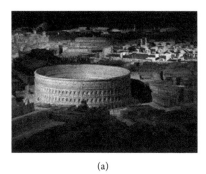 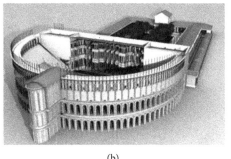 

(a)   (b)   (c)

FIGURE 3: 3D models of Rome; the Theatre of Pompey and pumps and the Forum of Augustus (http://www.unicaen.fr/rome). The virtual model makes it possible to visualize the hugeness of the complex and achieve a better understanding of the mechanical systems used in theatres in antiquity.

  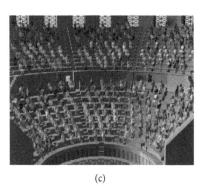

(a)   (b)   (c)

FIGURE 4: Shoots of virtual Roman audience reacting to the theatre play on stage [40].

synthetically, and comprehensively present the history, life and values of the Hellenic world in its broader geographical evolution (Figure 5) [28]. The Foundation itself has created a forum for archaeologists, historians, scientists, and artists to visualize their ideas and utilize the highest level of technology and resources for research and education within the context of Hellenic cultural heritage. The Foundation's public presence enhances its communication with the wide public, something that constitutes one of its fundamental objectives.

However, institutions of informal education, such as museums, research, and cultural centres, as in the case of (*FHW*), are now in a better position to make use of such advanced systems and investigate their educational potential while effectively shaping how they deliver public entertainment and education.

Many cultural heritage VR projects present the virtual reality systems, interaction devices and software used at the Foundation of the Hellenic World (FHW) (http://www.fhw.gr/fhw/index.php?lg=2&state=pages&id=80).

A particularly interesting project was designed for the Olympic History and Games in virtual reality productions for the Olympic Games in 2004 in Athens. Instead of focusing on only one production, several productions were created as a complementary series, finally concluding in a full-scale interactive representation of ancient Olympia and its Games. Significant effort has been made to recreate the feeling of the games and help the user/spectator to interact with the edutainment activity. This is clear from the creative approach

to interactive edutainment of the project, which is built on the famous Greek sculptor "*Feidias*" workshop. It is a highly interactive virtual experience that takes place at the construction site of the 15-meter-tall golden ivory statue of Zeus, Figure 6.

The visitors enter the two-story-high workshop and come in sight of an accurate reconstruction of an unfinished version of the famous statue of Zeus and walk among the sculptor's tools, scaffolding, benches, materials, and moulds used to construct it. The visitors take the role of the sculptor's assistants and actively help finish the creation of the huge statue, by using virtual tools to apply the necessary materials onto the statue. Interaction is achieved using the navigation wand of the VR system, onto which the various virtual tools are attached [25].

5.1.9. CAHRISMA Project. The work done in the context of the CAHRISMA project aimed to create Hybrid architectural heritage, where not only visual, but also acoustical aspects of the heritage are reconstructed. It integrates a virtual crowd simulation into a real-time photo realistic simulation of complex heritage edifices, where a crowd of virtual humans are able to move and interact within a virtual environment. The user can interact with the crowd, for example, by voice recognition. Another possible extension is the zoom feature which allows users to increase the number of visualized virtual humans [27, Pages 22–24]; [37, Pages 235–240].

 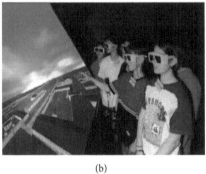 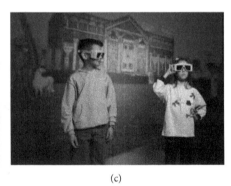

(a)   (b)   (c)

FIGURE 5: Young visitors immersed in the virtual learning environment of the Hellenic cultural heritage through immersive virtual archaeology [28].

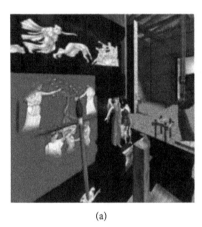  

(a)   (b)   (c)

FIGURE 6: *Feidias* Workshop; A creative approach to interactive edutainment [25].

5.1.10. Acropolis Restoration Service (YSMA) Project. This pilot project, inspired by existing educational programmes developed by the Department of Information and Education of the Acropolis Restoration Service (YSMA), explores further possibilities of advanced "physical modeling" of the most celebrated monuments of Western civilization—the Acropolis rock and the Parthenon temple [42, Pages 19–23]. Its aim is to present archaeological science as a contemporary educational instrument that facilitates an exciting and appealing form of historical inquiry for younger audiences. Another important advantage is making essential historical knowledge available and attractive to foreign students. The first stage of the project produced digital and physical models in variety of scales; the second stage focused on creating new educational "games" based on those models. The project is a collaborative work between YSMA and Victoria University of Wellington, New Zealand [43].

5.1.11. Metamuseum. The purpose of the project was to enable experts and visitors to communicate easily. The system provided knowledge exploration, using related information about and among the actual artifacts from several museums [44]. The project used a series of nonimmersive wall-screens at individual viewing stations in the museum. Each viewing station had a terminal with access to the data base. A specialist could input new data via the project's network. A visitor could use a PDA as a site guide. The Metamuseum focused more on the functions of the public museum [45].

5.1.12. The Enigma of the Sphinx Project. The user interacts with a game-like interactive "friendliness" and sense of presence virtual reality application. The interface consists of a large projection screen as the main display, a "magic wand", a stereo sound system and the user's voice for "casting spells" [46, Pages 106–108].

5.1.13. Jerusalem Temple Mount. The Jerusalem Temple Mount was created as an interactive simulation of the Herodian Mount for the Jerusalem Archaeological Park. The architectural design of the Temple Mount was created in solid modeling and the people in the simulation were authentically dressed static 2D figures from still photos provided courtesy of Archives and Collections, Universal Studios. The simulation is a real-time immersive fly-through visualization on an SGI Onyx2 IR3 [31].

5.1.14. Virtual Notre Dame. Virtual Notre Dame is a reconstruction of the Gothic Notre Dame Cathedral. This work is a nonimmersive, PC based network application using the internet. The realistic architecture rendered by Epic Unreal engine is normally used in creating video games [47].

5.2. Children TV Series/Programs: The Case of Sesame Workshop. After surveying the potential uses for multimedia in heritage education, it is interesting to apply some of these concepts to an existing and successful edutainment initiative. Perhaps the most well-known of these efforts is the internationally recognized Sesame Workshop, a nonprofit organization established over four decades ago in more than 150 countries, including many Arab states [48, Pages 103–105]. With the help of a cast of cheerful Muppet characters, the show has been dedicated to addressing children's critical development needs in terms of education, health, and social development. Sesame Workshop methodology has two complementary aspects, the television series and the educational outreach initiative and training.

The conceptual approach of "edutainment" in Sesame Workshop is a response to traditional education systems and represents an attempt to find the new channels to introduce more interactive learning styles. The Sesame Workshop adaptations have successfully integrated multiple cultural educational topics into a single program, or series of programs, thus addressing multiple cultural awareness topics. There are also few explanations of archaeology (what an archaeologist does) and several feature Indiana Jones parodies, in addition to Muppets visiting such historical sites such as the Great Wall in China, Figure 7, and the famous ancient Temples of Kyoto.

Sesame Street's success lies in their skillful weaving of characters and story lines with the delivery of cultural information. Coming in the form of relatable stories, the knowledge is thus a lot more accessible and memorable for children, making them more likely to talk about it or reenact it. Sesame Street has taken advantage of some of the latest technological advancements, with interactive e-games, extremely active social media channels, and mobile applications contributing to a complete educational experience. They have though been conservative in their application of the most cutting edge technology, and have yet to embrace the sort of Augmented Reality Technology that can bring different world to life within Sesame Street.

With the Muppets likeability, and the content-rich material that they provide, there remains significant potential to introduce heritage material using more virtual technologies. For example, the EU funded IST projects [6] are beginning to experiment with animation in an interactive experience, providing a way to truly draw children into different historical worlds within Sesame [49]. Actually, the rapid development of workstations makes it feasible to animate them in real time, which is required for VR Interactive Television, and video games applications. As the combination of artificial life with VR cannot exist without the growing development of computer animation techniques and corresponds to its most advanced concepts and techniques, and as several other works have been dealing with virtual humans in virtual heritage reconstructions, Sesame Street using the Muppet characters could start to invest more in these records projects, as was done by the UNESCO World Heritage Centre and the Archaeology Institute of America's curricula for teachers. Mixing such aesthetic ambiences with mobile virtual life augmentations in realtime, with the addition of compelling story lines and loveable characters, can develop the narrative patterns into an exciting new edutainment medium [50, Pages 183-184]. Sesame thus would be the perfect platform to begin incorporating more multimedia oriented approaches to heritage education, providing a physically and intellectually accessible channel for cultural exploration.

6. Discussion and Recommendations

The above reported case studies in this review help redress the lack of systematic design research into mainstream computing's ability to enhance informal learning. In general, recent advanced virtual museums can be classified by evaluating their capabilities of interactivity, immersion, and real-time interfaces. From a content perspective, while many museums and media organizations have designed multimedia curriculums for children dealing with cultural heritage, most of these sites and curriculums do not directly discuss the issue of preservation of culture, instead indirectly promoting an interest in the site itself (For instance, the British Museum offers a website for kids about the ancient Greek Olympic Games [51]. The Metropolitan Museum in New York holds lectures and storytelling sessions for kids about medieval history [52]. The Public Broadcasting Service (PBS), a nonprofit television and media organization in the USA, has also used the medium of television to teach children about heritage and supplement elementary school history curriculums. For American teachers has created "The Greeks," a multimedia site with videos, activities, and other information about all aspects of ancient Greek culture and history [53]. The site offers students interactive tours of ruins, such as the Parthenon, as they are now and images of how they might have looked when ancient Greeks were using them [54]).

General review of the range of projects in the field of Old World archaeology described as virtual heritage, shows numerous examples of virtual environments build as reconstructions of historic sites but sterile and devoid of population. However, beyond tools, we need a standard user-interface that can both run the exact heritage models being made by scholars in increasing numbers and be enhanced by the new tools, which might be added as plug-ins. This might be a high-quality but inexpensive proprietary games engine [55].

However, virtual gaming and TV film industry have shown ways to embrace imagined environments. Indeed an increasing number of fine digital materials are being produced for researchers and educators who want to incorporate heritage and archaeology into multidisciplinary studies. Up to the present, there have been few examples in the field of fully interactive, real-time models that have been published to the Internet. Generally, scholars have only been able to publish articles about their modeling projects with, at most, several color 2D illustrations. This presentation greatly hinders the overall effect of the project, and prevents greater interest and funding from being drawn. 3D models should be used in more effective and creative ways to improve interpretation in museums, and virtual museums, children TV productions, E-games, as well as in the classroom.

On the other hand, the above presented programs and projects illustrate the potentials and scenarios to promote

(a)   (b)   (c)

FIGURE 7: Sesame Street Muppet characters and some heritage TV segments.

cultural heritage and archaeology appreciation among children, as an essential step to the preservation of heritage in the future. We can also reflect on how EM can incorporate play and discovery into childhood heritage evolvement, in a way that is fun and developmentally appropriate for young children.

For example, passing through the 3D models created by ERATO project (the 3D visual models of theatres and the animation of the actors and audience included in the virtual reconstructions, modelled in 3D for a visual VR, musical instruments from the Hellenistic and Roman times, and Audible sound demonstrations of virtual performances with high degree of acoustical realism integrated with the visual restorations to form the virtual realizations of performances), and from other similar projects as ATHENA: *Ancient Theatres Enhancement for New Actualities*, they can support many digital children games and activities. But unfortunately, there is no coordination nor thought to further benefit from these many projects.

6.1. The Need for Multidisciplinary Team and Approach. The kind of change which could be accomplished is not clear cut, and it will require a multidisciplinary team to handle the various facets of the change. This multidisciplinary team can assist in producing new ideas for activities and games in EM, with the aim of establishing the required children and family awareness.

On all levels, heritage education requires the expertise of archaeologists, historical architects, educators, creative and art directors, scriptwriters, artists, painters, outreach initiatives, information and communication technologies (ICT) persons, TV, cinema and theatre persons, CRM specialists professional, conservators and cultural heritage institutions.

Methods to teach concepts and make students fully understand novel technologies and put them in practice are always challenging tasks. Reinforcement learning (RL) is one of the methodologies of machine learning and cognitive sciences. All RL methodologies require a balance between the research for new strategies and the use of already acquired knowledge [56, Pages 179-180]. Given the central place of constructivist learning theory and its influence on pedagogy, computer science and heritage persons and educators should pull through the theory, perform research, and analyze their educational proposals in terms of constructivism. Software

and language designers can be guided by constructivist principles, though the individuality of the construction by learners implies that no system will ever be universally easy-to-learn, and educators must learn how to teach these extant artifacts [57, Pages 49–53].

Such approach should include raising licensing standards for also childhood programs providing more family resource and support services and stimulating better collaboration between schools and the other heritage services. For that, community heritage education programs are needed. This while establishing cooperative relationships with heritage specialists, archaeological parks, and heritage centres, and homes is equally important. The concept of programs and campaigns is that, participants can use several tools to map and plot their heritage in combination with multimedia (field survey, drawing, 3D models, photography, script writing, interviews, video, digital illustration, animation, and theatre), then they can continue to interpret and promote it through demonstration, performance, exhibitions and creative documentation, websites games and writing. A collaborative approach between those different players at policy-making level and schools is a must, to support some projects or where specific networks or bodies are set up to promote children cultural heritage education programs and games. In the meantime there is a need to:

(i) conduct training and specialized workshops that can assists in changing the mindset of educators and teachers and to collaborate with new partners, to develop new resources and to implement new approaches in teaching "outside" the pencil and paper classroom. Online learning, e-commerce, public relations, and museum/collection sites would all benefit from integrating e-collaboration in different ways;

(ii) plan and develop a pedagogical approach for both the formal and informal cultural heritage education programs for students outside of school, with aalternatives methodologies in EM to enhance child interaction with cultural heritage and life in the community and environment;

(iii) design EM programs and campaigns, to help children's retrace the lost of their cultural heritage, to deepen their appreciation of cultural assets in their locality and to encourage them to take responsibility for the conservation and sustainability of their culture. For example, heritage specialist and educators can develop some concepts like "I am a heritage artist," "I am a heritage scientist." These programs and campaigns should be implemented with collaboration of archaeologists, CRM specialists' professional conservators, arts educators, artists, Creative and art directors, community and local societies and cultural heritage institutions. Some suggested topics and themes are: (1) cultural mapping: archaeological sites and architectural heritage. (2) folklore and lifestyle of rural and urban areas. (3) cultural heritage visual, oral, and aural performing and fine arts. (4) scriptural heritage (treatises on architecture, archaeology, aesthetics). (5) pre- and post-independence heritage philosopher and thinkers. (6) mode of transmission.

As a first step, the specialized technician and nontechnical users involved in heritage documentation and interpretation should discuss issues of interactivity in multimedia visualization production system, which can now more easily be achieved by the modern digital photographic and laser scanning technology, and can play a major role in the interpretation of the cultural heritage. However, it should be recognized and accepted that cultural heritage documentation is not only needed for proper conservation, but also foremost to raise public and especially children awareness.

Such investments are effectively useful and vastly improve the diffusion of heritage knowledge. For that, the thousands of documents of 3D models conducted around the world of 3D laser scanning, photogrammetry can be used as the first material in EM to create and design 3D animation for digital heritage children's edutainment games and activities. However, these games should be designed with the appropriate educational content from multidisciplinary and creative teams together with the childhood and heritage specialists.

As a recommendation, there is a need to design a project based on this critical issue of this section of this study. However, inhabited virtual heritage applications require careful balancing of computational resources between the visualization of environment and the visualization of people. There is also a need to design a special web site in which scholars can circulate and share their models and tool plug-ins. This can also facilitates the generation of historical and archaeological experiences using the techniques of computer animation, while reducing the need to reconstruct the historic sites.

These international examples of the fusion of EM with cultural heritage could be applied in the Arabic world, which is rich with world cultural heritage sites but transversely has lack of heritage awareness programs. These tools also exercise critical and creative thinking skills, where the past can be related to daily life. Explorations of archaeology also have great potential for encouraging children's investigative skills and inspiring in them a curiosity and appreciation for the our nonrenewable cultural heritage.

7. Summary and Concluding Remarks

Unlike formal education which uses a cognitive approach to impart information, EM projects facilitate affective and sensory learning, using experiential and participatory methodologies that can help children reconnect in a concrete and creative way to their cultural heritage. Potentially a virtual reality-based heritage experience gives the child the opportunity to feel he is present at significant places and times in the past, using a variety of senses to experience what it would have felt like to be there. Heritage EM, if we make the appropriated plans, can encourage children, parents, even educators to look for, explore and care for the wonders of our cultured heritage.

Virtual Site Museum's authentic database together with advanced VR technology contributed positively to both research and experience in the classroom and museums. However, For the application of technology to heritage to become a viable historical recreation tool, a combination of technological, economic and creative challenges must be overcome. The 3D models should be used in more creative and effective way to improve interpretation in museums, virtual museums, children TV productions, E-games, as well as in the classroom.

Specialized technicians and nontechnical involved in heritage should discuss the issues of "Heritage interactivity multimedia visualization production system," which can play a major role in the interpretation of the cultural heritage for children. The thousands of 3D model documents of 3D models like of the 3D laser scanning and photogrammetry should be used not only as tools for preservation and conservation, but also as the initial material in children heritage EM, to create 3D heritage edutainment games and activities, as directed by the multidisciplinary team of archaeologists, historian architects, CRM specialists', professional conservationists, arts educators, artists, creative & art directors, IT experts, and local arts foundations. In the meantime, there is a need to:

(i) design more EM projects and campaigns to help young people and children's retrace the lost of their cultural heritage, to deepen their appreciation of cultural assets in their locality and to encourage them to take social responsibility for the sustainability of their cultural assets and to participate in mapping and documenting their history and cultural assets. These initiatives should rely on local community partnerships, while objects in museum should be used as a resource base for teachers and educators, especially in the Middle East today;

(ii) establish and develop partnerships between cultural heritage institutions, researchers and digital games companies for archiving 3D documents of 3D digital models of laser scanning and photogrammetry of the world heritage sites, monuments, sculptures and artifacts, with the purpose of using them in EM. They can even share these documents with virtual gaming companies and TV and film industry producers to use them in documentaries, films, and television series;

(iii) develop an EM pedagogical approach for nonformal heritage education programs. There is a need for alternative EM approaches and methodologies to enhance child interaction with heritage and life in the community and environment. In the meantime, it is necessary to conduct specialized training workshops to orient educators towards more multidisciplinary collaborations, helping to develop new resources and implement new approaches to arts education;

(iv) develop a national and regional heritage EM supreme children council to take over planning to coordinate between all children related sectors such as ministries of cultural heritage and education, and civil socio-cultural associations. There is a need to craft a short, medium and long range plan to implement and monitor the national EM strategy, taking into consideration the comprehensive dimension in developing childhood sector and linking it to the national development plans. Promote collaborative approach between the different players at policy-making level as well as in EM and schools to improve heritage education—especially in the middle East countries—to support some projects or where specific networks or bodies are set up to promote heritage education programs.

Conflict of Interests

The author declares that there is no conflict of interests regarding the publication of this paper.

References

[1] Heritage 2012, 3rd International Conference on Heritage and Sustainable Development Overview, Porto, Portugal, June 2012.

[2] K. M. Kailash, *Curriculum Development for Cultural Heritage Studies*, 2001, http://ignca.nic.in/nl001703.htm.

[3] M. Fleer and J. Robbins, "A cultural-historical analysis of early childhood education: how do teachers appropriate new cultural tools?" *European Early Childhood Education Research Journal*, vol. 15, no. 1, pp. 103–119, 2007.

[4] Arts and Cultural Education at School in Europe, European Commission, The Education, Audiovisual and Culture Executive Agency (EACEA P9 Eurydice), 2009, http://eacea.ec .europa.eu/education/eurydice/documents/thematic_reports/ 113EN.pdf.

[5] Council of Europe, "The Council of Europe framework convention on the value of cultural heritage for society," Council of Europe Treaty Series No 199, Council of Europe, Faro, Portugal, 2005.

[6] Council of the European Union, "Resolution of the Council of 16 November 2007 on a European agenda for culture," *Official Journal of the European Union*, vol. 287, pp. 1–4, 2007, http://eur-lex.europa.eu/LexUriServ/LexUriServ.do?uri=OJ:C:2007:287: 0001:0004:EN:PDF.

[7] Council of Europe, "White paper on intercultural dialogue: 'living together as equals in dignity,'" The Council of Europe Ministers of Foreign Affairs at their 118th Ministerial Session, Strasbourg, France, 2008, http://www.coe.int/t/dg4/intercul-tural/source/white%20paper_final_revised_en.pdf.

[8] A. Bamford, *The Wow Factor: Global Research Compendium on the Impact of the Arts in Education*, Waxmann, Berlin, Germany, 2006, http://books.google.jo/books?id=ZEaxmwG9n4EC&print-sec=frontcover&hl=ar&source=gbs_ge_summary_r&cad=0#v= onepage&q&f=false.

[9] United Nations Educational, Scientific and Cultural Organization (UNESCO), "Road map for arts education," in *Proceedings of the World Conference on Arts Education: Building Creative Capacities for the 21st Century*, Lisbon, Portugal, March 2006, http://portal.unesco.org/culture/en/files/40000/ 12581058115Road_Map_for_Arts_Education.pdf/Road% 2BMap%2Bfor%2BArts%2BEducation.pdf.

[10] The Arab Gulf Programme for United Nations Development Organizations (AGFUND), http://www.agfund.org/en/Pages/ search.aspx?k=childhood

[11] The Arab Gulf Programme for United Nations Development Organizations (AGFUND), http://www.agfund.org/en/about/ Pages/Vision_Mission_Objectives.aspx.

[12] National Advisory Committee on Creative and Cultural Education (NACCCE), *All Our Futures: Creativity, Culture and Education*, http://sirkenrobinson.com/pdf/allourfutures.pdf.

[13] P. Shank and R. Kozma, "Learning chemistry through the use of a representation-based knowledge building environment," *Journal of Computers in Mathematics and Science Teaching*, vol. 21, no. 3, pp. 253–279, 2002.

[14] C. Heeter, "Technology enhanced learning," White paper for the Internet 2 Sociotechnical Summit, Michigan State University, Department of Telecommunication, 1999, http://commtechlab .msu.edu/reandd/collaboration/tech-paper/carrietech-paper3 .htm

[15] "Cross-curriculum dimensions, a planning guide for schools," http://schoolsonline.britishcouncil.org/sites/default/files/el/ 98010.pdf

[16] N. Sabnani, "The challenges of a sleeping giant," *Design Issues*, vol. 21, no. 4, pp. 94–105, 2005.

[17] D. Christopoulos and A. Gaitatzes, "Multimodal interfaces for educational virtual environments," in *Proceedings of the 13th Panhellenic Conference on Informatics (PCI '09)*, pp. 197–201, Corfu, Greece, September 2009.

[18] J. Einarsdottir, S. Dockett, and B. Perry, "Making meaning: children's perspectives expressed through drawings," *Early Child Development and Care*, vol. 179, no. 2, pp. 217–232, 2009.

[19] P. G. Ramsey, "Children's responses to differences," *NHSA Dialog*, vol. 11, no. 4, pp. 225–237, 2008.

[20] J. D. Bailey, "A practice model to protect the ethnic identity of international adoptees," *Journal of Family Social Work*, vol. 10, no. 3, pp. 1–11, 2007.

[21] I. P. Samuelsson and M. A. Carlsson, "The playing learning child: towards a pedagogy of early childhood," *Scandinavian Journal of Educational Research*, vol. 52, no. 6, pp. 623–641, 2008.

[22] M. R. Gruber and C. Glahn, "E-learning for arts and cultural heritage education in archives and museums, commission of the European communities," TeLearn-DigiCULT, Learning and Cultural Heritage, http://cordis.europa.eu/ist/telearn-digicult/index.html.

[23] F. Corona, F. Perrotta, E. T. Polcini, and C. Cozzarelli, "The new frontiers of edutainment: the development of an educational and socio-cultural phenomenon over time of globalization," *Journal of Social Sciences*, vol. 7, no. 3, pp. 408–411, 2011.

[24] J. Mihova and M. Fraser, "Scale(s) of cultural (re) productions," in *Digital Media and Its Applications in Cultural Heritage (DMACH '11)*, J. Al-Qawasmi, Y. Alshawabkeh, and F. Remondino, Eds., pp. 185–200, CSAAR Press, Amman, Jordan, 2011.

[25] A. Gaitatzes, D. Christopoulos, and G. Papaioannou, "Virtual reality systems and applications: the ancient olympic games," *Advances in Informatics*, Springer, New York, NY, USA, vol. 3746, pp. 155–165, 2005.

[26] P. Fleury and S. Madeleine, "Interactive visit of the city of Rome in the fourth century A.D.," in *Making History Interactive: Computer Applications and Quantitative Methods in Archaeology*, B. Frischer, J. W. Crawford, and D. Koller, Eds., pp. 67–75, Archaeopress, Oxford, UK, 2009.

[27] G. Papagiannakis, S. Schertenleib, B. O'Kennedy et al., "Mixing virtual and real scenes in the site of ancient Pompeii," *Computer Animation and Virtual Worlds*, vol. 16, no. 1, pp. 11–24, 2005.

[28] A. Gaitatzes, D. Christopoulos, A. Voulgari, and M. Roussou, "Hellenic cultural heritage through immersive virtual archaeology," Foundation of the Hellenic World, Foundation of the Hellenic World, Athens, Greece, http://www.fhw.gr/FoundationoftheHellenicWorld, http://www.fhw.gr/fhw/index.php?2&state=pages&id=106

[29] A. C. Addison, "Emerging trends in virtual heritage," *IEEE Multimedia*, vol. 7, no. 2, pp. 22–25, 2000.

[30] M. Roussou and D. Efraimoglou, "High-end interactive media in the museum," in *Proceedings of SIGGRAPH '99 Computer Graphics Conference*, pp. 59–62, ACM SIGGRAPH, 1999.

[31] A. Doyle, "Living in the past: a digital reconstruction provides valuable insight to Jerusalem's archaeological treasures," *Computer Graphics*, 2001, http://www.ust.ucla.edu/ustweb/Projects/Israel/compgraphics.pdf

[32] Y. S. Kim, T. Kesavadas, and S. M. Paley, "The virtual site museum: a multi-purpose, authoritative, and functional virtual heritage resource," *Presence: Teleoperators and Virtual Environments*, Special Issue on Virtual Heritage, vol. 15, no. 3, MIT Press, Cambridge, Mass, USA, pp. 245–261, 2006.

[33] T. Hall and L. Bannonw, "Designing ubiquitous computing to enhance children's learning in museums," *Journal of Computer Assisted Learning*, vol. 22, no. 4, pp. 231–243, 2006.

[34] Y. P. Lim, "Virtual Reality as a means for preserving digital heritage: Masjid Jamek," *International Journal of Interdisciplinary Social Sciences*, vol. 5, no. 9, pp. 119–128, 2010.

[35] C. I. Sedano, E. Sutinen, M. Vinni, and T. H. Laine, "Designing hypercontextualized games: a case study with LieksaMyst," *Educational Technology and Society*, vol. 15, no. 2, pp. 257–270, 2012.

[36] L. Plowman and C. Stephen, "A "benign addition"? Research on ICT and pre-school children," *Journal of Computer Assisted Learning*, vol. 19, pp. 149–164, 2003.

[37] G. Papagiannakis, A. Foni, and N. Magnenat-Thalmann, "Real-Time recreated ceremonies in VR restituted cultural heritage sites," in *Proceedings of the CIPA 19th International Symposium*, pp. 235–240, 2003.

[38] S. Madeleine and P. Fleury, "Reconstruction of ancient rome in interactive virtual reality," in *Proceedings of the Digital Media and its Applications in Cultural Heritage Conference (DMACH '11)*, J. Al-Qawasmi, Y. Alshawabkeh, and F. Remondino, Eds., pp. 169–183, Center for the Study of Architecture in the Arab Region; CSAAR Press, Amman, Jordan, 2011.

[39] N. Haddad, "Criteria for the assessment of the modern use of ancient theatres and odea," *International Journal of Heritage Studies*, vol. 13, no. 3, pp. 265–280, 2007.

[40] ERATO, http://historyoftheancientworld.com/2011/03/how-did-the-ancient-roman-theatres-sound/.

[41] http://www.euromedheritage.net/intern.cfm?menuID=12&submenuID=13&idproject=41.

[42] J. Mihova, "Parthenon marbles as embodiments of dramatic consciousness," *International Journal of Interdisciplinary Social Sciences*, vol. 2, no. 5, pp. 19–28, 2008.

[43] J. Mihova and M. Fraser, "Making sense of the multilayered past. An interactive visual interpretation of the Athenian acropolis and the parthenon," in *Proceedings of the 6th International Conference on History*, Athens Institute for Education and Research, Athens, Greece, 2009, http://vuw.academia.edu/MattFraser/Papers.

[44] R. Kadobayashi and K. Mase, "Seamless guidance by personal agent in virtual space based on user interaction in real world," in *Proceedings of the 3rd International Conference and Exhibition on The Practical Application of Intelligent Agents and Multi-Agent Technology (PAAM '98)*, London, UK, 1998.

[45] K. Mase, R. Kadobayashi, and R. Nakatsu, "Metamuseum: supportive augmented-reality environment for knowledge sharing," in *Proceedings of the International Conference on Virtual Systems and Multimedia (VSMM '96)*, Gifu, Japan, 1996.

[46] T. Abaci, R. de Bondeli, J. Cger et al., "The enigma of the sphinx," in *Proceedings of the International Conference on Cyberworlds*, pp. 106–113, IEEE Computer Society, 2003.

[47] G. Burdea and P. Coiffet, *Virtual Reality Technology*, John Wiley & Sons, Hoboken, NJ, USA, 2nd edition, 2003.

[48] N. Haddad, K. Haddad, and D. Labin, "The role of multi-media in early childhood education: a case study of Hikayat Simsim in Jordan," in *Proceedings of the 1st Conference on Childhood and the Family, Towards a Happy Childhood & Prosperous Family*, pp. 103–117, The Hashemite University, Zarqa, Jordan, 2005.

[49] CHARISMATIC IST Project, http://www.charismatic-project.com/.

[50] D. Gutierrez, B. Frischer, E. Cerezo, A. Gomez, and F. Seron, "AI and virtual crowds: populating the Colosseum," *Journal of Cultural Heritage*, vol. 8, no. 2, pp. 176–185, 2007.

[51] The British Museum, "The games at olympia," http://www.ancientgreece.co.uk/festivals/story/sto_set.html.

[52] The Metropolitan Museum of Art, "Museum kids: explore and learn," http://www.metmuseum.org/explore/museumkids.asp.

[53] Public Broadcasting Service, "The Greeks," http://www.pbs.org/empires/thegreeks/htmlver/.

[54] Public Broadcasting Service, "The acropolis experience," http://www.pbs.org/empires/thegreeks/acropolis/intro_html.html.

[55] http://www.garagegames.com/education.

[56] T. Conde, W. Tambellini, and D. Thalmann, "Behavioral animation of autonomous virtual agents helped by reinforcement learning," in *Intelligent Virtual Agents: 4th International Workshop (IVA '03), Kloster Irsee, Germany, September 15–17, 2003*, T. Rist, R. Aylett, D. Ballin, and J. Rickel, Eds., vol. 2792 of *Lecture Notes in Computer Science*, pp. 175–180, Springer, Berlin, Germany, 2003.

[57] M. Ben-Ari, "Constructivism in computer science education," *Journal of Computers in Mathematics and Science Teaching*, vol. 20, no. 1, pp. 45–73, 2001.

6

A Novel k-out-of-n Oblivious Transfer Protocol from Bilinear Pairing

Jue-Sam Chou

Department of Information Management, Nanhua University, No. 55, Section 1, Nanhua Road, Dalin Township, Chiayi County 62249, Taiwan

Correspondence should be addressed to Jue-Sam Chou, jschou@mail.nhu.edu.tw

Academic Editor: Mohamed Hamdi

Oblivious transfer (OT) protocols mainly contain three categories: 1-out-of-2 OT, 1-out-of-n OT, and k-out-of-n OT. In most cases, they are treated as cryptographic primitives and are usually executed without consideration of possible attacks that might frequently occur in an open network, such as an impersonation, replaying, or man-in-the-middle attack. Therefore, when used in certain applications, such as mental poker games and fair contract signings, some extra mechanisms must be combined to ensure the security of the protocol. However, after a combination, we found that very few of the resulting schemes are efficient enough in terms of communicational cost, which is a significant concern for generic commercial transactions. Therefore, we propose a novel k-out-of-n oblivious transfer protocol based on bilinear pairing, which not only satisfies the requirements of a k-out-of-n OT protocol, but also provides mutual authentication to resist malicious attacks. Meanwhile, it is efficient in terms of communication cost.

1. Introduction

An oblivious transfer (OT) is an important primitive for designing security services. It can be used in various applications like the signing of fair contracts, oblivious database searches, mental poker games, privacy-preserving auctions, secure multiparty computations [1], and so on. In 1981, Rabin [2] first proposed an interactive OT scheme in which the probability of the receiver's capability to decrypt a message sent by the sender is 1/2. Rabin used the proposed OT to design a 3-pass secret exchange (EOS) protocol, hoping that two parties can exchange their secrets fairly. In 1985, Even et al. [3] presented a more generalized OT, called 1-out-of-2 OT (OT_1^2), in which a sender sends two encrypted messages to a chooser with only one of which the chooser can decrypt. They also presented a contract-signing protocol by evoking OT_1^2 multiple times to prevent one party from obtaining the other party's contract signature without first showing his own. In 1986, Brassard et al. [4] further extended OT_1^2 into a 1-out-of-n OT (OT_1^n, also known as "all-or-nothing"), in which only one out of n sent messages can actually be obtained by the chooser. The authors pointed out

that their OT_1^n scheme can be used to implement a multiparty mental poker game [5] against a player coalition. In contrast to the interactive versions described above, Bellare and Micali [6] first proposed a noninteractive OT_1^2 scheme in 1989. In this scheme, a user obliviously transfers two messages to another party equipped with two public keys to decrypt one of the messages.

From 1999 to 2001, based on the above-mentioned interactive and noninteractive OT schemes, Naor and Pinkas proposed some related OT methods, such as an adaptive OT_k^n [7], proxy OT_1^2 [8], distributed OT_k^n [9], efficient OT_1^n [10], and efficient OT_k^n [11]. Here, OT_k^n is the final form of the OT schemes. In this form, from the n encrypted messages sent, the chooser can obtain k chosen messages in plaintext form without the sender's knowledge regarding which part of the messages are decrypted. In Naor and Pinkas's distributed OT_k^n schemes [9], the sender distributes two messages (M_0, M_1) among n servers, and the chooser contacts k ($k < n$) servers to receive one (M_σ, $\sigma = 0$ or 1) of them. The authors claimed that their schemes can protect the privacy of both parties. However, in 2007, Ghodosi [12] showed two possible attacks on these schemes. In the first attack, two collaborating servers can reveal the chooser's choice of σ, while, in the second attack, the chooser can learn both M_0 and M_1 by colluding with only a single server. In 2002, Mu et al. [13] proposed three OT_k^n schemes constructed using RSA encryption, a Nyberg-Rueppel signature, and an ElGamal encryption scheme, respectively. Two of these are interactive, while the other can be either interactive or noninteractive. The authors claimed that their schemes are complete, robust, and flexible and induce a significant improvement in communication cost. However, in 2006, Ghodosi and Zaare-Nahandi [14] showed that these schemes fail to satisfy the requirements of an oblivious transfer protocol. In 2004, Ogata and Kurosawa [15] proposed another OT_k^n scheme, based on an RSA blind signature, which can be employed in either an adaptive or a nonadaptive manner. The authors claimed that their scheme can be applied to oblivious key searching. In 2005, three OT_k^n schemes are proposed [16–18]. Among these, Chu and Tzeng's scheme [16] is the most efficient as it needs only 2 passes to send $1024k$ bits from the chooser to the sender, and $1024*(k + 1) + n*|Data|$ bits from the sender to the chooser, where Data is a message or ciphertext, and |Data| represents the bit length of Data. In 2006, Parakh [19] proposed an elliptic-curve-based algorithm allowing A to obliviously transfer his secrecy, n_A, to B with a 50% probability of success. However, we found that A can decide whether B can obtain his secret n_A (which is one-to-one mapped to Pn_A) by first assuming that $P_A = P_B$. Under this assumption, upon receiving $\{n_BP_B; n_B(n_AP_A) + R; n_BR\}$ from B, A can obtain B's one-time random variable R by computing $(n_B(n_AP_A) + R) - n_A(n_BP_B)$. Then, by computing $n_A(n_BR) = n_B(n_AR)$, A can obtain n_BK. Subsequently, by computing $(n_A(n_B R) + Pn_A) - n_BK$, A obtains Z_B, just as B does in step 5(b). Therefore, if A finds $Z_B = Pn_A$, it confirms that B can obtain n_A after the protocol runs; otherwise, it knows B cannot obtain the value of n_A. This violates B's privacy. In the same year, for coping with all possible attacks encountered in an open network, Kim and Lee [20] proposed two OT_1^2 protocols, which are modified from Bellare-Micali noninteractive OT_1^2 scheme [6] by appending the sender's signature to make the sender undeniable about what he sent and be authentic to the chooser. However, we found, other than the weaknesses pointed by Chang and Shiao [21], Kohnfelder's protocol still has the reblocking problem [22]. Because when modulus $n_A > n_B$, message M_A cannot be recovered by Bob. This makes legal Alice unable to be authenticated by Bob.

In 2007, Halevi and Kalai [23] proposed another OT_1^2 scheme by using smooth projective hashing and showed that the used RSA composite in their scheme need not be a product of safe primes. Also in 2007, Camenish et al. and Green and Hohenberger proposed two related OT schemes [24, 25], respectively. Both focus on the security of full simulatability for the sender and receiver to resist against selective-failure attack [7]. In 2009, Qin et al. [26] proposed two noninteractive OT_1^n schemes. However, in their protocols, a receiver has to interact with a third party to obtain the choice-related secret key each time it wants to select one of the n sent message. This makes their

scheme somewhat inconvenient and inconsistent with the meaning of noninteractive protocols as indicated in the title (this phenomenon can also be found in some proposed noninteractive OT schemes). In the same year, Chang and Lee [27] presented a robust OT_k^n scheme using both the RSA blind signature and Chinese Remainder Theorem. However, we found their scheme fails since the sender can decide which parts of the messages were chosen by the chooser. We will describe this weakness in Section 3.2. In addition, in 2011, Ma et al. [28] proposed an oblivious transfer using a privacy scheme for a timed-release receiver. Their scheme has a good timed-release property. However, it needs to call ZKP k times to learn k of the n sent messages. This makes their protocol less efficient. Moreover, it does not have mutual authentication. Therefore, when the sender and receiver want to communicate, they need a secure channel. Otherwise, without identity authentication, malicious attackers can simultaneously launch many ZKPs. This will degrade the system performance and may cause the system to suffer from a denial-of-service (DOS) attack (according to the definition in [29]).

After surveying all of the above-mentioned OT schemes, we found that almost all of them lack the consideration of adding security features. Only [2, 20] do consider the protection against all possible attacks. However, study [20] fails which we have described earlier. Hence, if we wish all of the proposed OT protocols, other than scheme [2], to be able to resist against various attacks, we should run them through secure channels. This would incur extra communicational overhead. For this reason, in this paper, we propose a novel interactive OT_k^n scheme that needs only two passes but can get rid of using a secure channel to avoid adding extra communicational overhead. It not only is simple in concept but also encompasses some essential security features such as mutual authentication, the prevention of man-in-the-middle (MIMA) attack, and replay attack. Thus, when compared with other interactive OT schemes, our scheme promotes not only in the communicational efficiency but also in the aspect of security.

The rest of this paper is organized as follows. The introduction has been presented in Section 1, and some preliminaries are shown in Section 2. In Section 3, we review Chang et al.'s scheme and show its weakness. After that, we show our protocol in Section 4. Then, the security analyses and communicational cost comparisons among related works and our scheme are made in Section 5. Finally, a conclusion is given in Section 6.

2. Preliminaries

In this section, we briefly introduce the security features of our OT_k^n scheme in Section 2.1, the principles of bilinear pairing in Section 2.2, and some intractable problems used in this paper in Section 2.3.

2.1. Security Features of Our OT_k^n Scheme. Just as traditional OT schemes, our OT_k^n also has two parties, the sender S and the chooser C. In the scheme, S obliviously transfers

n messages to C, and C can choose k messages among them without S's knowledge about which k messages were selected, where $n \geq 2$ and $k < n$. In addition, our scheme also possesses the following three security features which are needed in a traditional OT scheme.

(1) Correctness. After the protocol run, C should be able to obtain the valid data chosen by him before.

(2) Chooser's Privacy. In the protocol, each of the k chooser's choices should not be known to the sender or any third party. More precisely, each of the chooser's encrypted choice can be any valid choice with equal probability, that is, for an encrypted choice y and any valid choice x, $\Pr[x \mid y] = \Pr[x]$. This property is known as *Shannon perfect secrecy*.

(3) Sender's Privacy. At end of the protocol run, the chooser cannot get any knowledge about the other messages it did not choose. More formally, the ciphertexts sent by the sender are semantically secure [30]. The chooser can obtain a plaintext decrypted from its ciphertext only if it has the key offered by the sender.

Except for the above three properties, our interactive OT_k^n scheme also has the following three security features, (4) through (6), to guard against possible security threats.

(4) Impersonation Attack Resistance. Each party has to authenticate the counterpart. That is, it should be a mutual-authentication OT.

(5) Replaying Attack Resistance. An adversary could not obtain any messages by only replaying old messages sent by the sender.

(6) Man-in-the-Middle Attack (MIMA) Resistance. MIMA is an attack that an adversary eavesdropping on the communication line between two communicating parties uses as some means to make them believe that they each are talking to the intended party. But indeed, they are talking to the adversary.

2.2. Bilinear Pairing. Let G_1 be an additive group composed of points on an elliptic curve with order q, and let G_2 be a multiplicative group with the same order. A bilinear mapping is defined as $\hat{e} : G_1 \times G_1 \rightarrow G_2$ which must satisfy the following properties [31].

(1) Bilinear: a mapping $\hat{e} : G_1 \times G_1 \rightarrow G_2$ is bilinear if $\hat{e}(aP, bQ) = \hat{e}(P, Q)^{ab}$ for all $P, Q \in G_1$ and all $a, b \in Z_q^*$.

(2) Nondegenerate: the mapping does not map all pairs in $G_1 \times G_1$ to the identity in G_2.

(3) Computable: there is an efficient algorithm to compute $\hat{e}(P, Q)$ for any $P, Q \in G_1$.

(4) If P is a generator for G_1 then $\hat{e}(P, P)$ is a generator for G_2.

(5) Commutative: for all $P_1, P_2 \in G_1$, $\hat{e}(P_1, P_2) = \hat{e}(P_2, P_1)$.

(6) Distributive: for all $P_1, P_2, P_3 \in G_1$, $\hat{e}(P_1 + P_2, P_3) = \hat{e}(P_1, P_3)\hat{e}(P_2, P_3)$.

2.3. Some Diffie-Hellman Problems. Let $a, b, c, g \in_R Z_q^*$, let P be a base point of a group on an Elliptic curve, and let $G = \langle g \rangle$, $G_1 = \langle P \rangle$, and $G_2 = \langle g(= \hat{e}(P, P)) \rangle$ be three groups with each having a prime order q. Using these definitions, we describe some well-known intractable Diffie-Hellman problems [32] that will be used in this paper.

(1) The Computational Diffie-Hellman (CDH) Problem. In G, given (g, g^a, g^b), finding the element $C = g^{ab} \bmod q$.

(2) The Decisional Diffie-Hellman (DDH) Problem. In G, given (g, g^a, g^b, g^c), deciding whether $c = ab \bmod q$.

(3) The Bilinear Computational Diffie-Hellman (BCDH) Problem. Given (P, aP, bP, cP) in G_1, finding $\hat{e}(P, P)^{abc}$ in G_2.

According to Boneh and Franklin's study [31], the BCDH problem is no harder than the CDH problem in G (or equivalently G_2).

(4) Chosen-Target CDH (CTCDH) Problem. Let $H : \{0,1\}^* \rightarrow G$ be a hash function, let $T(\cdot)$ be a target oracle which returns a random element in G, and $(\cdot)^c$ a helper oracle which returns $T(j)^c$ when queried by $T(j)$, where c is an unknown random integer in Z_q^*. Also, let q_t be the number of queries to $T(\cdot)$ and q_h the number of queries to $(\cdot)^c$. The CTCDH problem is finding l pairs of $(j_1, v_1), \ldots,$ and (j_l, v_l), with each satisfying $v_i = (T(j_i))^c$, for $1 \leq i \leq l$ and $q_h < l \leq q_t$. Without loss of generality, we can let q_h and q_t be $l - 1$ and l, respectively. The CTCDH problem can then be rephrased as that after obtaining $T(j_1), \ldots, T(j_l)$ and $(j_1, v_1), \ldots, (j_{l-1}, v_{l-1})$ via querying the $T(\cdot)$ oracle and the helper oracle $(\cdot)^c$ correspondingly, trying to find the lth pair (j_l, v_l) without the knowledge of c. The CTCDH problem is proposed and considered as a hard problem by Boldyreva in 2002 [33]. Its former version in RSA is proved by Bellare et al. in [34].

3. Review of Chang et al.'s Protocol

In 2009, Chang et al. proposed a robust OT_k^n scheme based on CRT, hoping that their scheme can achieve the security requirements of a general OT_k^n scheme. However, we found their scheme cannot satisfy the chooser's privacy. In the following, we first review the scheme in Section 3.1 then show the weakness found in Section 3.2.

3.1. Review. We roughly describe the protocol by listing the relevant steps in the following (see [27] for more details).

Step 1. After receiving the request from Bob for all messages $a_1, a_2, \ldots, a_n$, Alice owning these n messages selects n

relatively prime integers, d_1, d_2, ..., d_n, and computes $D = d_1 * d_2 * \cdots * d_n$. She then constructs the congruence system

$$C \equiv a_1 \bmod d_1, \; C \equiv a_2 \bmod d_2, \ldots,$$
$$C \equiv a_n \bmod d_n. \tag{1}$$

Furthermore, Alice computes the following values: $T_1 = d_1^e \bmod N$, $T_2 = d_2^e \bmod N, \ldots$, and $T_n = d_n^e \bmod N$, where N be the product of two large primes and (e, d) be Alice public/private key pair satisfying $ed = 1 \bmod \varphi(N)$, by using her public key e. Finally, she publishes C and the n pairs of (ID_i, T_i), for $i = 1$ to n, in the public board.

Step 2. If Bob wants to learn k messages among them, he must select k pairs of (ID'_j, T'_j), for $j = 1$ to k, from the public board and first generate k corresponding random numbers r_1, r_2, ..., r_k, for each pair of (ID'_j, T'_j). Then, he subsequently computes the following:

$$\alpha_1 = r_1^e * T'_1 \bmod N, \; \alpha_2 = r_2^e * T'_2,$$
$$\bmod N, \ldots, \alpha_k = r_k^e * T'_k \bmod N, \tag{2}$$

by using Alice's public key e and sends $\{\alpha_1, \alpha_2, \ldots, \alpha_k\}$ back to Alice.

Step 3. Upon receiving the messages sent by Bob, Alice employs her private key d to compute $\beta_1 = \alpha_1^d = r_1 T_1'^d = r_1 d_1' \bmod N$, $\beta_2 = \alpha_2^d = r_2 T_2'^d = r_2 d_2' \bmod N$, ..., $\beta_k = \alpha_k^d = r_k T_k'^d = r_k d_k' \bmod N$ and then sends the results $\{\beta_1, \beta_2, \ldots, \beta_k\}$ to Bob.

Step 4. After receiving the messages from Alice, Bob computes the following values: $d_1' = r_1^{-1} * \beta_1 \bmod N, d_2' = r_2^{-1} * \beta_2 \bmod N, d_k' = r_k^{-1} * \beta_k \bmod N$. Consequently, Bob learns the demanded messages successfully by computing

$$b_1 = C \bmod d_1', \; b_2 = C \bmod d_2', \ldots,$$
$$b_k = C \bmod d_k'. \tag{3}$$

3.2. Weaknesses. Although Chang et al. claimed that their scheme can satisfy the security requirements demanded by the OT_k^n scheme, we found that Bob's privacy has been violated, since according to their protocol, Alice first sets n values of d_i ($i = 1$ to n), and Bob commits his k choices to the k values of α_j($j = 1$ to k). After computing the k values of β_j ($= 1$ to k), Alice can use each of the d_i^{-1}s ($i = 1$ to n) to compute $r_{ji} = \beta_j * d_i^{-1}$, for $j = 1$ to k and $i = 1$ to n. In addition, using each r_{ji}, Alice can compute the n values of $\alpha_i^{(*)} = (r_{ji} * d_i)^e$, for $i = 1$ to n, to compare with the k committed values, α_j. For example, suppose Bob chooses the first message, $T_1 = d_1^e \bmod N$, and Alice wants to guess which T_i Bob chose, Alice starts to use d_1^{-1} to compute $r_{11} = \beta_1 * d_1^{-1} \bmod N = \alpha_1^d (= r_1 * d_1) * d_1^{-1} \bmod N = r_1 \bmod N$. He will get $\alpha_1^{(*)} = (r_{11} * d_1)^e \bmod N = \alpha_1 = r_1^e * T_1$. That is, Alice will find a match, α_1, and knows that Bob chose the first message. Conversely, if Alice uses d_i^{-1}, ($i = 2$, n) to compute $r_{1i} = \beta_1 * d_i^{-1}$, he will get

$\alpha_i^{(*)} = (r_{1i} * d_i)^e \bmod N$, which is not equal to α_1. In other words, Alice cannot know the correct message T_1 that Bob chose. That is, once a pair, $(\alpha_i^{(*)}, \alpha_i)$, for example, has been matched, Alice knows that Bob chose the ith message. Hence, we can easily see that such explorations cost at most $n * k$ multiplications to obtain r_{ji}, and $n^2 * k$ multiplications and $n^2 * k$ exponentiations to yield all values of $\alpha_i^{(*)}$. Therefore, with at most $(n^2 * k + n * k)$ multiplications and $n^2 * k$ exponentiations, it is computationally feasible for Alice to decide which k values Bob selected, which violates Bob's privacy.

4. Proposed Protocol

In this section, we present our ID-based OT_k^n protocol based on bilinear pairings, which were proved and applied to cryptography by Boneh and Franklin in 2001 [31]. Our scheme consists of two phases: (1) an initialization phase and (2) an oblivious transfer phase. In the following, we first describe these two phases. Then, to demonstrate the chooser's privacy preservation, we use a misleading attack for an explanation. As the receiver's privacy preservation can be reasoned in a similar fashion, we omit its description here.

(1) Initialization Phase. In this phase, we adopt the same system parameters as the ones used in [31]. In addition, there also exists a trusted key generation center (KGC) which is assumed to be key-escrow-attack free. Initially, KGC chooses an additive group $G_1 = \langle P \rangle$ of order q, a multiplicative group $G_2 = \langle \hat{e}(P, P) \rangle$ of the same order, where $\hat{e}$ is a bilinear mapping, that is, $\hat{e} : G_1 \times G_1 \rightarrow G_2$, and three one-way hash functions: $H: \{0,1\}^* \rightarrow \{0,1\}^l$, $H_2 : G_1 \rightarrow \{0,1\}^l$, and H_1 which maps a string (a user's ID) to an element in G_1, that is, $H_1:\{0,1\}^* \rightarrow G_1$. Moreover, it selects $s \in Z_q^*$ as its private master key and computes the corresponding system public key as $P_{\mathrm{pub}} = sP$. Then, KGC publishes the system parameter set $\{G_1, G_2, q, \hat{e}, P, P_{\mathrm{pub}}, H, H_1, H_2\}$. After that, when a user U (sender/chooser) registers his identifier ID_U, KGC will compute a public/private key pair $U_{\mathrm{pub}}/U_{\mathrm{priv}}$ for him, where $U_{\mathrm{pub}} = H_1(ID_U)$ and $U_{\mathrm{priv}} = sU_{\mathrm{pub}}$.

(2) Oblivious Transfer Phase. In this phase, when a sender possessing n messages (m_1, $m_2, \ldots,$ and m_n) wants to obliviously transfer k messages of them (m_{σ_1}, $m_{\sigma_2}, \ldots,$ and m_{σ_k}) to a chooser, they together will execute the following steps, where the public/private key pairs of the sender and chooser are $S_{\mathrm{pub}}/S_{\mathrm{priv}}$ and $C_{\mathrm{pub}}/C_{\mathrm{priv}}$, respectively, and $\{\sigma_1, \sigma_2, \ldots, \sigma_k\} \subset \{1, 2, \ldots, n\}$ are the set of k choices selected by the chooser in advance. We also depict them in Table 1.

Step 1. The chooser randomly chooses two integers $a, b \in Z_q^*$ and computes $V = abC_{\mathrm{pub}}$, $V_j = bH(\sigma_j)C_{\mathrm{priv}}$, where $j = 1, 2, \ldots, k$ and V_j are the k random choices. After that, he generates a signature Sig on V by computing $h = H_2(V)$ and Sig $= hC_{\mathrm{priv}}$. Then, he sends ID_c, V, $V_1, \ldots, V_k$ together with Sig to the sender.

TABLE 1: The proposed k-out-of-n authentic OT protocol.

Sender $(S_{pub}/S_{priv}(= sS_{pub}))$	Chooser $(C_{pub}/C_{priv}(= sC_{pub}))$
	(1) Selects $, b \in_R Z_q^*$, computes $V = abC_{pub}$, for $j = 1$ to k, computes $V_j = bH(\sigma_j)C_{priv}$, computes $h = H_2(V)$ and Sig $= hC_{priv}$.
$\xleftarrow{\quad ID_C, V, V_1, \dots, V_k, Sig \quad}$	
(2) Computes $h = H_2(V)$ and verifies $\hat{e}(P, \text{Sig}) =?\hat{e}(P_{pub}, hC_{pub})$. If it does not hold, aborts. Selects $c \in_R Z_q^*$ and computes $U_j = cV_j$, for $j = 1, \dots, k$, and $ct_i = m_i \oplus \hat{e}(H(i)V, S_{priv})^c$, for $i = 1, \dots, n$.	
$\xrightarrow{\quad U_1, \dots, U_k, ct_1, \dots, ct_n \quad}$	
	(3) For $j = 1$ to k and $i = 1$ to n, computes $m_{\sigma_i} = ct_{\sigma_i} \oplus \hat{e}(U_j, S_{pub})^a$.

Step 2. After receiving IDc, V, $V_1, \dots,$ V_k and Sig from the chooser, the sender computes $h = H_2(V)$ and verifies the chooser's signature by checking whether the equation $\hat{e}(P, \text{Sig}) = \hat{e}(P_{pub}, hC_{pub})$ holds. If it holds, he believes that the chooser is the intended party as claimed. Then, the sender randomly chooses an integer $c \in Z_q^*$ and computes $U_j = cV_j$ and $ct_i = m_i \oplus \hat{e}(H(i)V, S_{priv})^c$, where $j = 1, \dots, k$, $i = 1, \dots, n$, and m_i are the n messages. He/She then sends $U_1, \dots, U_k, ct_1, \dots,$ and ct_n to the chooser.

Step 3. After receiving the message $U_1, \dots,$ $U_k, ct_1, \dots,$ and ct_n from the sender, the chooser can obtain the k intended messages by at most computing the equation, $m_{\sigma_j} = ct_{\sigma_j} \oplus \hat{e}(U_j, S_{pub})^a$, $nk - \cdot(k(k-1)/2)(= n + (n-1) + \cdots + (n - (k-1)))$ times.

(3) A Misleading Attack for Chooser's Privacy Preservation. To demonstrate the chooser's privacy more clearly, we take the following as a counterexample. According to step 1 in our protocol, the chooser computes $V_1, \dots, V_k$, where $V_j = bH(\sigma_j)C_{priv}$ and $j = 1$ to k. Since b and C_{priv} are both the same for V_i and V_j, a misleading attack may be that $V_i/V_j = H(\sigma_i)/H(\sigma_j)$. A malicious sender can pre-compute $H(\sigma_i)/H(\sigma_j)$ for each i, j in the interval $[1, n]$. After receiving $V_1, \dots, V_k$ from the chooser, he computes each V_i/V_j for all i, j in $[1, k]$ for a comparison with the precomputed values. Consequently, the sender may guess some or all of the chooser's choices. Therefore, the protocol cannot achieve chooser privacy. However, the mistake here is that both V_i and V_j are points in the additive group G_1. The division operation V_i/V_j is invalid because G_1 is an additive group.

5. Security Analysis

In this section, we use the following claims to show that our protocol not only is correct but also possesses the properties

of mutual authentication, chooser's privacy, and sender's privacy and can resist against active attacks such as relay attack, man-in-the-middle attack, and denial of service attack.

Claim 1. The proposed protocol is correct.

Proof. After the protocol runs, the chooser can exactly obtain the k messages which he/she selected by computing

$$
\begin{aligned}
ct_{\sigma_j} &\oplus \hat{e}(U_j, S_{pub})^a \\
&= ct_{\sigma_j} \oplus \hat{e}\left(cbH(\sigma_j)C_{priv}, S_{pub}\right)^a \\
&= ct_{\sigma_j} \oplus \hat{e}\left(H(\sigma_j)bcsC_{pub}, S_{pub}\right)^a \\
&= ct_{\sigma_j} \oplus \hat{e}\left(H(\sigma_j)abC_{pub}, sS_{pub}\right)^c \\
&= ct_{\sigma_j} \oplus \hat{e}\left(H(\sigma_j)V, S_{priv}\right)^c = m_{\sigma_j}.
\end{aligned}
\tag{4}
$$

$\square$

Claim 2. The proposed protocol can achieve mutual authentication.

Proof. We show the holdness of this claim by using the following two reasons.

(1) Apparently, it can be easily seen that the sender can authenticate the chooser by verifying the chooser's signature, Sig (as described in step 2 of the oblivious transfer phase).

(2) For that the ciphertext ct_i $(= m_i \oplus \hat{e}(H(i)V, S_{priv})^c)$ contains the sender's private key $S_{priv}(= sS_{pub})$, the chooser can compute the meaningful message m_{σ_j} only via using the sender's public key S_{pub} (also refer to the equation in claim 1). This means that only the true sender can produce the right ct_i and thus can be authenticated by the chooser using his public key.

$\square$

Claim 3. The proposed protocol can achieve the chooser's privacy.

Proof. Due to the fact that each of the chooser's k choices $\sigma_j \in \{1, 2, \ldots, n\}$ are first hashed and randomized by H and b respectively, and then signed as $V_j = bH(\sigma_j)C_{\text{priv}}$ by chooser C in step 1, where b is a random number. We argue that nobody except for the chooser can know the choice σ_j. Because even an attacker might steal the chooser's private key C_{priv}, he/she cannot obtain $bH(\sigma_j)$ from V_j owing to the hardness of ECDLP. That is, he cannot figure out $bH(\sigma_j)$, and therefore not to mention σ_j. More formally, let $\mathcal{A} = \{(b, \sigma_j) \in Z_q * Z_n \mid bH(\sigma_j)C_{\text{priv}} = V_j\}$; that is, $\mathcal{A}$ consists of all the possible ordered pairs (b, σ_j) satisfying the equation $bH(\sigma_j)C_{\text{priv}} = V_j$. If we are given a value V_j, then under fixed C_{priv}, there only exists a unique value $bH(\sigma_j)$ satisfying the equation. And for a given $bH(\sigma_j)$, under the definition of a collision-free one-way hash function, once σ_j has been determined, the value of b is determined as well. That is, the relationship between b and σ_j is one-to-one. Having this observation in mind and the dimension of σ_j is n, we can see that there are n (b, σ_j) pairs in $\mathcal{A}$. In other words, $\Pr[\sigma_j \mid V_j] = \Pr[\sigma_j] = 1/n$ which means that, under seeing a specific V_j, the choice σ_j of the chooser cannot be revealed other than guessing. This achieves the *Shannon perfect secrecy*. Therefore, the proposed protocol possesses chooser's privacy. □

Claim 4. The proposed scheme can achieve the sender's privacy.

Proof. Assume that malicious chooser $\hat{C}$ wants to obtain more than k messages in the protocol. If he/she could succeed, then, the sender's privacy is violated (see Section 2.1). However, we will prove that, other than his k chosen messages, it is computationally infeasible for $\hat{C}$ to obtain the $(k+1)$th message by using the following two arguments, (I) and (II). In argument (I), we show why $\hat{C}$ must follow the protocol to form the values of V and kV_js; otherwise, he/she cannot obtain the k chosen messages. In argument (II), we show that if $\hat{C}$ intends to obtain the $(k+1)$th message, he/she will face the intractable CTCDH problem under the assumption that $H(\cdot)$ is a random hash function. □

Argument (I). $\hat{C}$ must follow the protocol to form the values of $V(= ab\hat{C}_{\text{pub}})$ and $V_j(= bH(\sigma_j)\hat{C}_{\text{priv}})$, for $j = 1$ to k; otherwise, he cannot obtain the k chosen messages, $m_{\sigma_1}, \ldots, m_{\sigma_j}$.

In the following, we further divide this argument into three cases: (a) $\hat{C}$ fakes V but forms V_j honestly, (b) $\hat{C}$ fakes V_j but forms V honestly, and (c) $\hat{C}$ fakes both the values of V and V_j. (For each case's explanation, refer to Table 1.)

(a) $\hat{C}$ fakes V but forms V_j honestly. Assume that $\hat{C}$ is dishonest in forming V but forms V_j honestly as specified in the protocol. For example, without loss of generality, it replaces V with a specific $X \in G_1$ and computes $V_j = bH(\sigma_j)\hat{C}_{\text{priv}}$. Then, the sender will compute $U_j = cV_j$, $ct_i = m_i \oplus \hat{e}(H(i)X, S_{\text{priv}})^c$ and send them back to $\hat{C}$. As a result, $\hat{C}$ cannot decrypt $ct_{\sigma_j}(ct_{\sigma_j} = m_{\sigma_j} \oplus \hat{e}(U_j, S_{\text{pub}})^a)$ to obtain the k messages since $\hat{e}(U_j, S_{\text{pub}})^a$ is obviously not equal to $\hat{e}(H(\sigma_j)X, S_{\text{priv}})^c$ (refer to claim 1). Perhaps, for obtaining the k messages, $\hat{C}$ may try another way by computing $\hat{e}(H(i)X, S_{\text{priv}})^c$ expected to be equal to $\hat{e}(U_j, S_{\text{pub}})^a$. But this is computationally infeasible since $\hat{C}$ does not know both the sender's private key S_{priv} and the one-time secrecy c. To extract c from U_j is an ECDLP.

(b) $\hat{C}$ fakes V_js but forms V honestly. Assume that $\hat{C}$ is dishonest in forming V_js but forms V in the same manner as specified in the protocol. For example, without loss of generality, he replaces each V_j with a specified $X_j \in G_1$ and computes $V = ab\hat{C}_{\text{pub}}$. Then, the sender will compute $U_j = cV_j = cX_j$, $ct_i = m_i \oplus \hat{e}(H(i)V, S_{\text{priv}})^c = m_i \oplus \hat{e}(H(i)ab\hat{C}_{\text{pub}}, S_{\text{priv}})^c$, for $i = 1$ to n, and send them back to $\hat{C}$. As a result, $\hat{C}$ cannot decrypt ct_{σ_j} since $\hat{e}(U_j, S_{\text{pub}})^a = \hat{e}(cX_j, S_{\text{pub}})^a$ is obviously not equal to $\hat{e}(H(i)V, S_{\text{priv}})^c$. Perhaps, for obtaining the k messages, $\hat{C}$ may try another way by computing $\hat{e}(H(i)V, S_{\text{priv}})^c (= \hat{e}(H(i)ab\hat{C}_{\text{pub}}, S_{\text{priv}})^c)$ expected to be equal to $(U_j, S_{\text{pub}})^a$. But again this is computationally infeasible since $\hat{C}$ does not know both the sender's private key S_{priv} and the one-time secrecy c. Even he knows S_{priv}, extracting c from $U_j(= cX_j)$ is an ECDLP. Hence, $\hat{C}$ cannot compute the value $\hat{e}(H(i)V, S_{\text{priv}})^c$ to decrypt ct_{σ_j} for obtaining the k messages, m_{σ_j}.

(c) $\hat{C}$ fakes both the values of V and V_j. Without loss of generality, we assume that $\hat{C}$ replaces V with X and also fakes V_j as $H(\sigma_j)X$. Under this construction, the value of U_j computed by the sender would be $U_j = cV_j = cH(\sigma_j)X$ and the ciphertexts ct_{σ_j} would be $m_{\sigma_j} \oplus \hat{e}(H(\sigma_j)X, S_{\text{priv}})^c$, for $j = 1$ to k, or equivalently, $ct_{\sigma_j} = m_{\sigma_j} \oplus \hat{e}(cH(\sigma_j)X, S_{\text{priv}})$. Although, $\hat{C}$ knows the value of $cH(\sigma_j)X$ (since it just equals to U_j received from the sender), it still cannot compute $\hat{e}(cH(\sigma_j)X, S_{\text{priv}})$ without the knowledge of S_{priv}. From above description, we know that when the setting of V is X and V_j is $H(\sigma_j)X$, $\hat{C}$ cannot obtain m_{σ_j}. Not to mention, $\hat{C}$ might set V_j as $H(\sigma_j)Y$, where $Y(\neq X)$ is a random chosen element in G_1. In summary, $\hat{C}$ cannot obtain the k selected messages under the violation of setting both the values, V and V_j.

Argument (II). If $\hat{C}$ follows the protocol honestly to obtain k messages, but intends to extract the $(k+1)$th message then it will face the intractable CTCDH problem under the assumption that $H(\cdot)$ is a random hash function.

That $\hat{C}$ wants to obtain message m_i implies $\hat{C}$ would have the knowledge of $\hat{e}(H(i)V, S_{\text{priv}})^c$ ($= \hat{e}(U_j, S_{\text{pub}})^a$) (in fact, according to argument (I), an honest chooser C could know k of the n values, $\hat{e}(H(i)V, S_{\text{priv}})^c$, for $i = 1$ to n, since $\hat{e}(H(i)V, S_{\text{priv}})^c = \hat{e}(U_j, S_{\text{pub}})^a$, for $i = \sigma_j$ and $j = 1$ to k). Let $y^{(i)} \in G_2$ and $\hat{e}(H(i)V, S_{\text{priv}})^c = y^{(i)}$. According to argument (I), for obtaining the k chosen messages, $\hat{C}$ cannot change the structures of $V(= ab\hat{C}_{\text{pub}})$ and $V_j (= bH(\sigma_j)\hat{C}_{\text{priv}})$. Under this situation, $y^{(i)}$ only can be decomposed as $y^{(i)} = \hat{e}(H(i)ab\hat{C}_{\text{pub}}, S_{\text{priv}})^c = \hat{e}(abH(i)\hat{C}_{\text{priv}}, S_{\text{pub}})^c$ since $S_{\text{priv}} = sS_{\text{pub}}$ and $\hat{C}_{\text{priv}} = s\hat{C}_{\text{pub}}$. Moreover, under the assumption that $H(\cdot)$ is a random hash function and the fact that $\hat{C}$ has the knowledge of a, b, $\hat{C}_{\text{priv}}$, and S_{pub}, $y^{(i)}$ can be represented as $(g_i)^c$, where g_i equals to $\hat{e}(abH(i)\hat{C}_{\text{priv}}, S_{\text{pub}})$ and is a random element in G_2 due to the assumption that $H(\cdot)$ is a random hash function. Consequently, the problem $\hat{C}$ really faces is finding the $(k + 1)$th pair $(\sigma_{k+1}, (g_{\sigma_{k+1}})^c)$ with the knowledge of k pairs of $(\sigma_1, (g_{\sigma_1})^c), (\sigma_2, (g_{\sigma_2})^c), \ldots,$ and $(\sigma_k, (g_{\sigma_k})^c)$, where $(g_{\sigma_j})^c = \hat{e}(U_j, S_{\text{pub}})^a$, but without the knowledge of sender's one-time secrecy c (since it is an ECDLP for extracting c from $U_j(= cV_j)$). This is known as the intractable CTCDH problem introduced in Section 2.3 by letting $k = (l - 1)$. Therefore, the chooser cannot obtain the $(k + 1)$th message.

According to arguments I and II, we have proven claim 4 that our scheme has the sender's privacy.

Claim 5. The proposed scheme can resist against replay attack.

Proof. Suppose that an adversary intercepts a chooser's OT request (containing ID_C, V, V_j, and Sig) and replays it later. After receiving the sender's new response $(U_1, \ldots, U_k, ct_1, \ldots, ct_n)$ computed from the replayed V and V_j, the adversary cannot obtain the k selected messages by computing $m_{\sigma_j} = ct_{\sigma_j} \oplus \hat{e}(U_j, S_{\text{pub}})^a$ since he/she does not know the value of a embedded in the replayed message V. It is computationally infeasible for the adversary to extract a from $V = ab\hat{C}_{\text{pub}}$, due to the hardness of ECDLP. $\square$

Claim 6. The proposed scheme can resist against man-in-the-middle attack (MIMA).

Proof. MIMA is an attack that an adversary E intercepts the communication line between two communicating parties and uses some means to make them believe that they each are talking to the intended party as claimed. But indeed, they are talking to E. Figure 1 illustrates the scenario of such a MIMA. We first argue that the adversary E cannot succeed in this scenario since it cannot generate the valid message (2), $(\text{ID}_C, V', V_1', \ldots, V_k', \text{Sig}')$ as shown in the figure. More clearly, without the knowledge of chooser's private key C_{priv}, he/she cannot forge a valid signature Sig' in message (2) to be successfully verified by the sender since Sig' should be equal to $H_2(V) C_{\text{priv}}$. In addition, it is also hard for E to forge valid message (4), $(U_1', \ldots, U_k', ct_1', \ldots, ct_n')$, to be accepted by the chooser. Since that for embedding a meaningful m_i' into ct_i',

E must have the knowledge of $\hat{e}(H(i)V, S_{\text{priv}})^c$. Although E can choose another random nonce c' such that $U_j' = c'V_j$, it still has to know the sender's private key S_{priv} to form the valid $ct_i'(= m_i \oplus \hat{e}(H(i)V, S_{\text{priv}})^{c'})$. Therefore, without the knowledge of S_{priv}, E cannot launch such a MIMA attack. $\square$

Claim 7. The proposed scheme can resist a denial of service attack (DOS).

Proof. Our protocol has a built-in mutual authentication property; thus, it can prevent this kind of attack, as the sender needs only one hash and two bilinear pairing computations to authenticate the chooser in step (2). Once the sender finds that the authenticating equation $\hat{e}(P, \text{Sig}) = \hat{e}(P_{\text{pub}}, hC_{\text{pub}})$ does not hold, it aborts the procedure. $\square$

5.1. Communicational Cost Comparisons.

Generally, the communicational cost of a protocol run consists of three factors: (1) needed passes, (2) computational overhead, and (3) needed transmission data size (NTDS) or bandwidth consumption. It is well known that factor (1) is always dominant over factor (2). Hence, in this section, we focus only on factor (1) and (3) to demonstrate the communication cost comparisons among our nonadaptive OT_k^n protocol and the other same type OT_k^n protocols, such as Chu and Tzeng's [16] (which is to our best knowledge, the most efficient OT_k^n scheme up to date), Mu et al.'s [13], Naor and Pinkas's [7], and recent works [17, 18, 24, 27]. From factor (1), our scheme is the most efficient since it only requires two passes. As to factor (3), the data size transmitted in our scheme is also the minimal among such type of OT_k^n schemes. For demonstrating this in the following, we will first describe two underlying facts and used notations for making comparisons about factor (3).

Generally speaking, we have the following two facts for cryptosystems.

Fact 1. To the same security level, a RSA cryptosystem would require a key length of 1024 bits while an ECC-based cryptosystem only needs 160 bits.

Fact 2. The length of the ciphertexts for RSA, ElGamal, and ECC-based cryptosystems is 1024 bits, 1024 bits, and 160 bits, correspondingly.

Notations. We use |string/action| to represent the bit length of a *string*, or the required bit length that an *action* performs.

After the description of used facts and notations, we now use them to estimate the needed transmission data size (NTDS) of our scheme and the above-mentioned OT_k^n protocols. In our scheme, each of the variables V, $V_1, \ldots, V_k$, Sig, $U_1, \ldots, U_k$ transmitted between the chooser and sender is an ECC point. Thus, the NTDS from the chooser to the sender is estimated as $160 * (k + 2)$ bits and from the sender to the chooser is $160k + n * |\text{ciphertext}|$ bits. Naor and Pinkas's scheme [7] constructs their OT_k^n scheme by evoking an OT_1^2 primitive $\log n$ times. Thus, the needed number of passes is $\log n$ times the number of passes required in one of their OT_1^2's protocol run and

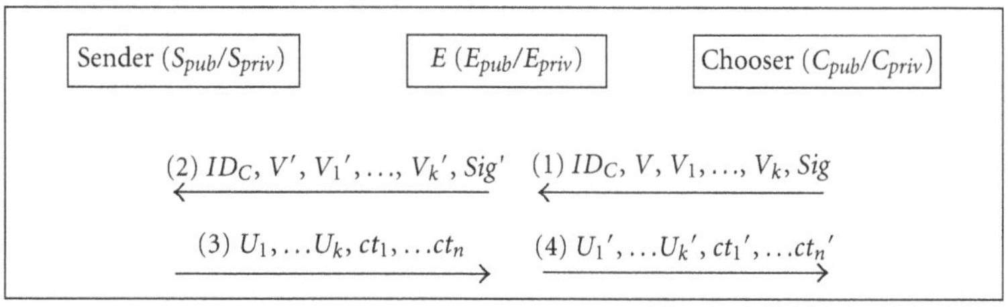

FIGURE 1: The scenario of MIMA attack.

TABLE 2: Needed rounds and data size comparisons among OT_k^n protocols.

Protocol	Passes	Size of message: $C \to S$ (bits)	Size of message: $S \to C$ (bits)	Mutual authentication
Ours	2	$160 * (k+2)$	$160k + n * |\text{ciphertext}|$	Yes
Naor and Pinkas [7]	$k * \log n\ OT_1^2$	depends on OT_1^2	depends on OT_1^2	No
Mu et al.'s scheme (1) [13]	3	$1024k$	$1024n + nk * |\text{ciphertext}|$	No
Mu et al.'s scheme (2) [13]	2	$1024 * 2n$	$n * |\text{ciphertext}|$	No
Chu and Tzeng [16]	2	$1024k$	$1024 * (k+1) + n * |\text{ciphertext}|$	No
Zhang and Wang [17]	2	$1024 * (k+3)$	$1024n + n * |\text{ciphertext}|$	No
Huang and Chang [18]	3	$1024k$	$(n+k) * |\text{ciphertext}|$	
Camenisch et al. [24]	$2 + k * \text{Pok}$	$|\text{Pok}| + k * |\text{BlindExtract}|$	$n * |\text{ciphertext}| + |\text{Pok}| + k * |\text{BlindExtract}|$	No
Chang and Lee [27]	4	$1024k$	$(n + 2k + 2) * 1024$	No
Ma et al. [28]	$k * (2 + \text{Pok})$	$k * 3|\text{ciphertext}|$	$k * (n * 2|\text{ciphertext}|)$	No

likewise the NTDS is about $\log n$ times of the NTDS that an OT_1^2's work demands. Therefore, their scheme has the most expensive communicational cost. As for Camenisch et al.'s protocol [24], the communicational cost is expensive as well due to the complexity of the protocol. In their protocol, the sender first sends n commitments to the chooser, and then the sender and the chooser together run a proof-of-knowledge (Pok) subprotocol for assuring the correctness of the commitments. If the proof is valid, the sender sends n ciphertexts to the chooser, and the chooser then runs the BlindExtract subprotocol k times with the help of the sender to extract the blind choices to decrypt the ciphertexts.

Consequently, the number of passes for executing protocol [24] is $2 + k * \text{Pok}$, where Pok represents the required passes for executing the proof-of-knowledge subprotocol. Besides, the NTDS from chooser to sender is estimated as $|\text{Pok}| + k * |\text{BlindExtract}|$ and from sender to chooser is $n * |\text{ciphertext}| + |\text{Pok}| + k * |\text{BlindExtract}|$. Similarly, the passes and NTDS of other studies can be estimated in the same manner. We show the comparison results in Table 2.

From Table 2, we can see that our scheme not only possesses the mutual authentication function but also is the most efficient in both needed passes and NTDS among these related. Therefore, our scheme can be gracefully used when applied in commercial applications (e.g., Kerschbaum et al.'s method [1] used OT scheme as a building block in constructing RFID benchmarking protocols).

6. Conclusion

An OT scheme which is secure and efficient in communicational cost is essential and eager for commercial applications. After reviewing most of the OT schemes, we found that, other than considering the protocol's correctness and privacy of both communication parties, almost all of them lack the security services, such as mutual authentication, and the prevention of replay, DOS, and main-in-the-middle attacks. Hence, they should run under a secure channel when applied in commercial applications. This will increase execution overhead. Therefore, to get rid of using the secure channel (for improving the communicational efficiency in some applications, such as mental poker playing, oblivious key searching), we propose a novel k-out-of-n oblivious transfer protocol by combining an OT scheme with a security mechanism based on bilinear pairing. We have proved that our scheme not only is correct but also possesses the properties of mutual authentication, the sender's privacy, and the chooser's privacy and can resist against replay and MIMA attacks. Further, we have compared our scheme with other nonadaptive k-out-of-n OT schemes in the aspects of needed passes, NTDS, and the function of mutual authentication and shown the result in Table 2. From Table 2, we can see that our scheme is the most efficient in communicational cost (including needed passes and NTDS). In addition, to our knowledge, it is the only OT_k^n scheme that has successfully integrated the function of mutual authentication nowadays.

References

[1] F. Kerschbaum, N. Oertel, and L. W. F. Chaves, "Privacy-preserving computation of benchmarks on item-level data using RFID," in *Proceedings of the 3rd ACM Conference on Wireless Network Security (WiSec '10)*, pp. 105–110, March 2010.

[2] M. O. Rabin, "How to exchange secrets with oblivious transfer," Tech. Rep. TR-81, Aiken Computation Lab, Harvard University, Cambridge, Mass, USA, 1981.

[3] S. Even, O. Goldreich, and A. Lempel, "A randomized protocol for signing contracts," *Communications of the ACM*, vol. 28, no. 6, pp. 637–647, 1985.

[4] G. Brassard, C. Crepeau, and J.-M. Robert, "All-or-nothing disclosure of secrets," in *Proceedings of the International Conference on Advances in Cryptology (CRYPTO '86)*, vol. 263 of *Lecture Notes in Computer Science*, pp. 234–238, 1986.

[5] J. S. Chou and Y. S. Yeh, "Mental poker game based on a bit commitment scheme through network," *Computer Networks*, vol. 38, no. 2, pp. 247–255, 2002.

[6] M. Bellare and S. Micali, "Non-interactive oblivious transfer and application," in *Proceedings of the International Conference on Advances in Cryptology (CRYPTO '89)*, vol. 435 of *Lecture Notes in Computer Science*, pp. 547–557, 1989.

[7] M. Naor and B. Pinkas, "Oblivious transfer with adaptive queries," in *Proceedings of the International Conference on Advances in Cryptology (CRYPTO '99)*, Lecture Notes in Computer Science, pp. 573–590, 1999.

[8] M. Naor, B. Pinkas, and R. Sumner, "Privacy preserving auctions and mechanism design," in *Proceedings of the 1st ACM Conference on Electronic Commerce*, 1999.

[9] M. Naor and B. Pinkas, "Distributed oblivious transfer," in *Proceedings of the International Conference on Advances in Cryptology (CRYPTO '00)*, vol. 1976 of *Lecture Notes in Computer Science*, 2000.

[10] M. Naor and B. Pinkast, "Oblivious transfer and polynomial evaluation," in *Proceedings of the 31st Annual ACM Symposium on Theory of Computing (FCRC '99)*, pp. 245–254, May 1999.

[11] M. Naor and B. Pinkas, "Efficient oblivious transfer protocols," in *Proceedings of the 12th annual ACM-SIAM symposium on Discret Mathematics (SODA '01)*, pp. 448–457, 2001.

[12] H. Ghodosi, "On insecurity of Naor-Pinkas' distributed oblivious transfer," *Information Processing Letters*, vol. 104, no. 5, pp. 179–182, 2007.

[13] Y. Mu, J. Zhang, and V. Varadharajan, "m out of n oblivious transfer," in *Proceedings of the 7th Australasian Conference on Information Security and Privacy (ACISP '02)*, vol. 2384 of *Lecture Notes in Computer Science*, pp. 395–405, 2002.

[14] H. Ghodosi and R. Zaare-Nahandi, "Comments on the 'm out of n oblivious transfer'," *Information Processing Letters*, vol. 97, no. 4, pp. 153–155, 2006.

[15] W. Ogata and K. Kurosawa, "Oblivious keyword search," *Journal of Complexity*, vol. 20, no. 2-3, pp. 356–371, 2004.

[16] C. K. Chu and W. G. Tzeng, "Efficient k-out-of-n oblivious transfer schemes with adaptive and non-adaptive queries," in *Proceedings of the 8th International Workshop on Theory and Practice in Public Key Cryptography (PKC '05)*, pp. 172–183, January 2005.

[17] J. Zhang and Y. Wang, "Two provably secure k-out-of-n oblivious transfer schemes," *Applied Mathematics and Computation*, vol. 169, no. 2, pp. 1211–1220, 2005.

[18] H. F. Huang and C. C. Chang, "A new design for efficient t-out-n oblivious transfer scheme," in *Proceedings of the 19th International Conference on Advanced Information Networking and Applications (AINA '05)*, pp. 28–30, March 2005.

[19] A. Parakh, "Oblivious transfer using elliptic curves," in *Proceedings of the 15th International Conference on Computing (CIC '06)*, pp. 323–328, November 2006.

[20] S. Kim and G. Lee, "Secure verifiable non-interactive oblivious transfer protocol using RSA and Bit commitment on distributed environment," *Future Generation Computer Systems*, vol. 25, no. 3, pp. 352–357, 2009.

[21] Y. F. Chang and W. C. Shiao, "The essential design principles of verifiable non-interactive OT protocols," in *Proceedings of the 8th International Conference on Intelligent Systems Design and Applications (ISDA '08)*, pp. 241–245, November 2008.

[22] L. M. Kohnfelder, "On the signature reblocking problem in public-key cryptography," *Communications of the ACM*, vol. 21, no. 2, p. 179, 1978.

[23] S. Halevi and Y. T. Kalai, "Smooth projective hashing and two-message oblivious transfer," Cryptology ePrint Archive 2007/118, 2007.

[24] J. Camenisch, G. Neven, and A. Shelat, "Simulatable adaptive oblivious transfer," in *Proceedings of the Annual International Conference on the Theory and Applications of Cryptographic Techniques*, vol. 4515 of *Lecture Notes in Computer Science*, pp. 573–590, 2007.

[25] M. Green and S. Hohenberger, "Blind identity-based encryption and simulatable oblivious transfer," Cryptology ePrint Archive 2007/235, 2007.

[26] J. Qin, H. W. Zhao, and M. Q. Wang, "Non-interactive oblivious transfer protocols," in *Proceedings of the International Forum on Information Technology and Applications (IFITA '09)*, pp. 120–124, May 2009.

[27] C. C. Chang and J. S. Lee, "Robust t-out-of-n oblivious transfer mechanism based on CRT," *Journal of Network and Computer Applications*, vol. 32, no. 1, pp. 226–235, 2009.

[28] X. Ma, L. Xu, and F. Zhang, "Oblivious transfer with timed-release receiver's privacy," *Journal of Systems and Software*, vol. 84, no. 3, pp. 460–464, 2011.

[29] W. Stallings, *Cryptography and Network Security—Principals and Practices*, Prentice Hall, Upper Saddle River, NJ, USA, 3rd edition, 2003.

[30] S. Goldwasser and S. Micali, "Probabilistic encryption & how to play mental poker keeping secret all partial information," in *Proceedings of the 40th annual ACM symposium on Theory of Computing (STOC '82)*, pp. 365–377, 1982.

[31] D. Boneh and M. K. Franklin, "Identity-based encryption from the Weil pairing," in *Proceedings of the International Conference on Advances in Cryptology (CRYPTO '01)*, vol. 2139 of *Lecture Notes in Computer Science*, pp. 213–229, 2001.

[32] D. R. Stinson, *Cryptography—Theory & Practice*, Chapman & Hall/CRC Taylor & Francis Group, 3rd edition, 2006.

[33] A. Boldyreva, "Threshold signatures, multisignatures and blind signatures based on the Gap-Diffie-Hellman-group signature scheme," in *Proceedings of the 6th International Workshop on Theory and Practice in Public Key Cryptography*, vol. 2567 of *Lecture Notes in Computer Science*, pp. 31–46, 2003.

[34] M. Bellare, C. Namprempre, D. Pointcheval, and M. Semanko, "The one-more-RSA-inversion problems and the security of chaum's blind signature scheme," in *Proceedings of Financial Cryptography (FC '01)*, vol. 2248 of *Lecture Notes in Computer Science*, pp. 319–338, 2003.

7

An Improved Fast Mode Decision Method for H.264/AVC Intracoding

Abderrahmane Elyousfi

Computer Science Department, National Engineering School of Applied Sciences, University Ibn Zohr, 80000 Agadir, Morocco

Correspondence should be addressed to Abderrahmane Elyousfi; elyousfiabdo@yahoo.fr

Academic Editor: Constantine Kotropoulos

An improved fast and efficient mode decision method for H.264/AVC intracoding is proposed, which is based on the analysis of the gravity center method and more efficient mode selection. In contrast to the fast mode decision method where the intramodes are determined by the gravity center of the block, the mass center vector is computed for the block and the subblocks formed by the proposed subsampling techniques. This method is able to determine all correlation directions of the block that correspond to the intraprediction mode directions of the H.264/AVC. On this basis, only a small number of intraprediction modes are chosen as the best modes for rate-distortion optimization (RDO) calculation. Different video sequences are used to test the performance of the proposed method. Experimental results reveal the significant computational savings achieved with slight peak signal-to-noise ratio (PSNR) degradation and bit-rate increase.

1. Introduction

The H.264/AVC video coding standard supports intraprediction for various block sizes. For the luma samples, H.264/AVC supports three block-size types in high profile: luma 4×4, luma 8×8, and luma 16×16. Intraluma 4×4 supports eight directional modes and DC mode. Figure 1 illustrates the 4×4 luma block and intraprediction directions. In Figure 1(b), eight out of the nine different intraprediction modes of luma 4×4 are shown (except DC mode). In each of the modes, the prediction pixels of the current block a-p can be obtained by the neighboring pixels A-M with a certain extrapolating operation. And the pixels A-M in Figure 1(a) belong to the reconstructed image (not the original lossless image). Except the DC mode (mean value prediction), the eight modes can be specified by their local texture direction [1]. Intraluma 8×8 shares the same prediction modes with intraluma 4×4 except that the coding block size is 8×8. Intraluma 16×16 contains three modes with directions: vertical, horizontal, and plane. For the chroma intraprediction, only 8×8 block is supported and the prediction modes are the same as those of intraluma

16×16 [1–6]. To select the optimal encoding mode for an MB, H.264/AVC video encoder calculates the rate distortion cost (denoted as RDcost) of every possible mode and chooses the mode having the minimum value, and this process is repeatedly carried out for all the possible modes for a given MB [7, 8]. Unfortunately, the computational burden of this type of exhaustively full searching algorithm is far more demanding than any other existing video coding standards.

Several fast intraprediction mode selection algorithms have been proposed [9–22]. In [15], hybrid method is used to achieve better performance than conventional edge detection methods by adapting these filters. Plus, several other improvements are also investigated. First, the sort operations at the stage of individual pixel processing are time consuming and summing method is used instead. Second, as the adaptation of the computation efficient summing method is used, more pixels can be applied to improve the filtering results with negligible time increase. Finally, local information is exploited to enhance the mode selection accuracy. Elyousfi [16] proposed a fast intramode selection algorithm for H.264/AVC that uses the gravity center vector of the block to determine the best intraprediction mode.

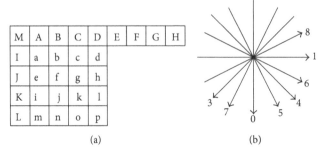

FIGURE 1: The 4 × 4 luma block and prediction directions. (a) For a 4 × 4 luma block, a to p are the pixels to be predicted, and A to M are the neighboring pixels that are available of prediction. (b) Eight prediction directions for intraprediction of 4 × 4 luma block.

In this paper, we present an improved gravity center method proposed by Elyousfi [16]. In [16], the authors use the idea that the direction of the gravity center vector of the block is perpendicular with the direction of the correlation of this block. However, the prediction precision of the above algorithm is hampered by the limitation that this algorithm is not applicable for all correlation directions of the block that correspond to intraprediction mode directions of H.264/AVC. In case of the blocks having a directional correlation such as horizontal-up, horizontal-down, vertical-left, and vertical-right direction, the gravity center vector direction of these blocks is not identified. From this, the gravity center method cannot determine all correlation directions of the block that correspond to intraprediction mode direction of H.264/AVC. Hence, as the best intraprediction mode direction is this that corresponds to the block correlation direction, the previous algorithm [16] cannot determine the best intraprediction mode candidates for RDO computation in intraprediction. Consequently, the previous algorithm [16] may increase the bit rate and/or may affect heavily the PSNR degradation.

This work proposes a novel adaptive fast and efficient intraprediction in H.264/AVC algorithm based on center of mass and two subsampling techniques. This method is able to determine all correlation directions of the block that correspond to the intraprediction mode directions of the H.264/-AVC. The technique of the mass center used in the previous work is also applied in this paper. That is, the block mass center direction is perpendicular to the block correlation direction. However, in this paper we indicate the block correlation directions that are perpendicular to the mass center direction of the block. We note that these correlation directions are horizontal, vertical, diagonal-right, and diagonal-left. Furthermore, after the analysis of the characteristics of the blocks having these correlation directions, we observed that these blocks are symmetric.

For the case of the blocks that their correlation directions are not perpendicular with the direction of the mass center vector of these blocks, the previous work [16] is not capable to determine these correlation directions. We note that these directions are horizontal-up, horizontal-down, vertical-left, and vertical-right. In this paper, in order to determine the correlation direction of these blocks with mass center direction

we formed their corresponding symmetric subblock. These subblocks are formed by subsampling the pixels of the block.

Two subsampling techniques are proposed in this paper. The first method named by ILHC (impair lines and half columns) and applied to vertical-left and vertical-right directional correlation blocks. The square subblock formed by this method (ILHC) is composed by the impair lines and the half columns in the middle of the block. The second method named by ICHL (impair columns and half lines) and applied to horizontal-up and horizontal-down correlation direction of the blocks. The square subblock formed by this method (ICHL) is composed by the impair columns and half lines in the middle of the block.

The mass center direction computed from the subblock formed by the ILHC method can determine if the block has vertical-left or vertical-right correlation direction. Also, the mass center direction computed from the subblock formed by the ICHL method can determine if the block has horizontal-up or horizontal-down correlation direction.

Based on the block correlation direction determined by the mass center method and subsampling techniques, the best intraprediction candidates are chosen for RDO calculation during intraprediction. The experiment results reveal that the proposed correlation direction detection algorithm can provide better coding performance and time reduction comparing to the previous algorithms.

This paper is organized as follows. The proposed fast and efficient intraprediction algorithm will be illustrated in Section 2. In Section 3, we present the experimental results and discuss the performance of the proposed algorithm, and, then, we conclude this paper in Section 4.

2. The Proposed Algorithm

In this section, the observations which motivate the basic idea of the proposed subsampling techniques will be discussed first. Then the proposed method will be introduced in detail, including the two proposed subsampling techniques and block correlation direction determination. Finally, to further reduce the computational complexity for intracoding in H.264/AVC, a fast intramode decision algorithm is introduced, while maintaining the original coding performance very well.

2.1. Observations and the Two Proposed Subsampling Techniques

2.1.1. Observations. We observed that when the block has a correlation direction, such as horizontal, vertical, diagonal-right, and diagonal-left, this block has a symmetry axis through the center of this block. The direction of this axis is perpendicular to the direction of the homogeneous pixels of the block. Figure 2 shows these four correlation directions and their corresponding symmetry axes for 5×5 blocks. Also, we observed that when the block has a correlation direction, such as horizontal-up, horizontal-down, vertical-left, and vertical-right, this block does not have a symmetry axis through the center of this block. We note that this is valid for all block sizes.

2.1.2. The Proposed ILHC Subsampling Method. The proposed ILHC subsampling method forms square subblocks by subsampling the pixels of the block with two main steps. In the first, it selects the impair lines of the block. In the second, it selects the half columns in the middle of the block.

Figure 3(a) shows the two 5×5 blocks and their corresponding square subblocks formed by ILHC subsampling method. We observed, from this figure, that the subblock formed by the proposed ILHC subsampling method for the block having, respectively, the vertical-left and vertical-right directional homogeneous pixels has a diagonal-left and diagonal-right directional homogeneous pixels. Hence, each subblock of these subblocks has a symmetry axis through the center of this subblock.

2.1.3. The Proposed ICHL Subsampling Method. The proposed ICHL subsampling method forms square subblocks by subsampling the pixels of the block with two main steps. In the first, it selects the impair columns of the block. In the second, it selects the half lines in the middle of the block.

Figure 3(b) shows the two 5×5 blocks and their corresponding square subblocks formed by ICHL subsampling method. from this figure we observed that the subblock formed by the proposed ICHL subsampling method for the block having, respectively, the horizontal-up and horizontal-down directional homogeneous pixels has diagonal-left and dia-gonal-right directional homogeneous pixels. Hence, each subblock of these subblocks has a symmetry axis through the center of this sub-block.

We conclude that the eight correlation directions of the block can be determined if we determine the vector direction of the symmetry axis of the block (or of the subblock formed by the subsampling techniques). In this paper we prove that this direction can be determined by the mass center method. In the next section, we detail the relationship between the symmetry axes direction and mass center direction of the block.

2.2. Block Symmetry Axes Direction Determination.
The principle of the mass center scheme is applied to the determination of the block symmetry axes. In this section, we prove

that the symmetry axes direction of the block is parallel to the mass center direction of the block.

2.2.1. Mass Center Theory. In this study, gray levels are regarded as the pixel mass. For a block, in a luma (or chroma) picture, we define the corresponding mass center vector, $\overrightarrow{G} = \{G_x, G_y\}$, as

$$
\begin{aligned}
G_x &= \frac{1}{S_I} \sum_{x=x_0}^{x_0+N} \sum_{y=y_0}^{y_0+M} x \times I_{x,y} \\
G_y &= \frac{1}{S_I} \sum_{x=x_0}^{x_0+N} \sum_{y=y_0}^{y_0+M} y \times I_{x,y},
\end{aligned}
\tag{1}
$$

where $I_{x,y}$ is the intensity of the pixel of location (x, y) of a block, (G_x, G_y) is the coordinate of the mass center of a block, (x_0, y_0) is the coordinate of the pixel up-left of a block, and $(M + 1, N + 1)$ is the block dimension. S_I represents the sum of block pixels intensity values; the formula of the equation used for computation of this sum is defined as follows:

$$
S_I = \sum_{x=x_0}^{x_0+N} \sum_{y=y_0}^{y_0+M} I_{x,y}.
\tag{2}
$$

The direction of the block mass center vector $(\overrightarrow{G})$ is computed by

$$
\text{Ang}\left(\overrightarrow{G}\right) = \frac{180}{\pi} \arctan\left(\frac{G_y}{G_x}\right).
\tag{3}
$$

2.2.2. Block Symmetry Axes Direction Determination with Mass Center Direction. A symmetry axes direction of the block can be obtained by using the mass center method. The following simple proof verifies that the mass center vector direction represents the symmetry axis direction of the block and is taken as the basis of the proposed algorithm.

Suppose that in an orthonormal coordinate system $(O, \overrightarrow{i}, \overrightarrow{j})$, the origin is chosen to be the block's center, i represents the horizontal direction to the right and j the vertical direction to the bottom, and each block $N \times N$, N is an impair value (i.e., $N = 2m + 1$ which $m = \{2, 4, 8\}$), and the possible correlation directions of this block are horizontal, vertical, diagonal-right, and diagonal-left direction; then the mass center vector direction is parallel to the symmetry axis direction of this block.

Proof. Vertical direction correlation block: we let L_v be the line through the origin O and parallel to the vector $V_{L_v} = (x, 0)$, where x is an integer number except zero. This line L_v is the symmetry axis of the vertical direction correlation block (see observation 1). Hence, all pixels in this block that are symmetrical with this line L_v have the same intensity and can be written as

$$
I_{x,y} = I_{x,-y}, \quad -m \le x, y \le m.
\tag{4}
$$

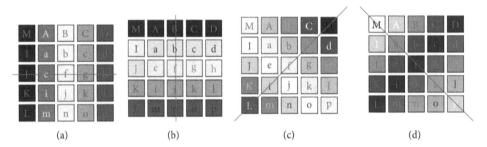

FIGURE 2: (a) The 5×5 block horizontal homogeneous pixels and their corresponding symmetry axes. (b) The 5×5 block vertical homogeneous pixels and their corresponding symmetry axes. (c) The 5×5 block diagonal-right homogeneous pixels and their corresponding symmetry axes. (d) The 5×5 block diagonal-left homogeneous pixels and their corresponding symmetry axes.

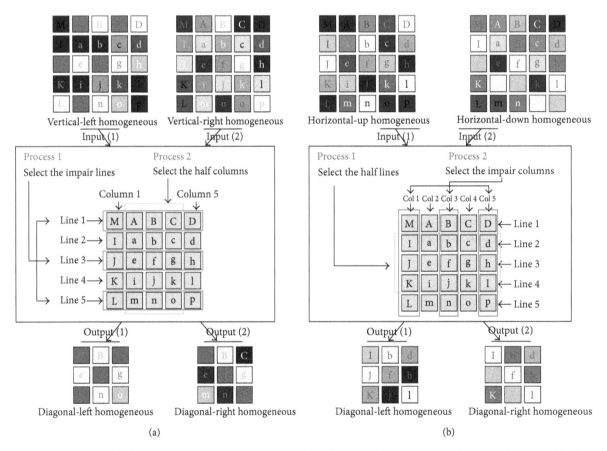

FIGURE 3: (a) The two 5×5 blocks and their corresponding square subblocks formed by ILHC method. (b) The two 5×5 blocks and their corresponding square subblocks formed by ICHL method.

The coordinates of the mass center of this block can be written as

$$G_x = \frac{1}{S_I} \sum_{x=-m}^{m} \sum_{y=-m}^{m} I_{x,y} \times x$$

$$= \frac{1}{S_I} \sum_{x=-m}^{m} N \times I_{x,0} \times x,$$

$$G_y = \frac{1}{S_I} \sum_{y=-m}^{m} \sum_{x=-m}^{m} I_{x,y} \times y$$

$$= \frac{1}{S_I} \sum_{y=1}^{m} \left[\sum_{x=-m}^{m} I_{x,y} \times y + \sum_{x=-m}^{m} I_{x,-y} \times (-y) \right]$$

$$= 0.$$

$$(5)$$

Hence, the mass center vector of this block is $\mathbf{G} = (\kappa, 0)$, where κ is a constant value. From these computations, we found that the direction of the mass center vector is parallel to the symmetry axis direction of this block.

Horizontal direction correlation block: we let L_h be the line through the origin O and parallel to the vector

$V_h = (0, y)$, where y is an integer number except zero. This line L_h is the symmetry line of the horizontal direction correlation block (see observation 1). The pixels of this block that are symmetrical with this line L_h have the same intensity. This later expression can be written by this equality

$$I_{x,y} = I_{-x,y}, \quad -m \le x, y \le m. \tag{6}$$

The coordinates of the mass center of this block can be written as

$$G_x = \frac{1}{S_I} \sum_{x=1}^{m} \left[\sum_{y=-m}^{m} I_{x,y} \times x + \sum_{y=-m}^{m} I_{-x,y} \times (-x) \right] = 0$$

$$G_y = \frac{1}{S_I} \sum_{y=-m}^{m} \sum_{x=-m}^{m} I_{x,y} \times y. \tag{7}$$

$$= \frac{1}{S_I} \sum_{y=-m}^{m} N \times I_{0,y} \times y.$$

From these computations, the mass center vector of horizontal direction correlation block is written by $\mathbf{G} = (0, \kappa)$, where κ is a constant value. Then the direction of this vector $\mathbf{G}$ is parallel to the symmetry axis of this block. □

2.3. Mass Center Direction and Intraprediction Mode Candidates in H.264/AVC. In H.264/AVC, intraprediction uses different block sizes, and each block has a limited number of the intraprediction direction. Hence, we use the angle of the mass center vector of the block to determine the intraprediction mode of this block.

2.3.1. 4 × 4 Luma Block Directional Correlation. The 4 × 4 luma blocks are more suitable to predict the pictures with significant details. There are nine prediction modes, the DC prediction mode and eight directional prediction modes. We classified these directional prediction modes into three classes: the first class, named by class 1, contains the mode 0: the vertical prediction mode, mode 1: the horizontal prediction mode, mode 3: the diagonal-left mode, and mode 4: the diagonal-right mode. The second class, named by class 2, contains the mode 5: the vertical-right mode and mode 7: the vertical-left mode. The third class, named by class 3, contain mode 6: the horizontal-down mode and mode 8: the horizontal-up mode. In the following, the corresponding

mass center direction of each mode of each classes modes prediction of the 4 × 4 blocks is determined:

$$I4 \times 4 = \begin{cases} \text{Mode 3} & \beta_1 \in \left] \dfrac{3\pi}{16} + k\pi, \dfrac{5\pi}{16} + k\pi \right] \\[2mm] \text{Mode 0} & \beta_1 \in \left] \dfrac{7\pi}{16} + k\pi, \dfrac{9\pi}{16} + k\pi \right] \\[2mm] \text{Mode 4} & \beta_1 \in \left] \dfrac{11\pi}{16} + k\pi, \dfrac{13\pi}{16} + k\pi \right] \\[2mm] \text{Mode 1} & \beta_1 \in \left[-\dfrac{\pi}{16} + k\pi, \dfrac{\pi}{16} + k\pi \right] \\[2mm] \text{Mode 5} & \beta_2 \in \left] \dfrac{11\pi}{16} + k\pi, \dfrac{13\pi}{16} + k\pi \right] \\[2mm] \text{Mode 7} & \beta_2 \in \left] \dfrac{3\pi}{16} + k\pi, \dfrac{5\pi}{16} + k\pi \right] \\[2mm] \text{Mode 6} & \beta_3 \in \left] \dfrac{11\pi}{16} + k\pi, \dfrac{13\pi}{16} + k\pi \right] \\[2mm] \text{Mode 8} & \beta_3 \in \left] \dfrac{3\pi}{16} + k\pi, \dfrac{5\pi}{16} + k\pi \right] \end{cases} \quad k = \{0, 1\}. \tag{8}$$

The angle β_1 is computed as $\beta_1 = \theta_1 - \pi/2$, where θ_1 is the angle of the 4 × 4 block mass center computed by (3). The angle β_2 is computed as $\beta_2 = \theta_2 - \pi/2$, where θ_2 is the mass center angle, computed by (3), for the subblocks formed by ICHL method. The angle β_3 is computed as $\beta_3 = \theta_3 - \pi/2$, where θ_3 is the mass center angle, computed by (3), for the subblocks formed by ILHC method.

2.3.2. 16 × 16 Luma Block Directional Correlation. In the case of 16 × 16 luma blocks, there are only horizontal and vertical prediction modes, plus a plane prediction and a DC prediction mode. So, to determine the prediction mode candidate, we associate the directional correlation for horizontal and vertical prediction modes to their corresponding areas of the block's mass center direction and the rest of this areas is associated with the plane mode.

Therefore, for each 16 × 16 luma block, the mass center direction of this block and their corresponding prediction modes are represented as follows. For each 16×16 luma block, let θ_4 be the mass center angle and let $\beta_4 = \theta_4 - \pi/2$; then

$$I16 \times 16 = \begin{cases} \text{Mode 1} & \beta_4 \in \left[-\dfrac{\pi}{8}, \dfrac{\pi}{8} \right] \cup \left[-\dfrac{\pi}{8} + \pi, \dfrac{\pi}{8} + \pi \right] \\[2mm] \text{Mode 0} & \beta_4 \in \left] \dfrac{3\pi}{8}, \dfrac{5\pi}{8} \right] \cup \left] \dfrac{3\pi}{8} + \pi, \dfrac{5\pi}{8} + \pi \right]. \end{cases} \tag{9}$$

2.4. Mode Decision Algorithm for Intraprediction. Based on the prediction mode determined by the mass center and subsampling techniques, the efficient and fast mode decision algorithms for intraprediction select a small number of the prediction modes as the best candidates to be used in RDO computation. So, we can determine the candidate mode for intracoding block size by the following rules.

Step 1. For each chroma block, two mass center directions are computed by using (3), one from component U and the other from component V. According to (9), the intraprediction mode for each component is selected.

Step 2. If these two intraprediction modes of the two components are identical; we chose this mode as the candidate intraprediction modes for RDO calculation; otherwise, the DC mode is the mode used in the RDO calculation.

Step 3. The direction of the mass center vector is computed for the 16 × 16 block by using (3). According to (9), the mode that corresponds to this direction is chosen as a candidate intraprediction mode for RDO computation. In addition to this mode, the DC mode is also chosen as the another intraprediction mode candidate for RDO computation.

Step 4. For each of the 4 × 4 luma blocks (total number is sixteen for a MB), the directions of the mass center vector of the 4 × 4 block, of the subblock formed by IHCL technique, and of the subblock formed by ICHL technique are computed by using (3).

Step 5. According to (8), the modes that correspond to these directions are chosen as a candidate intraprediction modes for RDO computation. In addition to these modes, the DC mode is also chosen as the other intraprediction mode candidate for RDO computation.

Step 6. For each of the 8 × 8 luma blocks (total number is four for a MB), the directions of the mass center vector of the 8×8 block, of the subblock formed by IHCL technique, and of the subblock formed by ICHL technique are computed by using (3).

Step 7. According to (8), the modes that correspond to these directions are chosen as a candidate intraprediction modes for RDO computation. In addition to these modes, the DC mode is also chosen as the another intraprediction mode candidate for RDO computation.

2.5. Computational Complexity Assessment. Table 1 summarizes the number of candidates selected for RDO computation by the fast intraprediction methods. As can be seen from Table 1, the encoder with the proposed algorithm would need to perform only $1 \times (1 \times 16 + 1 \times 4 + 2) = 22$ if one intraprediction mode is selected by the mass center method for each 4×4 luma blocks and one for each 8 × 8 luma block. The upper limit of RDO calculations in our algorithm is $1 \times (4 \times 16 + 4 \times 4 + 2) = 82$ if three intraprediction modes are selected by the mass center method for each 4 × 4 luma block and three for each 8 × 8 luma blocks.

From these data, our proposed algorithm significantly reduces the number of RDO calculation, compared with the method presented in [15] (between $1 \times (2 \times 16 + 2 \times 4 + 2) = 42$ and $2 \times (5 \times 16 + 5 \times 4 + 2) = 204$) and the method presented in [16] (between $1 \times (2 \times 16 + 1 \times 4 + 2) = 38$ and $2 \times (2 \times 16 + 5 \times 4 + 4) = 112$).

3. Experimental Results and Discussion

As the most previous methods do not support intra 8 × 8 block, this section presents simulation results based on Chen et al.'s algorithm [15], ELyousfi's algorithm [16],

and the proposed fast and efficient intraprediction algorithm in H.264/AVC.

3.1. Coding Conditions. All the algorithms were implemented into H.264/AVC reference software JM18.0 [23]. The system platform is the Intel (R) Core (TM)2 Duo CPU Processor of speed 3.4 GHz, 4.00 Gbytes RAM, and Microsoft Windows Vista. The simulation condition is as RD optimization is enabled, CABAC is enabled, GOP structure is full I, the number of frames of each sequence is 150, and FREXT Profile: high profile. The group of experiments were carried out on the test sequences with the 4 quantization parameters; that is, QP = 28, 32, 36, and 40. The averaged PSNR values of luma (Y) and chroma (U, V) are used and are based on the following equations:

$$\overline{\text{PSNR}} = 10 \times \log_{10} \left(\frac{255^2}{\overline{\text{MSE}}} \right), \tag{10}$$

where ($\overline{\text{MSE}}$) is the average mean square error [16].

The comparisons with the case of exhaustive search were performed with respect to the PSNR difference (ΔPSNR), the data bits rate difference (ΔBit), and the difference of coding time (ΔTime).

In order to evaluate the time saving of the fast prediction algorithm, the following calculation is defined to find the time differences. Let T_{JM} denote the coding time used by full search intraprediction algorithm of JM18.0 encoder and let T_{FI} be the time taken by the fast mode decision algorithm; the time difference is defined as

$$\Delta\text{Time} = \frac{T_{\text{FI}} - T_{\text{JM}}}{T_{\text{JM}}} \times 100\%. \tag{11}$$

PSNR and bit-rate differences are calculated according to the numerical averages between the RD-curves derived from JM18.0 encoder and the fast algorithm, respectively. The detailed procedures in calculating these differences can be found from a JVT document authored by Bjontegaard [24].

3.2. Coding Performances. In this experiment, a total number of 150 frames are used for each sequence, and the period of I-frames is set to 1; that is, all the frames in the sequence are intracoded. In all the I-frames structure encoding, for each MB in each frame of this sequence, intracoding is chosen as the possible coding modes in RDO operation; thus great time saving is expected by using the fast intracoding algorithms for this structure encoding. Table 2 shows the simulation results of the proposed algorithm and Chen et al.'s [15] and Elyousfi's [16] algorithms for various sequences with all intraframes type. Notice that in the table, positive values mean increments and negative values mean decrements.

The results show that the proposed schemes reduced execution time greater than 87.893% with only an average of 0.046 dB losses in PSNR and 0.616% increments in bitrate only. These results are compared to those obtained with Chen et al.'s [15] and Elyousfi's [16] algorithms where the time coding is reduced in average, respectively, to 63.183% and 79.689% with an average of 0.089 dB and 0.134 dB losses in

TABLE 1: Comparison of the number of candidate modes.

Algorithms	Luma 4×4	Luma 8×8	Luma 16×16	Chroma 8×8	Min and max number of RDO computation
Reference [15]	2–5	2–5	2	1-2	042–204
Reference [16]	2	1–5	2–4	1-2	038–112
Proposed	1–4	1–4	2	1	022–082

TABLE 2: Simulation results for all intraframes sequences.

Sequences		$\Delta Time$			$\Delta PSNR$			$\Delta Bitrate$		
Format	Name	Reference [15]	Reference [16]	Proposed	Reference [15]	Reference [16]	Proposed	Reference [15]	Reference [16]	Proposed
QCIF	Silent	−64.855	−87.711	−92.890	−0.088	−0.134	−0.044	0.994	1.219	0.327
	Container	−64.309	−80.062	−89.733	−0.106	−0.148	−0.050	1.020	1.369	0.488
	Foreman	−60.426	−74.167	−84.592	−0.119	−0.153	−0.048	1.952	2.682	1.203
	Hall	−68.100	−87.697	−93.747	−0.056	−0.129	−0.033	1.003	1.205	0.340
CIF	Foreman	−63.571	−75.347	−83.283	−0.103	−0.187	−0.069	2.884	3.110	1.084
	Coastguard	−61.330	−75.066	−82.891	−0.147	−0.159	−0.053	2.922	3.790	1.347
	Paris	−59.846	−76.884	−84.694	−0.085	−0.094	−0.031	1.470	2.178	0.728
	News	−66.109	−87.650	−93.455	−0.047	−0.127	−0.024	0.825	1.090	0.390
720 p	Crew	−67.466	−82.388	−90.176	−0.089	−0.107	−0.055	1.077	1.146	0.366
	Parkrun	−54.992	−71.105	−83.800	−0.072	−0.122	−0.058	0.962	1.130	0.288
	Shields	−64.004	−78.503	−87.561	−0.069	−0.113	−0.041	0.883	1.193	0.211
Average		−63.183	−79.689	−87.893	−0.089	−0.134	−0.046	1.454	1.828	0.616

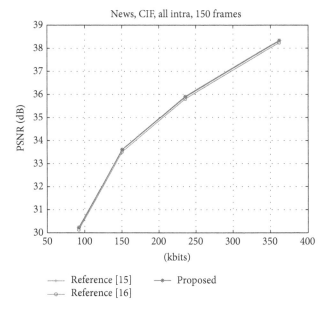

FIGURE 4: Comparison of PSNR for the all intrasequences of news.

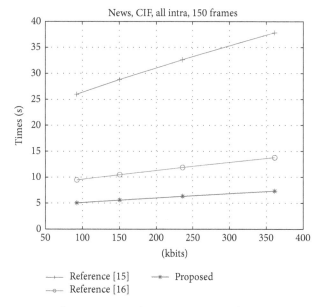

FIGURE 5: The computational time comparison of news all intrasequence.

PSNR and, respectively, 1.454% and 1.828% increments in bitrate.

The proposed schemes achieve faster encoding in intraprediction compared to the Chen et al.'s [15] and Elyousfi's [16], with little RD performance enhancement. Figures 4 and 5 show the RD performance and the computation time for the all I-frames sequence "News," respectively. In Figure 4, three RD curves resulting from the Chen et al.'s algorithm [15], Elyousfi's algorithm [16], and the proposed

schemes are nearly overlapping each other that our proposed algorithm has greater performances as compared to the other approaches in terms of PSNR and data bits but offers higher computation time saving as shown in Figure 5.

4. Conclusion

This paper presented an improved fast intraprediction in H.264/AVC algorithm based on mass center method and two subsampling techniques. Extensive experimental results show that the proposed method can achieve 87.893% total encoding time reduction with only 0.046 dB PSNR degradation and 0.616% bit rate increase on average. This performance is more efficient than most of the well-known fast intramode decision algorithms for H.264/AVC.

Conflict of Interests

The author declares that there is no conflict of interests regarding the publication of this paper.

References

[1] G. J. Sullivan, P. Topiwala, and A. Luthra, "The H.264/AVC advanced video coding standard: overview and introduction to the fidelity range extensions," in *Applications of Digital Image Processing XXVII*, vol. 5558 of *Proceedings Of SPIE*, pp. 454–474, Denver, Colo, USA, August 2004.

[2] ITU-T Recommendation H. 264 and ISO/IEC, 14496-10 (MPEG-4) AVC, "Advanced Video Coding for Generic Audiovisual Services," (version 1: 2003, version 2: 2004) version 3: 2005.

[3] T. Wiegand, G. J. Sullivan, G. Bjøntegaard, and A. Luthra, "Overview of the H.264/AVC video coding standard," *IEEE Transactions on Circuits and Systems for Video Technology*, vol. 13, no. 7, pp. 560–576, 2003.

[4] A. Puri, X. Chen, and A. Luthra, "Video coding using the H.264/MPEG-4 AVC compression standard," *Signal Processing: Image Communication*, vol. 19, no. 9, pp. 793–849, 2004.

[5] I. E. G. Richardson, *H. 264 and MPEG4 Video Compression: Video Coding for Next Generation Multimedia*, John Wiley & Sons, 2003.

[6] ISO/IEC, "Report of The Formal Verification Tests on AVC, (ISO/IEC, 14496-10—ITU-T Rec.H.264)," Tech. Rep. ISO/IEC JTC1/SC29/WG11 MPEG2003/N6231, ISO/IEC, Waikoloa, Hawaii, USA, 2003.

[7] G. J. Sullivan and T. Wiegand, "Rate-distortion optimization for: video compression," *IEEE Signal Processing Magazine*, vol. 15, no. 6, pp. 74–90, 1998.

[8] T. Wiegand, H. Schwarz, A. Joch, F. Kossentini, and G. J. Sullivan, "Rate-constrained coder control and comparison of video coding standards," *IEEE Transactions on Circuits and Systems for Video Technology*, vol. 13, no. 7, pp. 688–703, 2003.

[9] H. Li, K. N. Ngan, and Z. Wei, "Fast and efficient method for block edge classification and its application in H.264/AVC video coding," *IEEE Transactions on Circuits and Systems for Video Technology*, vol. 18, no. 6, pp. 756–768, 2008.

[10] A.-C. Tsai, A. Paul, J.-C. Wang, and J.-F. Wang, "Intensity gradient technique for efficient intra-prediction in H.264/AVC," *IEEE Transactions on Circuits and Systems for Video Technology*, vol. 18, no. 5, pp. 694–698, 2008.

[11] A.-C. Tsai, J.-F. Wang, J.-F. Yang, and W.-G. Lin, "Effective subblock-based and pixel-based fast direction detections for H.264 intra prediction," *IEEE Transactions on Circuits and Systems for Video Technology*, vol. 18, no. 7, pp. 975–982, 2008.

[12] K. Bharanitharan, B.-D. Liu, J.-F. Yang, and W.-C. Tsai, "A low complexity detection of discrete cross differences for fast H.264/AVC intra prediction," *IEEE Transactions on Multimedia*, vol. 10, no. 7, pp. 1250–1260, 2008.

[13] Y.-H. Huang, T.-S. Ou, and H. H. Chen, "Fast decision of block size, prediction mode, and intra block for H.264 intra prediction," *IEEE Transactions on Circuits and Systems for Video Technology*, vol. 20, no. 8, pp. 1122–1132, 2010.

[14] R. Su, G. Liu, and T. Zhang, "Fast mode decision algorithm for intra prediction in H.264/AVC with integer transform and adaptive threshold," *Signal, Image and Video Processing*, vol. 1, no. 1, pp. 11–27, 2007.

[15] C. Chen, J. Chen, T. Xia, Z. Ju, and L. Po, "An improved hybrid fast mode decision method for H. 264/AVC intra coding with local information," *Multimed Tools and Applications*, 2013.

[16] A. Elyousfi, "Gravity direction-based ultra-fast intraprediction algorithm for H.264/AVC video coding," *Journal Signal, Image and Video Processing*, vol. 7, no. 1, pp. 53–65, 2013.

[17] D. Quan and Y.-S. Ho, "Categorization for fast intra prediction mode decision in H.264/AVC," *IEEE Transactions on Consumer Electronics*, vol. 56, no. 2, pp. 1049–1056, 2010.

[18] K. Lim, S. Kim, J. Lee, D. Pak, and S. Lee, "Fast block size and mode decision algorithm for intra prediction in H.264/AVC," *IEEE Transactions on Consumer Electronics*, vol. 58, no. 2, pp. 654–660, 2012.

[19] J. W. Chen, C. H. Chang, C. C. Lin, Y. H. Yang, J. I. Guo, and J. S. Wang, "A condition-based intra prediction algorithm for H.264/AVC," in *Proceedings of the IEEE International Conference on Multimedia and Expo (ICME '06)*, pp. 1077–1080, Ontario, Canada, July 2006.

[20] F. Fu, X. Lin, and L. Xu, "Fast intra prediction algorithm in H.264/AVC," in *Proceedings of the 7th International Conference on Signal Processing Proceedings (ICSP '04)*, pp. 1191–1194, Beijing, China, September 2004.

[21] B.-G. Kim, "Fast selective intra-mode search algorithm based on adaptive thresholding scheme for H.264/AVC encoding," *IEEE Transactions on Circuits and Systems for Video Technology*, vol. 18, no. 1, pp. 127–133, 2008.

[22] J. Kim and J. Jeong, "Fast intra-mode decision in H.264 video coding using simple directional masks," in *Visual Communications and Image Processing*, vol. 5960 of *Proceedings Of SPIE*, pp. 1071–1079, Beijing China, July 2005.

[23] H. 264/AVC, "JM Reference Software Version 18.0," http://iphome.hhi.de/suehring/tml/download/.

[24] G. Bjontegaard, "Calculation of average PSNR differences between RD-curves," in *Proceedings of the 13-th VCEG Meeting*, Austin, Tex, USA, April 2001, Document VCEG-M33.

8

Macroblock Layer Rate Control Based on Structural Similarity and Mean Absolute Difference for H.264

Xiao Chen[1,2] and Dongjue Gu[2]

[1] Jiangsu Key Laboratory of Meteorological Observation and Information Processing, Nanjing University of Information Science and
   Technology, Nanjing 210044, China
[2] School of Electronic and Information Engineering, Nanjing University of Information Science and Technology, Nanjing 210044, China

Correspondence should be addressed to Xiao Chen; rainofsun@netease.com

Academic Editor: Costas Kotropoulos

In the process of the H.264 video coding, special attention should be paid to the subjective quality of the image. This paper applies the structural similarity (SSIM) based subjective evaluation to the rate control in the H.264 coding and proposes to combine the SSIM and the mean absolute difference (MAD) to perform the macroblock layer bit allocation instead of the MAD. Experimental results show that the proposed method is correlating better with the human visual system and thus achieves better subjective image quality.

1. Introduction

The JVT-G012 algorithm for the H.264 video coding uses the mean absolute difference (MAD) linear prediction model to solve the "chicken and egg dilemma" [1]. The basic unit layer number of bits (including the macroblock layer) is allocated averagely. As JM10.1 adopts the method, the distribution scheme mainly allocates the bit rate from the content of the complexity of the natural image. It has some disadvantages— it does not allocate the bit rate according to the human's subjective characteristic. The obtained image is not consistent with the subjective characteristics of the human eyes.

Some scholars made a lot of improvement to overcome these shortcomings. For example, Lu put forward the motion extrapolated coding complexity to allocate bits between the region of interest (ROI) and other regions which reduced the distortion in the ROI using the rate distortion optimized macroblock level bit allocation [2]. Han et al. used a content complexity factor to allocate the bits more accurately and a quantization parameter adaptation factor to adjust the current quantization parameter according to the encoded frames history information [3]. Chen and Lu put forward the frame complexity factor to optimize the frame layer target bit allocation [4]. Liu et al. combine an inter-frame subtraction with the background subtraction to detect the target region

[5]. To achieve the purpose of high-definition of the target region under the low bit rate, an optimized rate control scheme is proposed. But these methods are not, according to the HVS (human visual system) model, to allocate the bits of the macroblock.

Wang et al. proposed the SSIM (structural similarity) as a new indicator to measure the similarity of two images. It is a method used for evaluating the quality of image [6]. Due to the fact that the human visual can extract image structure information easily, the calculation of two-image structure similarity can be used as a standard to evaluate the image quality. The bigger the value is, the better the quality is. The biggest of the SSIM is 1. The SSIM is better than the MSE (Mean Squared Error) and the PSNR (peak signal to noise ratio) in the image similarity evaluation.

Cui et al. put forward an empirical model of the SSIM linear distortion model and combined it with the improved secondly rate-quantitative model using Lagrange multiplier method to get the closed solution of the SSIM optimal MB layer quantization [7]. Cui et al. also used the SSIM to guide the RDO frame mode selection [8]. Wang et al. put forward a method of interest video quality evaluation method [9]. The method presented the extraction of the frame's interest area to weigh the calculated SSIM of the block in the frame. Yang et al. introduced the SSIM as the distortion measurement for the H.264 interframe prediction [10]. Yang et al. found the myopia relationship between the SSIM and rate, and then it was integrated into SSE as distortion measure of RDO function and combined with human visual characteristics [11]. It built the distortion measure of RDO model combining the SSE with the SSIM. Cui and Zhu applied the SSIM based subjective distortion to RDO-based intramode decision in H.264 I frame coding, and they further proposed a frame layer adaptive Lagrange multiplier adjustment scheme to get better tradeoff between the rate and the SSIM distortion [12]. Wu et al. used the relationship between the reconstructed macroblock and the best prediction macroblock from mode selection [13]. Cui and Zhu put forward a kind of the adaptive skipped frame scheme by recovering the skip frame in the decoding port through the reference frame [14].

The above methods did not use the SSIM to allocate the bits of the macroblock layer. This paper will focus on how to use the SSIM theory to allocate the bit of the macroblock layer in order to improve the subjective video quality.

2. Improved Rate Control in MB

The pixels of the image are related. This contains the structural information of the image. In the observation of the image, the human eyes are more sensitive to changes of the structure information than individual pixel values. In the SSIM theory, the SSIM index is defined from the view of image composition, which reflects the scene object structure properties. It is independent of the brightness and contrast of the image. The distortion modeling is built as the combination of three different factors—brightness, contrast, and structure. The SSIM of the original image x to the distorted image y is defined as [6]

$$
\text{SSIM} = \frac{\left(2u_x u_y + c_1\right)\left(2\delta_{xy} + c_2\right)}{\left(u_x^2 + u_y^2 + c_1\right)\left(\delta_x^2 + \delta_y^2 + c_2\right)}, \tag{1}
$$

where u_x and u_y are the brightness mean of the images x and y, δ_x^2 and δ_y^2 are the standard deviation the images x and y, δ_{xy} is the covariance between them, and c_1 and c_2 are the small constants in order to avoid that the denominator is zero. In the calculation of frame SSIM, the general is to divide the image into the fixed size MBs and then calculate the SSIM of each MB. The SSIM measurement has a boundary, which is not more than 1. The closer the value is to 1, the better the subjective quality of the distorted image is. The higher SSIM value implies that the similarity between the distorted image and the original image is high, so the image quality is better. Therefore, the distortion of the ith MB in the P frame can be defined as 1-SSIM(i).

The MBs in the same position of the adjacent frames have strong temporal correlation and thus have the similar SSIM distortion characteristics. Therefore, the SSIM of the current MB can be estimated by the actual SSIM of the same position MB in the previous frame.

In the JVT-G012 algorithm for the H.264 video coding, the bit rate of the MB is allocated averagely. The obtained image is not consistent with the subjective characteristics

of the human eyes. This paper applies the SSIM based subjective evaluation to the rate control in the H.264 coding and proposes to combine the SSIM and the mean absolute difference to perform the MB layer bit allocation instead of the mean absolute difference.

The implementation of rate control for the MB layer mainly includes the bit allocation, calculations of the quantization parameter, and buffer control. First, we allocate the target bits according to the remaining bits, SSIM and MAD. Then, we calculate the quantization parameter and adjust it. Last, we perform rate-distortion-optimization (RDO) and update the model parameters.

Firstly, the bit $R(i)$ of the ith MB in the frame is allocated by

$$
R(i) = T_r \left[a \frac{[1 - \text{SSIM}(i)]^2}{\sum_{k=1}^{N} [1 - \text{SSIM}(k)]^2} + b \frac{\text{MAD}_{\text{EMV}}(i)^2}{\sum_{k=1}^{N} \text{MAD}_{\text{EMV}}(k)^2} \right], \tag{2}
$$

where i is the serial number of the MB in the frame, N is the total number of the MBs in the frame, and k is the loop variable. a and b are the weighted coefficients to allocate bits and $a + b = 1$. T_r is the remaining bits in the frame. SSIM(i) represents the SSIM of the ith MB in the frame; $\text{MAD}_{\text{EMV}}(i)$ represents the MAD of the ith MB in the frame. a and b are 0.4 and 0.6 after taking a lot of experiments.

Then, the quantization parameter of the current MB is computerized by using the quadratic R-D model. However, the inaccuracy of the model can produce the unexpected coded bits. Therefore, we adjust the current quantization parameter by the previous MB coding information, which can achieve more accurate rate control. In order to avoid the adjacent MBs' image quality jump too much, we adjust the quantization parameter. If the current macroblock is the first basic unit in the current frame, $\text{QP} = Q_{\text{apf}}$, Q_{apf} is the average quantization parameter of all the basic units in the previous frame. If the bit number of current frame is less than zero, the quantization parameter should be greater than that of the previous basic unit in order that the sum of generated bits is closed to the current frame bits. Therefore, $\text{QP} = \text{QP}_{\text{prev}} + 1$ where QP_{prev} is the quantization parameter of the previous macro block. Otherwise, using the quadratic model to compute a quantization parameter, $\text{QP} = \max\{\text{QP}_{\text{prev}} - 1, \min\{\text{QP}, \text{QP}_{\text{prev}} + 1\}\}$.

Finally, the algorithm has taken into account the coded frame information fully after the adjustment. We perform RDO and update the model parameters. In this paper, the SSIM is incorporated into the RDO framework as a quality metric [15] for all MBs in the current basic unit. For convenience, the method in reference 15 is called PRDO method.

3. Experimental Results and Discussions

The proposed algorithm in this paper is realized by enhancing the JM10.1 test model. The main experimenters are shown in Table 1. The purpose of the proposed algorithm is to improve the video subjective quality, so the original JM10.1 rate control algorithm is selected as a reference for the comparison,

(a)   (b)

FIGURE 1: The image subjective quality comparison of the 3rd (a) and 76th (b) frame for the carphone sequence.

because the bit allocation method in the JM10.1 algorithm is better than the original JVT-G012 algorithm. The proposed algorithm is also compared with the PRDO algorithm.

3.1. Subjective Visual Quality. Figures 1 and 2 give some subjective renderings for the carphone and foreman sequences of the proposed, JM10.1, and PRDO algorithms at the bit rate of 64 kbps. From the view of human being's eyes, the image

structure information of the proposed algorithm is better than the JM10.1 algorithm as shown in the figures (the top is original image, the middle is obtained from the proposed algorithm, and the bottom is obtained from JM10.1).

3.2. SSIM. Figures 3 and 4 show the SSIM comparison from the first to the one hundredth frame of the carphone and foreman sequences by using the proposed, JM10.1, and PRDO

(a)   (b)

FIGURE 2: The image subjective quality comparison of the 69th (a) and 82nd (b) frame for the foreman sequence.

TABLE 1: The main experimental parameters.

Coding mode	Format	Frame rate	Frame number	Target bitrate	Iframe circle	Search range	ME precision	Reference frame numer	Entropy coding	RDO
IPPP	QCIF	30 fps	100	64 kbps	20	16	1/4	1	CAVLC	on

algorithms. As can be seen from the figures, the proposed algorithm improves the SSIM of the video sequence. The SSIM obtained from the proposed algorithm is better than other two algorithms. So it has the better subjective video quality.

Tables 2, 3, and 4 show the average SSIM of the proposed, JM10.1, and PRDO algorithms for the carphone, crew, highway, claire, and foreman sequences at the bit rates of 64, 128, 256, and 512 kbps when the initial quantization parameter is set to 23, 28, and 33, respectively. According to tables,

the proposed algorithm gets better average SSIM than the other algorithms for all video sequences at all bit rates. So the proposed algorithm can achieve better subjective video quality than other algorithms during the video coding.

3.3. PSNR. Figures 5 and 6 show the PSNR comparison from the first to the one hundredth frame of the carphone and foreman sequences by using the proposed, JM10.1, and PRDO algorithms. As can be seen from figures, the PSNR differences

TABLE 2: Average SSIM comparison of the proposed, PRDO, and JM10.1 algorithms (QP = 23).

Sequence	Target bit rate (kbps)	JM10.1	PRDO	Proposed
Crew	64	0.6032	0.6113	0.6140
Carphone	64	0.7851	0.7926	0.7954
Highway	64	0.7810	0.7879	0.7908
Foreman	64	0.7365	0.7468	0.7500
Claire	64	0.7498	0.7569	0.7597
Crew	128	0.7495	0.7560	0.7581
Carphone	128	0.8252	0.8321	0.8348
Highway	128	0.8235	0.8341	0.8362
Foreman	128	0.8452	0.8515	0.8540
Claire	128	0.8015	0.8078	0.8107
Crew	256	0.8634	0.8694	0.8722
Carphone	256	0.8853	0.8911	0.8943
Highway	256	0.8481	0.8544	0.8565
Foreman	256	0.8984	0.9025	0.9058
Claire	256	0.8433	0.8494	0.8519
Crew	512	0.9249	0.9280	0.9305
Carphone	512	0.9105	0.9146	0.9173
Highway	512	0.8742	0.8787	0.8815
Foreman	512	0.9368	0.9402	0.8424
Claire	512	0.8566	0.8619	0.8648

TABLE 3: Average SSIM comparison of the proposed, PRDO, and JM10.1 algorithms (QP = 28).

Sequence	Target bit rate (kbps)	JM10.1	PRDO	Proposed
Crew	64	0.6330	0.6409	0.6434
Carphone	64	0.7703	0.7788	0.7819
Highway	64	0.7748	0.7815	0.7846
Foreman	64	0.7611	0.7686	0.7717
Claire	64	0.7135	0.7215	0.7250
Crew	128	0.7710	0.7791	0.7815
Carphone	128	0.8430	0.8497	0.8529
Highway	128	0.8142	0.8198	0.8219
Foreman	128	0.8263	0.8332	0.8359
Claire	128	0.7753	0.7829	0.7855
Crew	256	0.8614	0.8678	0.8706
Carphone	256	0.8770	0.8829	0.8864
Highway	256	0.8428	0.8477	0.8503
Foreman	256	0.8862	0.8908	0.8942
Claire	256	0.8319	0.8378	0.8409
Crew	512	0.9236	0.9275	0.9296
Carphone	512	0.9071	0.9122	0.9146
Highway	512	0.8694	0.8742	0.8775
Foreman	512	0.9328	0.9359	0.9380
Claire	512	0.8437	0.8491	0.8524

of three algorithms are very small. The proposed algorithm achieves a little higher PSNR than the other two algorithms.

3.4. Bit Rate. Tables 5, 6, and 7 show the bit rates of the proposed, JM10.1, and PRDO algorithms for the carphone, crew, highway, claire, and foreman sequences at the target bit rates of 64, 128, 256, and 512 kbps when the initial quantization parameter is set to 23, 28, and 33, respectively. As summarized in the tables, the proposed algorithm can control the bit rates more accurately than the other two algorithms.

The experimental results show that the proposed algorithm in this paper makes the macroblock layer bit rate

TABLE 4: Average SSIM comparison of the proposed, PRDO, and JM10.1 algorithms (QP = 33).

Sequence	Target bit rate (kbps)	JM10.1	PRDO	Proposed
Crew	64	0.6385	0.7461	0.7492
Carphone	64	0.7839	0.7908	0.7939
Highway	64	0.7540	0.7611	0.7641
Foreman	64	0.7572	0.7643	0.7670
Claire	64	0.6750	0.6835	0.6869
Crew	128	0.7683	0.7763	0.7787
Carphone	128	0.8333	0.8405	0.8434
Highway	128	0.7982	0.8050	0.8078
Foreman	128	0.8195	0.8266	0.8295
Claire	128	0.7860	0.7939	0.7972
Crew	256	0.8592	0.8657	0.8684
Carphone	256	0.8745	0.8801	0.8834
Highway	256	0.8274	0.8339	0.8366
Foreman	256	0.8820	0.8869	0.8893
Claire	256	0.8204	0.8256	0.8284
Crew	512	0.9142	0.9193	0.9214
Carphone	512	0.8974	0.9015	0.9037
Highway	512	0.8561	0.8608	0.8633
Foreman	512	0.9254	0.9334	0.9353
Claire	512	0.8419	0.8470	0.8499

TABLE 5: Bit rate comparison of the JM10.1, the PRDO, and the proposed algorithms (QP = 23).

Sequence	Target bit rate (kbps)	JM10.1 (kbps)	PRDO (kbps)	Proposed (kbps)
Crew	64	78.59	65.89	65.32
Carphone	64	64.38	64.42	64.26
Highway	64	64.83	64.71	64.54
Foreman	64	64.28	64.25	64.23
Claire	64	64.31	64.27	64.25
Crew	128	128.37	128.32	128.29
Carphone	128	128.60	128.53	128.47
Highway	128	129.71	129.43	129.27
Foreman	128	128.51	128.36	128.33
Claire	128	128.62	128.45	128.38
Crew	256	256.13	256.11	256.17
Carphone	256	256.34	256.27	256.21
Highway	256	257.07	256.89	256.77
Foreman	256	256.54	256.43	256.31
Claire	256	257.04	256.78	256.73
Crew	512	512.14	512.16	512.22
Carphone	512	512.25	512.21	512.16
Highway	512	512.34	512.24	512.21
Foreman	512	512.56	512.37	512.29
Claire	512	513.42	513.12	512.95

allocation more reasonable and improves the subjective image quality, which allocates the macroblock layer rate from the two angles of the image structure similarity and the close degree of the content. What is more, it improves the continuity of the video sequences. Compared with JM10.1 and PRDO, the video effect of the proposed algorithm is also better.

4. Conclusions

This paper presents a rate control algorithm for H.264 video coding by using the SSIM and the MAD to allocate the bit number of the macroblock, and then it performs some measurements to adjust the quantization parameter. The

TABLE 6: Bit rate comparison of the JM10.1, the PRDO, and the proposed algorithms (QP = 28).

Sequence	Target bit rate (kbps)	JM10.1 (kbps)	PRDO (kbps)	Proposed (kbps)
Crew	64	64.35	64.29	64.25
Carphone	64	64.38	64.31	64.29
Highway	64	64.96	64.72	64.57
Foreman	64	64.31	64.28	64.25
Claire	64	64.31	64.29	64.23
Crew	128	128.11	128.25	128.27
Carphone	128	128.57	128.36	128.31
Highway	128	129.30	128.98	128.79
Foreman	128	128.47	128.35	128.29
Claire	128	128.60	128.49	128.45
Crew	256	256.08	256.13	256.18
Carphone	256	256.44	256.31	256.19
Highway	256	257.53	257.12	256.88
Foreman	256	256.50	256.39	256.34
Claire	256	257.15	256.87	256.56
Crew	512	512.04	512.24	512.29
Carphone	512	512.07	512.05	512.13
Highway	512	512.21	512.19	512.17
Foreman	512	512.48	512.43	512.34
Claire	512	514.41	513.57	513.21

TABLE 7: Bit rate comparison of the JM10.1, the PRDO, and the proposed algorithms (QP = 33).

Sequence	Target bit rate (kbps)	JM10.1 (kbps)	PRDO (kbps)	Proposed (kbps)
Crew	64	64.35	64.29	64.31
Carphone	64	64.36	64.34	64.28
Highway	64	64.80	64.67	64.53
Foreman	64	64.26	64.31	64.25
Claire	64	64.34	64.43	64.32
Crew	128	128.10	128.17	128.25
Carphone	128	128.55	128.48	128.36
Highway	128	129.45	128.87	128.57
Foreman	128	128.50	128.46	128.41
Claire	128	128.58	128.44	128.39
Crew	256	256.10	256.31	256.24
Carphone	256	256.06	256.17	256.19
Highway	256	256.26	256.31	256.24
Foreman	256	256.46	256.35	256.21
Claire	256	257.16	256.88	256.63
Crew	512	512.04	512.21	512.26
Carphone	512	511.93	512.11	512.06
Highway	512	512.09	512.07	512.05
Foreman	512	512.38	512.28	512.26
Claire	512	504.10	512.25	512.23

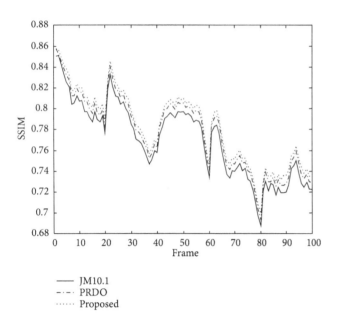

FIGURE 3: The SSIM of carphone.

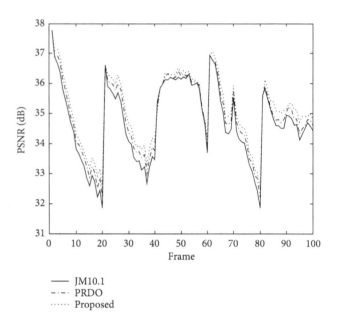

FIGURE 5: The PSNR of carphone.

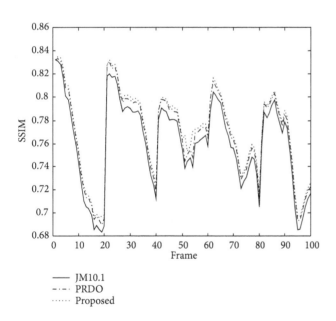

FIGURE 4: The SSIM of foreman.

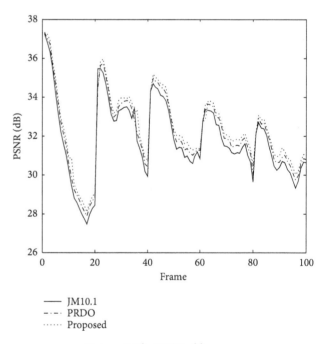

FIGURE 6: The PSNR of foreman.

experiment results show that the algorithm can improve the SSIM of the video sequence in the condition of ensuring the PSNR. So it can improve the subjective quality of the video sequence.

Conflict of Interests

The authors declare that there is no conflict of interests regarding the publication of this paper.

Acknowledgments

This work was supported by the Qing Lan Project and the Priority Academic Program Development of Jiangsu Higher Education Institutions.

References

[1] Zh. Li, F. Pan, K. P. Lim et al., "Adaptive basic unit layer rate control for JVT," in *Proceedings of the 7th Joint Video Team*

Meeting of ISO/IEC MPEG and ITU-T VCEG, Pattaya, Thailand, 2003.

[2] Y. Lu, H. Li, Y. Zhang, and H. Cui, "Consistent perceptual quality rate control in H.264 region of interest video coding," *Journal of Tsinghua University*, vol. 49, no. 1, pp. 90–93, 2009.

[3] Z. Han, K. Tang, and H. Cui, "Rate control method based on the standard H.264," *Journal of Tsinghua University*, vol. 48, no. 1, pp. 59–61, 2008.

[4] X. Chen and F. Lu, "A reformative frame layer rate control algorithm for H.264," *IEEE Transactions on Consumer Electronics*, vol. 56, no. 4, pp. 2806–2811, 2010.

[5] X. Liu, Y. Li, Y. Gao, and H. Zhang, "A coding strategy of H. 264 based on high- definition display of target region," *Computer Technology and Development*, vol. 20, no. 6, pp. 29–31, 2010.

[6] Z. Wang, A. C. Bovik, H. R. Sheikh, and E. P. Simoncelli, "Image quality assessment: from error visibility to structural similarity," *IEEE Transactions on Image Processing*, vol. 13, no. 4, pp. 600–612, 2004.

[7] Z. Cui, Z. Gan, and X. Zhu, "Structural similarity optimal MB layer rate control for H.264," in *Proceedings of the International Conference on Wireless Communications and Signal Processing (WCSP '11)*, November 2011.

[8] Z.-G. Cui and X.-C. Zhu, "Subjective rate-distortion performance improvement scheme for H.264 based on SSIM," *Journal of Electronics and Information Technology*, vol. 34, no. 2, pp. 433–439, 2012.

[9] Z. Wang, G. Hu, J. Ming, and H. Wu, "Video quality assessment based on SSIM and ROI," *Chinese Journal of Scientific Instrument*, vol. 30, no. 9, pp. 1906–1911, 2009.

[10] C.-L. Yang, H.-X. Wang, and R.-K. Liang, "Improved inter prediction based on structural similarity for H.264," *Chinese Journal of Computers*, vol. 32, no. 8, pp. 1603–1610, 2009.

[11] C.-L. Yang and D.-Q. Xiao, "Improvements for H.264 intra mode selection based on SSE and SSIM," *Journal of Electronics and Information Technology*, vol. 33, no. 2, pp. 289–294, 2011.

[12] Z. Cui and X. Zhu, "Subjective quality optimized intra mode selection for H.264 I frame coding based on SSIM," in *Proceedings of the 6th International Conference on Image and Graphics (ICIG '11)*, pp. 157–162, August 2011.

[13] G. Wu, Y. Fu, and S. Chien, "System design of perceptual quality-regulable H. 264 video encoder," in *Proceedings of The IEEE International Conference on Multimedia and Expo*, pp. 509–514, 2012.

[14] Z. Cui and X. Zhu, "SSIM-based content adaptive frame skipping for low bit rate H.264 video coding," in *Proceedings of the 12th International Conference on Communication Technology (ICCT '10)*, pp. 484–487, November 2010.

[15] T.-S. Ou, Y.-H. Huang, and H. H. Chen, "SSIM-based perceptual rate control for video coding," *IEEE Transactions on Circuits and Systems for Video Technology*, vol. 21, no. 5, pp. 682–691, 2011.

9

Adaptive Transformation for Robust Privacy Protection in Video Surveillance

Mukesh Saini,[1] Pradeep K. Atrey,[2] Sharad Mehrotra,[3] and Mohan Kankanhalli[1]

[1] *School of Computing, National University of Singapore, Singapore 117417*
[2] *Department of Applied Computer Science, The University of Winnipeg, MB, Canada R3T 5V9*
[3] *Information and Computer Science Department, University of California, Irvine, CA 92697-3425, USA*

Correspondence should be addressed to Mukesh Saini, mksaini@comp.nus.edu.sg

Academic Editor: Martin Reisslein

Privacy is a big concern in current video surveillance systems. Due to privacy issues, many strategic places remain unmonitored leading to security threats. The main problem with existing privacy protection methods is that they assume availability of accurate region of interest (RoI) detectors that can detect and hide the privacy sensitive regions such as faces. However, the current detectors are not fully reliable, leading to breaches in privacy protection. In this paper, we propose a privacy protection method that adopts adaptive data transformation involving the use of selective obfuscation and global operations to provide robust privacy even with unreliable detectors. Further, there are many implicit privacy leakage channels that have not been considered by researchers for privacy protection. We block both implicit and explicit channels of privacy leakage. Experimental results show that the proposed method incurs 38% less distortion of the information needed for surveillance in comparison to earlier methods of global transformation; while still providing near-zero privacy loss.

1. Introduction

In order to perform privacy-preserving CCTV monitoring, video data should be transformed in such a way that the information leaking the identity is hidden, but the intended surveillance tasks can be accomplished. The traditional approach of data transformation has been to detect the regions of interest (RoI) in the images (e.g., human faces) and selectively obfuscate them. This approach is an unreliable solution as the RoI detectors may sometimes fail. For example, even if a face detector is able to correctly detect the face in 99 (out of 100) frames, the undetected faces in the remaining frame will reveal the identity of the person in the video and result in his/her privacy loss.

In other set of works, global operations have been used for data transformation in which the whole video frame is transformed with same intensity, that is, same amount of blurring or quantization [1]. This approach is more appropriate in the context of data publication, where the published surveillance video is used by researchers for testing their algorithms. In contrast to the data publication scenario, CCTV

monitoring scenario has different requirements. In the case of CCTV monitoring, a human operator is required to watch the surveillance video feeds; although automated techniques may run in the background as shown in Figure 1. The automatic analysis can be performed using the original data, which is not accessible for viewing, unlike data publication. The original data may be encrypted and stored in a database which can be retrieved later in the event of emergency situations. The RoI information obtained using the detectors, along with the transformed data, can be presented to the human operators. Further, the RoI information can be used to adapt data transformation. We take this opportunity to explore an adaptive data transformation approach to combine the benefits of both selective obfuscation and global operations.

In this paper, to overcome the nonreliability of the RoI detectors, we examine the suitability of an adaptive approach of data transformation in order to provide near-zero privacy loss in a CCTV monitoring scenario. In the proposed privacy protection framework, data transformation is performed in two stages. In the first stage, automatic detectors (mainly

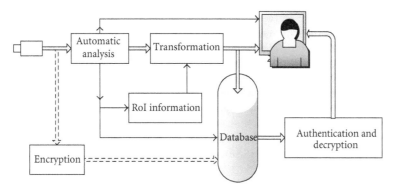

FIGURE 1: The automatic algorithms run on the original data. A transformed version can be showed to the CCTV operators.

blob and face detectors) are applied on the data for detection of evidences. The results from these detectors are used to adapt the global operation. The adaption is done in two dimensions: spatial (by using a space variant operation) and temporal (by providing a failure time window to the detectors). For privacy loss assessment, we adopt the model proposed in [2], as it considers both implicit and explicit identity leakage channels.

The main contributions of the paper are the following:

(i) an adaptive data transformation approach that uses space variant operations is proposed, which provides a near-zero privacy loss with minimal visual distortion;

(ii) the proposed method provides robust privacy preservation even with low-accuracy detectors.

Rest of the paper is organized as follows. We compare proposed work with previous works in Section 2. In Section 3, we describe proposed privacy protection method. Experimental results are analyzed in Section 4, and paper is concluded in Section 5.

2. Related Work

Most researchers [3–10] have used selective obfuscation to preserve privacy in surveillance videos. They have adopted the traditional approach, which is to detect the region of interest (e.g., face or blob) and hide it. Since this approach is limited by the accuracy of detectors, privacy cannot be guaranteed.

In Table 1, we present a comparison of the proposed work with other works in the following aspects: whether implicit identity leakage channels (e.g., location, time, and activity information) have been used for assessing privacy loss; whether a tradeoff between privacy loss and visual distortion of the whole frame due to data transformation has been examined, and which of the approaches (selective obfuscation or global operations) has been adopted. As shown in Table 1, our work is different from the works of other researchers in many aspects. First, we examine the implicit identity leakage channels, which have been ignored in the past. Second, the proposed privacy preserving method presents a tradeoff between utility and privacy in a given

TABLE 1: A comparison of the proposed work with the existing works.

The work	Implicit identity leakage channels used?	Utility/privacy tradeoff?	Approach adopted
Boyle et al. [1]	No	No	GO
Senior et al. [3]	No	No	SO
Moncrieff et al. [11]	No	No	SO
Fidaleo et al. [4]	No	No	SO
Wickramasuriya et al. [5]	No	No	SO
Koshimizu et al. [6]	No	No	SO
Spindler et al. [12]	No	No	SO
Thuraisingham et al. [7]	No	No	SO
Carrillo et al. [8]	No	No	SO
Paruchuri et al. [9]	No	No	SO
Qureshi [10]	No	No	SO
Saini et al. [2]	Yes	No	No transformation
Proposed work	Yes	Yes	SO and GO

SO: selective obfuscation; GO: global operations.

CCTV monitoring scenario. Finally, the proposed method examines an adaptive approach for data transformation. We use face and blob detectors to detect the regions in the image that need to be obfuscated. However, the inaccuracies of these detectors is overcome by adapting operations spatially as well as temporally in the video.

We differentiate the contributions in the paper from our past work [2] as follows. While in [2], we introduced the notion of implicit identity leakage channels and provided a computational model for identity leakage and privacy loss, in this paper we examine the appropriateness of data transformation operations in order to block these identity leakage channels. One approach could be to globally transform the data to provide a tradeoff between the privacy loss and utility loss. However, global data transformation operations are not appropriate in a CCTV monitoring scenario since the global operations introduce large amount of visual distortions in the video. Therefore, in this paper we propose an adaptive data transformation approach that combines benefits of selective obfuscation and global operations to provide robust privacy with minimal distortion. Further, we provide a tradeoff between the visual distortions due to data transformation and the privacy loss of the people present in the video.

3. Privacy Protection Method

In the previous works, it is identified that the identity leakage and privacy loss occur due to presence of the evidences information such as *who, what, when,* and *where.* An evidence can be learned from multiple sources. For example, the *where* evidence can be detected using text legends, familiar structures, symbols (company logos), and so forth. In order to robustly block the identity leakage, we need to remove/modify all the sources of evidence detection. In a surveillance scenario, relatively static regions of the camera view are known as the background, for example, rigid structures, fixed objects, doors, and exits. Anything that is not background is considered foreground, which generally corresponds to the humans walking in the camera view [13]. We observed that some of the sources of identity leakage are found in the background, while others are part of the foreground/object itself. Particularly, most of the sources of *where* and *when* evidences are embedded in the background; while the *who* and *what* evidences are usually found in the foreground. Further, we observe that the surveillance cameras are generally fixed, resulting in static background [14]. Since the background is mostly static, the sources which are part of background can be accurately detected manually and transformed. The foreground parts need to be automatically removed as they may appear at varying places in different frames.

Most sources of the evidences can be associated to a region in the image called evidence regions. For example, a rectangle encompassing a company logo, that can provide the company and its location information, is one evidence region for *where* evidence. Our aim is to transform the image such that all the evidence regions are obscured enough to block the identity information. However, the problem is that we may not be able to detect these regions accurately due to the limitations of the automatic techniques [15, 16]. In the proposed method, these inaccuracies are taken care of by using spatially and temporally adaptive data transformation. The quality of the transformed data is measured in terms of perceptual distortion D, which is computed as

$$D = 1 - SSIM, \quad (1)$$

where SSIM is the structural similarity index [17]. We use SSIM value over PSNR because this measure is more consistent with human eye perception [18, 19]. For the sake of completeness, we first provide a brief overview of selective

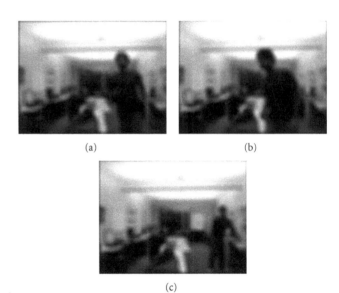

(a)   (b)

(c)

FIGURE 2: The images are blurred to hide the identity information.

obfuscation and global operations and then describe the proposed method.

3.1. Existing Approaches

3.1.1. Selective Obfuscation. In these methods, the evidence revealing image regions are selected using computer vision techniques and subsequently obfuscated. For example, Figure 3 shows the results of face detection for hiding the facial information. In the first image the face is detected properly, which helped in accurately removing the facial information. However, in the second image the face regions are incorrectly detected, while in the third image they are not detected at all. Note that if the face is left undetected and seen in even one frame, the identity is revealed. Hence, selective obfuscation methods do not provide robust privacy preservation.

3.1.2. Global Operations. To overcome the problem of unreliable vision algorithms, we can perform generalization on the whole image. For instance, we can coarsely quantize the image, scramble the color space, or blur the image. The problem with these methods is that they are generally too pessimistic; we need to determine the worst case transformation parameters (e.g., degree of blurring or quantization) and blur all the images to that amount, irrespective of the content of the image. This is in contrast to the fact that when the person is far from the camera, even little blurring might be sufficient. Figure 2 shows the result of this approach where the images are blurred to hide faces. From this figure, we observe that the image background gets distorted even when the object occupies a small portion of the image. The background information might be important for a surveillance person in order to understand the situation.

3.2. Proposed Adaptive Approach. We propose an adaptive method that uses global transformation according to the results of selective obfuscation. In this method, we first use

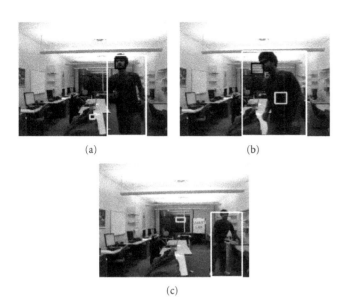

(a)   (b)

(c)

FIGURE 3: The results of the blob detection (white rectangle) and face detection (black rectangle).

face and blob detectors to approximate the location of the persons in the image and then use *space variant operation* to hide the identity. Figure 3 shows the results of blob detection and face detection on the same data. We can observe that a blob detector is generally more robust than the a face detector in detecting the presence of a person; although the boundaries may not be very accurate, we can still get a good approximation of the centroid of the region occupied by the person. This centroid information is used to perform a space variant operation. In the space variant operation, the operation parameters vary with the space according to a profile. Let r_i be the image region with evidence information and c_i the most probable (for face presence) point of the region, then the quality $\mathcal{Q}$ for a pixel p in region r_i is calculated as follows:

$$\mathcal{Q}(p) = \mathcal{Q}_0 f(\Delta(c_i, r_i)), \tag{2}$$

where f is the profile function, $\mathcal{Q}_0$ is the operation parameter for the centroid, and Δ is a distance function. In a ramp profile, for example, the transformation intensity decreases linearly with the distance from the centroid. This mechanism has the advantage that even if the approximate location of a person is determined, the evidence regions can be obscured with high probability without globally transforming the image.

The space variant operations are useful when the detectors are unable to detect the evidence regions correctly, but only provide an approximation of the region which can cause evidence detection. However, sometimes the detectors completely fail to detect persons in the video. We analyzed the failure pattern of the blob detector over a number of videos and made the following observations:

(i) when the person enters the camera view, the background model-based blob detector detects the person reliably;

(ii) the detector may fail to detect a person due to noise or lighting changes, and so forth;

(iii) the maximum number of contiguous frames in which the blob detector fails is limited.

One such failure pattern is shown in Figure 4 in which the person enters the camera view in 71th frame and leaves in 910th frame. The detector fails for the following frames: 220 to 230, 460 to 495, 710 to 740, and 810 to 830. To model this failure pattern, we define a failure window ω. If the number of contiguous frames in which the blob is not detected is less than ω, we assume that the person is present in the video, but the blob detector has failed to detect that person. In this situation we adopt the pessimistic approach and globally transform the whole image. If no blob is detected for more than ω contiguous frames, we conclude that the person has left the camera view and there is no need for a global transformation.

Note that our aim is to reduce the privacy loss when the data is presented to the surveillance operator for viewing. The automatic algorithms can still work on the original data, but human beings can only see the transformed data. Nonetheless, in emergency situations, a person with authority can access the original data. Figure 1 shows how the proposed method can be deployed in a surveillance system.

3.2.1. Description of Algorithm. The evidence regions can be divided into two groups:

(i) *static evidence regions:* these are the regions of the background that provide us evidence which can lead to identity. Let $R^s = \{r_1^s, r_2^s \ldots\}$ be the set of background evidence regions, which include any text legends, landmark or famous buildings, name plates, addresses, symbols and logos, and so forth;

(ii) *dynamic evidence regions:* these are the foreground regions that provide *who* and *what* evidence. Let $R^d = \{r_1^d, r_2^d, \ldots\}$ be the set of image regions detected as foreground using blob and face detectors. Each region is defined by a centroid, width, and height. Dynamic evidence regions may vary with time; therefore, these are calculated on-the-fly for the current frame.

The proposed method is described in Algorithm 1. The algorithm takes a video V and set of static evidence regions R^s as input and returns the transformed video V'. The important steps of the algorithm are explained below.

Statement 3. The function $DSR()$ estimates the dynamic evidence regions using blob and face detector. To detect the evidence regions, we tune the thresholds of the detectors to minimize the number of false negatives. In the experiments we show that we are able to obtain very low number of false negatives.

Statements 4 to 13. If no foreground is detected, there can be two cases: (1) there is no foreground region in the image; (2) the detector failed to detect the foreground. Whether current

Input: Original Video: $V = \{f_1, f_2 \ldots\}$
and set of static evidence regions: $R^s = \{r_1^s, r_2^s \ldots\}$;
Output: Transformed Video: $V' = \{f_{1'}, f_{2'} \ldots\}$
Description:
1: **for all** $f_i \in V$ **do**
2:     // Detect dynamic evidence regions
3:     $R^d = DSR(f_i)$;
4:     **if** $R^d == EMPTY$ **then**
5:         **if** $R^d == EMPTY$ for previous ω frames **then**
6:             $f_i^t = COPY(f_i)$;
7:             **for all** $r_j^s \in R^s$ **do**
8:                 $f_i^t = ST(f_i^t, r_j^s)$;
9:             **end for**
10:        **else**
11:            //Do the global transformation
12:            $f_i^t = GT(f_i)$;
13:        **end if**
14:    **else**
15:        //Foreground detected
16:        //Transform static regions
17:        $f_i^t = COPY(f_i)$
18:        **for all** $r_j^s \in R^s$ **do**
19:            $f_i^t = ST(f_i^t, r_j^s)$;
20:            $MARK(f_i^t, r_j^s) = TRUE$;
21:        **end for**
22:        //Transform dynamic regions
23:        **for all** frame $r_k^d \in R^d$ **do**
24:            //Calculate parameters for space variant operation
25:            $PRM = PE(r_k^d)$
26:            **if** $!MARK(f_i^t, r_k^d)$**then**
27:                $f_i^t = DT(f_i^t, r_k^d, PRM)$;
28:            **end if**
29:        **end for**
30:        //Data transformation over
31:    **end if**
32:    //Copy frame to output frame sequence
33:    $f_{i'} = COPY(f_i^t)$;
34: **end for**
35: **return** Transformed frame sequence $f_{i'}$ as Video V';

ALGORITHM 1: Adaptive data transformation.

frame belongs to the first case or the latter case is determined by examining the $DSR()$ output for the previous ω frames. If we do not detect any foreground regions in the previous ω frames, then it is very likely that there is no person in the image; hence, we only transform the static regions. On the other hand, if some foreground is detected within last ω frames, there are more chances of existence of a person in the image. In this case, we take the pessimistic approach and globally transform the whole image. In the function $ST()$, the static evidence regions of the images are obscured using a suitable transformation operation. An evaluation of three operations, namely, blurring, pixelization, and quantization is provided in the experimental results. Similarly, $GT()$ transforms the entire image globally.

Statements 17 to 21. When the foreground is detected, we selectively transform static and dynamic evidence regions. In this case, we first do the static transformation and then pass the image for transformation of dynamic evidence regions.

Statements 23 to 29. In these steps we transform the dynamic regions of the image. Only those regions are selected for the transformation that are not obscured during the static transformation. The dynamic transformation is done in two steps. In the first step, parameters of the dynamic region r_i^d (centroid, height, and width) are used to estimate ($PE()$) a probable area (PRM) (circular in our case), where the evidence could exist. The details of the parameter estimation are discussed in the experiments section. This area is then space-variantly transformed according to the probability of finding evidence information, that is, the subareas where the probability of finding evidence is less, they are transformed with less degree and vice versa. This space variant transformation operation (e.g., blurring, pixelization, etc.) is performed in function $DT()$; an implementation of which will be discussed with the experiments.

Space variant operations incorporate operating context in data transformation. For example, if the detectors being used are less accurate, a bigger area can be selected for dynamic transformation. Since the degree of transformation decreases with the distance from the center, we do not compromise much in the quality. By analyzing the frames over a temporal window and selecting a proper transformation function, we are able to accommodate temporary failures of the detector.

4. Experimental Results

We performed five experiments to demonstrate the efficacy of the proposed privacy protection method. In the first experiment we highlight the effect of nonfacial information on privacy loss. We also provide an evaluation of blurring, pixelization, and quantization transformation operations that are required to remove the static evidence regions, which provide *when* and *where* evidences. In the second experiment, we show the improved visual quality obtained using the proposed method for a near-zero privacy loss. It is shown that the proposed method that adaptively uses selective obfuscation and global operations is more reliable than the selective obfuscation alone, and it achieves better quality than the global transformation alone. It is also demonstrated how the spatial and temporal adaption can be used to overcome the inaccuracies of the detectors. In Experiment 3, we analyze how privacy loss and visual distortion are affected by varying ω. An attempt to improve the proposed method is made in Experiment 4 to overcome a special failure pattern that might occur in a multiperson scenario. Finally, we validate our conclusions with an experiment on 24 hours of real surveillance data in Experiment 5.

4.1. Data Set. Five video clips have been considered in our experiments. The description of the video clips is as follows:

(i) video 1: this video was recorded in a research lab. It shows name of the lab and two people doing various activities. The original video was shot for over one hour consisting of 200 key frames;

(ii) video 2: the video is recorded at the entrance of a department building. It has multiple *where* evidences in the form of text and logo. The video is of 45 minutes length, and it consists of 483 frames;

(iii) video 3: this is again a video recorded at a research lab where two people are doing some activities. It consists of 1095 frames;

(iv) video 4: this video was shot at the wash basin in a canteen. Two people are seen in the video at a time and it consists of 1520 frames;

(v) video 5: the video consists of 1200 frames which are taken from PETS data sets [20].

Figure 5 shows the background images for the five video clips used in this experiment. From the figure it can be

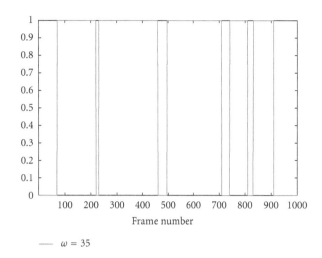

— $\omega = 35$

FIGURE 4: A failure pattern of blob detector, y-axis; 1 mean Detected correctly, 0 mean Failed.

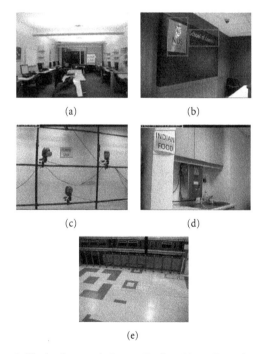

(a)   (b)

(c)   (d)

(e)

FIGURE 5: The background pictures for five videos. Green box shows *when* evidence and blue rectangle shows *where* evidence.

derived that: in video 1 and video 2, we can detect *what* and *where* evidences; in video 3 and video 4, we can detect *what*, *where*, and *when* evidences; but in video 5, we can only detect *what* evidence. To validate the conclusions in real scenarios, we also use 24 hours of real surveillance footage consisting of 28216 frames (video 6). The video frames are not shown due to privacy concerns. We can detect *what* evidence in the real video.

Experiment 1 (implicit identity leakage and static regions). A large amount of work assumes that privacy loss only occurs due to the presence of the facial information in the

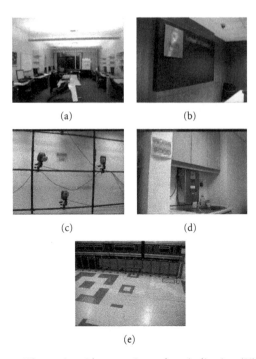

FIGURE 6: The static evidence regions after pixelization (Video 1–3, Video 2–8, Video 3–6, Video 4–9). Video 5 does not have any evidence region in background.

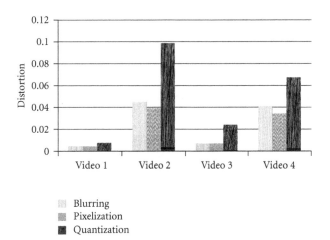

FIGURE 7: Different transformation operations to obscure the static evidence regions and corresponding distortion measures. Video 5 does not have any static evidence regions.

image. In this experiment we mainly highlight the limitations of the earlier privacy protection methods and show how the evidences found in the image can cause privacy loss even without facial information. To highlight the effect of the implicit channels alone, in this experiment we assume that the face is already removed from the videos and then calculate the privacy loss based on the model described in [2]. The associated cluster sizes depend on the scenario in which the video is recorded; however, for experimental purposes, we take the following values of clusters: $C_{what} = 10000$, $C_{what,when} = 3000$, $C_{what,where} = 20$, and $C_{what,when,where} = 5$.

TABLE 2: The privacy loss calculation for different video clips.

Video	Evidences	Identity leakage	Privacy loss
Video 1	*What; where*	$I_{what,where} = 2/20$	0.119
Video 2	*What; where*	$I_{what,where} = 1/20$	0.018
Video 3	*What; where; when*	$I_{what,where,when} = 2/5$	0.880
Video 4	*What; where; when*	$I_{what,where,when} = 1/5$	0.119
Video 5	*what*	$I_{what} = 6/10000$	0.002

In Table 2 we present the privacy loss that might occur from these video clips even when the face is not present.

It can be observed that if the adversary has the prior knowledge of the clusters, the nonfacial information can also cause significant privacy loss, and, therefore, we need to remove these evidences from the videos to minimize the privacy loss. We explore three operations to transform the static evidence regions: blurring, quantization, and pixelization. We perform these operations to the degree that the evidence is not detectable and compare the perceptual distortion they cause. The static evidence regions of the videos are shown as green and blue boxes in Figure 5; note that video 5 does not have any static evidence region. In Figure 7 we notice that pixelization performs equivalent or better than blurring and quantization operations. On average over all the videos, pixelization incurs 8% less distortion than blurring and 55% less distortion than quantization. The resulting pixelized images are shown in Figure 6. In the remaining experiments, we will use pixelization to obscure static evidence regions. This experiment only removes evidences from static background, we still need to consider *who* and *what* evidences which can be learned from the dynamic foreground.

Experiment 2 (space variant operation). In this experiment we examine the use of the techniques to remove evidences that are detected from the foreground. As mentioned before, the most common evidences that are found in the foreground of video frames are *what* (activities in our case) and *who* (face in our case). The identity leakage through *what* alone is negligible, hence we put more focus on the facial information removal. Also note that removing *what* evidence can severely affect the intended surveillance objective.

One extreme solution to overcome the nonreliability of the detectors is to globally transform the image. For example, we can blur the whole image irrespective of the location of the face. To evaluate this technique, we applied the operations on the whole video to the extent, where the face became unrecognizable in all the frames. Figure 8 shows the results of blurring and pixelization on the five videos. We observe that except for Video 5, blurring performs better than pixelization. This is probably because the distortion in the case of pixelization increases more rapidly compared to blurring as the faces are captured more close to the camera. The dips in the plots show the regions of high activity with multiple people. However, it cannot be avoided as the probability of privacy loss is also higher in those frames.

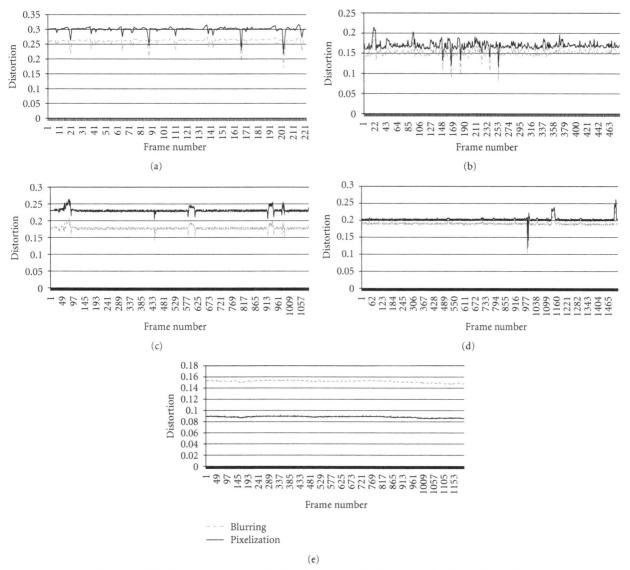

(a)

(b)

(c)

(d)

(e)

- - - Blurring
—— Pixelization

FIGURE 8: The distortion measures for blurring and pixelization using global transformation.

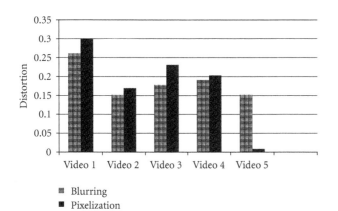

■ Blurring
■ Pixelization

FIGURE 9: Comparison of distortion due to blurring and pixelization for global transformation. If P is the degree of pixelization, and B is degree of blurring, we got following values: video 1: $B = 6$ and $P = 4$, video 2: $B = 13$ and $P = 8$, video 3: $B = 12$ and $P = 8$, video 4: $B = 12$ and $P = 8$, and video 2: $B = 6$ and $P = 3$.

The overall comparison of average distortion values for all five videos is shown in Figure 9.

The foreground regions only occupy a small part of the image, hence uniformly transforming the whole image is a very pessimistic approach. To overcome the non reliability of the face detectors, we propose to use more robust foreground detectors (e.g., blob detector) which can be made very reliable by reducing the threshold values, although at the cost of increased false positives. We conducted experiments with GMM-based adaptive background modeling to detect the blobs [21]. The results of the blob detection are shown in Figure 10. By reducing the threshold values we are able to detect foreground in most of the images.

However, transforming only the blob regions has two problems: (1) in some frames the blob may include the body of the person but still miss the face, for example, in Figure 10(a) and (2) the face only occupies small region of the blob, hence transforming whole blob region may be too

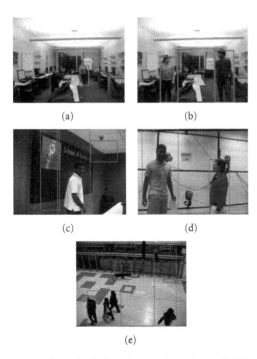

(a)　　　　　(b)

(c)　　　　　(d)

(e)

Figure 10: Results of blob detection on five videos. The blob detection works in the image where face detector fails.

pessimistic. From blob detection results and global transformation of the images, we make the following observations. (1) we need to apply more blurring/pixelization to obscure the frontal faces; however, the degree of blurring/pixelization could be less when the person is not directly looking at the camera. (2) the frontal face is generally found at 75% height of the blob. (3) the missed faces are within 125% of the height of the blob. These observations inspire us to use a space variant transformation, where the degree of transformation varies with the distance from the center of the estimated facial region.

In the implemented space variant transformation, a circular evidence region is estimated based on the inaccuracy of the detectors, and then different regions of the circle are transformed by different degrees of the transformation considering the distance from the center c_i (according to (2)). Based on the observations mentioned in the previous paragraph, the center (c_i) is determined as $(B_x + (3/2) * B_h, B_y + (1/2) * B_w)$, where (B_x, B_y) are the coordinates of the bottom-left corner of the blob with respect to the bottom-left corner of the image, and (B_w, B_h) are width and height of the blob. The radius of the circle is approximated as $(\max((1 + \mu) * B_h, (1 + 2 * \mu) * B_w))$, where μ is the fractional error margin which is 0.25 for the blob detector in our case. A less accurate blob detector would need higher value of margin μ. The circular region obtained above is divided into four concentric circles. The value of Q_0, that is, the transformation parameter for the innermost circle is chosen according to the results of the global transformation (Figure 9) as follows: Q_0 for blurring- 6, 13, 12, 12, and 6; for pixelization- 4, 8, 8, 8, and 3, respectively for five videos. The profile function f is chosen to be piecewise linear, and the function Δ is based on the Euclidean distance. With each

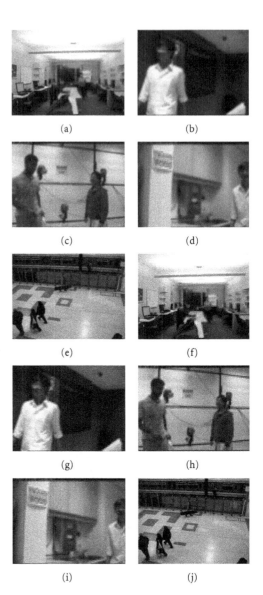

(a)　　　　　(b)

(c)　　　　　(d)

(e)　　　　　(f)

(g)　　　　　(h)

(i)　　　　　(j)

Figure 11: Key images from the transformed video using the proposed method. Row 1 shows the outputs of blurring, whereas row 2 shows the pixelization outputs.

outer circle, the blurring parameter is reduced by 5% and rounded to the nearest integer. The face detector output is also used to provide additional robustness. The implemented face detector provides a square facial region. In this case, the center is calculated as $(\text{Side}/2, \text{Side}/2)$, and radius is taken as $\max((1 + 2 * \mu) * \text{Side})$ to account for inaccuracy.

Again, these numbers may depend on the context of the surveillance and accuracy of the detectors. In the current experimental settings, these parameters are obtained to give near-zero privacy loss (no face recognition possible from the transformed data) for given videos and blob detector.

Now we evaluate the proposed method from the perspective of visual distortion. For evaluation of the proposed method, we implement Algorithm 1 (described in Section 3.2). Figure 11 shows the resulting output images. The resulting values of the distortion for video clips (of Figure 11) are shown in Figure 12. The variation in the

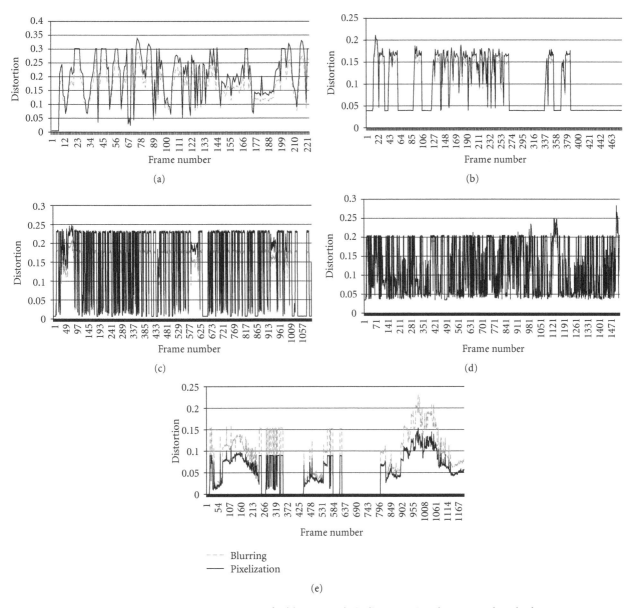

FIGURE 12: The distortion measures for blurring and pixelization using the proposed method.

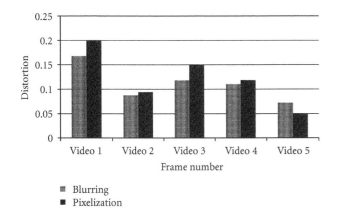

FIGURE 13: A comparison of distortion measure for pixelization and blurring for all video clips using the proposed method.

distortion is much more in comparison to global transformation. This is because when no blobs are detected, only static regions of the video are transformed; resulting in low distortion. On the other hand, sometimes blobs of large size are detected (probably due to increased false positive rate), which cause whole image to be transformed. It can be observed that even when the whole image is transformed, the distortion value using space variant method is less. This is due to the fact that in space variant operations less probable evidence regions are transformed mildly.It can be observed from Figure 13 that blurring provides a more effective solution for transforming the foreground regions. In Figure 14, a comparison of the proposed method with the global transformation is provided. The results show that we get 37% less distortion with proposed method in comparison to global method, still providing robust privacy protection.

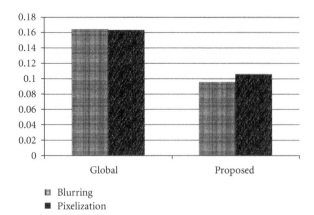

FIGURE 14: A comparison of global method and proposed method.

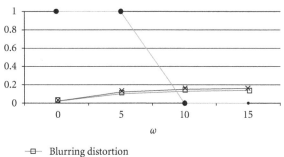

FIGURE 15: The effect of ω on privacy loss and visual distortion.

For the given video clips, we were able to remove the evidence information completely since the blob detector in our case never failed. However, there might be case that a low threshold blob detector may fail to detect the foreground. In the next experiment, we explore how different values of ω accommodate this failure.

Experiment 3 (effect of failure window on privacy loss and visual distortion). In this experiment, our objective is to find the value of failure window (ω) for which the visual distortion is minimum for a near-zero privacy loss. We perform blurring and pixelization operations globally on ω consecutive frames in the video after the blob detection fails. Experiment is done with four values of ω: 0, 5, 10, and 15. The result is shown in Figure 15. As can be seen in the figure that for the given video (Video 3 in this case) and the blob detector used in our experiment, at a value of $\omega = 10$ we obtain a near-zero privacy loss. With this value of ω, the distortion is less than 0.2 with both blurring and pixelization operations (although pixelization causes slightly more distortion than blurring). We have conducted this experiment only for Video 3 because only this video had such a failure of the blob detector.

Experiment 4 (when the blob detector fails). The solution provided in the previous experiment fails in situations, where one person is detected and other could not be detected. The

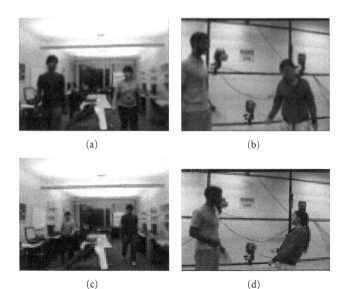

FIGURE 16: Output images from the pessimistic approach to overcome the failure of blob detector.

proposed method will only remove one person's identity. The other person will be left untransformed, and hence it might cause privacy loss. In this experiment we simulate such scenario by considering only the biggest blob detected in the video. Other blobs are assumed to be not detected. To improve the privacy loss in such scenarios, we use a very pessimistic approach of data transformation. Here we assume that someone is always there in the video and do global transformation when no blobs are detected. When the blob is detected, we do the space variant blurring according to the previous method; however, the image area outside estimated evidence region is globally transformed; unlike previous method where it is left unprocessed. Experiments show that this method performs better than global operations, but the perceptual quality is poorer in comparison to the normal space variant transformation discussed in previous experiments.

Figure 16 shows the output images for video 3 from the proposed algorithm. We notice that from Figures 16(a) to 16(c), we are able to hide the faces effectively even without global transformation. However, the method's success depends on the scenario and needs fine tuning. For example, in Figure 16(d) the other person's face is visible as it happens to fall in the outermost circle of the space variantly transformed first blob. Proper selection of the radius depends on the context and is out of scope of this paper. The qualitative results of the methods are provided in Figures 17 and 18. The figure can be compared with Figures 8 and 12 to conclude that the resulting video quality is worse than the normal space variant blurring is better than global transformation.

Experiment 5 (validation with real surveillance data). The five videos used in previous experiments cover various scenarios. The conclusions made for these scenarios are further validated by running the proposed method on real surveillance

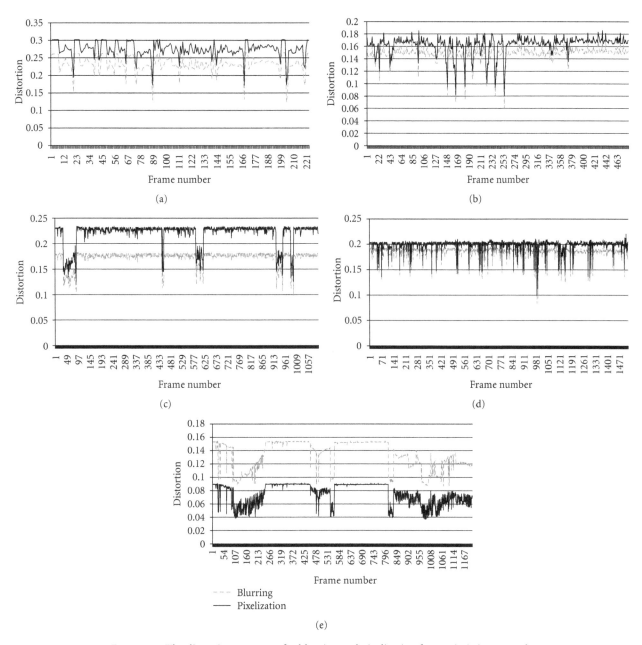

FIGURE 17: The distortion measures for blurring and pixelization for pessimistic approach.

footage of 24 hours, recorded at The University of Winnipeg. Since the video consists of 28216 frames, we omit the detailed distribution of the distortion values and provide the mean distortion in Figure 19 for the global method, the proposed method, and the pessimistic approach described in Experiment 4. A globally transformed background image of the video is shown in Figure 20. Other resulting figures are not shown due to privacy concerns.

We find that the results for real data are in agreement with our earlier conclusions. The proposed method causes less distortion than global transformation (63%) while the pessimistic approach causes more distortion than the proposed approach, though less than the global method.

Further, the distortion caused by blurring is 22% less than that of pixelization.

4.2. Further Discussion. The main goal of this paper is to introduce adaptive transformation in spatial as well as temporal domains to overcome inaccuracies of detectors and to achieve more robust privacy. To the best of our knowledge, this is the first attempt towards reliable privacy with unreliable detectors. It is important to note that a tracking based solution could also be used for temporal adaption; however, it would again be limited by the accuracy of the tracker. Also, in real scenarios, it is very difficult to initialize the tracking with a generic template, and the tracker fails as

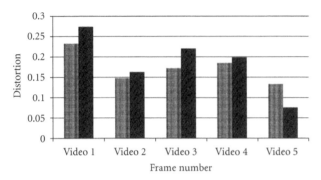

FIGURE 18: Mean distortion measures for blurring and pixelization for pessimistic approach.

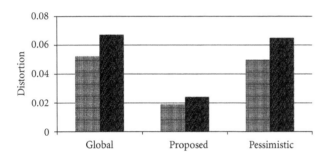

FIGURE 19: Mean distortion measures for blurring and pixelization for real surveillance data.

FIGURE 20: A globally transformed frame of real surveillance video.

soon as the person changes the posture. Therefore, we think that the proposed adaptive method is more robust.

5. Conclusions

The proposed adaptive approach of data transformation intelligently hides the evidence information in the video without much compromise with quality. It also provides robust privacy despite the inaccuracies of the detectors.

Experimental results are provided to support our claims. For the CCTV scenario, we explored the adaptive transformation method to capitalize on the benefits of a global transformation while adapting it with the output of unreliable detectors. The following are the important conclusions of the paper:

(i) pixelization is found to be better than blurring and quantization for transforming static evidence regions with 8% less distortion than blurring and 55% less distortion than quantization;

(ii) the proposed method is more reliable than the selective obfuscation based methods and has 38% lesser visual distortion than global transformation;

(iii) for foreground transformation using space variant operations, blurring provides 11% less distortion than pixelization.

In the future, we want to deploy these methods in real implementations and perform a user study-based evaluation of privacy loss and distortion. It would be interesting to know how much distortion is acceptable to maintain a desired surveillance quality. Also, we want to extend the work by modeling the failure pattern of the detectors for the scenarios with more dynamic background and foreground.

Acknowledgment

Dr. P. K. Atrey's research contribution was supported by the Natural Sciences and Engineering Research Council of Canada.

References

[1] M. Boyle, C. Edwards, and S. Greenberg, "The effects of filtered video on awareness and privacy," in *Proceedings of the ACM Conference on Computer Supported Cooperative Work*, pp. 1–10, December 2000.

[2] M. Saini, P. K. Atrey, S. Mehrotra, S. Emmanuel, and M. Kankanhalli, "Privacy modeling for video data publication," in *Proceedings of the IEEE International Conference on Multimedia and Expo (ICME '10)*, pp. 60–65, July 2010.

[3] A. Senior, S. Pankanti, A. Hampapur et al., "Enabling video privacy through computer vision," *IEEE Security and Privacy*, vol. 3, no. 3, pp. 50–57, 2005.

[4] D. A. Fidaleo, H. A. Nguyen, and M. Trivedi, "The networked sensor tapestry (nest): a privacy enhanced software architecture for interactive analysis of data in video-sensor networks," in *Proceedings of the 2nd ACM International Workshop on Video Sureveillance and Sensor Networks (VSSN '04)*, pp. 46–53, 2004.

[5] J. Wickramasuriya, M. Datt, S. Mehrotra, and N. Venkatasubramanian, "Privacy protecting data collection in media spaces," in *Proceedings of the 12th ACM International Conference on Multimedia*, pp. 48–55, usa, October 2004.

[6] T. Koshimizu, T. Toriyama, and N. Babaguchi, "Factors on the sense of privacy in video surveillance," in *Proceedings of the 3rd ACM Workshop on Continuous Archival and Retrievalof Personal Experiences (CARPE '06)*, pp. 35–43, 2006.

[7] B. Thuraisingham, G. Lavee, E. Bertino, J. Fan, and L. Khan, "Access control, confidentiality and privacy for video surveillance databases," in *Proceedings of the 11th ACM Symposium*

on Access Control Models and Technologies (SACMAT '06), pp. 1–10, June 2006.

[8] P. Carrillo, H. Kalva, and S. Magliveras, "Compression independent object encryption for ensuring privacy in video surveillance," in *Proceedings of the IEEE International Conference on Multimedia and Expo (ICME '08)*, pp. 273–276, June 2008.

[9] J. K. Paruchuri, S. C. S. Cheung, and M. W. Hail, "Video data hiding for managing privacy information in surveillance systems," *Eurasip Journal on Information Security*, vol. 2009, Article ID 236139, 7 pages, 2009.

[10] F. Z. Qureshi, "Object-video streams for preserving privacy in video surveillance," in *Proceedings of the 6th IEEE International Conference on Advanced Video and Signal Based Surveillance (AVSS '09)*, pp. 442–447, 2009.

[11] S. Moncrieff, S. Venkatesh, and G. West, "Dynamic privacy assessment in a smart house environment using multimodal sensing," *ACM Transactions on Multimedia Computing, Communications and Applications*, vol. 5, no. 2, pp. 1–29, 2008.

[12] T. Spindler, C. Wartmann, and L. Hovestadt, "Privacy in video surveilled areas," in *Proceedings of the ACM International Conference on Privacy, Security and Trust*, pp. 1–10, 2006.

[13] A. Elgammal, R. Duraiswami, D. Harwood, and L. S. Davis, "Background and foreground modeling using nonparametric kernel density estimation for visual surveillance," *Proceedings of the IEEE*, vol. 90, no. 7, pp. 1151–1163, 2002.

[14] H. Kruegle, *CCTV Surveillance: Analog and Digital Video Practices and Technology*, Butterworth-Heinemann, Boston, Mass, USA, 2006.

[15] R. Kasturi, D. Goldgof, P. Soundararajan et al., "Framework for performance evaluation of face, text, and vehicle detection and tracking in video: data, metrics, and protocol," *IEEE Transactions on Pattern Analysis and Machine Intelligence*, vol. 31, no. 2, pp. 319–336, 2009.

[16] E. Hjelmås and B. K. Low, "Face detection: a survey," *Computer Vision and Image Understanding*, vol. 83, no. 3, pp. 236–274, 2001.

[17] Z. Wang, A. C. Bovik, H. R. Sheikh, and E. P. Simoncelli, "Image quality assessment: from error visibility to structural similarity," *IEEE Transactions on Image Processing*, vol. 13, no. 4, pp. 600–612, 2004.

[18] S. Chikkerur, V. Sundaram, M. Reisslein, and L. J. Karam, "Objective video quality assessment methods: a classification, review, and performance comparison," *IEEE Transactions on Broadcasting*, vol. 57, no. 2, pp. 165–182, 2011.

[19] K. Seshadrinathan, R. Soundararajan, A. C. Bovik, and L. K. Cormack, "Study of subjective and objective quality assessment of video," *IEEE Transactions on Image Processing*, vol. 19, no. 6, Article ID 5404314, pp. 1427–1441, 2010.

[20] PETS, "Performance evaluation of tracking and surveillance," 2000-2011, http://www.cvg.cs.rdg.ac.uk/slides/pets.html.

[21] C. Stauffer and W. E. L. Grimson, "Adaptive background mixture models for real-time tracking," in *Proceedings of the IEEE Computer Society Conference on Computer Vision and Pattern Recognition (CVPR '99)*, vol. 2, pp. 246–252, June 1999.

10

Salt and Pepper Noise Removal with Noise Detection and a Patch-Based Sparse Representation

Di Guo,[1] **Xiaobo Qu,**[2] **Xiaofeng Du,**[1] **Keshou Wu,**[1] **and Xuhui Chen**[1]

[1] *School of Computer and Information Engineering, Fujian Provincial University Key Laboratory of Internet of Things Application Technology, Xiamen University of Technology, Xiamen 361024, China*
[2] *Department of Electronic Science, Xiamen University, Xiamen 361005, China*

Correspondence should be addressed to Di Guo; guodi@xmut.edu.cn

Academic Editor: Martin Reisslein

Images may be corrupted by salt and pepper impulse noise due to noisy sensors or channel transmission errors. A denoising method by detecting noise candidates and enforcing image sparsity with a patch-based sparse representation is proposed. First, noise candidates are detected and an initial guide image is obtained via an adaptive median filtering; second, a patch-based sparse representation is learnt from this guide image; third, a weighted l_1-l_1 regularization method is proposed to penalize the noise candidates heavier than the rest of pixels. An alternating direction minimization algorithm is derived to solve the regularization model. Experiments are conducted for 30%~90% impulse noise levels, and the simulation results demonstrate that the proposed method outperforms total variation and Wavelet in terms of preserving edges and structural similarity to the noise-free images.

1. Introduction

Noise is an evitable problem in image processing and computer vision. Images may be corrupted by impulse noise due to noisy sensors or channel transmission errors [1]. To improve the image quality, it is important to remove these noises.

Median [1] or adaptive median filtering (AMF) [2] is usually adopted to remove the impulse noise. Noise detection and pixel restoration are two main steps in impulse noise removal. In noise detection stage, noise candidates may be found in the spatial domain [2] or multiscale decomposition domain [3, 4]. In the spatial domain, the size of local window is adaptively set [5, 6] in a noise-aware way and a hypergraph can be defined as model relationship of a central pixel and its neighbor pixels [7]. In the multiscale decomposition domain, Wavelet transform has been adopted [3]. In pixel restoration stage, recovery methods can be applied in the spatial domain [2] or multiscale decomposition domain [4, 8]. In the spatial domain, pixels will be better recovered in the optimal direction if directional edges are taken into account [9, 10]. Fuzzy rules are also applied both in the spatial [11] or

Wavelet domain [8] to deal with the uncertainty of inaccurate recovery. When 50% pixels are corrupted by impulse noise, methods in [9, 10] have shown promising results, but these methods produce unsatisfactory images when noise level is higher than 50%. Methods in both [4, 5] restored reasonable images when 90% pixels are contaminated.

Images are recovered much better than typical impulse denoising methods if appropriate sparsity priors are applied [12–14]. Beyond traditional multiscale decomposition methods, for example, Wavelet [3, 4, 12], sparse representations of image model wider image priors such as geometric directions [15–17] or redundancy [18] among images. In impulse noise removal, noise is detected by a sparse representation in identity matrix [13], or images are restored by enforcing their sparsity in Wavelet domain [12] or finite difference domain [19]. Rather than using fixed basis or dictionary, data-driven dictionaries have been proposed to provide an adaptive sparse representation for a specific image [20, 21]. To further reduce the reconstruction error in impulse noise removal, adaptive sparse representation has been explored under the framework of dictionary learning [14, 22]. However, the dictionary training in iterations is time consuming.

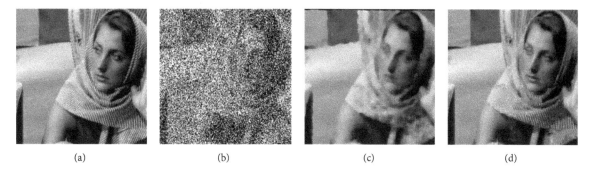

FIGURE 1: Restored image from 50% salt and pepper noise using median filtering and PANO. (a) Noise-free image, (b) noisy image with 50% salt and pepper noise, and (c) and (d) restored images using median filtering and PANO.

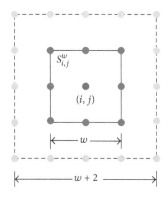

FIGURE 2: Window size of adaptive median filter (Initialize $w = 3$).

(1) Detect the noise candidate first, and only noisy pixels are heavily penalized in a weighted l_1-l_1 regularization model.

(2) Improve the similarity learning with a proper guide image, thus producing more accurate adaptive sparse representation of image patches.

(3) A numerical algorithm, alternating direction minimization with continuation, is developed to solve the new model accordingly.

The rest of this paper is organized as follows. The original PANO-based l_1-l_1 regularization model will be reviewed in Section 2.1. The new denoising approach is presented in Section 2.2. Experiments and results analysis are given in Section 3. Finally, Section 4 presents the conclusions.

2. Method

2.1. Review of PANO-Based Impulse Noise Removal Method. In the original PANO-based noise removal method [27], the image $\mathbf{x}$ is recovered from noisy observation $\mathbf{y}$ by solving a l_1-l_1 minimization model

$$\min_{\mathbf{x}} \lambda \|\mathbf{y} - \mathbf{x}\|_1 + \sum_{j=1}^{J} \|\mathbf{A}_j\mathbf{x}\|_1, \tag{1}$$

where $\sum_{j=1}^{J} \|\mathbf{A}_j\mathbf{x}\|_1$ promotes the sparsity of J groups of similar patches using PANO $\mathbf{A}_j$ ($j = 1, 2, \ldots, J$), $\|\mathbf{y} - \mathbf{x}\|_1$ removes the outliers, that is, impulse noise in images, and λ balances between the sparsity and outliers removal. A larger λ should be assigned since it is expected to smoothen images harder for heavier noise.

However, all the pixels of noisy observation $\mathbf{y}$ are penalized equally. This may change the pixels uncorrupted by noise. If the noise candidates are detected, the denoising performance is expected to be improved [28].

2.2. PANO-Based Impulse Noise Removal with Noise Detection and a Weighted l_1-l_1 Regularization Model (PANO-ND). In the proposed method, the salt and pepper noise are detected first and the locations of noise candidates are marked. With the location information, a weighted l_1-l_1 regularization

Recently, a fast adaptive sparse representation of images, called patch-based nonlocal operator (PANO) [23], has been proposed to make use of image self-similarity [24–26]. PANO searches similar patches in neighborhood; thus, the training phase is relatively fast. In our previous work, PANO was explored to reconstruct images from impulse noise corruption using an l_1-l_1 regularization model. By learning the similarity from images restored by median filtering, both strong edges and textures are recovered much better than total variation or Wavelet [27]. However, the denoising performance dropped when 50% pixels are contaminated with impulse noise.

In our experiments, we found two reasons for the reduction of denoising performance. First, many image structures are lost in the guide image thus affect learning the proper similarity. Second, noise-free pixels are also changed since the original PANO-based l_1-l_1 regularization model did not distinguish the noisy or noise-free pixels. Based on the two reasons, adaptive median filtering [2] is used to obtain a good guide image and to detect the noise candidates first. And a new model penalizing the noisy pixels more than noise-free ones is proposed to preserve the noise-free pixels.

In this paper, a novel denoising framework is proposed for salt and pepper noise removal based on adaptive sparse representation of similar image patches. The contributions of this paper are summarized as follows.

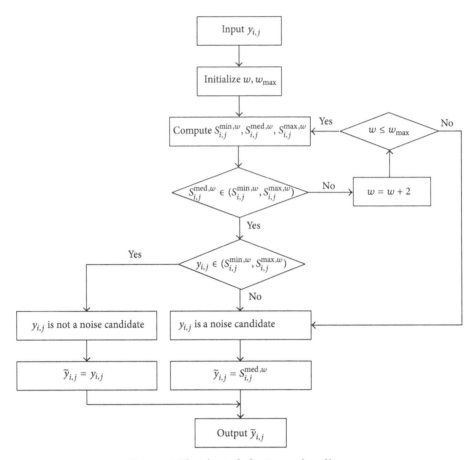

FIGURE 3: Flowchart of adaptive median filter.

model is proposed to preserve the noise-free pixels while removing noise. We call the proposed method PANO with noise detection (PANO-ND).

2.2.1. Noise Detection.
For the salt and pepper noise, the adaptive median filter (AMF) can be used to detect the noise candidates $y_{i,j}$ and replace each $y_{i,j}$ with the median of the pixels in a local window [2]. As shown in Figure 2, an adaptive structure of the filter ensures that most of the impulse noise is detected even at a high noise level provided that the window size is large enough [28].

Let $S_{i,j}^w$ be a window of size $w \times w$ centered at (i, j), and let $w_{max} \times w_{max}$ be the maximum allowable window size. Initialize $w = 3$ and compute $S_{i,j}^{\min,w}, S_{i,j}^{\text{med},w}, S_{i,j}^{\max,w}$ which denote the minimum, median, and maximum of the pixel values in $S_{i,j}^w$, respectively. When $S_{i,j}^{\text{med},w} \in (S_{i,j}^{\min,w}, S_{i,j}^{\max,w})$, that is, impulse noise does not dominate the window, we can judge $y_{i,j}$ is not a noise candidate if $y_{i,j} \in (S_{i,j}^{\min,w}, S_{i,j}^{\max,w})$, else we replace $y_{i,j}$ by $S_{i,j}^{\text{med},w}$ (*Median Filtering*); that is,

$$\widetilde{y}_{i,j} = \begin{cases} y_{i,j}, & \text{if } y_{i,j} \in \left(S_{i,j}^{\min,w}, S_{i,j}^{\max,w}\right) \\ S_{i,j}^{\text{med},w}, & \text{else.} \end{cases} \tag{2}$$

When $S_{i,j}^{\text{med},w} \notin (S_{i,j}^{\min,w}, S_{i,j}^{\max,w})$, that is, impulse noise dominates this window, we set $w = w + 2$ (*Adaptive*) and repeat the above steps.

When $w \geq w_{max}$, we replace $y_{i,j}$ by $S_{i,j}^{\text{med},w_{max}}$ (the algorithm is terminated when the maximum window size is reached). Notice that except for the noise candidates that are replaced by the median $S_{i,j}^{\text{med},w}$, the remaining pixels are left unchanged. The flowchart of AMF is summarized in Figure 3. In the proposed scheme, the noise candidates are detected using AMF.

The locations of detected noise candidates are stored in a set Ω whose complementary set $\overline{\Omega}$ stores locations of the rest of pixels. For an image $\mathbf{x} \in \mathbb{R}^{n \times 1}$, Ω and $\overline{\Omega}$ will be used to generate a diagonal matrix $\mathbf{W} \in \mathbb{R}^{n \times n}$ whose entries stand for weights on pixels in the regularization model.

2.2.2. Weighted l_1-l_1 Regularization Model.
In this paper, a weighted l_1-l_1 regularization model is proposed to solve the image reconstruction problem as follows:

$$\widehat{\mathbf{x}} = \arg\min_{\mathbf{x}} \lambda \|\mathbf{W}(\mathbf{y} - \mathbf{x})\|_1 + \sum_{j=1}^{J} \|\mathbf{A}_j \mathbf{x}\|_1, \tag{3}$$

where $\mathbf{y}$ is the noisy observation and $\mathbf{x}$ is the original image to be recovered; $\sum_{j=1}^{J} \|\mathbf{A}_j \mathbf{x}\|_1$ promotes the sparsity of J groups

FIGURE 4: Reconstructed *Barbara* images from 50% salt and pepper impulse noise. (a) Noise-free image, (b) noisy image, and (c)–(i) reconstructed images using AMF, TV, Wavelet, PANO, TV-ND, Wavelet-ND, and PANO-ND, respectively.

of similar patches using PANO $\mathbf{A}_j$ ($j = 1, 2, \ldots, J$); $\|\mathbf{y} - \mathbf{x}\|_1$ removes the outliers, that is, impulse noise in images; $\mathbf{W}$ is a diagonal matrix whose entries stand for weights on pixels; λ balances between the sparsity and outliers removal.

Let w_m be the mth diagonal entry of $\mathbf{W}$; a small weight w_i ($i \in \Omega$) is assigned for noise candidates and a large weight w_k ($k \in \overline{\Omega}$) for the rest of pixels; that is,

$$w_{i \in \Omega} > w_{k \in \overline{\Omega}}, \tag{4}$$

where Ω and $\overline{\Omega}$ contain the indexes of noise candidates and the rest of pixels, respectively. In this paper, we set $w_{k \in \overline{\Omega}} = 1$ for simplicity. The effect of $w_{i \in \Omega}$ will be analyzed in Section 3.3.

Compared with (1), noise candidates are distinguished from pixels and are expected to be suppressed according to the new model in (3). Therefore, the rest of the pixels are relatively preserved in the image reconstruction.

To solve the new regularization model, the alternating direction minimization with continuation [23] is modified

FIGURE 5: Reconstructed *House* images from 50% salt and pepper impulse noise. (a) Noise-free image, (b) noisy image, and (c)–(i) reconstructed images using AMF, TV, Wavelet, PANO, TV-ND, Wavelet-ND, and PANO-ND, respectively.

to solve the minimization problem with two l_1 regularization terms. A relaxed unconstraint form of (3) is written as

$$\min_{\mathbf{x},\boldsymbol{\alpha},\mathbf{z}}\sum_{j=1}^{J}\left(\left\|\boldsymbol{\alpha}_j\right\|_1 + \frac{\beta}{2}\left\|\boldsymbol{\alpha}_j - \mathbf{A}_j\mathbf{x}\right\|_2^2\right) \\ + \lambda\left(\|\mathbf{z}\|_1 + \frac{\beta}{2}\|\mathbf{z} - \mathbf{W}(\mathbf{y}-\mathbf{x})\|_2^2\right). \tag{5}$$

The solution of (5) approaches that of (3) as $\beta \to \infty$ [7]. For practical implementation, as β gradually increases, we use the previous solution as a "warm start" for the next alternating optimization.

When β is fixed, (5) can be solved in an alternating fashion as follows.

(1) For a fixed $\mathbf{x}$, solve

$$\min_{\boldsymbol{\alpha}}\sum_{j=1}^{J}\left(\left\|\boldsymbol{\alpha}_j\right\|_1 + \frac{\beta}{2}\left\|\boldsymbol{\alpha}_j - \mathbf{A}_j\mathbf{x}\right\|_2^2\right), \tag{6}$$

whose solution is obtained via soft thresholding for each $\boldsymbol{\alpha}_j$

$$\widehat{\boldsymbol{\alpha}}_j = S\left(\mathbf{A}_j\mathbf{x}, \frac{1}{\beta}\right) = \max\left(\left|\mathbf{A}_j\mathbf{x}\right| - \frac{1}{\beta}, 0\right)\frac{\mathbf{A}_j\mathbf{x}}{\left|\mathbf{A}_j\mathbf{x}\right|}, \tag{7}$$

and solve

$$\min_{\mathbf{z}}\|\mathbf{z}\|_1 + \frac{\beta}{2}\|\mathbf{z} - \mathbf{W}(\mathbf{y}-\mathbf{x})\|_2^2, \tag{8}$$

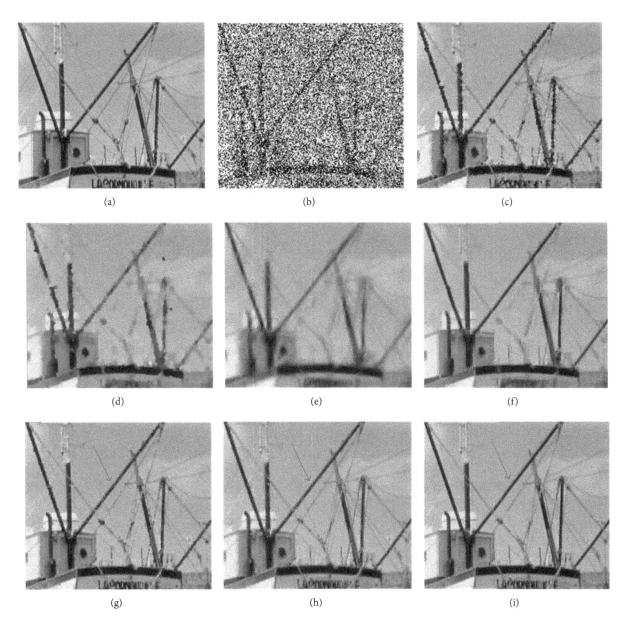

FIGURE 6: Reconstructed *Boat* images from 50% salt and pepper impulse noise. (a) Noise-free image, (b) noisy image, (c)–(i) reconstructed images using AMF, TV, Wavelet, PANO, TV-ND, Wavelet-ND, and PANO-ND, respectively.

whose solution is obtained via soft thresholding

$$\widehat{\mathbf{z}} = S\left(\mathbf{W}\left(\mathbf{y} - \mathbf{x}\right), \frac{1}{\beta}\right)$$

$$= \max\left(\left|\mathbf{W}\left(\mathbf{y} - \mathbf{x}\right)\right| - \frac{1}{\beta}, 0\right)\frac{\mathbf{W}\left(\mathbf{y} - \mathbf{x}\right)}{\left|\mathbf{W}\left(\mathbf{y} - \mathbf{x}\right)\right|}.$$

(9)

(2) For fixed $\boldsymbol{\alpha}_j$ $(j = 1, 2, \ldots, J)$ and $\mathbf{z}$, solve

$$\min_{\mathbf{x}} \sum_{j=1}^{J}\left\|\boldsymbol{\alpha}_j - \mathbf{A}_j\mathbf{x}\right\|_2^2 + \lambda\left\|\mathbf{z} - \mathbf{W}\left(\mathbf{y} - \mathbf{x}\right)\right\|_2^2, \quad (10)$$

which can be written as

$$\min_{\mathbf{x}} \sum_{j=1}^{J}\left\|\boldsymbol{\alpha}_j - \mathbf{A}_j\mathbf{x}\right\|_2^2 + \lambda\left\|\mathbf{W}\mathbf{y} - \mathbf{z} - \mathbf{W}\mathbf{x}\right\|_2^2. \quad (11)$$

The minimizer of (11) is given by the solution of the normal equation

$$\left(\sum_{j=1}^{J}\mathbf{A}_j^T\mathbf{A}_j + \lambda\mathbf{W}^T\mathbf{W}\right)\mathbf{x} = \sum_{j=1}^{J}\mathbf{A}_j^T\boldsymbol{\alpha}_j + \lambda\mathbf{W}^T\left(\mathbf{W}\mathbf{y} - \mathbf{z}\right),$$

(12)

which can be simplified as

$$\left(\mathbf{O} + \lambda\mathbf{W}^T\mathbf{W}\right)\mathbf{x} = \mathbf{v}_{\boldsymbol{\alpha}} + \lambda\mathbf{W}^T\mathbf{W}\mathbf{y} - \lambda\mathbf{W}^T\mathbf{z}, \quad (13)$$

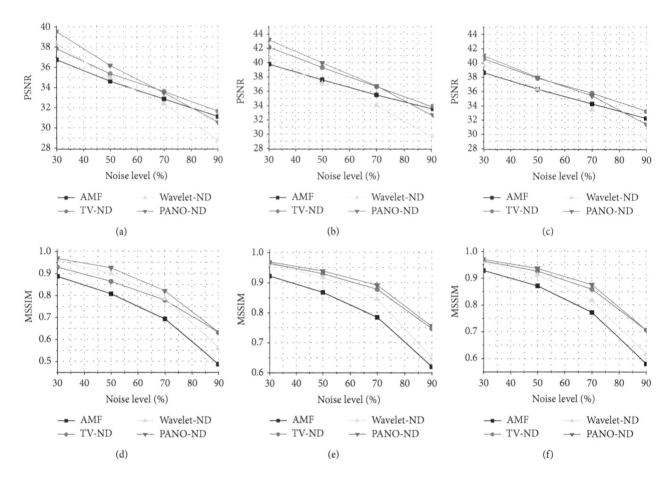

FIGURE 7: Quantitative measure at different noise levels. (a)–(c) PSNRs of *Barbara*, *House*, and *Boat* images, respectively; (d)–(f) MSSIMs of *Barbara*, *House*, and *Boat* images, respectively.

Initialization: Input the noise contaminated image **y**, the PANO $\mathbf{A}_j$ $(j = 1, \ldots, J)$, regularization parameter λ and tolerance of inner loop $\mu = 10^{-3}$. Initialize $\mathbf{x} = \mathbf{y}$, $\mathbf{z} = \mathbf{0}$, $\boldsymbol{\alpha}_j = \mathbf{0}$ for $j = 1, 2, \ldots, J$, $\beta = 2^4$ and $\mathbf{x}_{\text{last}} = \mathbf{0}$.

Main:
    While $\beta \leq 2^{14}$,
   Step 1. solve (7) to get $\boldsymbol{\alpha}_j$;
   Step 2. solve (9) to get **z**;
   Step 3. solve (13) to get **x**;
   Step 4. If $\|\mathbf{x}_{\text{last}} - \mathbf{x}\| > \mu \|\mathbf{x}_{\text{last}}\|$, go to *Step 1*;
      otherwise, go to *Step 5*;
   Step 5. $\beta \leftarrow 2\beta$, $\hat{\mathbf{x}} \leftarrow \mathbf{x}$, go to *Step 1*.
    End While

Output: $\hat{\mathbf{x}}$

ALGORITHM 1: PANO-based salt and pepper noise removal with noise detection.

---

and the term $\mathbf{v}_{\boldsymbol{\alpha}} = \sum_{j=1}^{J} \mathbf{A}_j^T \boldsymbol{\alpha}_j$ is an assembled image reconstructed from patches in all groups. One can use conjugate gradient to solve (13).

The algorithm is summarized in Algorithm 1 where **x** is updated in the subsequent iterations by following Step 1, 2, and 3.

3. Results

The proposed method is compared with AMF [2], sparsity-based denoising methods including TV [28, 29] and dual-tree complex Wavelet [12]. A suffix "ND" means that noise detection is applied in denoising. The proposed method PANO-ND is also compared with the original PANO [23].

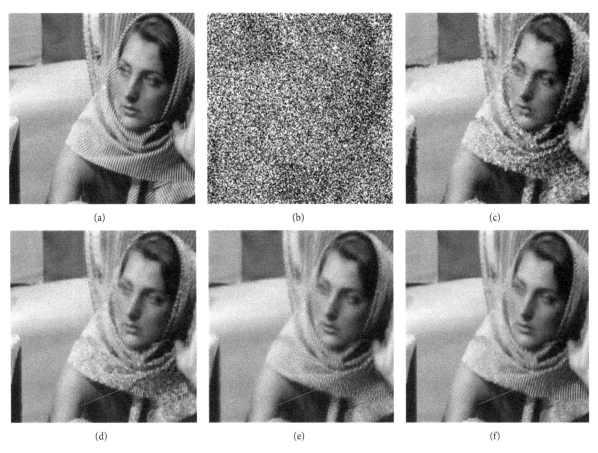

FIGURE 8: Reconstructed *Barbara* images from 70% salt and pepper impulse noise. (a) Noise-free image, (b) noisy image, (c)–(f) reconstructed images using AMF, TV-ND, Wavelet-ND, and PANO-ND, respectively.

Typical parameters of PANO-ND are the same as [23], including 16 similar patches in a group, patch size 8×8 and search region size 39×39. The similarity is first learnt form a denoised image using adaptive median filter, and then learnt twice from the denoised image for further reconstructions.

To quantitatively measure the denoising performance, the peak signal-to-noise ratio (PSNR) and mean measure of structural similarity (MSSIM) [30] are used. PSNR mainly measures the average pixel difference of the denoised and noise-free images. MSSIM focuses on the image structure consistency of denoised images to the original image. Higher PSNR and MSSIM mean better denoising performance. The regularization parameter λ of all sparsity-based methods is optimized to achieve the highest MSSIMs. Maximum window size of AMF is chosen as 39×39 since its performance is stable under all noise levels [28].

3.1. Effect of Noise Detection. Although edges are reconstructed better by exploring the image self-similarity in the original PANO (Figure 1(d)), all sparsity-based denoising methods fail to recover the image structures (Figures 4(d)–4(f)) when 50% or more pixels are corrupted without noise detection. By assigning noise candidates with a small weight, for example, 0.1 in experiments, all these methods have greatly improved the edge reconstruction (Figures 4(g)–4(i)).

Thus, noise detection is necessary for salt and pepper noise removal.

PANO-ND produces the most faithful images (Figure 4(i)) by clearly preserving edges of *Barbara* image among these methods. For *House* image (Figure 5) with more flat regions, between which exists a longer strong edge such as eave of the house, or pole in *Boat* image (Figure 6), they have more similar image groups; thus, the proposed method shows more advantage visually in restoring these edges.

In Table 1, we compared the performance of the AMF, Wavelet, PANO, and these methods with noise detection and weighted l_1-l_1 ($w = 0.1$). The proposed method achieves highest PSNRs and MSSIMs, indicating it performs better than the already existing ones. Therefore, PANO-ND significantly improves the edges and achieves better quantitative measures than other methods.

3.2. Different Noise Levels. How the performance varies for different noise levels is discussed. All the compared methods are with noise detection since its importance has been demonstrated. The denoising performance is quantitatively compared in Figure 7.

Under all noise levels, TV-ND achieves higher PSNRs and MSSIMs than AMF. Wavelet-ND obtains higher PSNRs than AMF for less than 50% noise and lower PSNRs when

FIGURE 9: Reconstructed *House* images from 70% salt and pepper impulse noise. (a) Noise-free image, (b) noisy image, (c)–(f) reconstructed images using AMF, TV-ND, Wavelet-ND, and PANO-ND, respectively.

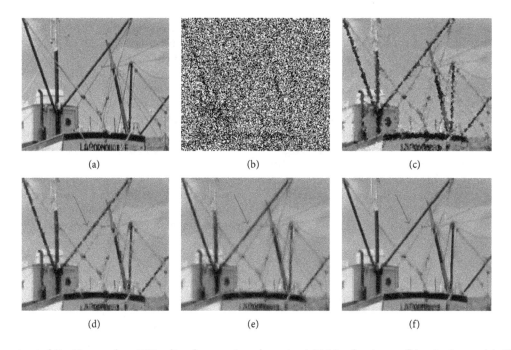

FIGURE 10: Reconstructed *Boat* images from 70% salt and pepper impulse noise. (a) Noise-free image, (b) noisy image, (c)–(f) reconstructed images using AMF, TV-ND, Wavelet-ND, and PANO-ND, respectively.

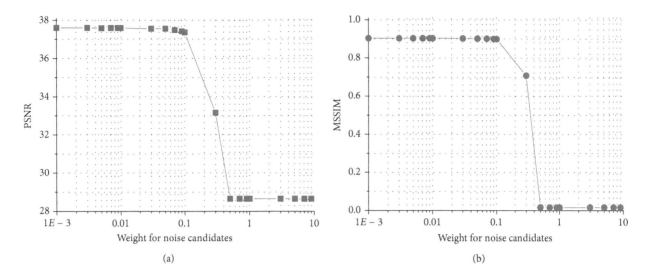

(a)   (b)

FIGURE 11: Quantitative measures versus the weight for noise candidates. Note: *House* image with 70% salt and pepper impulse noise is used in simulation and λ is 2.6.

TABLE 1: Quantitative measures for 50% salt and pepper impulse noise.

Images	Quantitative measure	l_1-l_1			Noise detection and weighted l_1-l_1			
		TV	Wavelet	PANO	AMF	TV	Wavelet	PANO
Barbara	PSNR	32.30	32.47	32.47	34.61	35.35	34.96	**36.18**
	MSSIM	0.6687	0.8884	0.7486	0.8080	0.8647	0.8991	**0.9262**
House	PSNR	35.52	32.14	35.87	37.61	39.32	37.08	**39.98**
	MSSIM	0.8096	0.7551	0.8537	0.8676	0.9293	0.9172	**0.9385**
Boat	PSNR	34.38	31.75	34.12	36.33	37.88	36.34	**37.99**
	MSSIM	0.7797	0.7167	0.822	0.8715	0.9266	0.9121	**0.9367**

the noise level is further increased. But the MSSIMs of Wavelet-ND are consistently larger than AMF for all noise levels, which implies that the image structures are better preserved. Comparing Wavelet-ND with TV-ND, the former leads to higher MSSIMs for *Barbara* image (Figure 7(d)) embedding fruitful textures while the latter obtains higher MSSIMs for *House* (Figure 7(e)) and *Boat* (Figure 7(f)) with more flat regions. The repeated small and directional patterns in clothes of *Barbara* image are usually considered as texture [31, 32]. Due to the directional Wavelet functions of the adopted dual-tree complex Wavelet, the Wavelet transform provides sparse representation of texture [33, 34]. On the contrary, total variation is good at sparsifying piece-wise constant image features [32, 35] and thus favors recovering flat regions in *House* and *Boat* images. Texture is easy to be lost when total variation is applied in noise removal [36]. Therefore, TV-ND is more suitable for images with flat regions while Wavelet-ND is better for image with fruitful textures.

The proposed PANO-ND outperforms both TV-ND and Wavelet-ND in terms of MSSIMs. PANO-ND achieves larger or comparable PSNRs when the noise level is below 90%. Besides, higher MSSIMs using PNAO-ND imply that image structures recovered by PANO-ND are more consistent to

those of noise-free images. As shown in Figures 8, 9, and 10, edges are recovered much clearer using PANO-ND than TV-ND. When the noise level approaches 90%, an extremely heavy noise, the PSNRs (lower than 34 dB) and MSSIMs (lower than 0.75) performance of all the methods are unsatisfactory since very limited information is available.

3.3. Effect of Weight for Noise Candidates. A smaller $w_{i\in\Omega}$ should be assigned to achieve better denoising performance. As shown in Figure 11, when $w_{i\in\Omega}$ becomes larger than 0.1, the quantitative measures reduce dramatically. One explanation is that, when $w_{i\in\Omega}$ and $w_{k\in\overline{\Omega}}$ are comparable, meaning $0.1 < w_{i\in\Omega}/w_{k\in\overline{\Omega}} < 1$, the penalization on noise candidates and the rest of pixels are in the same order; thus, noise candidates are not heavily suppressed in reconstruction. Therefore, $w_{i\in\Omega} \leq 10^{-1}$ is suggested.

3.4. Complexity Analysis. In this section, we tested the computation time of different methods in Table 2. The AMF is the fastest method, while PANO-ND is the most time-consuming method. Wavelet-ND runs faster than TV-ND but much slower than AMF.

Figure 12 shows the improvement in the MSSIM scores of these methods with increased complexity. The curve of

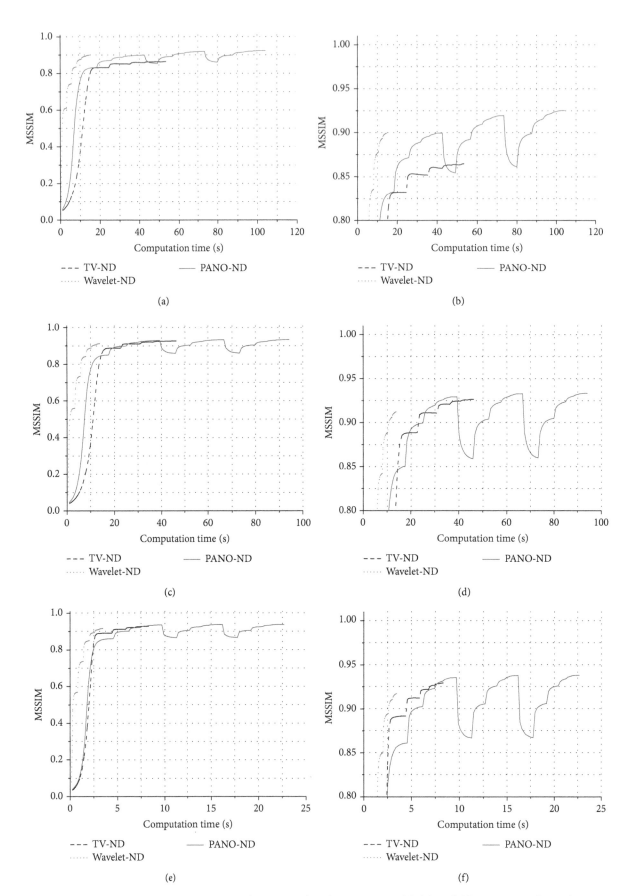

FIGURE 12: Figure 11 MSSIMs versus computation time from 50% salt and pepper noise. (a), (c), and (e) are MSSIMs for *Barbara*, *Boat*, and *House* images and (b), (d), and (f) are the zoom out part of (a), (c), and (e) when MSSIMs are greater than 0.8.

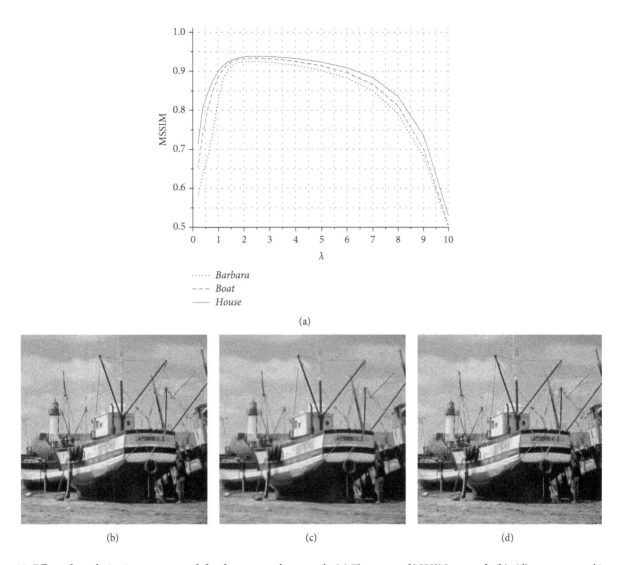

FIGURE 13: Effect of regularization parameter λ for the proposed approach. (a) The curve of MSSIM versus λ; (b)–(d) reconstructed images when $\lambda = 2, 1, 7$, respectively. Note: tests are performed at 50% impulse noise level.

TABLE 2: Computational time of different methods (units: seconds).

Images	Image size	AMF	TV-ND	Wavelet-ND	PANO-ND			
					1st recon.	2nd recon.	3rd recon.	Total
Barbara	512×512	0.37	49.21	11.34	40.15	28.89	28.86	97.90
Boat	512×512	0.37	42.32	10.39	37.56	25.80	25.74	89.10
House	256×256	0.07	7.61	3.00	9.19	6.29	6.19	21.67

Note: computations were performed on 2 Cores 2.7 GHz CPU desktop computer with 4 GB RAM. The alternating direction minimization with continuation is used to solve TV-ND, Wavelet-ND, and PANO-ND.

PANO-ND undergoes 3 peaks because the nonlocal similarity is learnt followed by reconstruction for 3 times. As to the first peak, PANO-ND gets higher or at least comparable MSSIM scores than other methods when the initial guide image is obtained using AMF. When this reconstructed image is further adopted as a guide image, PANO-ND keeps on achieving even higher MSSIM on the next two peaks for

Barbara image. For *Boat* and *House* image, it seems enough to only perform PANO-based reconstruction once.

3.5. Effect of λ. Effect of λ is discussed in Figure 13. MSSIMs versus λ are evaluated in Figure 13(a). With the increasing of λ, the MSSIMs increase first. Then MSSIMs hold similar for a range of λ ($\lambda \in [2, 4]$ for 50% noise level). When λ becomes too large ($\lambda > 4$ for 50% noise level), the MSSIMs decrease significantly. Reconstructed images with typical λ are shown in Figures 13(b)–13(d). The optimal result is achieved when $\lambda = 2$. The $\lambda = 1$ leads to oversmooth image in Figure 13(c) since a smaller λ encourages higher sparsity and fine image structures are lost. The $\lambda = 7$ results in some noise are not removed since the consistency between a noisy image **y** and its denoised version **x** is highly enforced. How to set an optimal λ is still unsolved which would be an interesting future work.

4. Conclusion

A new salt and pepper impulse noise removal method is proposed by first detecting noise candidates and then enforcing image sparsity with a patch-based sparse representation. A weighted l_1-l_1 regularization model is proposed to penalize the noise candidates heavier than other pixels. The proposed scheme significantly improves the denoising performance than the original PANO-based method under heavy noise. Compared with traditional impulse denoising methods, including adaptive median filtering, total variation and Wavelet, the new method shows obvious advantages on preserving edges and achieving higher structural similarity to the noise-free images. However, the nonlocal similarity is not accurate when noise level is high, for example, 90% noisy image, since initial guide image estimated from traditional adaptive median filtering is unsatisfactory. Future work includes the following.

(1) Taking advantage of nonlocal similarity in both noise detection and image restoration. A sparsity-based model to simultaneously extract impulse noise [13] and recover image will avoid introducing traditional adaptive median filtering; thus, it may improve the denoising performance when noise is heavy.

(2) Wedding adaptive geometric information [15, 16, 37] with image patch similarity may further improve the denoising performance.

(3) Given a specific image, how to automatically set the regularization parameters to trade the data consistency with sparsity remains open.

(4) Accelerate the proposed approach with advanced numerical algorithms [38–40] and hardware, for example, graphic processing units.

Conflict of Interests

The authors declare that there is no conflict of interests regarding the publication of this paper.

Acknowledgments

This work was supported in part by the National Natural Science Foundation of China (61302174, 61201045, and 61065007), Scientific Research Foundation for the Introduction of Talent at Xiamen University of Technology (YKJ12021R and YKJ12023R), Open Fund from Key Lab of Digital Signal and Image Processing of Guangdong Province (2013GDDSIPL-07 and 54600321), and Fundamental Research Funds for the Central Universities (2013SH002). The authors are grateful to the reviewers for their thorough advices which made this work more interesting.

References

[1] R. C. Gonzalez and E. Richard, *Digital Image Processing*, Prentice Hall, 2002.

[2] H. Hwang and R. A. Haddad, "Adaptive median filters: new algorithms and results," *IEEE Transactions on Image Processing*, vol. 4, no. 4, pp. 499–502, 1995.

[3] B. Deka and S. Choudhury, "A multiscale detection based adaptive median filter for the removal of salt and pepper noise from highly corrupted images," *International Journal of Signal Processing, Image Processing and Pattern Recognition*, vol. 6, pp. 129–144, 2013.

[4] P. S. J. Sree, P. Kumar, R. Siddavatam, and R. Verma, "Salt-and-pepper noise removal by adaptive median-based lifting filter using second-generation wavelets," *Signal, Image and Video Processing*, vol. 7, pp. 111–118, 2013.

[5] M. H. Hsieh, F. C. Cheng, M. C. Shie, and S. J. Ruan, "Fast and efficient median filter for removing 1–99% levels of salt-and-pepper noise in images," *Engineering Applications of Artificial Intelligence*, vol. 26, pp. 1333–1338, 2013.

[6] T.-C. Lin and Y. U. Pao-Ta, "Salt-pepper impulse noise detection and removal using multiple thresholds for image restoration," *Journal of Information Science and Engineering*, vol. 22, no. 1, pp. 189–198, 2006.

[7] R. Dharmarajan and K. Kannan, "A hypergraph-based algorithm for image restoration from salt and pepper noise," *International Journal of Electronics and Communications*, vol. 64, no. 12, pp. 1114–1122, 2010.

[8] A. Adeli, F. Tajeripoor, M. J. Zomorodian, and M. Neshat, "Comparison of the Fuzzy-based wavelet shrinkage image denoising techniques," *International Journal of Computer Science Issues*, vol. 9, pp. 211–216, 2012.

[9] Y. Dong and S. Xu, "A new directional weighted median filter for removal of random-valued impulse noise," *IEEE Signal Processing Letters*, vol. 14, no. 3, pp. 193–196, 2007.

[10] C.-T. Lu and T.-C. Chou, "Denoising of salt-and-pepper noise corrupted image using modified directional-weighted-median filter," *Pattern Recognition Letters*, vol. 33, no. 10, pp. 1287–1295, 2012.

[11] K. K. V. Toh, H. Ibrahim, and M. N. Mahyuddin, "Salt-and-pepper noise detection and reduction using fuzzy switching median filter," *IEEE Transactions on Consumer Electronics*, vol. 54, no. 4, pp. 1956–1961, 2008.

[12] S. Huang and J. Zhu, "Removal of salt-and-pepper noise based on compressed sensing," *Electronics Letters*, vol. 46, no. 17, pp. 1198–1199, 2010.

[13] X.-L. Wang, C.-L. Wang, J.-B. Zhu, and D.-N. Liang, "Salt-and-pepper noise removal based on image sparse representation," *Optical Engineering*, vol. 50, no. 9, Article ID 097007, 2011.

[14] Q. Liu, S. Wang, J. Luo, Y. Zhu, and M. Ye, "An augmented Lagrangian approach to general dictionary learning for image denoising," *Journal of Visual Communication and Image Representation*, vol. 23, pp. 753–766, 2012.

[15] E. Le Pennec and S. Mallat, "Sparse geometric image representations with bandelets," *IEEE Transactions on Image Processing*, vol. 14, no. 4, pp. 423–438, 2005.

[16] X. Qu, D. Guo, B. Ning et al., "Undersampled MRI reconstruction with patch-based directional wavelets," *Magnetic Resonance Imaging*, vol. 30, pp. 964–977, 2012.

[17] B. Ning, X. Qu, D. Guo, C. Hu, and Z. Chen, "Magnetic resonance image reconstruction using trained geometric directions in 2D redundant wavelets domain and non-convex optimization," *Magnetic Resonance Imaging*, vol. 31, pp. 1611–1622, 2013.

[18] M. Aharon, M. Elad, and A. Bruckstein, "K-SVD: an algorithm for designing overcomplete dictionaries for sparse representation," *IEEE Transactions on Signal Processing*, vol. 54, no. 11, pp. 4311–4322, 2006.

[19] J.-F. Cai, R. H. Chan, and C. Di Fiore, "Minimization of a detail-preserving regularization functional for impulse noise removal," *Journal of Mathematical Imaging and Vision*, vol. 29, no. 1, pp. 79–91, 2007.

[20] M. Elad and M. Aharon, "Image denoising via sparse and redundant representations over learned dictionaries," *IEEE Transactions on Image Processing*, vol. 15, no. 12, pp. 3736–3745, 2006.

[21] J. F. Cai, H. Ji, Z. Shen, and G. B. Ye, "Data-driven tight frame construction and image denoising," *Applied and Computational Harmonic Analysis*, 2013.

[22] L. Ma, J. Yu, and T. Zeng, "Sparse representation prior and total variation-based image deblurring under impulse noise," *SIAM Journal on Imaging Sciences*, vol. 6, pp. 2258–2284, 2013.

[23] X. Qu, Y. Hou, F. Lam, D. Guo, J. Zhong, and Z. Chen, "Magnetic resonance image reconstruction from undersampled measurements using a patch-based nonlocal operator," *Medical Image Analysis*, 2013.

[24] K. Dabov, A. Foi, V. Katkovnik, and K. Egiazarian, "Image denoising by sparse 3-D transform-domain collaborative filtering," *IEEE Transactions on Image Processing*, vol. 16, no. 8, pp. 2080–2095, 2007.

[25] Y. Hou, C. Zhao, D. Yang, and Y. Cheng, "Comments on image denoising by sparse 3-D transform-domain collaborative filtering," *IEEE Transactions on Image Processing*, vol. 20, no. 1, pp. 268–270, 2011.

[26] D. Huang, L. Kang, Y. Wang, and C. Lin, "Self-learning based image decomposition with applications to single image denoising," *IEEE Transactions on Multimedia*, vol. 16, pp. 83–93, 2014.

[27] D. Guo, X. Qu, M. Wu, J. Yan, X. Chen, and K. Wu, "Impulse artefacts removal with similarity-motivated sparse representation," submitted to *Electronics Letters*.

[28] R. H. Chan, C.-W. Ho, and M. Nikolova, "Salt-and-pepper noise removal by median-type noise detectors and detail-preserving regularization," *IEEE Transactions on Image Processing*, vol. 14, no. 10, pp. 1479–1485, 2005.

[29] M. Nikolova, "A variational approach to remove outliers and impulse noise," *Journal of Mathematical Imaging and Vision*, vol. 20, no. 1-2, pp. 99–120, 2004.

[30] Z. Wang, A. C. Bovik, H. R. Sheikh, and E. P. Simoncelli, "Image quality assessment: from error visibility to structural similarity," *IEEE Transactions on Image Processing*, vol. 13, no. 4, pp. 600–612, 2004.

[31] J.-F. Cai, R. H. Chan, and Z. Shen, "Simultaneous cartoon and texture Inpainting," *Inverse Problems and Imaging*, vol. 4, no. 3, pp. 379–395, 2010.

[32] J.-L. Starck, M. Elad, and D. L. Donoho, "Image decomposition via the combination of sparse representations and a variational approach," *IEEE Transactions on Image Processing*, vol. 14, no. 10, pp. 1570–1582, 2005.

[33] I. W. Selesnick, R. G. Baraniuk, and N. G. Kingsbury, "The dual-tree complex wavelet transform," *IEEE Signal Processing Magazine*, vol. 22, no. 6, pp. 123–151, 2005.

[34] R. Kwitt and A. Uhl, "Lightweight probabilistic texture retrieval," *IEEE Transactions on Image Processing*, vol. 19, no. 1, pp. 241–253, 2010.

[35] K. Bredies, K. Kunisch, and T. Pock, "Total generalized variation," *SIAM Journal on Imaging Sciences*, vol. 3, no. 3, pp. 492–526, 2010.

[36] A. Buades, B. Coll, and J. M. Morel, "A review of image denoising algorithms, with a new one," *Multiscale Modeling and Simulation*, vol. 4, no. 2, pp. 490–530, 2005.

[37] G. Peyre and S. Mallat, "Surface compression with geometric bandelets," *ACM Transactions on Graphics*, vol. 24, pp. 601–608, 2005.

[38] J.-F. Cai, S. Osher, and Z. Shen, "Linearized Bregman iterations for compressed sensing," *Mathematics of Computation*, vol. 78, no. 267, pp. 1515–1536, 2009.

[39] T. Goldstein and S. Osher, "The split Bregman method for L1-regularized problems," *SIAM Journal on Imaging Sciences*, vol. 2, pp. 323–343, 2009.

[40] W. Yin, S. Osher, D. Goldfarb, and J. Darbon, "Bregman iterative algorithms for l_1-minimization with applications to compressed sensing," *SIAM Journal on Imaging Sciences*, vol. 1, pp. 143–168, 2008.

11

Robust Signature-Based Copyright Protection Scheme Using the Most Significant Gray-Scale Bits of the Image

Mohammad Awrangjeb

Cooperative Research Centre for Spatial Information, Department of Infrastructure Engineering, University of Melbourne, VIC 3010, Australia

Correspondence should be addressed to Mohammad Awrangjeb, mawr@unimelb.edu.au

Academic Editor: Xian-Sheng Hua

The *most significant bit-* (MSB-) plane of an image is least likely to change by the most signal processing operations. This paper presents a novel multibit logo-based signature, using the most significant gray-scale bits, which is then used to develop an extremely simple but robust copyright protection scheme, where images along with their signatures are sent to a trusted third party when a dispute arises. Different ways of processing the MSB-plane before calculating the robust signature have been developed. This paper then presents an innovative classifier-based technique to test the robustness and uniqueness of any signature-based scheme. A new MSB-based attack, which would defeat our scheme most, has also been proposed. Experimental results have clearly demonstrated the superiority of the proposed scheme showing the high robustness of different MSB-based signatures over the existing signature-based schemes.

1. Introduction

For last few years, we have been using electronic commerce that includes online and offline distribution of multimedia data like images, audios, and videos. However, digital multimedia files can be easily manipulated using commercial graphics tools. Duplicating digital files has become as simple as clicking a button. Since maintaining an exact or manipulated duplicate of any digital data is easier than before, the enforcement of copyright protection has become more imperative than ever. Although copyright laws are being applied against abusers in order to ensure secure electronic commerce, the current problems with copyright protection obstruct the rapid evolution of computer and communication networks. As a result, the enhancement and further development of digital copyright protection is in central to the development of future communication networks [1]. There may be three types of solutions to the copyright protection problem: cryptographic tools, digital watermarking techniques, and digital signature-based techniques.

Cryptographic tools [2] can be used to encrypt a multimedia file using some secret key. The encrypted file is no more perceptually understandable and can be distributed to the users. Only the appropriate user that holds the secret key can decrypt and use this file. Such a technique while suitable for text documents is not suitable for multimedia data for the following two reasons. First, multimedia file size is much larger than that of text. Therefore, encrypting or decrypting a multimedia file is highly time consuming. Second, the encrypted media file is not useful in the public domain, for example, in the Internet. Because the encrypted file is not perceptually understandable and if the encrypted information is decrypted once, the information is no longer protected. However, the multimedia file provides an opportunity that the text document does not. That is, while no distortion is allowed in the signed text, some distortions are allowed in the signed multimedia file as long as it is perceptually similar to the original file.

Digital watermarking techniques take the opportunity of the abovementioned property of the media file. They embed a watermark such as logos, seals, or sequence numbers, into the original image. The embedded watermark should survive against both malicious and nonmalicious attacks depending on the applications. Latter, the embedded information is extracted from or detected in the watermarked image in order to verify the ownership [3–11].

Any watermarking technique should satisfy a number of essential properties [1, 5, 6]. However, many of the existing techniques do not satisfy some of the properties and, therefore, may not be applicable to build a proper copyright protection system [1, 8, 9]. They always distort the original image that might not be acceptable in some applications like medical imagery, law enforcement, and astrophysics research [7]. The amount of distortions increases with the increase of the embedding strength which though increases the chance of the survival of the watermark under different signal processing attacks. Some attacks like geometric distortions, collusion, and copy (averaging) attacks still challenge the robustness property. The watermark can also be removed using denoising [9]. Multiple watermarking (buyer's and seller's watermarks) in a single media is also problematic, since previous embedded watermark cannot be guaranteed to survive after the embedding of next watermark. Publicly verification of watermarking is another unsolved problem.

Digital signature-based copyright protection schemes [1, 12–15] combine the advantages of both digital watermarking and cryptographic solutions. This technique, in general, calculates a digital signature using a logo and the extracted features from the original image (see Figure 1). The signature may then be protected using cryptography and certified by a *trusted third party* (TTP). Later, the signature is used to retrieve the logo from the test image. The retrieved logo is compared with the original logo using some similarity measurement function and a decision is made based on a threshold.

The reason of using a logo as a watermark [16] or to calculate signature [1, 12–15] is because it is a true representative of a company, an owner, or a customer. In the verification phase, in addition to "yes" or "no" answer based on the threshold, logo-based copyright protection schemes also allow perceptual recognition of the logo. Watermarking techniques embedding logos [16] mainly embed small binary logos and are unable to use large multibit (e.g., gray-scale) logos due to limited embedding capacity. However, large multibit logos are more practical and offer greater security than small binary logos. In contrast, signature-based schemes may calculate signature using any type (e.g., binary, gray-scale) and size of logos. There are also other signature-based schemes [17, 18], which do not use logos.

There are many advantages of signature-based schemes over watermarking techniques. They cause no visual quality degradation to images as they do not embed any information. They offer cryptographic security and can sign any sizes of logos. They resolve multiple ownership claims by adding timestamp with the signature. They can use both buyer and seller logos while calculating the signature, thus providing practical usefulness of the copyright protection system in the network world. They can use any multibit logos that offer greater opportunity to survive than binary logos. In addition, they allow public verification when the signature is generated using public key cryptographic infrastructure.

Katzenbeisser [19] argued that watermarking alone is not sufficient to resolve rightful ownership of digital data;

therefore, a protocol relying on the existing cryptographic tools is necessary. Macq et al. [20] mentioned that watermarking along with registration authorities and transaction certifications are essential for digital right management of Internet distributed images. The signature-based schemes along with cryptographic tools can be considered as the complementary to the watermarking techniques to design a proper digital right management system.

In this paper, we propose a computationally inexpensive signature-based gray-scale image copyright protection scheme intuitively using the *most significant bit-* (MSB-) plane (MSB-based scheme), which is least likely to change by any image processing operation. The MSB-plane of an image can be chosen in different ways before calculating the signature using the bit-planes of the logo: (i) directly choosing the MSB-plane at a *region-of-interest* (ROI), (ii) choosing the MSB-planes of textured blocks, (iii) choosing the MSBs of DC coefficients of the MSB-plane, and (iv) choosing the MSB-plane after t-scale wavelet decomposition. Besides being image size invariant, the proposed scheme can be used with any n-bit logo. In order to prove the robustness and the uniqueness of this scheme, we also present a novel idea of finding a classifier to separate logo retrieval instances of attacked images with the original signature against all other possible alternatives. To avoid any bias, we further propose a new MSB-based attack, which would defeat our scheme most. We then present a comprehensive TTP management policy that uses classifier-based thresholds in order to minimize false alarms. Experimental results not only reveal very high logo retrieval rate and visual quality of the retrieved logos by the proposed scheme against those by the existing schemes [12, 13] that also use multibit logos but also show the weakness of the latter as they fail to produce any classifier as discussed above. Note that the proposed signature-based scheme along with some preliminary results was published in [21].

The rest of the paper is organized as follows: Section 2 presents the previous signature-based schemes using logos; Section 3 describes why we have chosen MSB bit-plane for the proposed scheme; Section 4 presents the proposed scheme; Section 5 presents the experimental results and then compares the proposed scheme with the existing schemes; finally Section 6 concludes the paper with future research directions.

2. Previous Works

Lee and Chen [13] calculated the signature of an image with a gray-scale logo using *vector quantization* (VQ) on the coarse scale of the image obtained by a t-scale wavelet transform. The scheme is publicly verifiable and robust to a wide variety of attacks. However, it is weak to high lossy compression and geometric distortions. It cannot calculate signature if the type of the logo and the image is different, for example, binary logo and gray-scale image. The size of the coarse image reduces exponentially as t increases. Compounded with the approximation due to VQ, this can potentially lead to a very poor quality of the retrieved logo, especially when

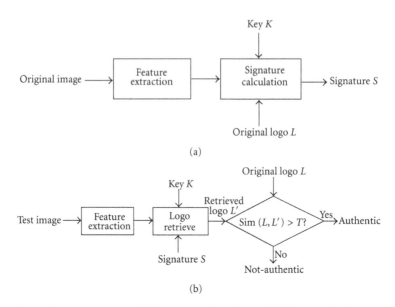

(a)

(b)

FIGURE 1: Signature-based scheme using logo: (a) signature calculation and (b) logo retrieval operation and verification.

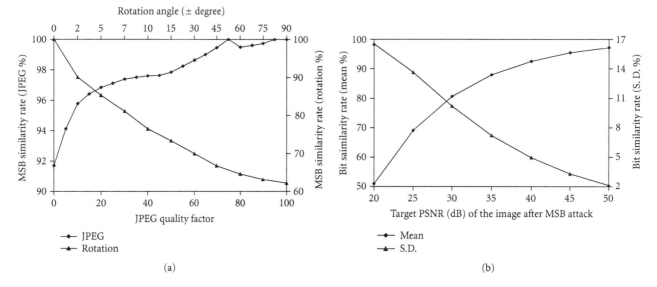

(a)

(b)

FIGURE 2: (a) Most significant bit (MSB) similarity rates of gray-scale image at different JPEG and rotation attacks; (b) mean and standard deviation of gray-scale MSB similarity under the newly proposed MSB attack. Note that the rotation angle axis in (a) is nonlinear.

the original image size is small as demanded by the WWW. Chen et al. [1] later extended this idea for binary logos by replacing VQ with a polarity table. However, uniqueness of the signature, where it should verify the corresponding image only, may not be guaranteed with binary logos.

Chang et al. [14] calculated signature with a gray-scale logo using torus automorphism functions. To survive in cropping attacks, the idea of using a rectangular *region-of-interest* (ROI) in the image was introduced in [12]. This technique can be used for cartoon graphics and survives on repainting. Nevertheless, it still cannot survive in high lossy compression and geometric distortions. It also cannot calculate signature if the type of the logo and the image is different, for example, binary logo and gray-scale image.

The scheme in [15] used visual secret sharing technique to calculate signature using binary logos. It offers cryptographic security and allows generating meaningful share. It also allows multiple owners to share the same image. However, robustness depends on the sorting algorithm; that is, if the image is modified moderately, the sorting algorithm may result different share. Consequently, it cannot survive in high JPEG compression and small geometric distortions.

All the above existing schemes offer very high time complexity. The time complexity increases, due to use of VQ encoding [13], torus automorphism [12, 14], permutation [1], or visual cryptography [15], with the increase of image size. Some of the above schemes [1, 13] incorporate digital signature including timestamp with the published image

FIGURE 3: Original images (a) Lena and (b) Elaine with their ROIs used; original logos (c) Monash and (d) NUS; mapped logos by TROI-based scheme [12] (e) Monash (15.19 dB, 53%) and (f) NUS (17.47 dB, 55%); and coded logos by VQ-based scheme [13] (g) Monash (23.40 dB, 64%) and (h) NUS (25.35 dB, 66%). Note that all images (512 × 512) and logos (64 × 64) are 8-bit gray-scale. Request granted to use logos for research purposes only.

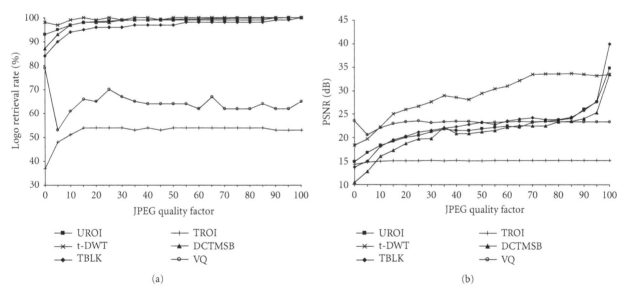

FIGURE 4: (a) Logo retrieval rate and (b) PSNR using Lena image and Monash logo by different approaches of the proposed MSB-based scheme and existing TROI-based [12] and VQ-based [13] schemes under different JPEG quality factors.

allowing public verification. Nonetheless, they increase the file size and the risk of losing copyright if the signature is removed from the header accidentally or intentionally.

3. Why the Most Significant Bit?

The MSBs are least likely to change by any image processing operation, for example, JPEG compression, filtering, and so forth. However, watermarking techniques cannot embed the watermark in the MSB-plane of an image. Because changes to MSBs introduce higher noticeable distortions. In the following experiments, we observed that the robustness of the MSB-based digital signature would be very high.

We conducted experiments on a large database of 1032 images [22], including the benchmark ones [23]. In each case, we measured the MSB similarity rate, which means the percentage of MSBs that remain unchanged under the attack. Figure 2(a) shows that on average more than 91%

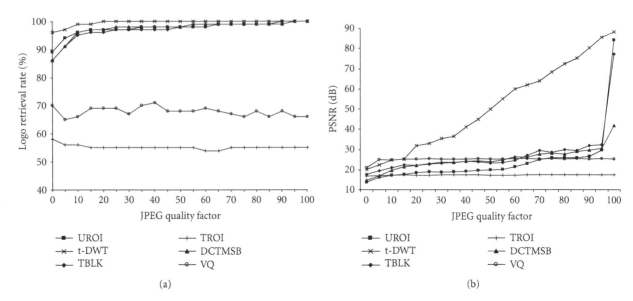

FIGURE 5: (a) Logo retrieval rate and (b) PSNR using Elaine image and NUS logo by different approaches of the proposed MSB-based scheme and existing TROI-based [12] and VQ-based [13] schemes under different JPEG quality factors.

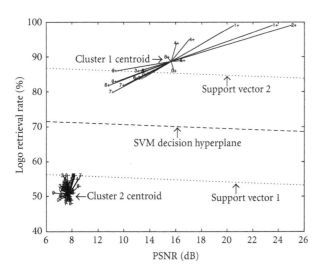

FIGURE 6: SVM classification and K-means clustering results by the UROI approach of the proposed MSB-based scheme. Note that the distance between support vectors by SVM [27] is $d = 30.2$ and cluster 1 and cluster 2 are positive and negative clusters, respectively, by K-means clustering algorithm [28]. Attack numbers 0–9 are referred using Table 3.

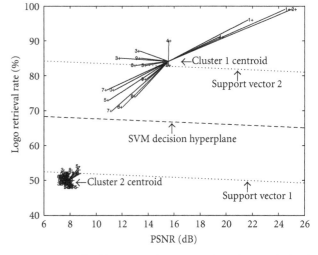

FIGURE 7: SVM classification and K-means clustering results by the TBLK approach of the proposed MSB-based scheme. Note that the distance between support vectors by SVM [27] is $d = 31.5$ and cluster 1 and cluster 2 are positive and negative clusters, respectively, by K-means clustering algorithm [28]. Attack numbers 0–9 are referred using Table 3.

of the gray-scale MSBs remained the same even when JPEG quality was set at the minimum; while more than 88% of the MSBs remained unchanged if the image is rotated by no more than ±5°. We further observed that under median filter, histogram equalization, salt and pepper noise, and Gaussian noise attacks on average more than 97%, 80%, 97%, and 90% of MSBs, respectively, remained unchanged, as shown in Table 1. In addition, we also tested the MSB similarity rate in the following four cases: (i) the MSB-plane at an ROI, (ii) the MSB-planes of textured blocks, (iii) the MSBs of DC coefficients of the MSB-plane, and (iv) the MSB-plane after

4-scale wavelet decomposition. Table 1 shows that histogram equalization and rotation attacks changed more MSBs than filtering and noising attacks. In StirMark attacks [24] like small random distortions, first three cases kept more than 80% MSBs unchanged and 4-level wavelet decomposition case is the most sensitive to these attacks. We will discuss how the MSBs were extracted in these four cases in Section 4.1.

In order to avoid any bias, we now propose a new attack, namely, the MSB attack, where for a given target image-quality, in *peak-signal-to-noise ratio* (PSNR), the maximum number of gray-scale MSBs are changed. We sort the pixels in

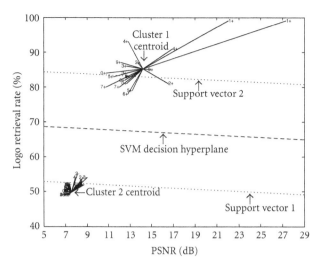

FIGURE 8: SVM classification and K-means clustering results by the DCTMSB approach of the proposed MSB-based scheme. Note that the distance between support vectors by SVM [27] is $d = 31.3$ and cluster 1 and cluster 2 are positive and negative clusters, respectively, by K-means clustering algorithm [28]. Attack numbers 0–9 are referred using Table 3.

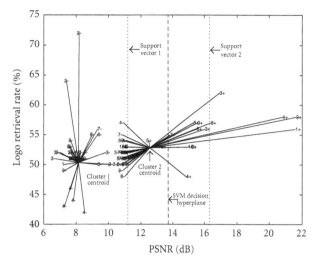

FIGURE 10: SVM classification and K-means clustering results by the existing TROI-based scheme [12]. Note that the distance between support vectors by SVM [27] is $d = 5.1$ and cluster 1 and cluster 2 are positive and negative clusters, respectively, by K-means clustering algorithm [28]. Attack numbers 0–9 are referred using Table 3.

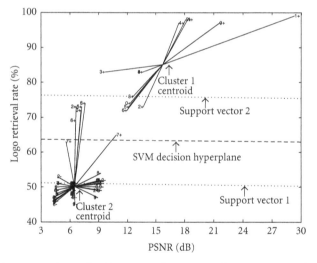

FIGURE 9: SVM classification and K-means clustering results by the t-DWT ($t = 4$) approach of the proposed MSB-based scheme. Note that the distance between support vectors by SVM [27] is $d = 25.1$ and cluster 1 and cluster 2 are positive and negative clusters, respectively, by K-means clustering algorithm [28]. Attack numbers 0–9 are referred using Table 3.

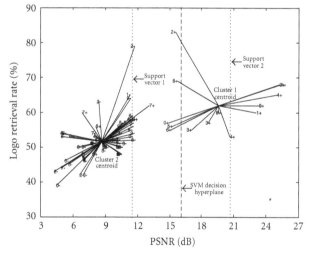

FIGURE 11: SVM classification and K-means clustering results by the existing VQ-based scheme [13]. Note that the distance between support vectors by SVM [27] is $D = 9.2$ and cluster 1 and cluster 2 are positive and negative clusters, respectively, by K-means clustering algorithm [28]. Attack numbers 0–9 are referred using Table 3.

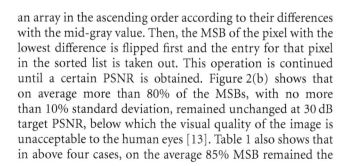

an array in the ascending order according to their differences with the mid-gray value. Then, the MSB of the pixel with the lowest difference is flipped first and the entry for that pixel in the sorted list is taken out. This operation is continued until a certain PSNR is obtained. Figure 2(b) shows that on average more than 80% of the MSBs, with no more than 10% standard deviation, remained unchanged at 30 dB target PSNR, below which the visual quality of the image is unacceptable to the human eyes [13]. Table 1 also shows that in above four cases, on the average 85% MSB remained the

same at 35 dB target PSNR, and among these cases 4-level DWT decomposition left most of the MSBs unchanged.

From Figure 2 and Table 1, it is observed that even when the images are distorted to a limit where the PSNR becomes as low as 15 dB to 30 dB, the majority of the MSBs still remain the same. This is because in signal processing attacks (JPEG, filtering, etc.), image pixels do not change their locations and thus majority of the MSBs do not change. On the other hand, in geometric attacks (rotation, scaling, etc.) image pixels change their locations and thus the MSB similarity rate drops even in small rotation angle change. In the case of high geometric distortions, it is possible to estimate the transformation parameters first [25] and then to reverse the transformation before using the MSBs for signature calculation.

4. Proposed Scheme

The proposed MSB-based scheme first selects a set of MSBs from the image and then calculates digital signature of an image for a logo. The signature is certified by the TTP. When a dispute arises between two images of two parties, both parties send their certified signatures and images along with their corresponding parameters to the TTP to judge.

4.1. Selecting the MSBs. The MSBs can be selected in different ways. In this section, we discuss four of them.

Consider an n-bit gray-scale image $I = \{i_b(x, y)\}$ of size $w_I \times h_I$ pixels where $1 \leq x \leq w_I$, $1 \leq y \leq h_I$, and $1 \leq b \leq n$. Similarly, consider an n-bit gray-scale logo $L = \{l_b(x, y)\}$ of size $w_L \times h_L$. Depending on the different ways of pre-processing the MSB-plane of the image, the MSB-based scheme may be named as different approaches.

    (i) UROI. The MSB-plane at an ROI of the image is chosen directly. Notice that an ROI can be user defined and can be located using reference points, for example, corners [26].

    (ii) TBLK. The MSB-planes of textured blocks at the ROI are chosen. We select 8×8 textured blocks from the image using the technique represented in [7]. The MSB-planes of the selected textured blocks are accumulated as a single MSB-plane, where textured blocks are first taken in row-wise and then in column-wise.

    (iii) DCTMSB. We can choose the MSBs of DC coefficients of MSB-plane. We divide the MSB-plane into 8×8 blocks before taking DCT. Then we take the MSB of DCT coefficients in original space order (without sorting them).

    (iv) t-DWT. The MSB-plane of LL_t after t-scale wavelet decomposition of the original image is chosen.

4.2. Signature Calculation. Let $M_I = \{m_j\}$, where $1 \leq j \leq z$, be the collective set of MSBs selected from I using one of the above approaches. Without any loss of generality, it is assumed that

$$z \geq n w_L h_L. \tag{1}$$

The signature S_I of I for L with M_I is thus calculated as

$$S_I(j = (b-1)w_L h_L + (y-1)h_L + x) = m_j \oplus l_b(x, y). \tag{2}$$

If the generality assumption in (1) cannot be met, m_j's could be reused iteratively once exhausted. Moreover, any color image can be signed using its gray-scale equivalent with even a colored logo after stripping it into three gray-scale

channels. Once the signature is calculated, the owner sends the following message, in the form of a triplet, to the TTP using public key cryptography:

$$M_{OT} = E_{T, \text{PUB}}(E_{O, \text{PRV}}([I, S_I, A_I])), \tag{3}$$

where $E_{T, \text{PUB}}$ and $E_{O, \text{PRV}}$ are the public and private key encryptions of the TTP and the owner respectively and A_I contains information about the MSB selection approach. On receiving the above message from the owner O at time TS, the message is first decrypted to receive the signature triplet as follows:

$$[I, S_I, A_I] = D_{O, \text{PUB}}(D_{T, \text{PRV}}(\text{Msg})), \tag{4}$$

where $D_{O, \text{PUB}}$ and $D_{T, \text{PRV}}$ are the public and private key decryptions of the owner and the TTP, respectively. The TTP verifies S_I for I using A_I, appends timestamp TS, and sends back the following message to the owner:

$$M_{TO} = E_{O, \text{PUB}}(E_{T, \text{PRV}}(S_I || \text{TS})), \tag{5}$$

where $E_{O, \text{PUB}}$ and $E_{T, \text{PRV}}$ are the public and private key encryptions of the owner and the TTP, respectively. The owner decrypts the above message with his private key as

$$S_I^c = E_{T, \text{PRV}}(S_I || \text{TS}) = D_{O, \text{PRV}}(M_2), \tag{6}$$

where $D_{O, \text{PRV}}$ is the private key decryptions of the owner. We name S_I^c as the certified signature for the image I.

4.3. Signature Verification. When a dispute arises for two images I_i and I_j between two persons P_1 and P_2, they send the following messages claiming the ownership to the TTP:

$$M_{P_1 T} = E_{T, \text{PUB}}\left(E_{P_1, \text{PRV}}\left(I_i, L_1, S_{I_i}^c, A_{I_i}\right)\right),$$
$$M_{P_2 T} = E_{T, \text{PUB}}\left(E_{P_2, \text{PRV}}\left(I_j, L_2, S_{I_j}^c, A_{I_j}\right)\right), \tag{7}$$

where $E_{P_1, \text{PRV}}$ and $E_{P_2, \text{PRV}}$ are the private key encryptions of P_1 and P_2, respectively. The TTP decrypts the above messages as

$$\left[I_i, L_1, S_{I_i}^c, A_{I_i}\right] = D_{P_1, \text{PUB}}(D_{T, \text{PRV}}(M_{P_1 T})),$$
$$\left[I_j, L_2, S_{I_j}^c, A_{I_j}\right] = D_{P_2, \text{PUB}}(D_{T, \text{PRV}}(M_{P_2 T})), \tag{8}$$

where $D_{P_1, \text{PUB}}$ and $D_{P_2, \text{PUB}}$ are the public key decryptions of P_1 and P_2, respectively. The TTP then decrypted the certified signatures $S_{I_i}^c$ and $S_{I_j}^c$ with its public key; this ensures the certificates have been issued by the TTP and the timestamps have not been changed afterwards their generation:

$$S_{I_i} || \text{TS}_i = D_{T, \text{PUB}}\left(S_{I_i}^c\right), \qquad S_{I_j} || \text{TS}_j = D_{T, \text{PUB}}\left(S_{I_j}^c\right). \tag{9}$$

The TTP recalculates the signatures S_{I_i} and S_{I_j} and compares with the existing ones. This check ensures that encrypted signatures $S_{I_i}^c$ and $S_{I_j}^c$ have been generated for images I_i and I_j, respectively.

TABLE 1: *Most significant bit* (MSB) similarity rate under different attacks.

Attacks	PSNR (dB)	MSB similarity rate (%)				
		MSB-plane	ROI[1]	Text blocks[2]	DC of MSB[3]	DWT $(t = 4)$[4]
Average filter[5]	28.23	96.4	95.6	96.0	96.3	99.6
BPM (25 dB)	22.94	89.0	91.0	85.0	89.4	97.0
Gauss. (G) filter[5]	36.99	98.8	98.6	99.0	98.8	100
G filter[5] & noise	20.19	90.2	89.4	85.0	89.5	98.2
G noise	20.40	90.8	89.8	85.0	89.3	98.2
Histogram equal.	16.51	80.0	79.0	92.4	84.3	80.8
JPEG (quality 0)	22.87	90.8	90.0	87.0	87.3	94.2
JPEG (quality 5)	25.13	93.8	92.6	91.0	93.3	96.0
JPEG (quality 10)	27.49	95.4	94.6	94.0	96.5	98.6
LSRD[6]	20.16	85.0	88.0	75.0	88.7	92.0
Median filter[5]	29.65	97.4	96.6	98.0	97.3	99.4
Motion filter[5]	26.02	95.2	94.2	92.0	95.5	98.8
MSB (30 dB)	30.00	81.0	75.0	75.0	79.6	93.0
MSB (35 dB)	35.00	85.0	86.0	82.0	89.2	98.0
Rot.-crop (2°)	17.15	88.0	88.6	81.0	93.5	89.6
Rot.-scale (2°)	14.18	84.4	86.0	75.0	89.8	85.6
Salt and pepper	17.95	97.8	97.4	98.0	96.8	98.0
Self similarities	26.04	90.0	95.0	90.0	90.2	99.0
Small rand. dist.	16.27	83.0	83.0	80.0	87.0	75.0
unZign	29.08	97.0	97.0	96.0	99.7	100
Wiener filter[5]	34.61	97.8	97.6	98.0	97.8	100

[1] Region-of-interest.
[2] 512 textured blocks 8×8 were chosen from each image.
[3] MSB-plane was divided into 8×8 blocks before taking DCT.
[4] 4-level wavelet decomposition.
[5] 3×3 window.
[6] Latest small random distortion.

4.3.1. Finding Disputable Images. Let $L = S^{-1}(I, S_I, A_I)$ denote the logo retrieval operation using the inverse process in (2) (see Figure 1(b)). The TTP has to confirm whether images I_i and I_j are disputable before taking a final decision based on the timestamps TS_i and TS_j. Two images are disputable if they are the same image or one is an attacked version of another. To do that the TTP executes the following two test cases:

$$TC_1 = S^{-1}\left(I_i, S_{I_j}, A_{I_j}\right) \mid S^{-1}\left(I_j, S_{I_j}, A_{I_j}\right),$$
$$TC_2 = S^{-1}\left(I_j, S_{I_i}, A_{I_i}\right) \mid S^{-1}\left(I_i, S_{I_i}, A_{I_i}\right), \quad (10)$$

where the logo retrieved from I_i using signature and feature of I_j is compared against the logo of P_2, and vice versa. If the *logo retrieval rate* (LRR), which is the percentage of unchanged bits, and the PSNR (with respect to original logos L_1 and L_2) of above two test cases TC_1 and TC_2 are above certain *identification thresholds* (Th_{LRR}, Th_{PSNR}), then the images are considered as disputable.

4.3.2. Verification. If I_i and I_j are proved to be disputable, then the TTP compares timestamps TS_i and TS_j. The image is authenticated for P_1 if $TS_i < TS_j$ or for P_2 if $TS_i < TS_j$.

4.4. Estimating Identification Thresholds. To avoid the risk of error due to arbitrary selection of identification thresholds (Th_{LRR}, Th_{PSNR}), we propose the following innovative classifier-based threshold estimation technique, which can also be used to test the robustness and uniqueness of any signature-based scheme. The lower the value of (Th_{LRR}, Th_{PSNR}), the lower the scheme is robust.

Let $TD = \{[I_i, S_{I_i}, A_{I_i}]\}$ be a large image *training database* and let $B_i = \{I_i(j)\}$ be a set of *attacked* images from I_i for all i. Let

$$TC(a, b, c, d, j) = S^{-1}(I_a(j), S_{I_b}, A_{I_c}) \mid S^{-1}(I_d, S_{I_d}, A_{I_d}) \quad (11)$$

be a *test case* where the logo retrieved from the jth attacked image of I_a using the signature of I_b and the feature of I_c is compared against the logo used to sign I_d, $1 \leq a, b, c, d \leq |TD|$, and $1 \leq j \leq |B_a|$. Let the positive (C_+) and negative (C_-) classes be defined as

$$C_+ = \{\forall a, \forall j : TC(a, a, a, a, j)\},$$
$$C_- = \{\forall a, \forall b, \forall c, \forall d, \forall j : TC(a, b, c, d, j)\} - C_+. \quad (12)$$

Note that the LRR and PSNR of all the test cases in (C_+) should ideally be significantly higher than those in (C_-). Any

TABLE 2: Experimental results (PSNR in dB and LRR in %) by different approaches of the proposed MSB-based scheme and existing TROI-based [12] and VQ-based [13] schemes against various attacks using Lena image and Monash logo.

| Attacks | PSNR | Proposed MSB-based scheme | | | | | | | | Existing schemes | | | |
| | | UROI | | TBLK | | DCTMSB | | t-DWT[1] | | TROI [12] | | VQ [13] | |
		PSNR	LRR	PSNR	LRR	PSNR	LRR	PSNR	LRR	PSNR	LRR	PSNR	LRR
Affine (XY)[5]	20.66	19.30	96	14.44	88	14.09	94	10.52	88	14.73	54	14.79	58
Avg. filter[2]	36.85	20.58	99	21.41	96	22.04	99	30.20	100	14.97	53	23.08	60
BPM (25 dB)	22.94	14.36	91	12.97	85	11.19	89	15.18	96	13.85	56	23.67	73
Cropping	10.67	∞	100	13.16	94	13.75	87	6.69	71	15.19	53	15.57	83
Gauss. (G) filter[2]	36.89	20.58	99	21.43	96	22.04	99	30.20	100	14.97	53	23.12	60
G filter[2] & noise	26.56	16.37	94	16.24	91	16.23	96	24.67	100	14.69	55	23.07	61
G noise	23.03	14.59	90	14.54	89	14.49	95	22.09	99	14.52	57	23.45	66
Histogram equal.	19.36	13.08	86	14.16	89	12.00	86	18.79	98	16.94	62	17.10	55
JPEG (quality 0)	24.88	14.96	93	13.73	84	10.51	87	18.42	98	14.30	37	23.64	79
JPEG (quality 5)	28.23	16.89	95	15.06	90	12.81	93	16.75	97	14.86	48	20.65	53
LSRD[3]	20.16	12.66	88	11.92	72	10.87	86	14.19	95	13.81	55	21.76	70
Median filter[2]	37.20	20.57	99	20.95	96	21.47	99	21.01	99	15.27	53	23.27	61
Motion filter[2]	22.27	12.85	90	12.54	78	13.73	89	14.01	94	11.58	53	17.62	63
Print-copy-scan	11.63	10.98	72	10.64	71	10.00	72	10.07	78	13.20	61	20.72	71
Print-scan	12.52	11.36	74	10.83	72	10.08	73	10.37	87	14.10	63	22.17	69
MSB (30 dB)	30.00	10.82	75	10.28	77	8.15	76	13.91	94	15.13	53	23.14	62
MSB (35 dB)	35.00	13.36	86	12.57	85	11.65	87	18.68	98	15.16	53	23.35	62
MSB (40 dB)	40.00	15.75	92	15.28	91	15.87	94	24.16	100	15.18	53	23.39	64
Rot.-crop (2°)	19.48	16.12	89	10.26	73	11.84	86	11.61	91	13.37	53	19.74	64
Rot.-scale (2°)	19.33	16.22	89	10.21	73	11.70	85	11.36	90	13.34	53	19.65	64
Rot.-scale (5°)	11.66	11.41	82	10.38	70	10.27	70	5.68	62	11.03	52	6.86	60
RCR[4] (1 in 10)[5]	34.06	23.82	99	23.42	97	22.39	99	25.40	100	15.11	53	23.43	61
Salt and pepper	18.55	20.56	97	20.43	98	30.60	100	17.38	98	12.99	53	23.04	65
Scaling (×0.5)[5]	33.98	19.07	98	19.63	94	21.13	98	30.81	100	15.02	53	23.41	62
Scaling (×2)[5]	39.34	24.73	99	23.70	98	24.13	99	23.64	100	15.16	53	23.49	66
Self similarities	26.04	16.47	95	15.21	90	11.37	90	25.61	100	16.71	57	23.47	66
Small rand. dist.	16.27	10.98	83	11.45	72	12.92	84	6.75	71	11.55	53	16.31	69
unZign	29.08	18.18	97	18.48	94	21.69	98	∞	100	14.68	54	23.38	65
Wiener filter[2]	41.32	23.81	99	22.11	98	23.27	99	30.66	100	15.25	53	24.00	66

[1] Decomposition level $t = 4$.
[2] 3×3 window.
[3] Latest small rand. dist.
[4] Row-col-removal.
[5] Resized to original.

efficient classifier can now be used to separate the positive and negative classes based on the LRR and PSNR of all the test cases and the values of $(\text{Th}_{\text{LRR}}, \text{Th}_{\text{PSNR}})$ can then be estimated synergistically from this classifier.

4.5. Robustness and Uniqueness Tests. The identification thresholds $(\text{Th}_{\text{LRR}}, \text{Th}_{\text{PSNR}})$ defined in the previous section is useful for determination of robustness and uniqueness properties of a scheme. A scheme is not robust to a particular attack if the logo retrieved from the corresponding attacked image offers low PSNR and LRR with respect to $(\text{Th}_{\text{LRR}}, \text{Th}_{\text{PSNR}})$. In that case, the corresponding (PSNR, LRR) entry

in C_+ causes a false negative alarm by the classifier. We need to consider all the tests cases of C_+, as defined by (12), in robustness tests. On the other hand, a scheme fails uniqueness test to a particular attack if the signature calculated from image I_d verifies the corresponding attacked version of a different image I_a. In that case, the corresponding (PSNR, LRR) entry in C_-, as defined by (12), is high with respect to $(\text{Th}_{\text{LRR}}, \text{Th}_{\text{PSNR}})$ and causes a false-positive alarm by the classifier. Therefore, we need to consider only the following test cases of the class C_- in uniqueness tests:

$$C'_- = \{\forall a, \forall d \neq a, \forall j : \text{TC}(a, b, c, d, j)\}. \quad (13)$$

TABLE 3: Attacks considered while designing the classifier.

	Attacks	PSNR (dB)	
Number	Name	Lena	Elaine
0	Affine[1]	20.66	18.69
1	Blurring[2]	36.89	42.74
2	Cropping[3]	10.67	9.64
3	Histogram equal.	19.36	18.23
4	JPEG (quality 5)	28.23	28.02
5	Rot.-crop 2°	19.48	17.68
6	Rot.-scale 2°	19.33	17.58
7	Rot.-scale 5°	11.66	11.53
8	Small rand. dist.	16.27	18.55
9	MSB attack	35.00	35.00

[1] Resized to original after XY-shearing.
[2] Gaussian filter.
[3] Cropping excluding ROI.

5. Performance Study

We implemented the proposed MSB-based scheme and existing TROI-based [12] and VQ-based [13] schemes with MATLAB 7 and tested their robustness using all the watermarking benchmark images in [23] with different logos against many attacks including those in stirMark 4.0 [24]. However, as we decided almost the same performance for each pair of a benchmark image and a logo, only results obtained using "Lena" and "Elaine" images signed by Monash and NUS logos, respectively (shown in Figure 3), are presented. Where necessary, the attacked images were resized to original. In fact, a corner matching technique can be used to undo the geometric transformations before verifying the copyright information [26].

We used the following two metrics to evaluate the performance: (i) PSNR determines the visual quality of the attacked media or retrieved logo with respect to its original copy; (ii) LRR determines the percentage of bits that are correctly retrieved from the given image using the given signature.

In Section 5.1, we present different types of attacks we considered in our experiments. Section 5.2 presents the detail classifier setup by different signature-based schemes. Section 5.3 presents the experimental results and discussions. Finally, Section 5.4 provides detail discussions on the overall performance of different signature-based schemes.

5.1. Attacks. All the attacks we tested to prove the efficacy of the proposed schemes are in Table 2. Below, we represent some attacks that require detail discussions. If not mentioned, the attack was done using MATLAB 7.

5.1.1. BPM Attack. In *blind pattern matching* (BPM) attack, we divided Lena image into 4×4 nonoverlapping blocks. For each block, the most similar 4×4 block was found out from Elaine image at 25 dB. The block with PSNR greater than or equal to 25 dB was considered as a similar one. Total 15736 blocks were replaced when the attacked image PSNR

became 22.94 dB. In the same way, when we attacked Elaine image using Lena image, we replaced total 16371 blocks and attacked image PSNR was 21.99 dB.

5.1.2. Print-Copy-Scan. We printed each image using a 1200 dpi laser printer. The printed image was then photocopied and scanned using a 300 dpi and 8-bit gray-scale scanner. Finally, it was resized to 512×512. The PSNR of Lena image after print-copy-scan attack was 11.63 dB and that of Elaine image was 19.56 dB.

5.1.3. MSB Attack. We attacked each image by flipping its MSB-plane. Maximum MSBs were changed at a particular PSNR. First, we found absolute difference of each pixel to flip its MSB. Second, we sorted the absolute differences in the ascending order. Finally, we flipped the MSB of the pixel with lowest absolute difference first. We continued flipping until the PSNR is decreased beyond a particular value. Since this attack changes the maximum number of MSBs for a given target PSNR, the proposed MSB-based scheme should suffer the most. However, we observed that most images cannot be degraded to less than 20 dB even if all of its MSBs were flipped. After the MSB attack at 30 dB the MSB similarity rate for Lena image was 73% and for Elaine image was 70%.

5.1.4. unZign Attack. The image was divided into 8×8 blocks. A pixel was selected randomly from each block and was either deleted or repeated randomly. All blocks were then put back in their original positions. The PSNR of Lena image after unZign attack was 29.08 dB and that of Elaine image was 29.79 dB.

5.1.5. Self-Similarities. This attack was done by stirMark 4.0 in RGB space of the image. The image was then converted to its gray-scale equivalent. The PSNR of Lena image after this attack was 26.04 dB and that of Elaine image was 25.48 dB.

5.2. Classifiers. In order to design classifiers for the different approaches, that is, UROI, TBLK, DCTMSB, and t-DWT, of the proposed MSB-based and existing TROI-based [12] and VQ-based [13] schemes, we used 10 different types of attacked images as shown in Table 3. We assigned numbers to the attacks for later references. The image Lena was signed using Monash logo and the image Elaine was signed with NUS logo. Then, different attacked images of Lena and Elaine were sent after signing with different logos with different or same A_I for verification. For UROI approach and TROI-based scheme, A_I indicates the same or different ROIs; while for t-DWT approach and VQ-based scheme, A_I indicates the same or different decomposition levels; and for TBLK approach, A_I indicates same or different set of textured blocks. We had total 8 different types of data points with two pairs of images and logos (Lena-Monash and Elaine-NUS). Therefore, maximum 160 logo retrieval instances (20 in C_+ and 140 in C_-) were used while designing each classifier. However, in the case of DCTMSB approach, there were total 80 instances (20 in C_+ and 60 in C_-); since for the same type and size (8-bit, 64×64) of logo, the image was

TABLE 4: Attacked images along with their corresponding retrieved logos using Lena image and Monash logo by different approaches of the proposed MSB-based scheme and existing TROI-based [12] and VQ-based [13] schemes.

	Affine[2]	BPM[3]	Blurring[4]	Crop.[5]	Hist. Eq.	JPEG (5)	PCS[6]	Rot.-crop 2°	unZign
Attacks[1] →									
Schemes[7] ↓	20.66	22.94	36.89	10.67	19.36	28.23	11.63	19.48	29.08
UROI	19.30, 96	14.36, 91	20.58, 99	∞, 100	13.08, 86	16.89, 95	10.98, 72	16.12, 89	18.18, 97
TBLK	14.44, 88	12.97, 85	21.43, 96	13.16, 94	14.16, 89	15.06, 90	10.64, 71	10.26, 73	18.48, 94
DCTMSB	14.09, 94	11.19, 89	22.04, 99	13.75, 87	12.00, 86	12.81, 93	10.00, 72	11.84, 86	21.69, 98
t-DWT ($t = 4$)	10.52, 88	15.18, 96	30.20, 100	6.69, 71	18.79, 98	16.75, 97	10.07, 78	11.61, 91	∞, 100
TROI [12]	14.73, 54	13.85, 56	14.97, 53	15.19, 53	16.94, 62	14.86, 48	13.20, 61	13.37, 53	14.68, 54
VQ [13]	14.79, 58	23.67, 73	23.12, 60	15.57, 83	17.10, 55	20.65, 53	20.72, 71	19.74, 64	23.38, 65

[1] Attacked images with PSNR (dB).
[2] Resized to original after XY-shearing.
[3] PSNR of similar blocks (4×4) ≥ 25 dB.
[4] Gaussian filter.
[5] Cropping excluding ROI.
[6] Print-copy-scan.
[7] Retrieved logos with PSNR (dB) and LRR (%).

divided into blocks of the same size (4×2) before taking DCT, assuming the image size (512×512) also remained the same. On the other hand, for VQ-based scheme, there were total 120 instances (20 in C_+ and 100 in C_-); since with different decomposition levels t, logo retrieval operation was not possible from a smaller codebook (due to larger t) using the indices set containing higher indices values, while it was possible from a bigger codebook (due to smaller t) using the indices set containing lower indices values.

We used *support vector machines* (SVMs) with linear kernel [27] and K-means clustering [28] separately for classification. Results by both SVM classification and K-means clustering are useful for the determination of the robustness and the uniqueness properties of the proposed and existing schemes. SVM results, especially, enabled to find out the values for identification thresholds (Th_{LRR}, Th_{PSNR}), defined in Section 4.3. The more the accuracy of the classification and the distance d between the support vectors of the SVM for a scheme, the more the scheme is robust (i.e., the two classes are well separated).

In the robustness test, the distance from a data point in C_+ (corresponding to an attack) to the SVM decision hyperplane is used to decide different levels of robustness (high, medium, low, and no). For example, if the data point is correctly classified and resides outside the nearest support vector (i.e., far away from the decision plane), then the robustness against the corresponding attack is high. If the data point is correctly classified but stays in the space between the nearest support vector and the decision plane and then the robustness against the corresponding attack is medium (when close to the support vector) or low (when close to the decision plane). If the data point is on the other side of the hyper plane (misclassified), then the copyright scheme is not robust to the corresponding attack. In the uniqueness test, if a data point in C'_- (corresponding to an attack) is incorrectly classified then the scheme does not possess the uniqueness property under this attack.

5.3. Experimental Results. We will present the experimental results in two parts. In Section 5.3.1, we present the robustness of the proposed and existing schemes in terms of PSNR

TABLE 5: Experimental results (PSNR in dB and LRR in %) by different approaches of the proposed MSB-based scheme and existing TROI-based [12] and VQ-based [13] schemes against various attacks using Elaine image and NUS logo.

| Attacks | PSNR | Proposed MSB-based scheme | | | | | | | | Existing schemes | | | |
| | | UROI | | TBLK | | DCTMSB | | t-DWT[1] | | TROI [12] | | VQ [13] | |
		PSNR	LRR	PSNR	LRR	PSNR	LRR	PSNR	LRR	PSNR	LRR	PSNR	LRR
Affine (XY)[5]	18.69	13.86	90	17.33	88	14.48	86	17.84	92	16.40	56	21.12	61
Avg. filter[2]	34.09	19.17	98	22.90	97	24.43	98	27.01	99	17.51	56	25.32	69
BPM (25 dB)	21.99	12.79	88	15.61	84	14.57	86	17.25	93	16.62	55	23.29	55
Cropping	9.64	∞	100	41.95	99	16.55	81	12.17	70	17.47	55	7.78	48
Gauss. (G) filter[2]	42.74	23.58	99	26.51	99	27.32	99	33.09	100	17.50	55	25.35	68
G filter[2] & noise	20.05	12.84	88	15.83	85	17.15	92	25.46	99	15.59	55	25.26	68
G noise	20.09	12.57	88	15.80	85	16.92	92	25.68	99	15.65	55	25.19	70
Histogram equal.	18.23	16.97	96	19.82	95	18.37	94	21.20	97	14.72	56	22.76	65
JPEG (quality 0)	25.14	13.69	89	17.74	86	14.63	86	20.26	96	16.85	58	21.13	70
JPEG (quality 5)	28.02	16.20	94	19.53	91	17.00	91	22.27	97	17.14	56	25.02	65
LSRD[3]	14.94	10.99	75	12.28	76	12.23	75	11.84	71	12.30	53	15.57	58
Median filter[2]	24.37	13.95	91	18.07	88	14.97	87	27.34	99	16.53	56	25.27	67
Motion filter[2]	25.54	14.61	93	19.00	84	18.54	94	19.41	95	17.14	55	24.35	65
Print-copy-scan	19.56	13.49	90	16.04	88	15.64	92	15.75	90	15.99	56	20.27	50
Print-scan	22.32	15.48	94	19.71	93	20.43	95	21.39	96	16.32	57	24.62	68
MSB (30 dB)	30.00	8.52	66	11.59	65	12.81	74	20.01	96	17.10	50	24.83	68
MSB (35 dB)	35.00	9.85	78	13.96	79	15.04	85	24.26	99	17.39	51	25.25	68
MSB (40 dB)	40.00	11.51	86	15.77	87	17.81	92	30.23	100	17.46	53	25.33	66
Rot.-crop (2°)	17.68	13.84	84	16.26	85	14.36	81	14.89	86	15.13	56	20.08	65
Rot.-scale (2°)	17.58	13.79	84	16.06	85	14.26	81	14.85	86	15.10	56	19.92	66
Rot.-scale (5°)	11.53	11.73	76	11.29	76	11.10	68	11.24	65	13.29	54	13.05	62
RCR[4] (1 in 10)[5]	25.20	14.48	92	18.57	89	15.72	89	29.28	99	16.68	56	25.34	69
Salt & pepper	22.60	25.61	99	25.23	99	34.72	100	22.98	99	16.24	54	25.04	72
Scaling (×0.5)[5]	25.09	14.39	92	18.29	89	15.97	90	∞	100	16.72	57	25.36	67
Scaling (×2)[5]	25.66	14.24	92	18.63	89	15.50	89	28.58	100	16.76	57	25.31	68
Self similarities	25.48	14.63	92	18.44	89	15.33	88	29.52	100	16.82	56	25.36	68
Small rand. dist.	18.55	11.99	85	16.12	84	13.62	84	17.24	91	15.10	54	20.40	67
unZign	29.79	19.02	97	23.80	97	24.03	98	33.09	100	17.26	55	25.35	68
Wiener filter[2]	36.52	20.10	98	20.96	97	25.12	99	27.90	99	15.20	52	24.45	67

[1] Decomposition level $t = 4$.
[2] 3×3 window.
[3] Latest small random distortion.
[4] Row-col-removal.
[5] Resized to original.

and LRR under different attacks. In Section 5.3.2, we present the classifiers from which we can evaluate overall robustness and uniqueness of the respective signature-based schemes.

5.3.1. Robustness Results. In this section, we first present and discuss robustness results of the proposed and existing schemes under different attacks. We then detail the results for two attacks—JPEG which is the most common unintentional attack and newly proposed MSB attack which would defeat our scheme the most.

Table 2 shows the logo retrieval results using Lena image and Monash logo by different approaches of the MSB-based scheme and existing TROI-based [12] and VQ-based [13] schemes. Table 4 shows the attacked images along with their

corresponding retrieved logos using Lena image and Monash logo. Table 5 and Table 6 present the same, respectively, using Elaine image and NUS logo.

We observed that all the approaches of the proposed scheme performed almost the same except the t-DWT approach which was sensitive to geometric distortions. In contrast, both the TROI-based and VQ-based schemes were very much sensitive to geometric attacks and the former did not survive under high JPEG lossy compression (quality less than 10). In most of the cases, the PSNR and in all the cases the LRR of the retrieved logos by the proposed scheme were higher than those by the TROI-based scheme. In the remaining few cases, the PSNR of the retrieved logos by the proposed scheme were lower. In most of the cases,

TABLE 6: Attacked images along with their corresponding retrieved logos using Elaine image and NUS logo by different approaches of the proposed MSB-based scheme and existing TROI-based [12] and VQ-based [13] schemes.

	Affine[2]	BPM[3]	Blurring[4]	Crop.[5]	Hist. Eq.	JPEG (5)	PCS[6]	Rot.-crop 2°	unZign
Attacks[1] →									
Schemes[7] ↓	18.69	21.99	42.74	9.64	18.23	28.02	19.56	17.68	29.79
UROI									
	13.86, 90	12.79, 88	23.58, 99	∞, 100	16.97, 96	16.20, 94	13.49, 90	13.84, 84	19.02, 97
TBLK									
	17.33, 88	15.61, 84	26.51, 99	41.95, 99	19.82, 95	19.53, 91	16.04, 88	16.26, 85	23.80, 97
DCTMSB									
	14.48, 86	14.57, 86	27.32, 99	16.55, 81	18.37, 94	17.00, 91	15.64, 92	14.36, 81	24.03, 98
t-DWT ($t = 4$)									
	17.84, 92	17.25, 93	33.09, 100	12.17, 70	21.20, 97	22.27, 97	15.75, 90	14.89, 86	33.09, 100
TROI [12]									
	16.40, 56	16.62, 55	17.50, 55	17.47, 55	14.72, 56	17.14, 56	15.99, 56	15.13, 56	17.26, 55
VQ [13]									
	21.12, 61	23.29, 55	25.35, 68	7.78, 48	22.76, 65	25.02, 65	20.27, 50	20.08, 65	25.35, 68

[1] Attacked images with PSNR (dB).
[2] Resized to original after XY-shearing.
[3] PSNR of similar blocks (4×4) ≥ 25 dB.
[4] Gaussian filter.
[5] Cropping excluding ROI.
[6] Print-copy-scan.
[7] Retrieved logos with PSNR (dB) and LRR (%).

the LRR by the MSB-based scheme was higher than the VQ-based scheme; while in many cases, the PSNR by the latter was higher due to its VQ coding. However, it is no way an indication to the superiority of the existing schemes for these kinds of attacks; because the logo quality degrades severely during the torus-mapping and VQ coding, as shown in Figures 3(e)–3(h), and as a consequence the PSNR and LRR remained almost unchanged irrespective of logos.

Table 7 presents the MSB-attacked images along with their corresponding retrieved logos using Lena image and Monash logo by the proposed MSB-based scheme and existing TROI-based [12] and VQ-based [13] schemes. Table 8 presents the same using Elaine image and NUS logo. Among the approaches of the proposed scheme, DWT-based approach showed the highest resistance against the MSB attack. The proposed scheme survived down to PSNR 30 dB of the attacked image. Lee and Chen [13] argued that the visual quality of the image is unacceptable to the human eyes if the PSNR is less than 30 dB. Moreover, we observed that the proposed scheme performed better if the PSNR of the MSB attacked image increases, while for the existing schemes

the PSNR and LRR of the retrieved logos remained almost unchanged irrespective of the PSNR of the attacked images. However, since the distortion in an image is more noticeable in the mid-gray region and sensitivity changes parabolically as the gray value fluctuates on the both sides of mid-gray level [7], as a precaution to the MSB attack, we suggest excluding mid-gray pixels during signature calculation.

Figure 4(a) plots the LRR and Figure 4(b) plots the PSNR of the retrieved logos using Lena image and Monash logo against different JPEG quality factors. Figure 5(a) and Figure 5(b) plot the same using Elaine image and NUS logo. We found that the t-DWT approach performed the best among different approaches of the MSB-based scheme and existing TROI-based and VQ-based schemes. Both the LRR and PSNR increased with the increase of JPEG quality factor for the proposed scheme, while for the existing schemes they remained almost the same. While the proposed scheme always offered higher LRR; it outperformed the existing schemes in term of the PSNR when JPEG quality factor was greater than 70. This result is consistent with the observation made in motivation.

TABLE 7: MSB attacked images along with their corresponding retrieved logos using Lena image and Monash logo by different approaches of the proposed MSB-based scheme and existing TROI-based [12] and VQ-based [13] schemes.

MSB Attacked[1] Images[2] → Schemes[3] ↓	20.00, 28	25.00, 54	30.00, 73	35.00, 85	40.00, 92	45.00, 97	50.00, 99
UROI	3.99, 17	8.00, 58	10.82, 75	13.36, 86	15.75, 92	18.98, 96	22.46, 99
TBLK	3.84, 30	7.59, 63	10.28, 77	12.57, 85	15.28, 91	18.33, 95	21.93, 98
DCTMSB	3.31, 31	5.57, 57	8.15, 76	11.65, 87	15.87, 94	19.46, 98	23.53, 99
t-DWT ($t = 4$)	7.15, 73	9.87, 86	13.91, 94	18.68, 98	24.16, 100	∞, 100	∞, 100
TROI [12]	12.36, 51	14.92, 52	15.13, 53	15.16, 53	15.18, 53	15.19, 53	15.19, 53
VQ [13]	20.25, 63	22.34, 62	23.14, 62	23.35, 62	23.39, 64	23.40, 65	23.40, 64

[1] Images with PSNR <30 dB are unacceptable [13].
[2] With target PSNR (dB) and MSB similarity rate (%).
[3] Retrieved logos with PSNR (dB) and LRR (%).

5.3.2. Classification Results (Robustness and Uniqueness). In this section, we present and discuss classification results of the proposed and existing schemes. We can infer the overall robustness and uniqueness of each scheme from the respective classifier.

Figures 6, 7, 8, 9, 10, and 11 present classification results using SVM with linear kernel [27] and K-means clustering [28] separating the positive and negative classes of test cases, defined in the Section 4.3, for the MSB-based scheme and existing TROI-based [12] and VQ-based [13] schemes. Though we conducted the experiments with all entries in C_-, for clarity we show C'_-, as defined in (13), instead of C_- in Figure 6 to Figure 11. Table 9 shows the classification results obtained by SVM and K-means. If for a scheme a data point in C_+ corresponding to an attack is misclassified by a classifier, then the scheme is decided not to be robust under that attack. Similarly, if for a scheme a data point in C'_- corresponding to an attack is misclassified by a classifier, then the scheme is decided not to be unique under that attack. While the classes could be distinctively separated (no misclassification) with a large distance d between the support vectors for UROI ($d = 30.2$), TBLK ($d = 31.4$), and DCTMSB ($d = 31.4$) approaches of the proposed scheme; the SVM classifier for t-DWT approach resulted in 5% positive misclassification with a large $d = 25.0$ and the classifiers for the TROI-based ($d = 10.0$) and

VQ-based ($d = 9.2$) schemes resulted in 20% and 30% positive misclassifications, respectively. We found no miss by K-means clustering for UROI, TBLK, and DCTMSB approaches, while for t-DWT approach and TROI- and VQ-based schemes, we found 35% positive, 26% negative, and 30% positive miss, respectively. Logo quality degradation due to torus-mapping and VQ coding constitute this problem for the existing schemes. Note that no misclassification and the large separation between positive and negative classes for UROI, TBLK, and DCTMSB approaches of the MSB-based scheme is so significant that simple PSNR-only (vertical) or LRR-only (horizontal) linear classifier can be used as well. Considering classification and clustering results and the distance from the SVM decision hyperplane to a corresponding entry of a particular attack, we took the decision of robustness and uniqueness tests. From Table 9, we see that UROI and DCTMSB approaches are highly robust and TBLK approach is moderately robust; while TROI-based scheme failed both robustness and uniqueness tests, and t-DWT approach and VQ-based scheme failed robustness test. We found that TBLK and t-DWT approaches are highly sensitive to geometric attacks.

5.4. Comparisons and Discussions. Table 10 presents comparisons among the different approaches of the proposed MSB-based scheme and the existing TROI-based [12] and

TABLE 8: MSB attacked images along with their corresponding retrieved logos using Elaine image and NUS logo by different approaches of the proposed MSB-based scheme and existing TROI-based [12] and VQ-based [13] schemes.

MSB Attacked Images[1,2] → Schemes[3] ↓	20.00, 31	25.00, 54	30.00, 70	35.00, 81	40.00, 88	45.00, 92	50.00, 95
UROI	6.41, 26	7.04, 46	8.52, 66	9.85, 78	11.51, 86	13.21, 91	14.93, 94
TBLK	7.59, 23	9.45, 44	11.59, 65	13.96, 79	15.77, 87	17.79, 91	19.49, 94
DCTMSB	8.04, 33	10.41, 56	12.81, 74	15.04, 85	17.81, 92	20.00, 95	21.51, 97
t-DWT ($t = 4$)	13.21, 79	16.31, 90	20.01, 96	24.26, 99	30.23, 100	37.98, 100	∞, 100
DCT	15.86, 91	20.43, 97	26.21, 99	34.59, 100	44.10, 100	69.20, 100	∞, 100
TROI [12]	16.25, 45	16.72, 49	17.10, 50	17.39, 51	17.46, 53	17.47, 53	17.47, 54
VQ [13]	19.20, 49	23.28, 61	24.83, 68	25.25, 68	25.33, 66	25.34, 66	25.34, 68

[1] Images with PSNR <30 dB are unacceptable [13].
[2] With target PSNR (dB) and MSB similarity rate (%).
[3] Retrieved logos with PSNR (dB) and LRR (%).

TABLE 9: Results and decisions for different approaches of the proposed MSB-based scheme and existing TROI-based [12] and VQ-based [13] schemes by the *support vector machines* (SVM) [27] and K-means clustering algorithm[28].

Schemes	Size of training set		Number of miss (%) by SVM		by K-means		Distance[1]	To individual attacks (robustness: h = high, m = moderate, l = low, and n = no robustness; and f = uniqueness fail)[2,3]										
	C_+	C_-	C_+	C_-	C_+	C_-	d	0	1	2	3	4	5	6	7	8	9	Over[4]
UROI	20	140	0 (0)	0 (0)	0 (0)	0 (0)	30.2	h	h	h	h	h	h	h	m	m	h	h
TBLK	20	140	0 (0)	0 (0)	0 (0)	0 (0)	31.5	m	h	h	h	h	l	l	l	l	m	m
DCTMSB	20	60	0 (0)	0 (0)	0 (0)	0 (0)	31.3	m	h	h	h	h	m	m	l	m	h	h
t-DWT	20	140	1 (5)	0 (0)	7 (35)	0 (0)	25.1	n	h	n	m	h	n	n	n	n	h	n
TROI [12]	20	140	6 (30)	0 (0)	0 (0)	36 (26)	5.1	n, f	l, f	n, f	m, f	l, f	n, f	n, f	n, f	n, f	m, f	n, f
VQ [13]	20	100	11 (55)	0 (0)	6 (30)	0 (0)	9.2	n	m	n	l	h	n	n	n	n	m	n

[1] Distance between support vectors.
[2] Robustness: correctly classified by both SVM and K-means with h = high PSNR and LRR, m = moderate PSNR and LRR, and l = low PSNR and LRR; no robustness: n = any false negative by SVM or K-means; and uniqueness fail: f = any false positive by SVM or K-means.
[3] Attack numbers 0-9 are referred using Table 3; and
[4] Overall decision.

TABLE 10: Comparisons of different approaches of the proposed scheme and existing schemes [12, 13].

Issues	Existing		Approaches of the proposed MSB-based scheme			
	TROI [12]	VQ [13]	UROI	TBLK	DCTMSB	t-DWT
Transparency	yes	yes	yes	yes	yes	yes
Robustness	no	no	high	moderate	high	no
Uniqueness	no	yes	yes	yes	yes	yes
Unambiguous	no	no	yes	yes	yes	no
Security	yes	yes	yes	yes	yes	yes
Blindness	semi-blind	blind	semi-blind	semi-blind	semi-blind	semi-blind
Multiple logo	yes	yes	yes	yes	yes	yes
Publicly verifiable	no	yes	no	no	no	no
StirMark resistance	no	no	moderate	low	moderate	no
MSB attack resistance	moderate	high	moderate	moderate	moderate	high
Scalability[1]	no	no	yes	yes	yes	yes
Signature addition[2]	no	yes	no	no	no	no
JPEG quality < 10	low	high	high	high	high	high
Operation domain	spatial	DWT	spatial	spatial	DCT	DWT
Time complexity	high	high	constant	low	low	low
Algorithm simplicity	no	no	yes	yes	yes	yes
Region-of-interest used	yes	no	yes	no	no	no

[1] Signature calculation using different types of image and logo.
[2] With image header.

VQ-based [13] schemes. The MSB-based scheme possesses *transparency* because it does not embed any information to the published image. UROI, TBLK, and DCTMSB approaches are robust, while *t*-DWT approach failed. In contrast, due to very low PSNR and LRR both TROI-based and VQ-based schemes are not robust and TROI-based scheme failed uniqueness test. The security of the MSB-based scheme is the same as the security of the digital signature and the digital timestamp. The classification and clustering results showed that UROI, TBLK, and DCTMSB approaches are *unambiguous* due to correctly classification by SVM with a large *d* between the support vectors and no miss by *K*-means, while *t*-DWT approach is ambiguous due to positive misclassification by both SVM and TROI. In contrast, the existing schemes are ambiguous because of high positive misclassifications. In our experiments, we also used the polynomial kernel for TROI-based and VQ-based schemes and found high misclassifications. The MSB-based scheme is not *blind* as the TTP finds whether images are disputable by comparing signatures calculated from them before taking the decision based on the timestamps. The TROI-based scheme is also not *blind* too; because as the published image does not contain any information, the original image must be used to find out the corresponding signature from the owner's database. On the other hand, the VQ-based scheme is *blind* as it adds the signature with the image header before publishing. However, this signature addition not only increases the file size but also creates severe problem of losing copyright if an attacker removes the signature from the image header. The MSB-based scheme can handle multiple logos (*multiple watermarking*) like the existing schemes. An image

may be signed using the same or different types of logos by the same owner.

The scheme by Lee and Chen [13] is publicly verifiable as it adds the signature with the image header. On the other hand, the ownership dispute is handled through the TTP by the MSB-based scheme. In TROI-based scheme, the owner keeps the security parameters secret himself. The existing schemes and *t*-DWT approach is not much robust as they offer low PSNR and LRR against stirMark attacks. However, *t*-DWT approach and VQ-based schemes showed high robustness to MSB attack, while UROI, TBLK, and DCTMSB approaches and TROI-based scheme showed moderate robustness. Any type and size of logos can be signed with an 8-bit gray-scale image by the MSB-based scheme, while the TROI-based and VQ-based schemes can sign only 8-bit gray-scale logos. The existing schemes are highly time consuming due to use of torus mapping and VQ encoding. In contrast, the MSB-based scheme is simple due to use of the MSB-plane; especially, the UROI approach is the simplest as it does not involve any transform domain operation. The proposed scheme also presents a comprehensive TTP management policy in order to secure the e-commerce.

6. Conclusions

This paper has proposed an MSB-based image copyright protection scheme, which relies on a TTP to offer the following advantages over the existing schemes: (i) any type and size of images and logos can be used; (ii) extremely low computational complexity, due to use of exclusive-OR operations for signature calculation, enables real time applications; (iii) robust to almost all kinds of attacks; (iv) the comprehensive TTP management policy ensures secure e-commerce.

The existing signature-based schemes that can sign images with multibit logos are not robust against geometric attacks and neither a linear nor a polynomial kernel of the SVM can classify them correctly. Among the approaches of the proposed MSB-based scheme, t-DWT approach is the best against the newly proposed MSB attack and JPEG. Nevertheless, this approach fails to be correctly classified due to its weakness against geometric attacks. On the other hand, classifiers designed by the UROI, TBLK, and DCTMSB approaches are excellent in the sense that they offer no misclassification and simple PSNR-only or LRR-only classifier can be used.

References

[1] T. H. Chen, G. Horng, and W. B. Lee, "A publicly verifiable copyright-proving scheme resistant to malicious attacks," *IEEE Transactions on Industrial Electronics*, vol. 52, no. 1, pp. 327–334, 2005.

[2] W. Stallings, *Cryptography and Network Security: Principles and Practice*, Prentice Hall, Englewood Cliffs, NJ, USA, 2nd edition, 1999.

[3] I. J. Cox, J. Kilian, F. T. Leighton, and T. Shamoon, "Secure spread spectrum watermarking for multimedia," *IEEE Transactions on Image Processing*, vol. 6, no. 12, pp. 1673–1687, 1997.

[4] M. Kutter, F. Jordan, and F. Bossen, "Digital watermarking of color images using amplitude modulation," *Journal of Electronic Imaging*, vol. 7, no. 2, pp. 326–332, 1998.

[5] R. K. Sharma and S. Decker, "Practical challenges for digital watermarking applications," in *Proceedings of the IEEE 4th Workshop on Multimedia Signal Processing*, pp. 237–242, October 2001.

[6] I. J. Cox, M. L. Miller, and A. L. Mckellips, "Watermarking as communications with side information," *Proceedings of the IEEE*, vol. 87, no. 7, pp. 1127–1141, 1999.

[7] M. Awrangjeb and M. S. Kankanhalli, "Reversible watermarking using a perceptual model," *Journal of Electronic Imaging*, vol. 14, no. 1, Article ID 013014, pp. 1–8, 2005.

[8] S. Craver, N. Memon, B. L. Yeo, and M. M. Yeung, "Resolving rightful ownerships with invisible watermarking techniques: limitations, attacks, and implications," *IEEE Journal on Selected Areas in Communications*, vol. 16, no. 4, pp. 573–586, 1998.

[9] K. Ratakonda, R. Dugad, and N. Ahuja, "Digital image watermarking: issues in resolving rightful ownership," in *Proceedings of the International Conference on Image Processing (ICIP '98)*, vol. 2, pp. 414–418, October 1998.

[10] C. I. Podilchuk and W. Zeng, "Image-adaptive watermarking using visual models," *IEEE Journal on Selected Areas in Communications*, vol. 16, no. 4, pp. 525–539, 1998.

[11] M. Awrangjeb and G. Lu, "A robust content-based watermarking technique," in *Proceedings of the IEEE 10th Workshop on Multimedia Signal Processing (MMSP '08)*, pp. 713–718, Cairns, Australia, October 2008.

[12] C. C. Chang, K. F. Hwang, and M. S. Hwang, "Robust authentication scheme for protecting copyrights of images and graphics," *IEE Proceedings: Vision, Image and Signal Processing*, vol. 149, no. 1, pp. 43–50, 2002.

[13] W. B. Lee and T. H. Chen, "A public verifiable copy protection technique for still images," *Journal of Systems and Software*, vol. 62, no. 3, pp. 195–204, 2002.

[14] C. C. Chang, J. Y. Hsiao, and C. L. Chiang, "An image copyright protection scheme based on torus automorphism," in *Proceedings of the 1st International Symposium on Cyber Worlds*, pp. 217–224, November 2002.

[15] C. C. Chang and J. C. Chuang, "An image intellectual property protection scheme for gray-level images using visual secret sharing strategy," *Pattern Recognition Letters*, vol. 23, no. 8, pp. 931–941, 2002.

[16] H. Quan and S. Guangchuan, "A semi-blind robust watermarking for digital images," in *Proceedings of the IEEE International Conference on Accoustics, Speech, and Signal Processing*, vol. 2, pp. 541–544, April 2003.

[17] C. Y. Lin and S. F. Chang, "A robust image authentication method distinguishing JPEG compression from malicious manipulation," *IEEE Transactions on Circuits and Systems for Video Technology*, vol. 11, no. 2, pp. 153–168, 2001.

[18] C. S. Lu and H. Y. M. Liao, "Structural digital signature for image authentication: an incidental distortion resistant scheme," *IEEE Transactions on Multimedia*, vol. 5, no. 2, pp. 161–173, 2003.

[19] S. Katzenbeisser, "On the design of copyright protection protocols for multimedia distribution using symmetric and public-key watermarking," in *Proceedings of the 12th International Workshop on Database and Expert Systems Applications*, pp. 815–819, 2001.

[20] B. Macq, J. Dittmann, and E. J. Delp, "Benchmarking of image watermarking algorithms for digital rights management," *Proceedings of the IEEE*, vol. 92, no. 6, pp. 971–983, 2004.

[21] M. Awrangjeb and M. Murshed, "Robust signature-based geometric invariant copyright protection," in *Proceedings of the IEEE International Conference on Image Processing (ICIP '06)*, pp. 1961–1964, Atlanta, Ga, USA, October 2006.

[22] Free Foto.com, 2005, http://www.freefoto.com.

[23] "Photo database," 2005, http://www.petitcolas.net/fabien/watermarking/image_database/.

[24] F. A. P. Petitcolas, "Watermarking schemes evaluation," *IEEE Signal Processing Magazine*, vol. 17, no. 5, pp. 58–64, 2000.

[25] M. Awrangjeb, G. Lu, and M. Murshed, "Global geometric distortion correction in images," in *Proceedings of the IEEE 8th Workshop on Multimedia Signal Processing (MMSP '06)*, pp. 435–440, Victoria, Canada, October 2006.

[26] M. Awrangjeb and G. Lu, "A robust corner matching technique," in *Proceedings of the IEEE International Conference onMultimedia and Expo (ICME '07)*, pp. 1483–1486, Beijing, China, July 2007.

[27] N. Cristianini and J. S. Taylor, *An Introduction to Support Vector Machines and other Kernel-Based Learning Methods*, Cambridge University Press, New York, NY, USA, 1st edition, 2000.

[28] G. A. F. Seber, *Multivariate Observations*, Wiley, New York, NY, USA, 1984.

12

Video Pulses: User-Based Modeling of Interesting Video Segments

Markos Avlonitis and Konstantinos Chorianopoulos

Ionian University, 49100 Corfu, Greece

Correspondence should be addressed to Konstantinos Chorianopoulos; choko@ionio.gr

Academic Editor: Deepu Rajan

We present a user-based method that detects regions of interest within a video in order to provide video skims and video summaries. Previous research in video retrieval has focused on content-based techniques, such as pattern recognition algorithms that attempt to understand the low-level features of a video. We are proposing a pulse modeling method, which makes sense of a web video by analyzing users' *Replay* interactions with the video player. In particular, we have modeled the user information seeking behavior as a time series and the semantic regions as a discrete pulse of fixed width. Then, we have calculated the correlation coefficient between the dynamically detected pulses at the local maximums of the user activity signal and the pulse of reference. We have found that users' *Replay* activity significantly matches the important segments in information-rich and visually complex videos, such as lecture, how-to, and documentary. The proposed signal processing of user activity is complementary to previous work in content-based video retrieval and provides an additional user-based dimension for modeling the semantics of a social video on the web.

1. Introduction

The web has become a very popular medium for sharing and watching video content [1]. Moreover, many organizations and academic institutions are making lecture videos and seminars available online. Previous work on video retrieval has investigated the content of the video and has contributed a standard set of procedures, tools, and data-sets for comparing the performance of video retrieval algorithms (e.g., TRECVID), but they have not considered the interactive behavior of the users as an integral part of the video retrieval process. In addition to watching and browsing video content on the web, people also perform other "social metadata" tasks, such as sharing, commenting videos, replying to other videos, or just expressing their preference/rating. User-based research has explored the association between commenting and microblogs, primarily tweets, or other text-based and explicitly user-generated content. Although there are various established information retrieval methods that collect and manipulate text, they could be considered burdensome for the users, in the context of video watching. In many cases,

there is a lack of comment density when compared to the number of viewers of a video. There are a few research efforts to understand user-based video retrieval without the use of social metadata.

In our research, we have developed a method that utilizes more so implicit user interactions for extracting useful information about a video. Our goal is to analyze the aggregated user interactions with the video using a stochastic pulse modeling process.

2. Related Work

Content semantics is an important concept that facilitates the retrieval of information from rich, yet complex, content, such as video. Semantic research in multimedia details two broad categories of approaches: content-based and user-based. Content-based methods extract meaning by analyzing the video itself (e.g., scene change, sound, and closed captioning). Alternatively, user-based methods extract meaning by analysis of the user activity on the video. Of these user-based actions, there are two subcategories; they can be explicit, like comments, annotations, and ratings, or implicit, such as play/pause events or seeking/scrubbing behavior [2]. One such set of experiments involves associating or finding a video's table of contents. Just like a book or a web site with many pages has a user navigation metaphor based on an index or a table of contents, a video needs structure to facilitate user through numerous scenes. Video table of contents is perceived by people to have high value for finding information, yet are seldom used for navigation when one is available [3]. Scenes are generally provided to the user with a set of thumbnails, which are called key-frames, if they are fixed pictures, or skims, if they are short videos [4]. A collection of still images has become popular in many applications, because it is easy to display and delivers a set of images, which stand as a table of contents for a video.

Besides the research interest in scene extraction, there have been also commercial systems that provide similar functionality. Many commercially available online players and devices, such as YouTube (Figure 1), provide thumbnails to facilitate user's navigation in each video. Nevertheless, most of the techniques that extract thumbnails at regular time intervals or from each shot are inefficient, because there might be too many shots in a video. In the case of Google YouTube, there is a very large number of thumbnails, which depending on the length of the video might be captured every second (for a three-minute video) or every five seconds (for an hour of video). Therefore, the selection of the thumbnails is actually completely random and stands for neither the content nor the semantics of the content.

2.1. Content-Based Semantics. Content-based information retrieval uses automated techniques to analyze actual video content. It uses images' colors, shapes, textures, sounds, motions, events, objects, or any other information that can be derived from only the video itself. Some techniques have combined the videos' metadata [5] with picture [6] or sound [7], while other researchers provide affective annotation [8, 9] or navigation aids [10]. Even though content-based techniques have begun to emphasize the importance of user perception, they do not take into account people's actual browsing and sharing behavior. Moreover, low-level features (e.g., color and camera transitions) often fail to capture the high-level semantics (e.g., events, actors, and objects) of the video content itself, yet such semantics are often what guide users, particularly nonspecialist users, when navigating [9] within or between videos [10].

According to Money and Agius [11], another classification for video summarization takes into account information from the videos during its production stage; this is called internal summarization as seen in SmartSkip by Drucker et al. [6]. Likewise, external summarization analyzes exterior information during any stage of the video lifecycle; however, most external summarization techniques ignore user activity with the video. Other approaches focus on personalization with the user. Hjelsvold et al. [12] employed hotspots and hyperlinks to match the content to the user profile. Although their framework is based on users' preferences, it requires

FIGURE 1: Google YouTube provides several thumbnails for each video. Moreover, a thumbnail is used to represent related videos on the right. The selection (as well as the number) of these thumbnails is important for effective user navigation.

extra user effort in order to build a profile. Overall, since it is very difficult to detect scenes and extract meaning from videos, previous research has attempted to model video in terms of better-understood concepts, such as text and images [13].

To evaluate methods for understanding video content, researchers and practitioners have been cooperating for more than a decade on a large-scale video library and tools for analyzing the content of video. The TRECVID (TREC Video Retrieval Evaluation: http://trecvid.nist.gov/) workshop series provides a standard-set of videos, tools, and benchmarks, which facilitate the incremental improvement of sense making for videos [14].

In summary, content-based techniques facilitate the discovery of a specific scene, the comprehension of a video in a limited time, and the navigation in multiple videos simultaneously. Again, here the video content is analyzed rather than the metadata associated with people or how people manipulated and consumed the video. Finally, content-based techniques are not applicable to some types of web video, such as lecture and how-to instruction, with a visually flat structure, or are semantically complex respectively.

2.2. User-Based Semantics. In comparison to the more so legacy content-based techniques, there are fewer works on user-based analysis of information retrieval for video content. One explanation for this imbalance is not the importance of content-based, but it is the relatively newer interest in the social web, the sharing, and the use of videos online. Nevertheless, there is a growing body of research and interest on user-based retrieval of video.

User interaction with video has been a basic element of multimedia research for many years. Yu et al. [15] suggested that viewers unintentionally leave footprints during their video-browsing process. They proposed ShotRank, a concept that measures the interestingness or importance of each video shot combining video content analysis and user log mining. Their work, influenced by the PageRank and centrality metrics, assumes there exists a short path in each video. Similarly, Syeda-Mahmood and Ponceleon [16] suggested that user interaction with video is a Markov-model chain of affect-based probability, and they developed a media player-based learning system called the MediaMiner. MediaMiner featured the common play, pause, and random seek into the video via a slider bar, fast/slow forward, and fast/slow backward as well. They modeled implicit user activity according to the user's sentiment (e.g., user is bored, or interested) nowadays is not the main motivation for watching video content. For example, there is a growing number of lecture and how-to videos, which are being watched for their informational value.

Finally, social video interactions on web sites are very suitable for applying community intelligence techniques. In the seminal user-based approach to web video, Shaw and Davis [17] proposed that video representation might be better modeled after the actual use made by the users. Notably, Yew and Shamma [2] have recognized the importance of scrubs (fast forward and rewind), but they have only included counts in their classifier and not the actual timing of the scrub events. Thus, we propose to leverage implicit user activity (e.g., pause/play, seek/scrub), in order to dynamically identify video segments of interest.

In summary, as more media is posted and viewed in online contexts, we assert the importance of analyzing the implicit behavior of consumption along with the traditional video signal and contemporary social metadata.

3. Methodology

We employed an open data-set [18], which has been created in the context of a controlled user experiment (23 users, approximately 400 user interactions within each video), in order to ensure well-defined user-based semantics and noise-free user activity data. Previous work has highlighted the evidence of correlation between the local maximum of user activity and the regions of interest [19], but it has not provided a statistical measure of this correlation, which is the focus of this work. Next, we developed a user activity model for analyzing user interactions as a time-based signal. Since there are no similar works in user activity modeling of implicit user interactions within web video, we have developed a pulse modeling process, which is straightforward to replicate for the same set videos or different ones.

In the initialization phase, we consider that every video is associated with four distinct time series of length equal to the video duration in seconds. Each series corresponds to the four distinct buttons of *Play/Pause*, *Skip*, and *Replay*.

It is our aim to construct a general formalism to treat the statistical properties of the aforementioned discrete signals as well as correlation properties between them. We have adapted established techniques from similar signal processing domains such as material science and seismology (see, e.g., [20] and references therein). Let us consider N user interactions and denote with $\mathbf{r}$ the position vectors of those actions in the time domain. The type of the button pushed is labeled by m. The discrete system of user's actions can be formally characterized by discrete densities as follows:

$$\rho^m(\mathbf{r}) = \sum_j^N \delta^m (\mathbf{r} - \mathbf{r_j}),\qquad(1)$$

which is actually a counter of the series of pulses (here modeling the users' actions) of definite width the centers

of which are determined by the position vectors $\mathbf{r}$ in time. The complete knowledge of the user's actions system is attributed to the fourth-dimension density function $\rho(\mathbf{r_1},\mathbf{r_2},\mathbf{r_3},\mathbf{r_4})dv_1 dv_2 dv_3 dv_4$ interpreted as being the joint probability to find the first button action in a time volume element dv_1 at $\mathbf{r_1}$, the second button action in a time volume element dv_2 at $\mathbf{r_2}$, the third button action in a time volume element dv_3 at $\mathbf{r_3}$, and the fourth button action in a time volume element dv_4 at $\mathbf{r_4}$. One possible way to take into account time correlation between the different bottom user actions is to assume that

$$\rho(\mathbf{r_1},\mathbf{r_2},\mathbf{r_3},\mathbf{r_4}) = \rho^1(\mathbf{r_1})\,\rho^2(\mathbf{r_2})\,\rho^3(\mathbf{r_3})$$
$$\times \rho^4(\mathbf{r_4})\,(1 - d(\mathbf{r_1},\mathbf{r_2},\mathbf{r_3},\mathbf{r_4})),\qquad(2)$$

where $d(\mathbf{r_1},\mathbf{r_2},\mathbf{r_3},\mathbf{r_4})$ corresponds to the correlation function in a homogeneous system and which in a first approximation can be considered of higher order. To this end, in the rest of the paper, we assume the simplest case of uncorrelated button actions. On the other hand pair correlation functions between pulse signals may be treated as usual with the well-known Pearson correlation coefficient.

Initially, the user activity signal is created as follows: each time user presses the *Replay* (*Skip*) button; the moments matching the replayed (skipped) segment of the video are incremented by one. We assume that the user replays a video either because there is something interesting or because there is something difficult to understand, while the user skips a video because there is nothing of interest. In this way, an experimental time series is constructed for each button and for each video—a depiction of users' activity patterns over time. In order to extract pattern characteristics for each time series, that is, scenes with high user activity, the following methodology, consistes of four distinct stages (see Table 1), was used.

In the first stage, we use simple procedure in order to average out user activity noise (Figure 2). In the context of probability theory the noise removal can be treated with the notion of the moving average [21]: from a time series $s^{\exp}(t)$ a new smoother time series $s_T^{\exp}(t)$ may be obtained as

$$s_T^{\exp}(t) = \frac{1}{T}\int_{t-T/2}^{t+T/2} s^{\exp}(t')\,dt',\qquad(3)$$

where T denotes the averaging "window" in time. The larger the averaging window T is, the smoother the signal will be. Schematically the procedure is depicted in Figure 2. The procedure of noise removal of the experimentally recording signal $s^{\exp}(t)$ is of crucial importance for the following reasons: first, in order to reveal trends of the corresponding signals (regions of high user activity) and second in order to estimate local maxima for the second stage, as explained in the next paragraph. It must be noted that the optimum size of the averaging window T is completely defined from the variability of the initial signal. Indeed, T should be large enough in order to average out random fluctuations of the user's activities and small enough in order to reveal, and not disturb, the bell-like localized shape of the user's signal which in turn will demonstrate the area of high user activity.

TABLE 1: Overview of the user activity modeling and analysis.

Stage	User activity signal processing
1	Smoothness procedure
2	Pulse construction at local maximums
3	Construction of approximated reference pulses
4	Determination of correlation between pulse signals

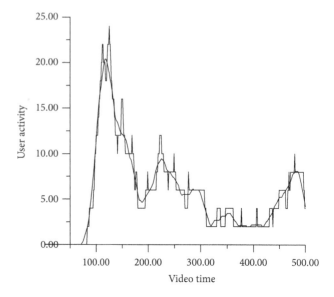

FIGURE 2: The user activity signal is approximated with a smooth signal. The y-axis is the measured user activity while the x-axis is the relative video time in seconds. The same notation is used throughout the paper.

In the second stage, we construct a pulse series from the above constructed user activity smooth signal (Figure 3). The pulse signal is to be compared with the corresponding pulse signal, which models the regions of interest of each video as explained in the third stage. The idea to construct a pulse signal from a time series is not new and several methods may be found in the literature (see, e.g., in [22] and references therein). At the basis of all those formalisms is the need to construct an analytical signal that models local areas of a given signal with significant value in contrast with the rest of the domain where almost zero values are encountered. Instead of pulses, other functional, for example, Gaussian-like, could be also used. In our analysis, the shape of the localized functional had no effect and as a result we kept the pulses since the following analysis was easier. Here, in order to construct the pulse signal the exact location of the pulses is defined by means of the generalized local maxima of the experimental smooth signal (Figure 4). By the term generalized local maxima, we mention the center of the corresponding bell-like area of the average signal, since the nature of our signal may cause more than one peak at the top of the bell. Although the height of the pulse does not affect our results, the width of the pulse D is a parameter that must be treated carefully. In particular, the variability of the average signal determines the order of the pulse width D. Here, we propose that the pulse width should be equal to the average half of the widths of the bell-like regions of the signals (see Figure 3(b)). In the context of our controlled experiment, this is a safe assumption, but it requires further elaboration in different experimental setups or in the field (e.g., data-mining of real video usage data). Moreover, we are providing a more detailed analysis of the interplay between the parameters in Section 5.

In the third stage we construct the corresponding pulse signal $s_{kf}(t)$ which models the regions of interest of each video (Figure 3). For compatibility reasons and without loss of generality the shape of the pulses (width and high) is the same as for $s_{kf}^{exp}(t)$. On the other hand, the exact locations of the pulses are defined as the center of the corresponding regions of interest as defined in the data-set.

It is our aim to examine whether the two signals (user activity and reference pulses) are correlated, for example, whether the patterns revealed from the user's activity are correlated with objective regions of interest of each video. In order to check this hypothesis the cross-correlation coefficient was used which estimates the degree to which two series are correlated (e.g., [21]). The values of the correlation coefficient range from −1 to 1. Perfect uncorrelated time series has zero correlation coefficient, while positive or negative

correlations may be scored as follows (we refer to absolute values): from 0.1 to 0.3 low correlation, from 0.3 to 0.5 medium correlation, and from 0.5 to 1 strong correlation. It is noted that the determination of the cross-correlation coefficient as well as the proposed signal process methodology was carried out via simple codes developed with standard math libraries in the C programming environment.

4. Results

We have focused on the analysis of the video seeking behavior, such as *Replay* and *Skip* the previously described smoothening procedure. An exploratory analysis with time series probabilistic tools verified what is visually depicted in the case of Video A, which is a lecture video (Figure 4). While the *Replay* signal has a quite regular pattern with a small number of regions with high user's activity, the *Skip* signal is characterized by a large number of merely random and abnormal local maxima of user's activity. We have also considered the use of the *Play/Pause* buttons, but there were few interactions. In the following, we present the results of the *Replay* signal analysis for four videos.

The analysis of the user activity signal was based on an exploration of several alternative averaging window sizes. The results of the pulse modeling methodology are depicted in Tables 2 to 5. The smoothed signals are plotted with the solid black curve. The pulse signals were extracted from the corresponding local maxima that are depicted with the red discontinued pulse signal while the pulse signals that model the regions of interest of each video are depicted with the blue solid pulse. Although the correlation of the constructed pulse signals for each video is visually evident in the graphs (figures embedded in Tables 2 to 5), the cross-correlation coefficient was used in order to establish the respective quantitative

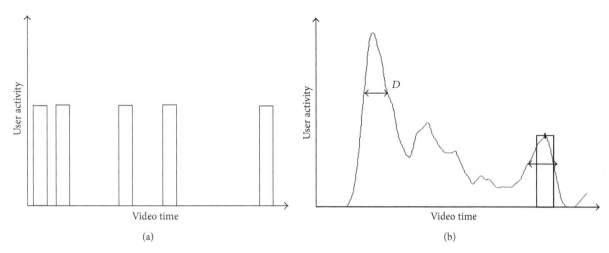

FIGURE 3: The pulse of reference (a), which is based on manually selected video scenes, is compared to the experimental pulse (b), which is created at the local maximum of the (smooth) user activity signal. The optimum pulse width D is also depicted schematically.

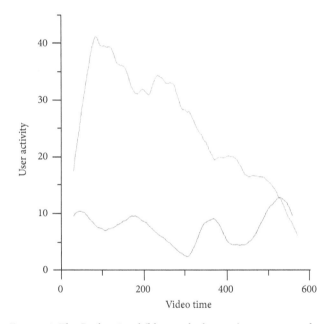

FIGURE 4: The *Replay* signal (blue, at the bottom) was compared to the *Skip* (red, at the top), in order to understand which one is closer to the semantics of the video. The higher values of the *Skip* signal stand for the popularity of the respective user activity.

measures. Indeed, the cross-correlation coefficients that we estimated were 0.67, 0.58, 0.76, and 0.62 correspondingly, indicating strong correlation between the two signals (reference and user signal). The pulse modeling process has identified the majority of the manually selected video scenes with high accuracy, but a few scenes were still not detected. In Tables 2, 3, 4, and 5, the video scenes (S1,...,S5) detected by the algorithm (user activity pulse modeling) are compared to the reference video scenes.

The most important parameter in the analysis of the user activity signal is the averaging window T and the relationship it has with the (1) skipping step, (2) video duration, and (3) number of user interactions. It must be noted that several values of the averaging window T were checked and the empirical relation $T \approx D$ was found, as the optimal one since it removes the underline signal noise without affecting user's activity characteristics. It is notable that if the skipping step was not fixed (e.g., random seek with a progress bar), then the analysis of the user activity signal would have required a dynamic size of the averaging window T, which would have made the process much more complex. In summary, the above results demonstrate the efficacy of this approach and provide a small set of parameters (video browsing actions, averaging window duration T, and pulse width D) that need to be further explored, as it is discussed next.

5. Discussion

In this work, we focused on an application for detecting important video segments, because it plays several roles in understanding video semantics. In particular, the important segments provide an additional navigation mechanism and an abstract of the video, either thumbnails or skims. The idea to interpret user's actions as a sum of discrete pulses as was mentioned before is borrowed from other fields, for example, material science [23]. Actually what is common is the existence of different populations (here different types of buttons) of discrete nature (discrete user's actions) and their patterning or morphogenesis in the corresponding space (here patterning of user's actions within the video duration). Note that since populations are discrete in nature the corresponding emerged patterns are also discrete thus resulting in theoretical models by means of pulses of definite width.

The determination of the optimum averaging window as well as the corresponding width pulse is of crucial importance and the analysis shows that these are dynamic-like variables meaning that their values require a careful balance between video and user activity attributes. On the one hand, a lengthy video might require a wider averaging window, in order to

TABLE 2: Video A is a lecture video (http://www.youtube.com/watch?v=8LebAtvulIY). The pulse width D is 60 seconds and the smoothing window T is 60 seconds. The pulse modeling is reported with respect to the center of each pulse.

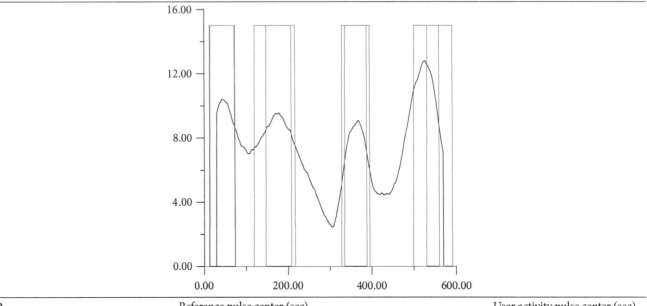

A	Reference pulse center (sec)	User activity pulse center (sec)
S1	43	44
S2	150	
S3	187	178
S4	358	365
S5	561	530

TABLE 3: Video B is a documentary video (http://www.youtube.com/watch?v=tSV2kAfkp5A). The pulse width D is 50 seconds and the smoothing window T is 40 seconds. The pulse modeling is reported with respect to the center of each pulse.

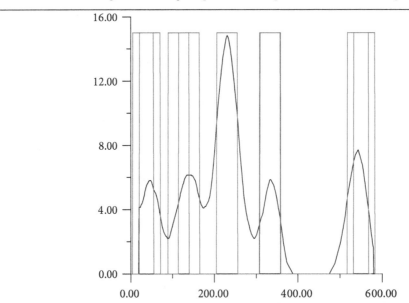

B	Reference pulse center (sec)	User activity pulse center (sec)
S1	30	46
S2	115	140
S3	231	231
S4	333	334
S5	558	543

TABLE 4: Video C is a lecture video (http://www.youtube.com/watch?v=Z09ythJT9Wk). The pulse width *D* is 50 seconds and the smoothing window *T* is 50 seconds. The pulse modeling is reported with respect to the center of each pulse.

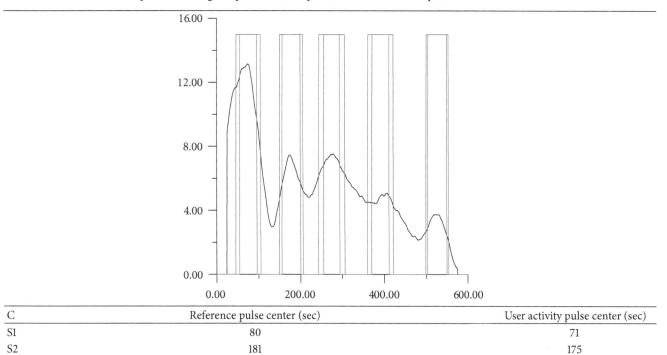

C	Reference pulse center (sec)	User activity pulse center (sec)
S1	80	71
S2	181	175
S3	269	281
S4	386	396
S5	528	524

TABLE 5: Video D is a cooking (how-to) video (http://www.youtube.com/watch?v=LzkYvtqlT5I). The pulse width *D* is 30 seconds and the smoothing window *T* is 25 seconds. The pulse modeling is reported with respect to the center of each pulse.

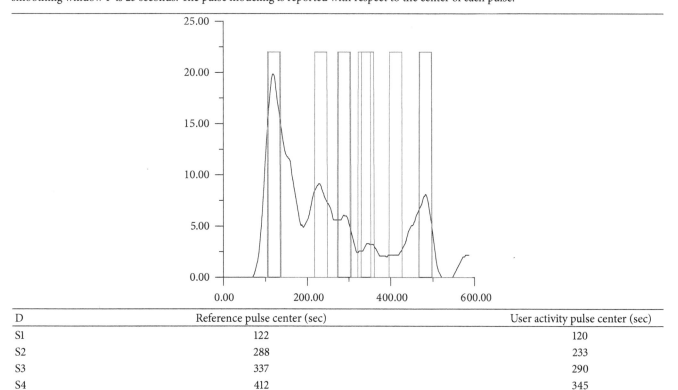

D	Reference pulse center (sec)	User activity pulse center (sec)
S1	122	120
S2	288	233
S3	337	290
S4	412	345
S5	482	483

limit the possible number of detected scenes. For example, a typical one-hour lecture with many users would have produced too many local maximums, which could be filtered with a wider averaging window (e.g., ten minutes). On the other hand, the larger the number and the variability of the users' activity signal, the smaller the averaging window. Indeed, if a dense users' activity is recording (during the video time), then a small averaging window must be used in order to catch this dense activity, while a larger averaging window may result to a mutual overlapping of two different regions of interest. Further research should also explore these basic signal attributes (smoothing window T and pulse width D) in the context of other real systems. In this way, our knowledge about the user activity signal attributes could complement the experimental understanding we have described in this work.

We have only employed four videos in the experimental procedure. Previous work on content-based information retrieval from videos has emphasized the number of videos employed in similar experiments, because the respective algorithms treated the content of those videos. In this user-based work, we are not concerned with the content of the videos, but with the user activity on the videos. Nevertheless, it is worthwhile to explore the effect of more videos and interaction types. Therefore, the small number of videos used in the study is not an important limitation, but further research has to elaborate on different genres of video (e.g., news, sports, and comedy) and the semantic label of the interaction (e.g., answering who, what, and how).

Another significant open research issue is the number of thumbnails. We have already shown that Google YouTube (Figure 1) provides so many thumbnails that the user has to navigate through them by scrolling. This research issue has already concerned SmartSkip's developers [6]. They started out with ten thumbnails and after an early prototype test; they reduced the number of thumbnails to eight. According to the final user test, they suggested to reduce the number of thumbnails even further to five. Nevertheless, the number of scenes depends on several parameters, such as the type and length of the video. Therefore, it is unlikely that there are a fixed number of scenes that describe a particular video. If the required number of scenes is different for each video, then, besides the scene extraction technique, we need a method to select the most important of them.

6. Conclusion

In this research, we validated a method for scene detection in web videos. Our main goal is to understand the semantics of video content from users' interactions with the video player. In particular, we found that the aggregation of user *Replay* interactions with the video player stands for the most important segments of a video. The results of this type of study can be used to develop systems that understand important video's scenes, generate thumbnails, and create a video summary. We decided to explore a user-based approach, because previous works have already analyzed content-based methods and because of a growing number of web videos and the respective user interactions.

A direction for further research would be to perform data mining on a large-scale web-video database. Nevertheless, we found that the experimental approach is more flexible than data mining for the development phase of a new video retrieval system. In particular, the iterative and experimental approach is very suitable for user-centric information retrieval, because it is feasible to explore and associate user behavior with the respective data-logs. Moreover, in contrast to data mining in large data-sets, a controlled experiment has the benefit of keeping a clean set of data that does not need several steps of filtering, before it becomes usable for any kind of simple user heuristic. Finally, we suggest that user-based content analysis has the benefits of continuously adapting to evolving users' preferences, as well as providing additional opportunities for the personalization of content. For example, researchers might be able to apply several personalization techniques, such as collaborative filtering, to the user activity data. In this way, implicit video pragmatics is emerging as a new playing field for improving user experience on social multimedia on the web.

Conflict of Interests

The authors declare that there is no conflict of interests regarding the publication of this paper.

Acknowledgment

The work reported in this paper has been partly supported by Project CULT (http://cult.di.ionio.gr/). CULT (MC-ERG-2008-230894) is a Marie Curie project of the European Commission (EC) under the 7th Framework Program (FP7).

References

[1] M. Cha, H. Kwak, P. Rodriguez, Y. Ahnt, and S. Moon, "I tube, you tube, everybody tubes: analyzing the world's largest user generated content video system," in *Proceedings of the 7th ACM SIGCOMM Internet Measurement Conference (IMC '07)*, pp. 1–14, ACM, San Diego, Calif, USA, October 2007.

[2] J. Yew and D. A. Shamma, "Know your data: understanding implicit usage versus explicit action in video content classification," in *5th Multimedia on Mobile Devices 2011; and Multimedia Content Access: Algorithms and Systems*, vol. 7881 of *Proceedings of SPIE*, San Francisco, Calif, USA, January 2011.

[3] E. G. Toms, C. Dufour, J. Lewis, and R. Baecker, "Assessing tools for use with webcasts," in *Proceedings of the 5th ACM/IEEE Joint Conference on Digital Libraries*, pp. 79–88, ACM Press, New York, NY, USA, June 2005.

[4] B. T. Truong and S. Venkatesh, "Video abstraction: a systematic review and classification," *ACM Transactions on Multimedia Computing, Communications and Applications*, vol. 3, no. 1, article 3, 2007.

[5] Y. Takahashi, N. Nitta, and N. Babaguchi, "Video summarization for large sports video archives," in *Proceedings of the 13th Annual ACM International Conference on Multimedia*, pp. 820–828, ACM, Singapore, 2005.

[6] S. M. Drucker, A. Glatzer, S. de Mar, and C. Wong, "Smartskip: consumer level browsing and skipping of digital video content," in *Proceedings of the SIGCHI Conference on Human Factors in*

Computing Systems (CHI '02), pp. 219–226, Minneapolis, Minn, USA, April 2002.

[7] F. C. Li, A. Gupta, E. Sanocki, L. W. He, and Y. Rui, "Browsing digital video," in *Proceedings of the SIGCHI Conference on Human Factors in Computing Systems (CHI '00)*, vol. 2, pp. 169–176, April 2000.

[8] L. Chen, G. Chen, C. Xu, J. March, and S. Benford, "EmoPlayer: a media player for video clips with affective annotations," *Interacting with Computers*, vol. 20, no. 1, pp. 17–28, 2008.

[9] C. Crockford and H. Agius, "An empirical investigation into user navigation of digital video using the VCR-like control set," *International Journal of Human Computer Studies*, vol. 64, no. 4, pp. 340–355, 2006.

[10] J. Kim, H. Kim, and K. Park, "Towards optimal navigation through video content on interactive TV," *Interacting with Computers*, vol. 18, no. 4, pp. 723–746, 2006.

[11] A. G. Money and H. Agius, "Analysing user physiological responses for affective video summarisation," *Displays*, vol. 30, no. 2, pp. 59–70, 2009.

[12] R. Hjelsvold, S. Vdaygiri, and Y. Léauté, "Web-based personalization and management of interactive video," in *Proceedings of the 10th International Conference on World Wide Web (WWW '01)*, pp. 129–139, 2001.

[13] R. Yan and A. G. Hauptmann, "A review of text and image retrieval approaches for broadcast news video," *Information Retrieval*, vol. 10, no. 4-5, pp. 445–484, 2007.

[14] C. G. M. Snoek and M. Worring, "Concept-based video retrieval," *Foundations and Trends in Information Retrieval*, vol. 2, no. 4, pp. 215–322, 2008.

[15] B. Yu, W. Y. Ma, K. Nahrstedt, and H. J. Zhang, "Video summarization based on user log enhanced link analysis," in *Proceedings of the 11th ACM International Conference on Multimedia (MULTIMEDIA '03)*, pp. 382–391, ACM Press, New York, NY, USA, November 2003.

[16] T. Syeda-Mahmood and D. Ponceleon, "Learning video browsing behavior and its application in the generation of video previews," in *Proceedings of the 9th ACM International Conference on Multimedia (MULTIMEDIA '01)*, pp. 119–128, ACM Press, New York, NY, USA, October 2001.

[17] R. Shaw and M. Davis, "Toward emergent representations for video," in *Proceedings of the 13th Annual ACM International Conference on Multimedia (MULTIMEDIA '05)*, pp. 431–434, ACM, New York, NY, USA, 2005.

[18] C. Gkonela and K. Chorianopoulos, "VideoSkip: event detection in social web videos with an implicit user heuristic," *Multimedia Tools and Applications*, 2012.

[19] K. Chorianopoulos, "Collective intelligence within web video," *Human-Centric Computing and Information Sciences*, vol. 3, article 10, 2013.

[20] I. Groma, F. F. Csikor, and M. Zaiser, "Spatial correlations and higher-order gradient terms in a continuum description of dislocation dynamics," *Acta Materialia*, vol. 51, no. 5, pp. 1271–1281, 2003.

[21] E. Vanmarcke, *Random Fields, Analysis and Synthesis*, MIT Press, Cambridge, Mass, USA, 1983.

[22] A. Papoulis, *Probability, Random Variables, and Stochastic Processes*, McGraw-Hill Kogakusha, Tokyo, Japan, 9th edition, 1965.

[23] M. Zaiser, M. C. Miguel, and I. Groma, "Statistical dynamics of dislocation systems: the influence of dislocation-dislocation correlations," *Physical Review B*, vol. 64, no. 22, Article ID 224102, 9 pages, 2001.

13

Application Layer Systematic Network Coding for Sliced H.264/AVC Video Streaming

Sajid Nazir,[1] Vladimir Stanković,[1] Ivan Andonović,[1] and Dejan Vukobratović[2]

[1] Department of Electronic and Electrical Engineering, University of Strathclyde, Glasgow G1 1XQ, UK
[2] Department of Power, Electronics and Communication Engineering, University of Novi Sad, 21000 Novi Sad, Serbia

Correspondence should be addressed to Sajid Nazir, nazirsajid@yahoo.com

Academic Editor: Vaggelis Kapoulas

Application Layer Forward Error Correction (AL-FEC) with rateless codes can be applied to protect the video data over lossy channels. Expanding Window Random Linear Codes (EW RLCs) are a flexible unequal error protection fountain coding scheme which can provide prioritized data transmission. In this paper, we propose a system that exploits systematic EW RLC for H.264/Advanced Video Coding (AVC) slice-partitioned data. The system prioritizes slices based on their PSNR contribution to reconstruction as well as temporal significance. Simulation results demonstrate usefulness of using relative slice priority with systematic codes for multimedia broadcast applications.

1. Introduction

H.264 Advanced Video Coding (AVC) [1] is currently the most commonly used video coding standard, which is gaining widespread use in the emerging communication standards and applications.

Two key challenges of multimedia communication applications over wireless networks are high and varying error characteristics of underlying communications channels and huge heterogeneity of users' equipment.

One of the solutions is to use channel coding techniques which could recover the original data despite losses. The latest state-of-the-art solutions like those based on Reed Solomon (RS) codes are inflexible because the code rate has to be fixed in advance. Moreover, the encoding and decoding operations are quite complex especially for large Galois Field. For such codes, the error characteristics of the channel must be known in advance in order to adjust the code rate to it. This solution does not extend well to multiple receivers as then only a worst-case erasure channel can be assumed for all receivers.

To enable communications in the presence of packet losses, rateless Digital Fountain Raptor codes [2] have become standardized solution in many wireless systems such as Digital Video Broadcasting-Handheld (DVB-H) [3–5], Multimedia Broadcast Multicast Service (MBMS), and mobile Worldwide Interoperability for Microwave Access (WiMax) [6].

Another class of rateless codes which have been gaining increased popularity for applications in wireless broadcast/cellular networks are Random Linear Codes (RLCs) [7, 8]. RLCs show near-capacity performance over erasure channels even for low codeword lengths [9, 10]. In addition, the emerging networking concepts, such as hybrid broadcast/cellular networks (with users equipped with multiple interfaces) or device-to-device communications, offer a number of opportunities for achieving network coding gains using RLC [11].

Traditional solutions for reliable multimedia delivery use multiple independent Reed Solomon (RS) codes with different rate allocation over importance classes [12, 13]. These solutions do not have the rateless property and thus have to be designed for the worst channel conditions, and they cannot explore network coding gains over network topologies by packet processing in intermediate nodes.

For applications where short message lengths represent a natural choice (such as multimedia delivery) and where wireless multihop communications are encountered, the RLC scheme represents a more efficient and versatile approach. Such realizations are expected to result in increased throughput of wireless multihop broadcast/cellular networks [8]. Due to all this, RLCs have been considered as a unique rateless/network coding solution [14–18] for emerging wireless systems, such as Long-Term Evolution-Advanced (LTE-A) and DVB-NGH (Next Generation Handheld). (See [19] for performance/complexity comparison between Raptor codes [2] and RLCs.)

The inherent disadvantage of RLC is that RLC suffers from high decoding complexity of the Gaussian Elimination decoding as codeword length increases. However, even with very short codeword lengths that admit efficient implementation, RLC performance matches that of Raptor codes of higher codeword lengths [19, 20].

Both Raptor codes and RLC are "all or nothing" codes that equally protect the entire stream. For embedded and scalable sources where different parts of the stream have different importance to reconstruction, unequal error protection (UEP) is beneficial. Expanding Window Fountain (EWF) codes as a class of UEP FEC codes for scalable video delivery are proposed in [21]. EWF codes are based on the idea of creating a set of "nested windows" over a source block. This EW concept is extended to RLC, and performance limits are presented in [22]. The suitability of nonsystematic EW RLC for transmission of data-partitioned H.264/AVC has been investigated in [4].

As compared to the data partitioning H.264/AVC feature [1], slicing has an advantage that the size of slices can be tailored to the application. The slicing feature of H.264/AVC can be used to partition video stream into classes of decreasing importance (for video reconstruction) with a very small decrease in overall performance.

A scheme has been proposed in [23] based on macroblock classification into three slice groups and UEP of H.264/AVC streams. The ordering of macroblocks into three slice groups is done by examining their contribution to the video quality. The three slice groups are then protected with UEP using RS coding. In [24], a slice sorting by relevance (SSR) algorithm for prioritizing slices based on their contribution to the reconstruction is used together with RS coding. The work in [24] is later extended in [25] and proposes an algorithm termed Concealment Driven Slice Ordering with RS codes. The ordering of slices is based on error propagation effect and the rate devoted to each slice.

The proposed work differs from the earlier work in the method of prioritizing slices and choice of systematic rateless codes for channel coding. The slice-partitioned video stream can provide an advantage with respect to H.264 Scalable Video Coding (SVC) [26] of better coding efficiency and compliance with the AVC standard. The layered video can be protected by EW RLC codes that can provide a different degree of protection to each layer/window.

Building on our prior work [4, 19, 20, 22], the focus of this study is to analyse the use of the EW approach with systematic RLC as component codes for UEP of the slice-partitioned H.264/AVC video. Systematic RLCs have the advantage of supporting more efficient encoding and decoding procedures compared to nonsystematic RLC.

In contrast to [24], where priority layers are built based purely on distortion information, in this paper, we propose a new cost function that takes into account the frame play out deadline and temporal error propagation to better prioritize slices into quality layers.

Our simulation results show that EW RLC can be used to effectively protect the different priority windows for reliable video transmission over packet erasure channels. Significant performance gains are obtained compared to the equal error protection scheme and the benchmark scheme that prioritizes the sliced stream in an ad hoc fashion.

The rest of the paper is structured as follows. The relevant background on RLC and the slicing feature of H.264/AVC is covered in Section 2. The proposed system is described in Section 3. The results are presented in Section 4 and conclusion and future research in Section 5.

2. Background

In this section, we give a brief background on slicing in H.264/AVC [1, 27] and overview of RLC [7] and EW RLC [22] coding scheme.

2.1. Slicing in H.264/AVC. H.264/AVC provides many error-resilience features to mitigate the effect of lost packets during transmission.

One such scheme available in the baseline profile is slicing [27], which enables the partitioning of a frame into two or more independently coded sections, called slices. Each slice in a frame can have either a fixed number of assigned macroblocks (MBs) or fixed data rate. Each coded slice is independently decodable; however, the slices have different contribution (importance) to the video reconstruction. Thus, arranging the slices in decreasing order of their contribution to reconstruction can be used to provide a layered video stream suitable for UEP.

2.2. Random Linear Codes (RLCs). RLC applied over a source message produces encoded packets as random linear combinations of message packets with coefficients randomly selected from a given finite field GF(2^q). For example, using RLC over a source message x of length K, an encoded packet ω is obtained as $\omega = \sum_{i=1}^{K} \alpha_i \cdot x_i$, where α_i is a randomly selected element of GF(2^q). The resulting encoded packet ω is of the same length (b bits) as the source message packets. In addition, to each encoded packet, ω a header information is attached that contains the so-called global encoding vector $\mathbf{g} = \{\alpha_1, \alpha_2, \dots, \alpha_k\}$ consisting of randomly selected finite field coefficients. The header requirements in a unicast point-to-point setup can be relaxed if a pair of synchronized random number generators (RNGs) is used at the transmitter and the receiver and only the RNG seed is communicated within each encoded packet header. The encoding procedure is repeated at the transmitter in a rateless fashion.

Thus, each encoded symbol is a linear combination of all or a subset of the original source symbols. An RNG seed carried in the header of the encoded symbol can be used at the decoder to recover the coefficients used at the encoder.

Encoding procedure is simple to implement, and, for sufficiently large finite field used for creating linear combinations of source symbols, RLC codes perform as near-optimal erasure codes (one-byte field GF(256) is usually sufficiently good [7]).

For practical network coding, RLC is used at source nodes for encoding the source message packets and at intermediate network nodes for random recombining of incoming and/or buffered encoded packets. The source nodes and intermediate nodes may produce encoded packets in a rateless fashion, until the requirements of receiving nodes are met (which may be confirmed by feedback messages), or in the delay-constrained applications, until a new source block is scheduled for transmission.

After sufficient linearly independent coded symbols have been received, the decoder can recover the original source symbols.

The RLC use is hindered by the decoding complexity of Gaussian Elimination decoding, which is polynomial in the number of symbols. However, for short lengths of the source messages, the decoding complexity is acceptable (see [19, 28] and references therein).

A systematic code is any error-correcting code in which the input data is embedded in the encoded symbol. The advantage of such codes is that the receiver does not need to recover the original source symbol in case of correct reception.

When erasure rates are low, it is effective to use systematic RLC, which further reduce the decoding complexity, since the received systemic packets can be used to reduce the effective code length before Gaussian Elimination decoding.

2.3. EW RLC [22]. In [21], EWF codes as a class of UEP fountain codes are proposed. EWF codes are based on the idea of creating a set of "nested windows" over the source block. The rateless encoding process is then adapted to use this windowing information while producing encoded packets. In this paper, we use the main concept of EWF to create EW RLC [22] from consecutive source blocks containing fixed number of symbols (data packets).

First, we define a set of windows over the groups of source symbols of unequal importance. Coding is then performed over progressively increasing source block subset windows aligned with this "most to least importance" subsets.

The general layout of a window structure with three importance classes is shown in Figure 1. The window with the most important subset of encoded data is W_1, and the importance of data additionally included in windows progressively decreases as we proceed to W_3. The subset data of W_1 is contained in all the subsequent windows and is hence the best protected. Apart from W_1, each window in addition to some of its own data also encloses all the data of the higher importance windows. Conventional RLC is applied on each window.

The encoding process for EW RLC has one important initial step that is to first select a window from which

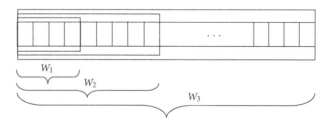

FIGURE 1: Expanding window structure with three windows.

the RLC encoded symbol is to be generated. This selection of a window is determined by probability of selection of a window which is a preassigned parameter keeping in mind the importance of different layers and the data rate available. After a window is selected, the encoding is the standard RLC encoding performed over the source packets contained in that particular window only [22]. The window selection procedure is independently repeated for each created encoded packet.

In [22], analytical performance of EW RLC is given together with comparison with traditional nonoverlapping UEP RLCs that use independent code for each window. In [4, 20], nonoverlapping window (NOW) and EW have been used to provide unequal error protection to the data partitioned H.264/AVC video data. It is shown in [4] that the performance of EW is better as compared to NOW because in NOW each window is independently decoded and thus the low priority windows do not contribute to recovery of the high priority windows.

3. The Proposed System

In this section, we propose a system for optimally protecting the slice-partitioned H.264/AVC video data with systematic EW RLC. We assume that the encoded video stream is transmitted over a packet loss channel. That is, all packets that arrive at the application-layer RLC decoder are correct, while those with bit errors are discarded by error detection codes, such as Cyclic Redundancy Check (CRC) codes present at the lower layer in the protocol stack (e.g., physical or link layer). We further assume that error detection capability of the employed CRC codes is perfect, which is usual assumption [7, 9–11, 24]. Thus, the application layer-to-application layer channel is modeled as packet erasure channel with random packet drop statistics.

In order to increase error resilience, we encode a video sequence using slicing with a fixed slice size of 600 bytes. That is, after the H.264/AVC encoding, we obtain the video data in which each frame including the IDR (instantaneous decoder refresh) is divided into slices of 600 ± 3 bytes, except for the last slice of each frame which can have a lesser size. The size of 600 bytes is chosen here to keep the number of RLC symbols per codeword low in order to reduce the decoding complexity of Gaussian Elimination. See [11, 28] for discussion about acceptable block lengths for real-time RLC decoding. The resulting slices carry different importance to reconstruction which has been used to achieve UEP (see [24, 29] and references therein).

After source coding, EW RLC coding takes place. Since systematic RLCs are used, first all encoded symbols (from all the slices) are transmitted without any coding. Because of possible errors/erasures in the channels, some packets will be missing at the decoder.

To correct these erasures, RLC redundancy packets are generated next.

Before RLC, the priority of each slice is obtained by dropping it from the Group of Pictures (GOPs) data and measuring the resulting peak signal-to-noise ratio (PSNR), as a frame-by-frame average of the entire GOP, by actual decoding. This also takes into account the error propagation effect to the subsequent frames due to loss of a slice in an earlier frame. That is, the cumulative PSNR of the GOP is measured by dropping each slice in turn starting at the first P frame. After having obtained the cumulative PSNR values for each slice (as dropped), the difference from the full-decoding PSNR of the GOP is measured. Determining PSNR drop can easily be done during the encoding process with negligible added complexity (see [24]).

The results are shown in Figure 2 for the first GOP (having 16 frames and the encoding structure IPPPP...) of the standard CIF Foreman sequence. It can be seen from Figure 2 that the importance of the slices on total frame-averaged PSNR generally decreases as we move towards the end of the GOP. Similar results are shown in Figure 3 for the first GOP (having 64 frames and the encoding structure IPPPP...) for the Paris sequence. As can be seen from the figures, the PSNR drop values for Paris sequence are larger due to large GOP size.

Thus, we can sort the slices into multiple priority layers and assign a higher degree of protection to the important layers as compared to the layers containing less significant slices. Such layering enables a prioritized data transmission with UEP schemes and was used before in [24, 29].

Purely grouping the slices into priority classes based on the PSNR decrease shown in Figure 2, as done in [24, 29], does not take into account real-time frame playout deadline (frames coming sooner should be given a higher priority).

Motivated by this, we redefine a cost function used in [29], to take into account not only the drop in cumulative PSNR for each slice, but also the temporal importance of a slice:

$$W(\text{slice}) = D(\text{slice}) - w * \tau(\text{slice}), \qquad (1)$$

where $D(\text{slice})$ represents the drop in the cumulative PSNR (see y-axis of Figure 2). The value of $\tau(\text{slice})$ represents the playout time deadline of the slice (frame) relative to the playout time of the first IDR in the GOP. That is, $\tau(\text{slice})$ of the IDR frame is set to zero, and each subsequent frame adds its playout time duration to this value. w is a constant that trades off the distortion $D(\text{slice})$ and remaining playout time.

In this way, we create a system to assign a priority to all the slices trading off importance of the slices to reconstruction and playout time deadline. After computing $W(\text{slice})$ for all the slices in a GOP and selecting threshold values $T_1 > T_2 > \cdots > T_{L-1}$, we group the slices into L layers.

The first layer includes IDR and slices with $W(\text{slice}) \geq T_1$, the second layer includes all remaining slices with $W(\text{slice}) \geq T_2$, and so forth. In addition, our algorithm also puts at least one slice per frame to the first layer, if none is selected (from a frame) based on the above criteria alone. This helps to stop the error propagation effect further and thus improves resulting PSNR. Such selections may be needed for frames which occur towards the end of GOP as can be seen from Figure 2.

In the proposed scheme, we can create L windows using a threshold $(L-1)$-tuple $T_1, \ldots, T_{L-1}$, and allocate different protection to each window. Note that the slices would already be in their decoding order within each layer. However, within each window, the slices will need to be restored to the original order to enable decoding by the AVC decoder.

After determining thresholds and assigning slices to the L windows, the size of each layer is fixed. Then, the remaining task is to find the optimal allocation of redundancy to each layer, or equivalently probability of window selection. We express the probability of window selection as an L-tuple where ith entry denotes probability of selection of a packet from layer i. For example, let $L = 2$ and the vector of selection probabilities as $[0.6, 0.4]$, this implies that the first window, W_1, will have a selection probability of 0.6, whereas W_2 will have a selection probability of 0.4. That is, in average, redundant packets from W_1 will comprise 60% of the overall redundancy.

To find optimal packet selection vector, we maximize the expected PSNR using analytically computed probabilities of decoding error performance. That is,

$$\max_{\pi} \text{PSNR}(\pi) = \sum_{i=0}^{L} P(i) \text{psnr}(i), \qquad (2)$$

where $P(i)$ is probability that layer i will be the highest layer recovered, $P(0)$ is the probability that nothing is recovered, $\text{psnr}(i)$ is the PSNR of the reconstruction if all layers up to and including layer i are recovered, π is an L-tuple vector of window selection probabilities that determines the UEP allocation scheme, and $\text{PSNR}(\pi)$ is the expected PSNR when UEP scheme π is used.

In the above maximization, we made assumption that, if decoding of window i fails, none of the packets from window $j \geq i$ can be used for reconstruction. This is true for nonsystematic EW RLC and approximation for systematic EW RLC.

Analytical expressions for probabilities $P(i)$ assuming a random channel loss model for EW RLC as derived in our prior work [22] are as follows:

$$P(l) = \begin{cases} 1 - P_{d,N}(1), & l = 0, \\ \prod_{i=1}^{l} P_{d,N}(i) \cdot (1 - P_{d,N}(l+1)), & 1 \leq l \leq L-1, \\ \prod_{i=1}^{L} P_{d,N}(i), & i = L, \end{cases} \qquad (3)$$

where the desired decoding probabilities $P_{d,N}(l)$ are expressed as

$$P_{d,N}(l) = \sum_{\substack{(n_1,n_2,...,n_L): \\ 0 \le N_1 \le N_2 \le \cdots N_L = N}} P_{r(\xi),N}(n) P_{d,N}(l \mid n). \quad (4)$$

The expression for $P_{r(\xi),N}$ is as given:

$$P_{r(\xi),N}(n) = \frac{N!}{n_1! n_2! \cdots n_L!} \Gamma_1^{n_1} \Gamma_2^{n_2} \cdots \Gamma_L^{n_L}, \quad (5)$$

whereas

$$P_{d,N}(l \mid n)$$
$$= P_r(R_l = K_l) + P_r(R_{l+1} = K_{l+1}, R_l < K_l)$$
$$+ \cdots + P_r(R_L = K, R_l < K_l, R_{l+1} < K_{l+1} \cdots R_{L-1} < K_{L-1}), \quad (6)$$

where Γ_i is the probability of selection of the ith window, R_is are random variables denoting the number of received packets from window i, and K_i is the number of source packets in widnow i.

The optimization method is exhaustive search and scales linearly with the number of UEP schemes being used.

For error concealment, we repeat the last correctly decoded frame to replace frames for which the base layer is not decoded properly.

4. Results and Analysis

In this section, we present our simulation results. For simplicity, we consider the case of $L = 2$ layers: high-priority layer (HPL) that contains more important slices, whose $W(\text{slice}) \ge T$, and low-priority layer (LPL) that contains less important slices for which $W(\text{slice}) < T$, where T is the chosen threshold.

The thresholds determine the source rate for each layer. For example, a lower T would result in a lower source rate (and, hence, error-free performance) for the base layer. Thus, T_is are set based on available clients' bandwidths as well as desired error-free performance levels. In practice, transmitter can dynamically adapt the source rate per layer to varying channel conditions of different clients by changing T_i's.

The video sequence *Foreman* in the CIF format is encoded using the H.264/AVC software JM version 16.2 [30]. First, we use the GOP size of 16 frames with a frame structure IPPP..., with a fixed slice size of 600 bytes. We compare three schemes: one is the proposed UEP scheme optimized using (1). The second scheme is the benchmark scheme, where we put all the slices of IDR and the first slice of each frame in HPL and all other slices in LPL. The third is the equal error protection (EEP) scheme that protects all slices equally. Note that the benchmark scheme is a low-complexity scheme where prioritization is done in an ad hoc manner; it still uses the same systematic EW RLC for protection of the two layers.

The proposed scheme is designed in accordance with the algorithm described in Section 3 with $T = 0.78$ and $w = 2.5$. The sizes, number of packets (same as the number of slices in a layer), and resulting PSNR values for both configurations are shown in Table 1.

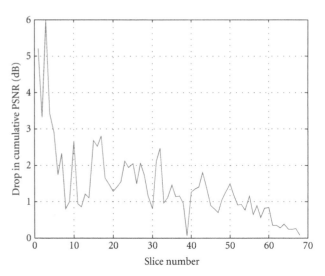

FIGURE 2: Drop in PSNR for non-IDR slices-Foreman sequence GOP16.

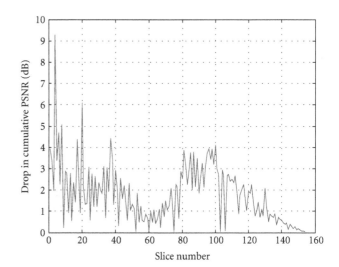

FIGURE 3: Drop in PSNR for non-IDR slices-Paris sequence GOP64.

For this selection of T, the proposed UEP scheme has larger HPL than the benchmark.

Note, however, that a smaller HPL for the proposed scheme could be obtained by suitably selecting parameter T and w in (1).

All schemes are compared at the same transmission bitrate. For an L-layer scheme, the overhead cost needed to describe a UEP solution is $7 \times L$ plus $(L-1) * 8 * 2$ to convey T_is and w_is. For $L = 2$ used in this paper, this number is only 30 bits and has not been taken into consideration.

The proposed schemes are simulated with transmission of EW RLC for 1000 runs and the results averaged. The total number of packets to be transmitted for each run is 100. Because of the employed systematic RLC, the transmission takes place in two phases. In Phase I, we transmit 77 packets consisting of the source symbols. In Phase II, we transmit additional packets in accordance with EW RLC. Note that Phase I will be the same for all the three schemes, whereas, in

TABLE 1: Layer sizes and PSNR contributions for $T = 0.78$ and $w = 2.5$ for Foreman sequence.

Layer	Proposed			Benchmark		
	Size (bytes)	Pkt	PSNR (dB)	Size (bytes)	Pkt	PSNR (dB)
HPL	21818	42	27.6	13042	24	23.14
LPL	19218	35	36.39	27994	53	36.39
Total	41036	77	36.39	41036	77	36.39

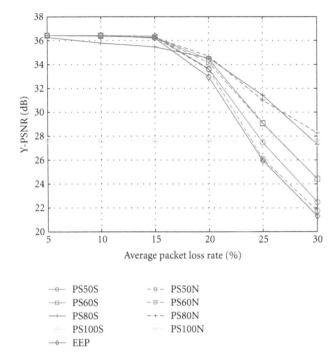

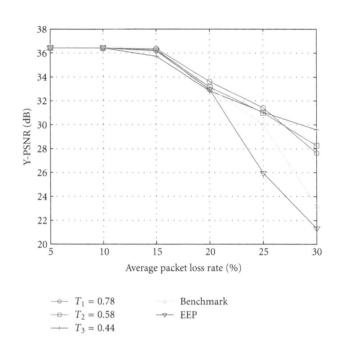

FIGURE 4: Comparison between systematic and nonsystematic EW RLC codes.

FIGURE 6: Optimized results for three values of T for the Foreman sequence.

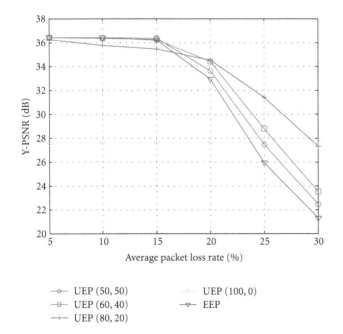

FIGURE 5: PSNR versus average PLR for the proposed scheme and the EEP scheme.

Phase II, the probability of selection can govern a prioritized transmission of HPL. The important phenomenon seen here is that, since each slice is independently decodable, the PSNR obtained in the case when RLC decoding of LPL fails and decoding of HPL succeeds is higher than the PSNR of successfully decoded HPL due to useful packets that are received from LPL during Phase I.

This gain comes from the correct reception of additional LPL symbols from Phase I even with failure of LPL decoding. The simulations have been performed for different packet loss rates (PLRs) and different probabilities of window selection to evaluate the performance of the slicing feature to overcome losses.

In the case of nonsystematic codes, if the first window W_1 (or W_2) does not get decoded, the entire GOP is considered to be lost. However, in case of systematic codes, it is still possible for the H.264/AVC decoder to decode the GOP as long as its IDR frame has been received correctly. In case of loss of IDR with systematic codes, the entire GOP is lost. The PSNR for such cases is obtained by using the last frame of the previously decoded GOP to replace all frames of the lost GOP.

The various configurations are used to create different UEP schemes based on protecting the constituent windows with different protection, based on probabilistically selecting a window for each output symbol at the transmitter. An increase in the selection probability of window 1 (W_1) will improve its robustness at a cost of a decrease in robustness of the succeeding layer(s). The EEP scheme is the case where only the largest window is selected with 100% probability. This means that all of the data is protected with no preference for the data considered important, that is, window W_1.

In Figure 4, we present the results of comparison between the systematic codes and nonsystematic codes. The scheme PS60S is a scheme with probability of W_1 selection equal 0.6 (i.e., probability to select a symbol from HPL is 0.6), and the suffix S indicates systematic codes. Similarly, scheme PS80N has probability of W_1 selection of 0.8 with nonsystematic codes. It can be seen from the figure that the systematic codes generally have better results than the nonsystematic codes for the error range and data rates shown.

Systematic codes, in general, do not provide improvement compared to nonsystematic codes. Systematic codes however reduce the decoding complexity since with systematic codes the decoder operates with the matrix that has reduced number of rows (reduced, by the number of correctly received systematic packets). Thus, Figure 4 demonstrates that there is no loss in performance due to systematic codes.

Figure 5 shows PSNR versus PLR for the proposed systematic EW RLC scheme. The numbers shown in brackets represent the selection probability of each of the two windows, for example, UEP (60, 40) represents a code in which a symbol from W_1 will be selected for transmission with probability 0.60. As can be seen from the figure, the results of UEP schemes are significantly better than the EEP schemes for high loss rates.

UEP (100, 0) is a scheme in which only W_1 is protected and sent. The scheme is constrained in that it cannot achieve higher PSNR than 27.6 dB (see Table 1). However, the decoding failures, that is, when the entire GOP data fails to be decoded, will be much less for UEP (100, 0), since HPL is protected strongest which facilitates each GOP to be received with high probability, though at basic quality level. This scheme could thus prove useful in higher PLR. Also, note that, for this scheme, in Phase I of transmission, only the systematic codes in the HPL will be transmitted and, in Phase II, the encoded symbols come from HPL alone.

The PSNR results are improving with an increase in probability of selection of W_1 because at higher probabilities of selection of W_1, the decoding of HPL has high chance to be successful. As described earlier, the PSNR with decoding of HPL is enhanced by systematic LPL packets.

In Table 2, the details of HPL size and PSNR contributions for the three schemes created with selecting three different values of T are shown. Intuitively, when the threshold T is lowered, the number of packets selected for HPL is higher. In Figure 6, we present the optimized results for the schemes created in Table 2. The results for the EEP scheme and benchmark are also shown for comparison. For each PLR, we found the optimal proposed UEP and the optimal benchmark UEP using (2). It can be seen from the figure that the proposed method leads to significant gains

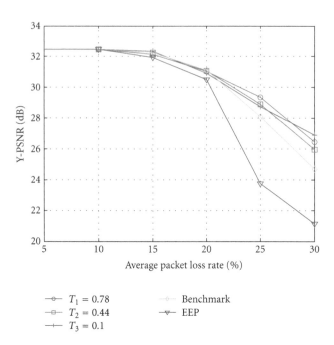

FIGURE 7: Optimized results for three values of T for the Paris sequence.

for high PLRs compared to the EEP and the benchmark scheme. The selection of T governs the size of HPL. If the size of selected HPL is small it will have relatively lower PSNR compared to a larger HPL. Lower T leading to a larger HPL, is thus better for higher PLRs, which is expected since a large HPL (with higher PSNR) is better protected, and for LPL anyway there is not enough bandwidth.

Similar results obtained for the CIF Paris video sequence are shown in Figure 7. Note that, for high PLR, it is better to reduce T resulting in large HPL. In any case, varying T, one can effectively design HPL/LPL sizes for different PLR.

A larger GOP size may be required for applications such as DVB-H [4]. We encode the same Foreman sequence with a GOP size of 64 frames. For this configuration, the total source packets are 161. The total number of sent packets is kept as 209 packets. In Figure 8, we present the optimized results for the schemes created using two different values of w as shown. Both schemes have the value of $T = 3.1$; however, based on different value of w, different slices are selected for HPL for each scheme. The scheme $w_1 = 2.5$ has better performance than $w_2 = 0$, especially at high packet loss, this comes from the fact that the former scheme prioritizes slices taking into account frame position in the sequence, which reduces error propagation. The benchmark scheme is created according to the selection criteria as used previously. EEP scheme performs the worst of all the schemes. The results for $w_1 = 2.5$ and $w_2 = 0$ are close at the lower PLR. The reason for this is that, with systematic codes, if the HPL is decodable, then the packets received correctly (which could be from HPL or LPL) in Phase-I also contribute to improve the PSNR.

The Paris sequence encoded with similar parameters is used to investigate the effect of w on performance. The

TABLE 2: Layer sizes and PSNR contributions for configurations with different values of T.

Layer	$T_1 = 0.78$			$T_2 = 0.58$			$T_3 = 0.44$		
	Size (bytes)	No. of packets	PSNR (dB)	Size (bytes)	No. of packets	PSNR (dB)	Size (bytes)	No. of packets	PSNR (dB)
HPL	21818	42	27.6	23598	45	28.25	25366	48	29.55
LPL	19218	35	36.39	17438	32	36.39	15670	29	36.39
Total	41036	77	36.39	41036	77	36.39	41036	77	36.39

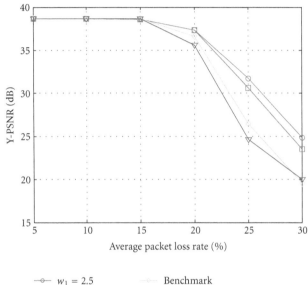

FIGURE 8: Optimized results for two values of w for the Foreman sequence.

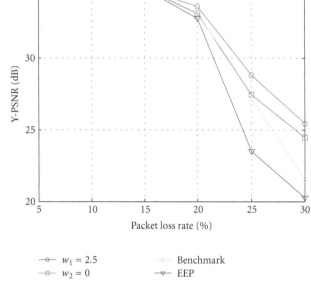

FIGURE 9: Optimized results for two values of w for the Paris sequence.

optimized results are presented in Figure 9 for the schemes created using two different values of w along with Benchmark and EEP scheme. The results are similar to those in Figure 8 for the Foreman sequence, which confirms the analysis carried out earlier.

From the last two figures, we conclude that w is a useful parameter to improve source packet allocation (compared to the $w = 0$ case). We tested several different values of w and report our results for the several typical cases that show achievable performance boundaries by varying w. One can see from the figures that effect of w is small—up to 1 db.

5. Conclusions and Future Work

In this paper, we proposed the systematic EW RLC scheme to protect the sliced-partitioned video data under various channel conditions at different probabilities of window selection. We proposed a novel slice prioritization method that takes into account PSNR contribution of a slice as well as position of its frame within GOP. The simulations for two layers show that UEP schemes perform better as compared to the EEP scheme and ad hoc prioritization, achievable

with a minimal selection (one slice) of video data from each frame. Such reduced selections may be advantageously used in video-on-demand applications. The decoding complexity of RLC can be easily managed in the proposed scheme by an adaptive scheme which dynamically selects the slice size. The proposed schemes are hence suitable for real-time multimedia mobile applications.

Acknowledgment

This work has been accepted in part for presentation at *IEEE ICON-2011* [29].

References

[1] T. Wiegand, G. J. Sullivan, G. Bjøntegaard, and A. Luthra, "Overview of the H.264/AVC video coding standard," *IEEE Transactions on Circuits and Systems for Video Technology*, vol. 13, no. 7, pp. 560–576, 2003.

[2] A. Shokrollahi, "Raptor codes," *IEEE Transactions on Information Theory*, vol. 52, no. 6, pp. 2551–2567, 2006.

[3] "ETSI TS 102 005, digital video broadcasting (dvb): specification for the use of video and audio coding in dvb services delivered directly over ip protocols," ETSI Tech. Spec., 2006.

[4] S. Nazir, D. Vukobratovic, and V. Stankovic, "Expanding window random linear codes for data partitioned H.264 video transmission over DVB-H network," in *Proceedings of the IEEE International Conference on Image Processing (ICIP-IEEE '11)*, Brussels, Belgium, September 2011.

[5] C. Hellge, E. Guinea Torre, D. Gmez-Barquero, T. Schierl, and T. Wiegand, "HDTV and 3DTV services over DVB-T2 using multiple PLPs with SVC and MVC," in *Proceedings of the 61st Annual IEEE Broadcast Symposium*, Alexandria, Va, USA, October 2011.

[6] L. Al-Jobouri, M. Fleury, and M. Ghanbari, "Raptor coding of H.264 data-partitioned video over a WiMAX channel," in *Proceedings of the IEEE International Conference on Consumer Electronics (ICCE '11)*, pp. 341–342, January 2011.

[7] D. S. Lun, M. Médard, R. Koetter, and M. Effros, "On coding for reliable communication over packet networks," *Physical Communication*, vol. 1, no. 1, pp. 3–20, 2008.

[8] J. Jin, B. Li, and T. Kong, "Is random network coding helpful in WiMAX?" in *Proceedings of the 27th IEEE Communications Society Conference on Computer Communications (INFOCOM '08)*, pp. 191–195, Phoenix, Ariz, USA, April 2008.

[9] D. Vukobratović and V. Stankovic, "Unequal error protection random linear coding strategies for erasure channels," *IEEE Transactions on Communications*, vol. 60, no. 5, pp. 1243–1252, May 2012.

[10] "ETSI TS 126 346, universal mobile telecommunications system (umts); multimedia broadcast/multicast service (mbms); protocols and codecs," ETSI Tech. Spec., 2005.

[11] R. Ahlswede, N. Cai, S. Y. R. Li, and R. W. Yeung, "Network information flow," *IEEE Transactions on Information Theory*, vol. 46, no. 4, pp. 1204–1216, 2000.

[12] A. Albanese, J. Blomer, J. Edmonds, M. Luby, and M. Sudan, "Priority encoding transmission," in *Proceedings of the IEEE FOCS*, pp. 604–612, Santa Fe, NM, USA, November 1994.

[13] U. Horn, K. Stuhlmüller, M. Link, and B. Girod, "Robust internet video transmission based on scalable coding and unequal error protection," *Signal Processing*, vol. 15, no. 1, pp. 77–94, 1999.

[14] Y. Lin, B. Liang, and B. Li, "Priority random linear codes in distributed storage systems," *IEEE Transactions on Parallel and Distributed Systems*, vol. 20, no. 11, pp. 1653–1667, 2009.

[15] K. Nguyen, T. Nguyen, and S. C. Cheung, "Video streaming with network coding," *Journal of Signal Processing Systems*, vol. 59, no. 3, pp. 319–333, 2010.

[16] M. Halloush and H. Radha, "Network coding with multi-Generation mixing: analysis and applications for video communication," in *Proceedings of the IEEE International Conference on Communications (ICC '08)*, pp. 198–202, Beijing, China, May 2008.

[17] X. Liu, G. Cheung, and C. N. Chuah, "Structured network coding and cooperative wireless ad-hoc peer-to-peer repair for WWAN video broadcast," *IEEE Transactions on Multimedia*, vol. 11, no. 4, pp. 730–741, 2009.

[18] N. Thomos, J. Chakareski, and P. Frossard, "Randomized network coding for UEP video delivery in overlay networks," in *Proceedings of the IEEE International Conference on Multimedia and Expo (ICME '09)*, pp. 730–733, New York, NY, USA, July 2009.

[19] S. Nazir, D. Vukobratovic, and V. Stankovic, "Performance evaluation of Raptor and Random Linear Codes for H.264/AVC video transmission over DVB-H networks," in *Proceedings of the IEEE ICASSP*, Prague, Czech Republic, May 2011.

[20] S. Nazir, D. Vukobratovic, and V. Stankovic, "Unequal error protection for data partitioned H.264/AVC video streaming with Raptor and Random Linear Codes for DVB-H networks," in *Proceedings of the International Conference on Multimedia and Expo*, Barcelona, Spain, July 2011.

[21] D. Vukobratovic, V. Stankovic, D. Sejdinovic, L. Stankovic, and Z. Xiong, "Scalable video multicast using expanding window fountain codes," *IEEE Transactions on Multimedia*, vol. 11, pp. 1094–1104, 2009.

[22] D. Vukobratović and V. Stanković, "Unequal error protection random linear coding for multimedia communications," in *Proceedings of the IEEE International Workshop on Multimedia Signal Processing (MMSP '10)*, pp. 280–285, Saint Malo, France, October 2010.

[23] N. Thomos, S. Argyropoulos, N. V. Boulgouris, and M. G. Strintzis, "Robust transmission of H.264/AVC streams using adaptive group slicing and unequal error protection," *Eurasip Journal on Applied Signal Processing*, vol. 2006, Article ID 051502, 2006.

[24] E. Baccaglini, T. Tillo, and G. Olmo, "Slice sorting for unequal loss protection of video streams," *IEEE Signal Processing Letters*, vol. 15, pp. 581–584, 2008.

[25] T. Tillo, E. Baccaglini, and G. Olmo, "Unequal protection of video data according to slice relevance," *IEEE Transactions on Image Processing*, vol. 20, no. 6, pp. 1572–1582, 2011.

[26] H. Schwarz, D. Marpe, and T. Wiegand, "Overview of the scalable video coding extension of the H.264/AVC standard," *IEEE Transactions on Circuits and Systems for Video Technology*, vol. 17, no. 9, pp. 1103–1120, 2007.

[27] ITU-T Recommendation H.264. Advanced video coding for generic audiovisual services. 2010.

[28] H. Shojania and B. Li, "Random network coding on the iPhone: fact or fiction?" in *Proceedings of the 19th International Workshop on Network and Operating Systems Support for Digital Audio and Video (NOSSDAV '09)*, pp. 37–42, Williamsburg, Va, USA, June 2009.

[29] S. Nazir, D. Vukobratovic, and V. Stankovic, "Scalable broadcasting of sliced H.264/AVC over DVB-H networks," in *Proceedings of the IEEE International Conference on Networks (ICON '11)*, Singapore, December 2011.

[30] H.264/AVC Reference Software, http://iphome.hhi.de/suehring/tml/.

14

2D+t Wavelet Domain Video Watermarking

Deepayan Bhowmik and Charith Abhayaratne

Department of Electronic and Electrical Engineering, The University of Sheffield, Sheffield S1 3JD, UK

Correspondence should be addressed to Charith Abhayaratne, c.abhayaratne@sheffield.ac.uk

Academic Editor: Chong Wah Ngo

A novel watermarking framework for scalable coded video that improves the robustness against quality scalable compression is presented in this paper. Unlike the conventional spatial-domain (t + 2D) water-marking scheme where the motion compensated temporal filtering (MCTF) is performed on the spatial frame-wise video data to decompose the video, the proposed framework applies the MCTF in the wavelet domain (2D + t) to generate the coefficients to embed the watermark. Robustness performances against scalable content adaptation, such as Motion JPEG 2000, MC-EZBC, or H.264-SVC, are reviewed for various combinations of motion compensated 2D + t + 2D using the proposed framework. The MCTF is improved by modifying the update step to follow the motion trajectory in the hierarchical temporal decomposition by using direct motion vector fields in the update step and implied motion vectors in the prediction step. The results show smaller embedding distortion in terms of both peak signal to noise ratio and flickering metrics compared to frame-by-frame video watermarking while the robustness against scalable compression is improved by using 2D + t over the conventional t + 2D domain video watermarking, particularly for blind watermarking schemes where the motion is estimated from the watermarked video.

1. Introduction

Several attempts have been made to extend the image water-marking algorithms into video watermarking by using them either on frame-by-frame basis or on 3D decomposed video. The initial attempts on video watermarking were made by frame-by-frame embedding [1–4], due to its simplicity in implementation using image watermarking algorithms. Such watermarking algorithms consider embedding on selected frames located at fixed intervals to make them robust against frame dropping-based temporal adaptations of video. In this case, each frame is treated separately as an individual image; hence, any image-watermarking algorithm can be adopted to achieve the intended robustness. But frame-by-frame watermarking schemes often perform poorly in terms of flickering artefacts and robustness against various video processing attacks including temporal desynchronization, video collusion, video compression attacks, and so forth. In order to address some of these issues, the video temporal dimension is exploited using different transforms, such as discrete Fourier transform (DFT), discrete cosine transform (DCT),

or discrete wavelet transform (DWT). These algorithms decompose the video by performing spatial 2D transform on individual frames followed by 1D transform in the temporal domain. Various transforms are proposed in 3D decomposed watermarking schemes, such as 3D DFT domain [5], 3D DCT domain [6], and more popularly multiresolution 3D DWT domain watermarking [7, 8]. A multilevel 3D DWT is performed by recursively applying the above-mentioned procedure on low-frequency spatiotemporal subband. Various watermarking methods similar to image watermarking are then applied to suitable subbands to balance the imperceptibility and robustness. 3D decomposition-based methods overcome the issues like temporal desynchronization, video format conversion, and video collusion. However, such naive subband decomposition-based embedding strategies without considering motion element of the sequence during watermark embedding often result in unpleasant flickering visual artefacts. The amount of flickering in watermarked sequences varies according to the texture, colour, and motion characteristics of the video content as well as the watermark strength and the choice of frequency subband used for watermark embedding. At the same time, these schemes are also fragile to video compression attacks, which consider motion trajectory during compression coding.

In order to address such issues stated above, we have extended image watermarking techniques into video considering the motion and texture characteristics of the video sequence using wavelet-based motion compensated 2D + t + 2D filtering. The proposed approach is evolved from the motion compensated temporal filtering- (MCTF-) based wavelet domain video decomposition concept. MCTF has been successfully used in wavelet-based scalable video coding research [9, 10]. The idea of MCTF was originated from 3D subband wavelet decomposition, which is merely an extension of spatial domain transform into temporal domain [11]. But 3D wavelet decomposition alone does not decouple motion information and it is addressed by using temporal filtering along the motion trajectories. This MCTF-based video decomposition technique motivates a new avenue in transform domain video watermarking. Few attempts have already been made to investigate the effect of motion in video watermarking by incorporating motion compensation into video watermarking algorithms [12–14]. In these investigations, the sequence is first temporally decomposed into Haar wavelet subbands using MCTF and then spatially decomposed using the 2D DCT transform resulting in the decomposition scheme widely known as t + 2D.

In this paper, we aim to advance further by investigating along the line of MCTF-based wavelet coding to propose a robust video watermarking scheme against scalable content adaptation, such as Motion JPEG 2000, MC-EZBC, or H.264-SVC, while keeping the imperceptibility. Apparent problems of direct use of MCTF and t + 2D decompositions in watermarking are three fold.

(1) In scalable video coding research, it is evident that video with different texture and motion characteristics leading to its spatial and temporal features perform differently on t + 2D domain [9] and its alternative 2D + t domain [15], where MCTF is performed on 2D wavelet decomposition domain. Further, in 3D subband decomposition for video watermarking, the use of MCTF is only required for subbands where the watermarks are embedded. Hence, the motion estimation and compensation on full spatial dimension (t + 2D case) add unnecessary complexity to the watermarking algorithm.

(2) Conventional MCTF is focused on achieving higher compression and thus gives more attention on the prediction-lifting step in MCTF. However, for watermarking, it is necessary to follow the motion trajectory of content into low-frequency temporal subband frames, in order to avoid motion mismatch in the update step of MCTF when these frames are modified due to watermark embedding.

(3) t + 2D structure offers better energy compaction in the low-frequency temporal subband, keeping most of the coefficient values to very small or nearly zero in high-frequency temporal subbands. This is very useful during compression but leaves very little room for

watermark embedding in high-frequency temporal subbands. Therefore, for a robust algorithm, most of the MCTF domain watermarking schemes, mentioned before, embed the watermark in the lowpass temporal frames. On the other hand, 2D + t provides more energy in high-frequency subbands, which enables the possibility to embed and recover the watermark robustly using highpass temporal frames which improves the overall imperceptibility of the watermarked video.

To overcome these shortcomings, we propose MCTF-based 3D wavelet decomposition scheme for video sequences and offer a flexible 2D + t + 2D generalized motion compensated temporal-spatial subband decomposition scheme using a modified MCTF scheme for video watermarking. Using the framework, we study and analyze the merits and the demerits of watermark embedding using various combinations of 2D + t + 2D structure and propose new 2D + t video watermarking algorithms to improve the robustness performance against quality scalable video compression.

The rest of the paper is organized as follows. In Section 2, the modified MCTF scheme is presented along with the new 2D + t + 2D subband decomposition framework. The video watermarking algorithms using the implementation of different subband decomposition schemes are proposed in Section 3. The analysis of the framework is described in Section 4. The experimental results are shown and discussed in Section 5 followed by the conclusions in Section 6.

2. Motion Compensated Spatiotemporal Filtering

The generalized spatiotemporal decomposition scheme consists of two modules: (1) MCTF and (2) 2D *spatial frequency decomposition*. To capture the motion information accurately, we have modified the commonly used lifting-based MCTF by tracking interframe pixel connectivity and use the 2D wavelet transform for spatial decomposition. In this section, first we describe the MCTF with implied motion estimation and then propose the 2D + t + 2D general framework.

2.1. MCTF with Implied Motion Estimation. We formulate the MCTF scheme giving more focus into the motion trajectory-based update step as follows. Let I_t be the video sequence, where t is the time index in display order. We consider two consecutive frames I_{2t} and I_{2t+1}, as the current frame (c) and the reference frame (r), respectively, following the video coding terminology. In traditional motion estimation for lifting-based MCTF [9], I_{2t+1} frame usually partitioned into nonoverlapping blocks and for each block, motion is estimated from I_{2t} frame using a block matching algorithm. In this case only, two types of pixel connectivity are considered, (1) pixels are connected or (2) unconnected. In the case of several pixels are connected to the same pixel in the reference frame, only one of them is categorized as a connected pixel. The temporal frames are derived using the subband analysis pair by replacing the I_{2t} as the low-frequency temporal frame (L) and I_{2t+1} as the high-frequency temporal frame (H).

Connected pixels:

$$
\mathrm{L}[m - \mathcal{H}^{c \to r}, n - \mathcal{V}^{c \to r}]
$$
$$
= \frac{1}{\sqrt{2}} I_{2t+1}[m, n] + \frac{1}{\sqrt{2}} I_{2t}[m - \mathcal{H}^{c \to r}, n - \mathcal{V}^{c \to r}],
$$
$$
\mathrm{H}[m, n] \tag{1}
$$
$$
= \frac{1}{\sqrt{2}} I_{2t+1}[m, n] - \frac{1}{\sqrt{2}} I_{2t}[m - \mathcal{H}^{c \to r}, n - \mathcal{V}^{c \to r}],
$$

where $\mathcal{V}^{c \to r}$ and $\mathcal{H}^{c \to r}$ represent the motion vector fields: vertical and horizontal displacements of the nonoverlapping blocks, respectively.

Unconnected pixels:

$$
\mathrm{L}[m, n] = \frac{2\, I_{2t}[m, n]}{\sqrt{2}}. \tag{2}
$$

For the unconnected pixels in I_{2t+1}, the scaled displaced frame differences are substituted to form the temporal high subband.

As stated in the introduction, such a traditional scheme gives more attention on the prediction-lifting step in MCTF to reduce the prediction error in high-frequency subband. This is useful in a compression scenario. However, in the case of watermarking, we account the object motion within low-frequency temporal frames to avoid motion mismatch in update step when these frames are modified due to watermark embedding. To address this, we have used MCTF with implied motion estimation, which allows opportunity to embed the watermark in any chosen low- or high-frequency temporal frame. At the same time, as opposed to the traditional scheme, we consider the relative contributions of one-to-many connected pixels and this is important to capture the motion information accurately during MCTF operation.

In the proposed scheme, the I_{2t} frame is partitioned into nonoverlapping blocks and for each block, vertical and horizontal displacements are quantified and represented as motion vector fields $\mathcal{V}^{c \to r}$ and $\mathcal{H}^{c \to r}$, respectively. Figure 1 shows an example how the four nonoverlapping blocks in the current frame (I_{2t}) are moved in different direction in the next frame (I_{2t+1}). In the I_{2t} frame, each block can be one of two types, namely, inter- and intrablocks, where the motion is only estimated for the former block type. Similarly, in the I_{2t+1} frame, any pixel can be one of three types, namely, one-to-one connected (point A), one-to-many connected (point B and C), and unconnected (point D) (as shown in Figure 1), depending on its connectivity to pixels in the I_{2t} frame. The connectivity follows the implied motion vector fields $\mathcal{V}^{c \to r}$ and $\mathcal{H}^{c \to r}$, which are simply the directional inverse of the original motion vector fields, $\mathcal{V}^{c \to r}$ and $\mathcal{H}^{c \to r}$.

Current frame for motion estimation (I_{2t})

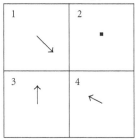

Reference frame for motion estimation (I_{2t+1})

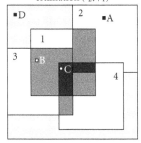

☐ Unconnected pixels
☐ One-to-one connected pixels
■ ▨ One-to-many connected pixels

FIGURE 1: Pixel connectivity in I_{2t} and I_{2t+1} frames.

Considering these block and pixel classifications, the lifting steps for pixels at positions $[m, n]$ in frames I_{2t} and I_{2t+1} (i.e., $I_{2t}[m, n]$ and $I_{2t+1}[m, n]$) performing the temporal motion compensated Haar wavelet transform are defined as follows.

Forward Transform

The Prediction Step. For one-to-one connected pixels,

$$
I'_{2t+1}[m, n] = I_{2t+1}[m, n] - I_{2t}[m + \mathcal{H}^{c \to r}, n + \mathcal{V}^{c \to r}]. \tag{3}
$$

For one-to-many connected pixels,

$$
I'_{2t+1}[m, n] = I_{2t+1}[m, n] - \frac{1}{J} \sum_{i=0}^{J-1} I_{2t}[m + \mathcal{H}_i^{c \to r}, n + \mathcal{V}_i^{c \to r}], \tag{4}
$$

where J is the total number of connections.

For unconnected pixels,

$$
I'_{2t+1}[m, n] = I_{2t+1}[m, n]. \tag{5}
$$

The last case is similar to the no prediction case as in intrablocks used in conventional MCTF.

The Update Step. For interblocks, every pixel in an interblock is one-to-one connected with a unique pixel in I_{2t+1}. Then, the update step is computed as

$$
I'_{2t}[m, n] = I_{2t}[m, n] + \frac{1}{2} I'_{2t+1}[m - \mathcal{H}^{c \to r}, n - \mathcal{V}^{c \to r}]. \tag{6}
$$

For intrablocks, as there are no motion compensated connections with I_{2t+1},

$$I'_{2t}[m, n] = I_{2t}[m, n]. \tag{7}$$

Finally, these lifting steps are followed by the normalization step:

$$I''_{2t}[m, n] = \sqrt{2} I'_{2t}[m, n],$$
$$I''_{2t+1}[m, n] = \frac{1}{\sqrt{2}} I'_{2t+1}[m, n]. \tag{8}$$

The temporally decomposed frames I''_{2t} and I''_{2t+1} are the first level low- and highpass frames and are denoted as L and H temporal subbands. These steps are repeated for all frames in L to obtain LL and LH subbands and continued to obtain the desired number of temporal decomposition levels.

Inverse Transform

For the inverse transform, the order of operation of steps is reversed as stated follows.

First, the decomposed coefficients are passed through an unnormalization step followed by the inverse lifting steps:

$$I'_{2t}[m, n] = \frac{1}{\sqrt{2}} I''_{2t}[m, n],$$
$$I'_{2t+1}[m, n] = \sqrt{2} I''_{2t+1}[m, n]. \tag{9}$$

The inverse update step:

$$I_{2t}[m, n] = \begin{cases} I'_{2t}[m, n] - \frac{1}{2} I'_{2t+1}[m - \mathcal{H}^{c \sim r}, n - \mathcal{V}^{c \sim r}] \\ \qquad\qquad\qquad\qquad \text{for interblocks,} \\ I'_{2t}[m, n] \qquad\qquad \text{for intrablocks.} \end{cases} \tag{10}$$

The inverse prediction step:

$$I_{2t+1}[m, n] = \begin{cases} I'_{2t+1}[m, n] + I_{2t}[m + \mathcal{H}^{c \sim r}, n + \mathcal{V}^{c \sim r}] \\ \qquad\qquad \text{for one-to-one connected pixels,} \\ I'_{2t+1}[m, n] + \frac{1}{J} \sum_{i=0}^{J-1} I_{2t}[m + \mathcal{H}_i^{c \sim r}, n + \mathcal{V}_i^{c \sim r}] \\ \qquad\qquad \text{for one-to-many connected pixels,} \\ I'_{2t+1}[m, n] \qquad \text{for unconnected pixels.} \end{cases} \tag{11}$$

2.2. 2D + t + 2D Framework. In a 3D video decomposition scheme, t + 2D is achieved by performing temporal decomposition followed by a spatial transform whereas in case of 2D + t, the temporal filtering is done after the spatial 2D transform. Due to its own merit and demerit, it is required to analyze both the combinations in order to enhance the video

watermarking performance. A common flexible reconfigurable framework, which allows creating such possible combinations, is particularly useful for applications like video watermarking. Here, we propose the 2D + t + 2D framework by combining the modified motion compensated temporal filtering with spatial 2D wavelet transformation.

Let $(s_1 t s_2)$ be the number of decomposition levels used in the 2D + t + 2D subband decomposition to obtain a 3D subband decomposition with motion compensated t temporal levels and s spatial levels, where $s = s_1 + s_2$. In such a scheme, first the 2D DWT is applied for an s_1 level decomposition. As a result, a new sequence is formed by the low-frequency spatial LL subband of all frames. Then, the sequences of spatial LL subbands are temporally decomposed using the MCTF with implied motion estimation into t temporal levels. Finally, each of the temporal transformed spatial LL subbands are further spatially decomposed into s_2 wavelet levels.

For a *t-s* motion compensated temporal subband decomposition, the values of s_1 and s_2 are determined by considering the context of the choice of temporal-spatial subbands used for watermark embedding. From now onwards, in this paper, we will use exact values of s_1, t, s_2 to represent various combinations of spatiotemporal decomposition, that is, $s_1 t s_2$. For example, $s_1 = 0$, $t = 3$, $s_2 = 2$ (032), and $s_1 = 2$, $t = 3$, $s_2 = 0$ (230) parameter combinations result in t + 2D and 2D + t motion compensated 3D subband decompositions, respectively. The same amount of subband decomposition levels can be obtained by also using the parameter combination $s_1 = 1$, $t = 3$, $s_2 = 1$ (131) using the proposed generalized scheme implementation. The combination $s_1 = 0$, $t = 0$, $s_2 = 2$ (002) allows 2D decomposition of all frames for frame-by-frame watermark embedding. The realizations of these examples are shown in Figure 2. We use the notation (LLL, LLH, LH, H) to denote the temporal subbands after a 3 level decomposition. We have described the use of this framework in combination with watermarking algorithms, in the next section.

3. Video Watermarking in 2D + t + 2D Spatiotemporal Decomposition

We propose a new video watermarking scheme by extending the wavelet-based image watermarking algorithms into 2D + t + 2D framework. In this section, we briefly revisit the wavelet-based image watermarking algorithms followed by the proposed video watermarking scheme. Then, we carry on to analyze various combinations in the proposed video decomposition framework to decide unique video embedding parameters, such as (1) choice of temporal subband selection and (2) motion estimation parameters, to retrieve the motion information from watermarked video.

3.1. Wavelet-Based Watermarking. Due to its ability for efficient multiresolution spatiofrequency representation of the signals, the DWT became the major transform for spread-spectrum image watermarking [16–22]. A broad classification of such wavelet-based watermarking algorithms can be found in [23]. In this paper, we have chosen commonly

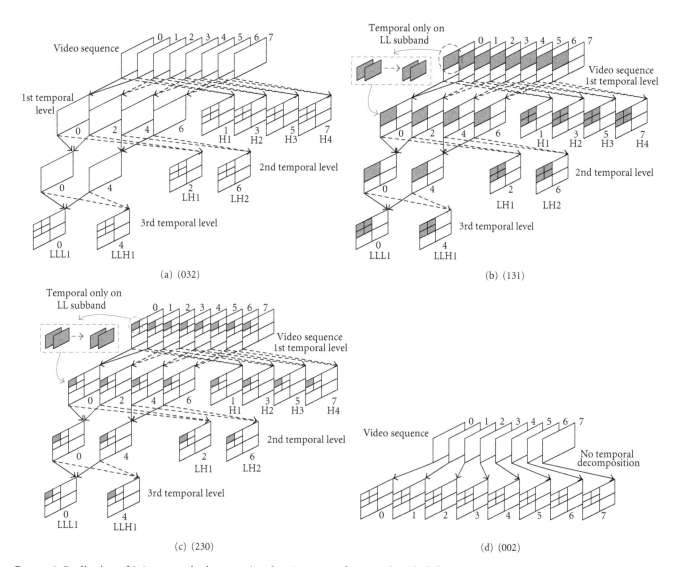

FIGURE 2: Realization of 3-2 temporal schemes using the 2D + t + 2D framework with different parameters: (a) (032), (b) (131), (c) (230), and (d) (002).

used example algorithms to represent nonblind and blind watermarking algorithmic classes.

3.1.1. The Nonblind Case. A magnitude alteration-based additive watermarking is chosen as a nonblind case. In such an algorithm, coefficient values are increased or decreased depending on the magnitude of the coefficient, by making the modified coefficient a function of the original coefficient:

$$C'_{s,t}[m,n] = C_{s,t}[m,n] + \alpha C_{s,t}[m,n] W, \quad (12)$$

where $C_{s,t}[m,n]$ is the original decomposed coefficient at s,t spatiotemporal subband, α is the watermark weighting factor, W is the watermark value to be embedded, and $C'_{s,t}[m,n]$ is the corresponding modified coefficient.

3.1.2. The Blind Case. In this category, we used an example blind watermarking algorithm as proposed in [20, 24], by modifying various coefficients towards a specific quantization step, δ. The method modifies the median coefficient by using a nonoverlapping 3×1 running window, passed through the entire selected subband of the wavelet decomposed image. At each sliding position, a rank-order sorting is performed on the coefficients C_1, C_2, and C_3 to obtain an ordered list $C_1 < C_2 < C_3$. The median value C_2 is modified to obtain C'_2 as follows:

$$C'_2 = f(\gamma, C_1, C_3, \delta, W), \quad (13)$$

where W is the input watermark sequence, γ is the weighting parameter, $f()$ denotes a nonlinear transformation, and $\delta = (\gamma(|C_1| + |C_3|)/2)$ is the quantization step.

3.2. The Proposed Video Watermarking Scheme. The new video watermarking scheme uses the above algorithms on spatial-temporal decomposed video. The system block diagrams for watermark embedding, a nonblind extraction

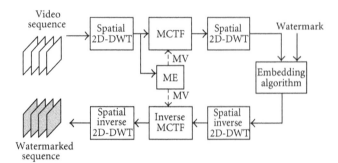

FIGURE 3: System blocks for watermark embedding scheme in 2D + t + 2D spatiotemporal decomposition.

process, and a blind extraction process are shown in Figures 3, 4(a), and 4(b), respectively.

3.2.1. Embedding. To embed the watermark, first spatiotemporal decomposition is performed on the host video sequence by applying spatial 2D-DWT followed by temporal MCTF for a 2D + t (230) or temporal decomposition followed by spatial transform for a t + 2D (032). In both the cases, the motion estimation (ME) is performed to create the motion vector (MV) either on the spatial domain (t + 2D) or on the approximation subband in the frequency domain (2D + t) as described in Section 2.2. Other combinations, such as 131 and 002, are achieved in a similar fashion. After obtaining the decomposed coefficients, the watermark is embedded either using nonblind (12) or a blind watermarking algorithm (13) by selecting various temporal low- or highpass frames (i.e., LLL or LLH, etc.) and spatial subband within the selected frame. Once embedded, the coefficients follow inverse process of spatiotemporal decomposition in order to reconstruct the watermarked video.

3.2.2. Extraction and Authentication. The extraction procedure follows a similar decomposition scheme as in embedding and the system diagram for the same is shown in Figure 4. The watermark coefficients are retrieved by applying 2D + t + 2D decomposition on watermarked test video. For a nonblind algorithm, the original video sequence is available at the decoder and hence the motion vector is obtained from the original video. After spatiotemporal filtering on test and original video, the coefficients are compared to extract the watermark. In case of a blind watermarking scheme, the motion estimation is performed on the test video itself without any prior knowledge of original motion information. The temporal filtering is then done by using the new motion vector and consequently the spatiotemporal coefficients are obtained for the detection.

The authentication is then done by measuring the Hamming distance (H) between the original and the extracted watermark:

$$H(W, W') = \frac{1}{L} \sum_{i=0}^{L-1} W_i \oplus W_i', \qquad (14)$$

where W and W' are the original and the extracted watermarks, respectively. L is the length of the sequence and $\oplus$ represents the XOR operation between the respective bits.

4. The Framework Analysis in Video Watermarking Context

Before approaching to the experimental results, in this section, we aim to address the issues related to MCTF-based video watermarking of the proposed framework. Firstly, to improve the imperceptibility, an investigation is made about the energy distribution of the host video in different temporal subbands, which is useful to select the temporally decomposed frames during embedding. Then, an insight is given to motion retrieval for a blind watermarking scheme, where no prior motion information is available during watermark extraction and this is crucial for the robustness performance.

4.1. On Improving Imperceptibility. In wavelet domain watermarking research, it is a well-known fact that embedding in high-frequency subbands offers better imperceptibility and low-frequency embedding provides higher robustness. Often wavelet decompositions compact most of the energy in low-frequency subbands and leave less energy in high-frequencies and due to this reason, high-frequency watermarking schemes are less robust to compression. Therefore, increase in energy distribution in high-frequency subbands can offer a better watermarking algorithm.

In analyzing our framework, the research findings show that different 2D + t + 2D combinations can vary the energy distribution in high-frequency temporal subbands and this is independent of video content. To show an example, we used *Foreman* sequence and decomposed using 032, 131, and 230 combinations in the framework and calculate the sum of energy for first two GOP each with 8 temporal frequency frames, namely, LLL, LLH, LH 1, LH 2, H1, H2, H3, and H4. In all cases, we calculate the energy for the low-frequency (LL_s) subband of spatial decomposition. Other input parameters are set to 8 × 8 macroblock, a fixed-size block matching motion estimation with ±16 search window. The results for percentage of energy (of a GOP) in each temporally decomposed frame are shown in Figure 5 and the histograms of the coefficients for 032, 131, and 230 of LLL and LLH are shown in Figure 6. The inner graph in Figure 6 represents the zoomed version of the local variations by clipping the y-axis to show the coefficient distribution more effectively. From the results, we can rank the energy distribution in high-frequency temporal subbands as: (230) > (131) > (032). This analysis guides us to select optimum spatiotemporal parameter in the framework to improve the robustness while keeping better imperceptibility. We have performed the experimental simulation on 8 test videos: (*Foreman, Crew, News, Stefan, Mobile, City, Football, and Flower garden*) and all of them follows a similar trend.

4.2. On Motion Retrieval. In an MCTF-based video watermarking scheme, motion information contributes at large for

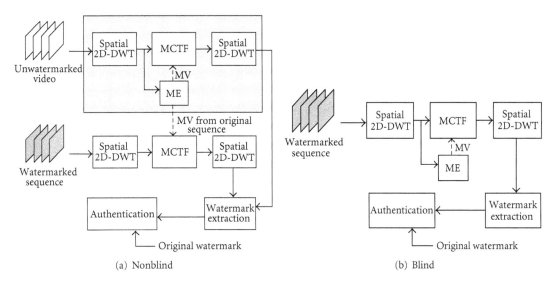

(a) Nonblind   (b) Blind

FIGURE 4: System blocks for watermark extraction scheme in 2D + t + 2D spatiotemporal decomposition.

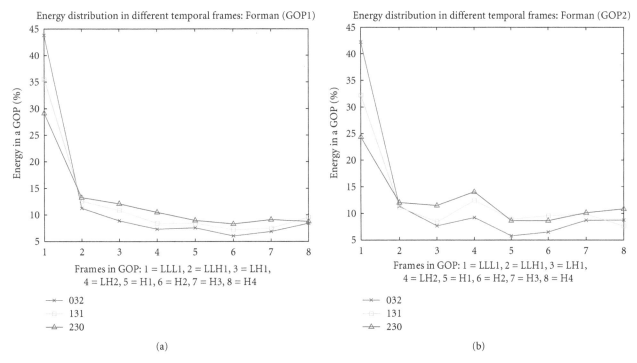

(a)   (b)

FIGURE 5: Percentage of energy (of a GOP) in each temporally decomposed frame. Energy calculation considers the energy of the coefficients at LL_s for first two GOP each with 8 temporal low and high frequency frames of *Foreman* sequence. (a) GOP1 and (b) GOP2.

temporal decomposition along motion trajectory. The watermark embedding modification in the temporal domain causes motion mismatch, which affects the decoder performance. While original motion information is available for a nonblind watermarking scheme, motion estimation must be done in the case of a blind video watermarking scheme. In this case, the motion vectors are expected to be retrieved from the watermarked video without any prior knowledge of the original motion vector (MV). Our study shows that, in such a case, more accurate motion estimation is possible by choosing the right 2D + t + 2D combination along with an

optimum choice of macro block (MB) size. At the same time, we investigate the performance, based on motion search range (SR). Experimental performance shows that effectively SR has lesser contribution towards motion retrieval. The experiment set is organized by studying the watermarking detection performance by measuring Hamming distance of a blind watermark embedding at LL_s spatial subband on LLL and LLH temporal frames. The watermark extraction is done by using various combinations of MB and SR to find the best motion retrieval parameters. The results are shown in Tables 1 and 2 using average of the first 64 frames from Foreman and

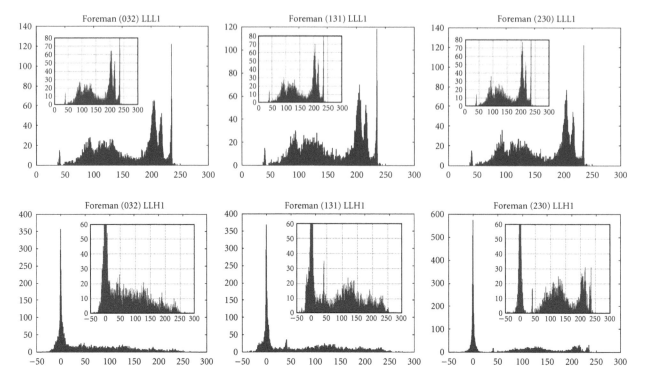

FIGURE 6: Histogram of coefficients at LL_s for 3 rd level temporal low and high-frequency frames (GOP 1) for *Foreman* sequence. *Row* (1) and (2) represents LLL and LLH temporal frames, respectively, and *Column* (1), (2) and (3) shows 032, 131, and 230 combinations of 2D + t + 2D framework.

TABLE 1: Hamming distance for blind watermarking by estimating motion from watermarked video using different macro block size (MB) and search range (SR). Embedding at LL_s on frame: (a) LLL and (b) LLH on *Foreman* sequence (average of first 64 frames).

(a) LLL

	MV from watermarked video: MB/SR						
	32×32	16×16	16×16	8×8	8×8	4×4	4×4
	$/\pm64$	$/\pm64$	$/\pm32$	$/\pm32$	$/\pm16$	$/\pm16$	$/\pm8$
032	0.02	0.03	0.02	0.03	0.03	0.04	0.04
131	—	0.02	0.03	0.03	0.03	0.08	0.07
230	—	—	—	0.03	0.03	0.08	0.07

(b) LLH

	MV from watermarked video: MB/SR						
	32×32	16×16	16×16	8×8	8×8	4×4	4×4
	$/\pm64$	$/\pm64$	$/\pm32$	$/\pm32$	$/\pm16$	$/\pm16$	$/\pm8$
032	0.15	0.29	0.29	0.40	0.39	0.49	0.49
131	—	0.22	0.21	0.29	0.28	0.44	0.44
230	—	—	—	0.23	0.22	0.30	0.30

Crew CIF size video sequences, respectively, for 032, 131, and 230 spatiotemporal decompositions. Due to the limitations in macroblock size and integer pixel motion search, 32 × 32 MB search is excluded for 131 decomposition and 32 × 32, 16 × 16 MB searches are excluded for 230 decomposition. It is noted that, in the video compression schemes, 16 × 16 is the most commonly used MB while in this paper we have used various other MB sizes to investigate the effect on watermark retrieval.

The results show that for an MB size more than 8 × 8, 2D + t outperform t + 2D. In this context, the spatiotemporal decompositions can be ranked as (230) > (131) > (032). In the case of 131 or 230, the motion is estimated in hierarchically downsampled low-frequency subband. Therefore,

TABLE 2: Hamming distance for blind watermarking by estimating motion from watermarked video using different macro block size (MB) and search range (SR). Embedding at LL_s on frame: (a) LLL and (b) LLH on *Crew* sequence (average of first 64 frames).

(a) LLL

	MV from watermarked video: MB/SR						
	32×32	16×16	16×16	8×8	8×8	4×4	4×4
	$/\pm 64$	$/\pm 64$	$/\pm 32$	$/\pm 32$	$/\pm 16$	$/\pm 16$	$/\pm 8$
032	0.03	0.06	0.05	0.09	0.09	0.09	0.09
131	—	0.03	0.03	0.07	0.07	0.14	0.13
230	—	—	—	0.03	0.03	0.15	0.12

(b) LLH

	MV from watermarked video: MB/SR						
	32×32	16×16	16×16	8×8	8×8	4×4	4×4
	$/\pm 64$	$/\pm 64$	$/\pm 32$	$/\pm 32$	$/\pm 16$	$/\pm 16$	$/\pm 8$
032	0.17	0.24	0.23	0.36	0.36	0.48	0.47
131	—	0.16	0.16	0.23	0.23	0.41	0.38
230	—	—	—	0.17	0.17	0.28	0.27

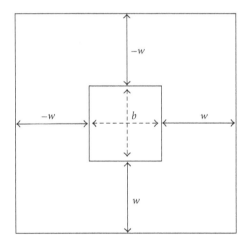

FIGURE 7: Exhaustive search complexity for a motion block.

number of motion vector reduces accordingly for a given macroblock size. This offers two-fold advantages.

(1) Complexity. The search range during the motion estimation is either half or quarter size of the full-resolution motion estimation. As a result, the searching time and computation complexity reduces significantly as follows: Let us assume motion is estimated for MB of $b \times b$ with SR $w \times w$ as shown in Figure 7. The complexity, $\mathcal{O}$, is calculated based on the number of search operations as given in (15):

$$\mathcal{O} = T(2w + 1)^2, \tag{15}$$

where $T = MN$ is total number of pixels. As motion is estimated only on the downsampled low-frequency component, we can rewrite (15) as

$$\mathcal{O} = \frac{M}{s_1} \frac{N}{s_1} (2w + 1)^2, \tag{16}$$

where s_1 is the 1st spatial decomposition in the proposed scheme. Now, SR $w \times w$ is a constant considering any given column in Tables 1 and 2 and hence it is evident that the complexity is inversely proportional to s_1^2:

$$\mathcal{O} \propto \frac{1}{s_1^2}(2w + 1)^2,$$
$$\propto \frac{1}{s_1^2}. \tag{17}$$

Therefore, the complexity of various spatiotemporal decomposition can be ranked as $(230) < (131) < (032)$, that is, complexity of proposed 2D + t scheme is much lesser when compared to traditional t + 2D.

(2) MV Error Reduction. At the same time, for blind motion estimation, less number of motion vector needs to be estimated at the decoder resulting in more accurate motion estimation and higher robustness. It is evident from Tables 1 and 2 that if the same number of motion vectors are considered, that is, 32×32 MB for 032, 16×16 MB for 131, and 8×8 MB for 230, the robustness performance is comparable for all three combinations. However, in LLL subband of 2D + t, for a smaller MB, such as 4×4, more motion mismatch is observed as motion estimation is done in a spatially decomposed region. Now, using the analysis, above, we have designed experiments to verify our proposed video watermarking schemes for improved imperceptibility as well as robustness against scalable video compressions.

5. Experimental Results and Discussion

We used the following experimental setup for the simulation of watermark embedding using the proposed generalized 2D + t + 2D motion compensated temporal-spatial subband scheme. In order to make the watermarking strength constant across subbands, the normalization steps in the MCTF

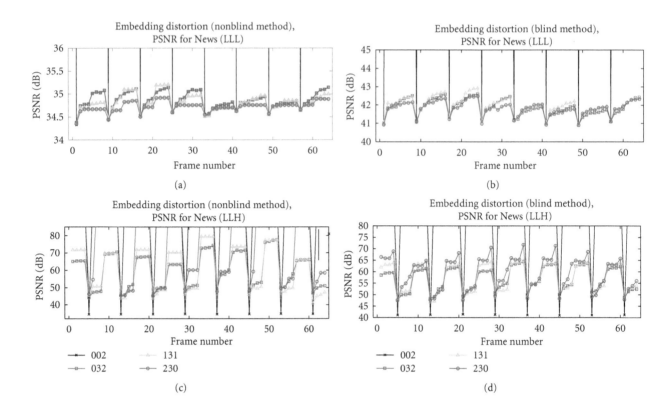

FIGURE 8: PSNR for nonblind and blind watermarking on LLL and LLH temporal subbands for *News* sequence. (a) LLL (nonblind), (b) LLL (blind), (c) LLH (nonblind), and (d) LLH (blind).

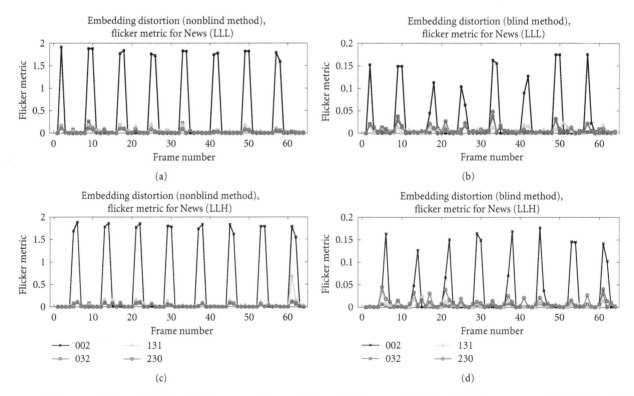

FIGURE 9: Flicker metric for nonblind and blind watermarking on LLL and LLH temporal subbands for *News* sequence. (a) LLL (nonblind), (b) LLL (blind), (c) LLH (nonblind), and (d) LLH (blind).

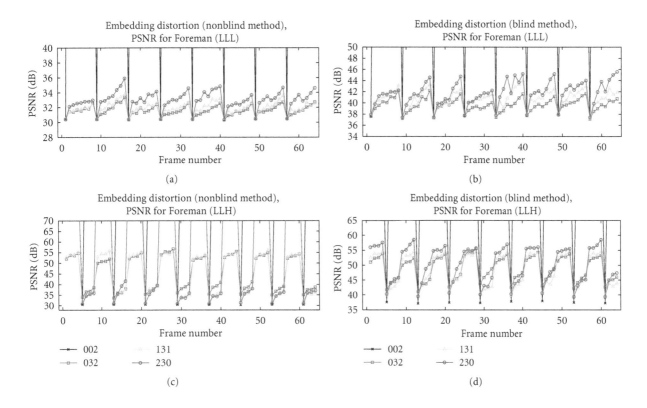

FIGURE 10: PSNR for nonblind and blind watermarking on LLL and LLH temporal subbands for *Foreman* sequence. (a) LLL (nonblind), (b) LLL (blind), (c) LLH (nonblind), and (d) LLH (blind).

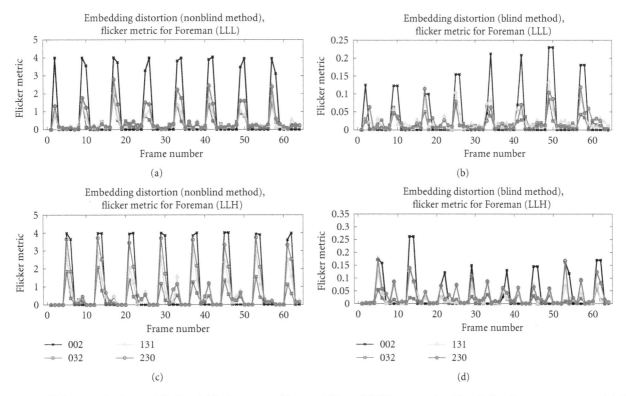

FIGURE 11: Flicker metric for nonblind and blind watermarking on LLL and LLH temporal subbands for *Foreman* sequence. (a) LLL (nonblind), (b) LLL (blind), (c) LLH (nonblind), and (d) LLH (blind).

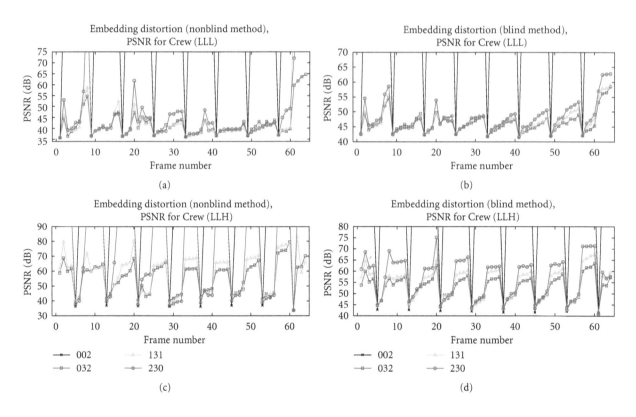

FIGURE 12: PSNR for nonblind and blind watermarking on LLL and LLH temporal subbands for *Crew* sequence. (a) LLL (nonblind), (b) LLL (blind), (c) LLH (nonblind), and (d) LLH (blind).

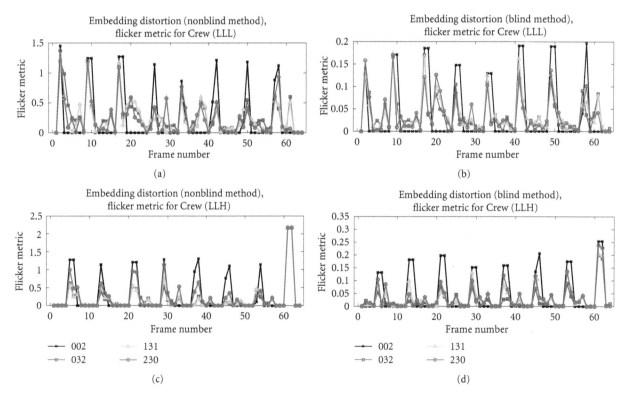

FIGURE 13: Flicker metric for nonblind and blind watermarking on LLL and LLH temporal subbands for *Crew* sequence. (a) LLL (nonblind), (b) LLL (blind), (c) LLH (nonblind), and (d) LLH (blind).

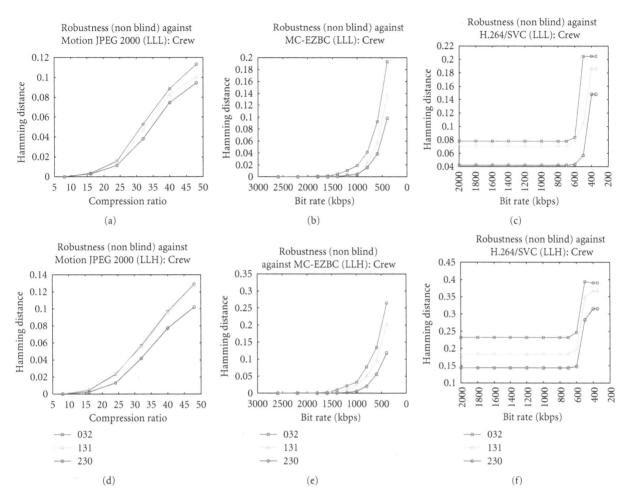

FIGURE 14: Robustness performance of nonblind watermarking scheme for *Crew* sequence. *Columns* (1), (2) and (3) show robustness against Motion JPEG 2000, MC-EZBC, and H.264-SVC, respectively. *Rows* (1) and (2) represent the embedding on temporal subbands LLL & LLH, respectively.

and the 2D DWT were omitted. There are two different sets of results obtained to show the embedding distortion and the robustness performance using luma component of 8 test video sequences (4 : 2 : 0 YUV): (*Foreman, Crew, News, Stefan, Mobile, City, Football, and Flower garden*). However, within the scope of this paper, three test sequences are chosen to show the results according to their object motion activity, that is, high-motion activity (*Crew*), medium-motion activity (*Foreman*), and low-motion activity (*News*). We have used one nonblind and one blind watermarking scheme as example cases, described in Section 3.1. For the simulations shown in this work, the four combinations (032), (230), (131), and (002) were used. In each case, the watermark embedding is performed on the low-frequency subband (LL_s) of 2D spatial decompositions due to its improved robustness performance against compression attacks in image watermarking. In these simulations, the 9/7 biorthogonal wavelet transform was used as the 2D decompositions.

Based on the analysis in the previous section, here we explored the possibility of watermark embedding in high-frequency temporal subband and investigate the robustness performance against compression attacks, as high-frequency

subband can offer improved imperceptibility. In the experiment sets, we chose third temporal level highpass (LLH) and lowpass (LLL) frames to embed the watermark. Other video decomposition parameters are set to (1) 64 frames with GOP size of 8, (2) 8×8 macro block size, and (3) a search window of ±16. The choice of macro block size and search window are decided by referring the motion retrieval analysis in Section 4.2.

For embedding distortion measure, we used peak signal to noise ratio (PSNR) and also measured the amount of flicker introduced due to watermark embedding. Fan et al. [25] defined a quality metric to measure flicker in intracoded video sequences. In our experiments, we have measured flicker in a similar way by calculating the difference between average brightness values of previous and current frames and used the flicker metric in the MSU quality measurement tool [26]. The flicker metric here compares the flicker content in the watermarked video with respect to the original video. In these metrics, higher PSNR represents lower embedding distortion and for flicker, the lower values correspond to the better distortion performance. On the other hand, the watermarking robustness is represented by Hamming

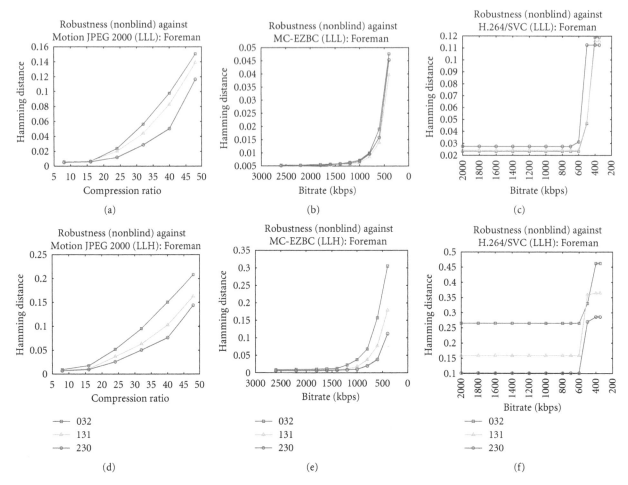

FIGURE 15: Robustness performance of nonblind watermarking scheme for *Foreman* sequence. *Columns* (1), (2) and (3) show robustness against Motion JPEG 2000, MC-EZBC, and H.264-SVC, respectively. *Rows* (1) and (2) represent the embedding on temporal subbands LLL & LLH, respectively.

distance as mentioned in (14) and lower Hamming distance corresponds to better detection performance. Various scalable coded quality compression attacks are considered, such as Motion JPEG 2000, MC-EZBC scalable video coding, and H.264/AVC scalable extension (H.264-SVC). In these experiments, low-frequency spatial LL subband are selected within LLL and LLH temporal subbands. Therefore, the scheme is robust against respective spatial and temporal scalability. For example, the algorithm is robust against spatial scalability up to quarter resolution and temporal scaling up to LH and H frames. The results show the mean value of Hamming distance for average of first 64 frames of test video set.

The experiments are divided into two sets, one for embedding distortion analysis and the other for robustness evaluation. In all the experimental setup, we considered two watermarking algorithms, one each from nonblind (Section 3.1.1) and blind (Section 3.1.2) category. The weighting parameters α and γ are set to 0.1. In case of nonblind algorithm, the level adaptive thresholding as described in [22] is taken into account to avoid watermark embedding in small or nearly zero coefficients to minimize the false detection. The watermarking payload is set to 2000

bits and 2112 bits using a binary logo for all combinations and every sequences for nonblind and blind watermarking methods, respectively.

5.1. Embedding Distortion Analysis. The embedding distortion results in terms of PSNR are shown in Figures 8, 10, and 12 for *News, Foreman,* and *Crew* sequences, respectively, for nonblind and blind watermarking methods. In each of the figures, *x-axis* shows the frame number and *y-axis* represents the PSNR. The flickering results are shown in Figures 9, 11, and 13 for *News, Foreman,* and *Crew* sequences, respectively. In these figures, the *y-axis* represents the flicker metric as discussed in the previous section.

From the results for LLL subband, it is evident that although the PSNR performances are comparable, proposed MCTF-based methods ((032), (131), and (230)) outperform the frame-by-frame embedding (002) in addressing the flickering problem. In all four combinations, the sum of energy in LLL subband are similar and resulting in comparable PSNR. However, in the proposed methods, the error (i.e., PSNR) is propagated along the GOP due to hierarchical temporal decomposition along the motion trajectory and the error

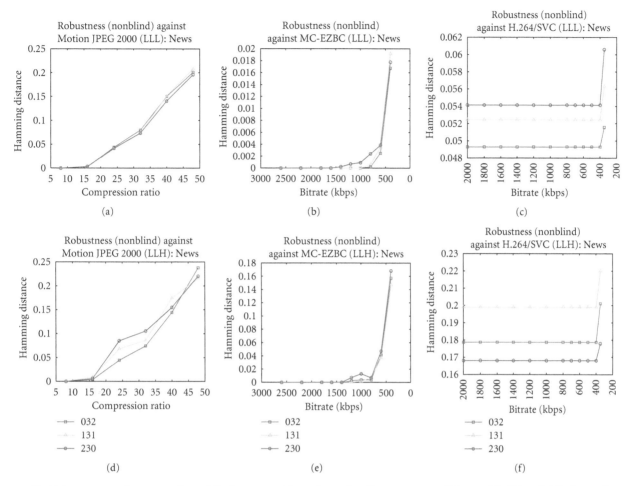

FIGURE 16: Robustness performance of non-blind watermarking scheme for *News* sequence. *Columns* (1), (2) and (3) show robustness against Motion JPEG 2000, MC-EZBC, and H.264-SVC, respectively. *Rows* (1) and (2) represent the embedding on temporal subbands LLL and LLH, respectively.

propagation along the motion trajectory addressed the issues related to flickering artifacts. On the other hand, for LLH subband, due to temporal filtering, the sum of energy is lesser and the four combinations can be ranked as 032 < 131 < 230 < 002. Hence, the PSNR and flickering performance for this temporal subband can be ranked as 032 > 131 > 230 > 002. Therefore, while choosing a temporally filtered high-frequency subband, such as LLH, LH, or *H*, the proposed MCTF approach also outperforms the frame-by-frame embedding in terms of PSNR while addressing the flickering issues. It is evident that flickering due to frame-by-frame embedding is increasingly prominent in the sequences with lower motion (e.g., *News > Foreman > Crew*) and is successfully addressed by the proposed MCTF-based watermarking approach.

5.2. Robustness Performance Evaluation. The robustness results for the nonblind watermarking method are shown in Figures 14, 15, and 16 for *Crew, Foreman,* and *News* sequences, respectively. The *x*-axis represents the compression ratio (Motion JPEG 2000) or bitrates (MC-EZBC and H.264-SVC) and *y*-axis shows the corresponding Hamming

distances. *Columns* (1) and (2) show the results for the LLL and LLH frame selections, respectively. The robustness performances shows that 2D + t, for example, any combination of temporal filtering on spatial decomposition (i.e., (131) and (230)) outperforms a conventional t + 2D scheme. The experimental robustness results for blind watermarking method are shown in Figures 17, 18, and 19 for *Crew, Foreman,* and *News* sequences, respectively. *Column 1* shows results for the LLL temporal subband while results for LLH are shown in *Column 2*. The rows represent various scalability attacks, Motion JPEG 2000, MC-EZBC, and H.264-SVC, respectively. In this case, the motion information is obtained from the watermarked test video. Similar to the nonblind watermarking 2D + t again outperforms a conventional t + 2D scheme such as in [14]. We now analyze the obtained results by grouping it by selection of temporal subband, by embedding method, and by compression scheme.

5.2.1. Selection of Temporal Subband. The low-frequency temporal subband (LLL) offers higher robustness in comparison to high-frequency LLH subband. This is due to more

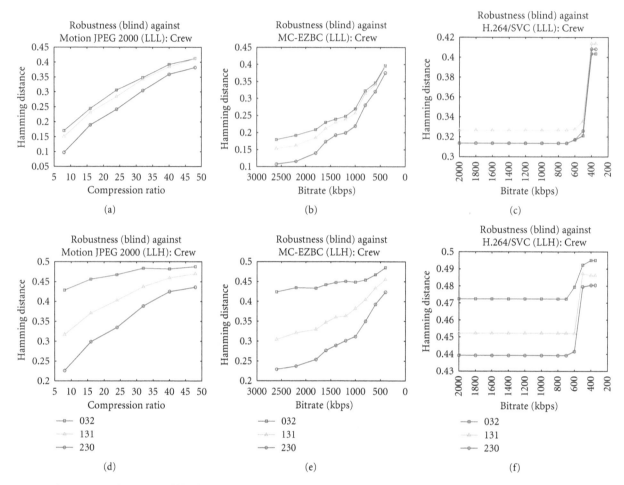

FIGURE 17: Robustness performance of blind watermarking scheme for *Crew* sequence. *Columns* (1), (2) and (3) show robustness against Motion JPEG 2000, MC-EZBC, and H.264-SVC, respectively. *Rows* (1) and (2) represent the embedding on temporal subbands LLL and LLH, respectively.

energy concentration in LLL subband after temporal filtering. Within the temporal subbands, in LLL subband, various spatiotemporal combinations perform equally as the energy levels are nearly equal for 032, 131, and 230. However, 230 performs slightly better due to lesser motion-related error in spatially scaled subband. On the other hand, for LLH subband, we can rank the robustness performance as 230 > 131 > 032 as a result of the energy distribution ranking of these combinations in Section 4.1.

5.2.2. Embedding Method. For a nonblind case, the watermark extraction is performed using the original host video and hence the original motion vector is available at the extractor which makes this scheme more robust to various scalable content adaptation. On the other hand, as explained before, the blind watermarking scheme neither have any reference to original video sequence nor any reference motion vector. The motion vector is estimated from the watermarked test video itself which results in comparatively poor robustness. The effect of motion related error is more visible in LLH subband as the motion compensated temporal highpass frame is highly sensitive to motion estimation accuracy and

so the robustness performance. As discussed in Section 4.2 in case of a 2D + t (i.e., 230), the error due to motion vector is lesser compared to t + 2D scheme and hence offers better robustness (230 > 131 > 032).

5.2.3. Compression Scheme. We have evaluated our proposed algorithm against various scalable video compression schemes, that is, Motion JPEG 2000, MC-EZBC, and H.264-SVC. First two video compression schemes are based on wavelet technology whereas more recent H.264-SVC uses layered scalability using base layer coding of H.264/AVC.

In Motion JPEG 2000 scheme, the coding is performed by applying 2D wavelet transform on each frame separately without considering any temporal correlation between frames. In the proposed watermarking scheme, the use of 2D wavelet transform offers better association with Motion JPEG 2000 scheme and hence provides better robustness for 2D + t combination for LLL and LLH. Also in the case of LLH subband, a better energy concentration offers higher robustness to Motion JPEG 2000 attacks. The robustness performance against Motion JPEG 2000 can be ranked as 230 > 131 > 032.

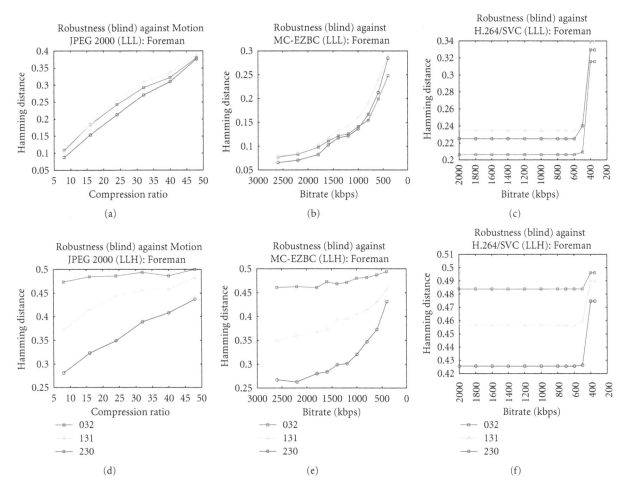

FIGURE 18: Robustness performance of blind watermarking scheme for *Foreman* sequence. *Columns* (1), (2) and (3) show robustness against Motion JPEG 2000, MC-EZBC, and H.264-SVC, respectively. *Rows* (1) and (2) represent the embedding on temporal subbands LLL and LLH, respectively.

MC-EZBC video coder uses motion compensated 1D wavelet transform in temporal filtering and 2D wavelet transform in spatial decomposition. In compression point of view, MC-EZBC usually encodes the video sequences in t + 2D combination due to better energy compaction in low-frequency temporal frames. But in watermarking perspective, higher energy in high-frequency subband can offer higher robustness. The argument is justified from the robustness results where results for LLL subbands are comparable, but a distinctive improvement is observed in LLH subband and based on the results the robustness ranking for MC-EZBC can be done as 230 > 131 > 032.

Finally, we have evaluated the robustness of the proposed scheme against H.264-SVC, which uses inter- /intramotion compensated prediction followed by an integer transform with similar properties of DCT transform. Although the proposed watermarking and H.264-SVC video coding scheme do not share any common technology or transform, the robustness evaluation of the proposed method, against H.264-SVC, has been carried for the completeness of the paper for different scalable video compression schemes. The results provide acceptable robustness. However, for a blind watermarking scheme in LLH subband, proposed schemes

performs poorly due to blind motion estimation. Similar to previous robustness results, based on energy distribution and motion retrieval argument, here we can rank the spatiotemporal combinations as 230 > 131 > 032. In a specific example case, H.264-SVC usually gives preference to intraprediction to the sequences with low global or local motion, as in *News* sequence and hence exception in robustness performance to H.264-SVC is noticed for the proposed scheme.

It is evident that, due to close association between the proposed scheme and MC-EZBC, robustness of the proposed scheme offers best performance against MC-EZBC-based content adaptation. To conclude this discussion, we suggest that a choice of 2D + t watermarking scheme improves the imperceptibility and the robustness performance in a video watermarking scenario for a nonblind as well as a blind watermarking algorithm.

6. Conclusions

In this paper, we have presented a new motion compensated temporal-spatial subband decomposition scheme, based on

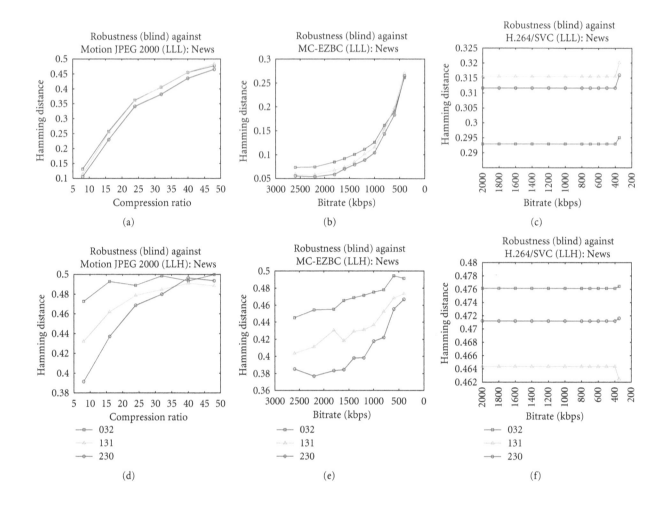

FIGURE 19: Robustness performance of blind watermarking scheme for *News* sequence. *Columns* (1), (2) and (3) show robustness against Motion JPEG 2000, MC-EZBC, and H.264-SVC, respectively. *Rows* (1) and (2) represent the embedding on temporal subbands LLL and LLH, respectively.

the MCTF with implied motion estimation for video watermarking. The MCTF was modified by taking into account the motion trajectory in obtaining an efficient update step. The proposed 2D + t domain watermarking offers improved robustness against scalable content adaptation compared to state-of-the-art conventional t + 2D video watermarking scheme in a nonblind as well as a blind watermarking scenario. The robustness performance is evaluated against scalable coding-based quality compressions attacks, including Motion JPEG 2000, MC-EZBC, and H.264-SVC (scalable extension). The proposed subband decomposition also provides low complexity as MCTF is performed only on subbands where the watermark is embedded.

Acknowledgment

This work is funded by the UK Engineering and Physical Sciences Research Council (EPSRC) by an EPSRC-BP Dorothy Hodgkin Postgraduate Award (DHPA).

References

[1] F. Hartung and B. Girod, "Watermarking of uncompressed and compressed video," *Signal Processing*, vol. 66, no. 3, pp. 283–301, 1998.

[2] H. Inoue, A. Miyazaki, T. Araki, and T. Katsura, "Digital watermark method using the wavelet transform for video data," in *Proceedings of the 1999 IEEE International Symposium on Circuits and Systems (ISCAS '99)*, vol. 4, pp. V-247–V-250, June 1999.

[3] G. Doërr and J. L. Dugelay, "A guide tour of video watermarking," *Signal Processing*, vol. 18, no. 4, pp. 263–282, 2003.

[4] M. P. Mitrea, T. B. Zaharia, F. J. Preteux, and A. Vlad, "Video watermarking based on spread spectrum and wavelet decomposition," in *Wavelet Applications in Industrial Processing II*, vol. 5607 of *Proceedings of the SPIE*, pp. 156–164, 2004.

[5] F. Deguillaume, G. Csurka, J. J. O'Ruanaidh, and T. Pun, "Robust 3D DFT video watermarking," in *Security and Watermarking of Multimedia Contents*, vol. 3657 of *Proceedings of the SPIE*, pp. 113–124, 1999.

[6] J. H. Lim, D. J. Kim, H. T. Kim, and C. S. Won, "Digital video watermarking using 3D-DCT and intracubic correlation," in

Security and Watermarking of Multimedia Contents III, vol. 4314 of *Proceedings of the SPIE*, pp. 64–72, 2001.

[7] S. J. Kim, S. H. Lee, K. S. Moon et al., "A new digital video watermarking using the dual watermark images and 3D DWT," in *Proceedings of the IEEE Region Conference (TENCON '04)*, vol. 1, pp. 291–294, 2004.

[8] P. Campisi and A. Neri, "Video watermarking in the 3D-DWT domain using perceptual masking," in *IEEE International Conference on Image Processing (ICIP '05)*, pp. 997–1000, September 2005.

[9] S. J. Choi and J. W. Woods, "Motion-compensated 3-D subband coding of video," *IEEE Transactions on Image Processing*, vol. 8, no. 2, pp. 155–167, 1999.

[10] S. T. Hsiang and J. W. Woods, "Embedded video coding using invertible motion compensated 3-D subband/wavelet filter bank," *Signal Processing*, vol. 16, no. 8, pp. 705–724, 2001.

[11] C. I. Podilchuk, N. S. Jayant, and N. Farvardin, "Three-dimensional subband coding of video," *IEEE Transactions on Image Processing*, vol. 4, no. 2, pp. 125–139, 1995.

[12] P. Vinod and P. K. Bora, "Motion-compensated inter-frame collusion attack on video watermarking and a countermeasure," *IEE Proceedings on Information Security*, vol. 153, no. 2, pp. 61–73, 2006.

[13] P. Vinod, G. Doërr, and P. K. Bora, "Assessing motion-coherency in video watermarking," in *Proceedings of the Multimedia and Security Workshop*, pp. 114–119, September 2006.

[14] P. Meerwald and A. Uhl, "Blind motion-compensated video watermarking," in *Proceedings of the IEEE International Conference on Multimedia and Expo (ICME '08)*, pp. 357–360, June 2008.

[15] Y. Andreopoulos, A. Munteanu, J. Barbarien, M. Van Der Schaar, J. Cornelis, and P. Schelkens, "In-band motion compensated temporal filtering," *Signal Processing*, vol. 19, no. 7, pp. 653–673, 2004.

[16] F. Huo and X. Gao, "AWavelet based image watermarking scheme," in *Proceedings of the IEEE International Conference on Image Processing*, pp. 2573–2576, Atlanta, Ga, USA, 2006.

[17] C. Jin and J. Peng, "A robust wavelet-based blind digital watermarking algorithm," *Information Technology Journal*, vol. 5, no. 2, pp. 358–363, 2006.

[18] M. A. Suhail, M. S. Obaidat, S. S. Ipson, and B. Sadoun, "A comparative study of digital watermarking in JPEG and JPEG 2000 environments," *Information Sciences*, vol. 151, pp. 93–105, 2003.

[19] M. Barni, F. Bartolini, and A. Piva, "Improved wavelet-based watermarking through pixel-wise masking," *IEEE Transactions on Image Processing*, vol. 10, no. 5, pp. 783–791, 2001.

[20] L. Xie and G. R. Arce, "Joint wavelet compression and authentication watermarking," in *Proceedings of the International Conference on Image Processing (ICIP '98)*, vol. 2, pp. 427–431, October 1998.

[21] D. Kundur and D. Hatzinakos, "Digital watermarking using multiresolution wavelet decomposition," in *Proceedings of the IEEE International Conference on Acoustics, Speech and Signal Processing (ICASSP '98)*, vol. 5, pp. 2969–2972, May 1998.

[22] J. R. Kim and Y. S. Moon, "Robust wavelet-based digital watermarking using level-adaptive thresholding," in *International Conference on Image Processing (ICIP '99)*, pp. 226–230, October 1999.

[23] D. Bhowmik and C. Abhayaratne, "A framework for evaluating wavelet based watermarking for scalable coded digital item adaptation attacks," in *Wavelet Applications in Industrial Processing VI*, vol. 7248 of *Proceedings of the SPIE*, San Jose, Calif, USA, January 2009.

[24] P. Meerwald, "Quantization watermarking in the JPEG2000 coding pipeline," in *Proceedings of the 5th International Working Conference on Communication and Multimedia Security*, pp. 69–79, 2001.

[25] X. Fan, W. Gao, Y. Lu, and D. Zhao, "Flicking reduction in all intra frame coding," Tech. Rep. JVT-E070, 2002.

[26] MSU Graphics & Media Lab VG, MSU Quality Measurement Tool, http://www.compression.ru/video/.

15

Mining Local Specialties for Travelers by Leveraging Structured and Unstructured Data

Kai Jiang,[1] Like Liu,[2] Rong Xiao,[2] and Nenghai Yu[1]

[1] *MOE-Microsoft Key Laboratory of Multimedia Computing and Communication, University of Science and Technology of China, Anhui, Hefei 230027, China*
[2] *Microsoft Research Asia, Tower 2, No. 5 Dan Ling Street, Haidian District, Beijing 100080, China*

Correspondence should be addressed to Kai Jiang, kaijiang@mail.ustc.edu.cn

Academic Editor: Lei Wu

Recently, many local review websites such as Yelp are emerging, which have greatly facilitated people's daily life such as cuisine hunting. However they failed to meet travelers' demands because travelers are more concerned about a city's local specialties instead of the city's high ranked restaurants. To solve this problem, this paper presents a local specialty mining algorithm, which utilizes both the structured data from local review websites and the unstructured user-generated content (UGC) from community Q&A websites, and travelogues. The proposed algorithm extracts dish names from local review data to build a document for each city, and applies *tfidf* weighting algorithm on these documents to rank dishes. Dish-city correlations are calculated from unstructured UGC, and combined with the *tfidf* ranking score to discover local specialties. Finally, duplicates in the local specialty mining results are merged. A recommendation service is built to present local specialties to travelers, along with specialties' associated restaurants, Q&A threads, and travelogues. Experiments on a large data set show that the proposed algorithm can achieve a good performance, and compared to using local review data alone, leveraging unstructured UGC can boost the mining performance a lot, especially in large cities.

1. Introduction

The notion of *SoLoMo* (social local mobile) has induced an explosion of mobile technologies and applications. Under this trend, many local review social network services such as Yelp [1], Dianping [2], and Baidu Shenbian [3] are emerging. These websites enable users to explore, search, share and review local business entities, and indeed provide valuable information for people's daily life. Take cuisine hunting for instance, these applications may provide a great answer to the question "What are the fabulous restaurants nearby and what are the featured dishes in these restaurants?" That might satisfy local residents, but for a traveler, that's not enough. What makes travelers different from local residents is that instead of nearby restaurant and their featured dishes, a traveler is more concerned about the local specialties of the city. A local specialty means a dish is so special in some way that it seldom found in other cities. It may be the ingredients, flavor or cooking style that makes the dish special, and the local specialty often reveals the local culture and lifestyle. Thus, to experience local specialties is always an important task for travelers. Unfortunately, current local review services cannot meet travelers' demands well, because of the following.

(1) Current local review services tend to recommend restaurants of high rank to users, but a city's local specialties are not necessarily provided in high-ranked restaurants. So the user will not be able to discover the specialties.

(2) In some cities, especially large ones, restaurants' quantity can be very large and their varieties can be vast. In these cities, the local specialties may be overwhelming and cannot be found by travelers. For example, Baidu Shenbian contains 49903 restaurant pages in Beijing, and these restaurants cover almost all dish varieties in China, such as Chuan-Style, Xiang-Style, Lu-Style and even foreign dish varieties,

such as Italian-Style, Korean-Style, and Japanese-Style. It is very hard for a traveler to dig into this vast information to find out what is the specialty of Beijing.

To solve this problem, this paper propose a local specialty mining algorithm, which utilizes both the structured data from local review websites and the unstructured data from community Q&A websites and travelogues. We have noticed that many travelers may ask information about travel destinations on Q&A websites such as Yahoo! Answers [4], and after the trip travelers like to record their travel experience in travelogues. We believe the community Q&A data and travelogues can reveal valuable information about travel destinations, so these unstructured user-generated content (UGC) are adopted into our mining algorithm.

Our method first extracts dish names from restaurants' featured dishes information in the local review data. After that the dish names are filtered to remove trivial dish names, noises, and spams. After the dish filtering, a document is built for each city. The words in the document are dishes that are recommended by the city's restaurants. Then *tfidf*-weighting algorithm is applied to these documents to rank dishes. As for the unstructured UGC, locations are first extracted from Q&A threads and travelogues, and then the correlation of dishes and cities are calculated. The *tfidf*-ranking score generated from local review data and city-dish correlation score generated from unstructured UGC are combined to generate the final ranking score. Dishes with high-ranking score are considered as local specialties. Duplicate dishes in top local specialties are merged and reranked to form the final local specialty mining results. After the mining process, a recommendation service is built which can recommend local specialties to a traveler, and for each local specialty, its associated restaurants, Q&A threads, and travelogues are ranked and presented. Extensive experiments demonstrate that leveraging both structured local review data and unstructured UGC can achieve a good local specialty mining performance, thus the effectiveness of our method is proven.

The contributions of this paper are as follows. (1) To the best of our knowledge, this is the first paper addressing the novel problem of local specialty mining and is of particular interest for travelers. (2) This paper presented a method that leverages both structured local review data and unstructured UGC, which generates a good mining performance. (3) A recommendation service is built to recommend local specialties to travelers. The local specialties' associated restaurants, Q&A threads, and travelogues are also presented to travelers, so that these information can facilitate travelers' cuisine hunting.

The remainder of this paper is organized as follows. Section 2 reviews some related works. Section 3 formulates the local specialty mining problem, and gives an overview of the proposed mining algorithm. The local specialty mining algorithm is elaborated in Section 4, followed by the description of the recommendation service in Section 5. In Section 6, the experiment's settings are first introduced, and then the effectiveness of the proposed algorithm is evaluated, and finally the results are reported, followed by some

discussions. Section 7 concludes the paper and presents some future research directions.

2. Related Work

There are some research efforts which are related to our work. Here we give these works a brief description from three directions.

UGC as Contextual Information. There are some works focused on landmark and tourism attraction mining for travel recommendation. These works adopted user-generated content such as blogs, user reviews, and user ratings, to serve as contextual information. Gao et al. [5] build a tourism recommendation service by mining landmarks from geotagged photos in photo sharing websites such as Flickr. In the landmark mining process, Yahoo Travel Guide [6] is adopted as a context information to decide whether the tags from photo sharing websites are travel related, and in the landmark ranking process, user-generated reviews and ratings in Yahoo Travel Guide is also brought into use. Ji et al. [7] harvest travel related photos and blogs from Windows Live Space [8], and associate the photos with extracted locations from the textual information such as photos' titles, tags, and blogs. After that, both the photos' visual information and the location hierarchy are used to rank and recommend attractions.

Travelogue Mining. There're many works which are dedicated to extract location related information by mining the large volume of user-generated travelogue [9–12]. Ye et al. [9] are focused on identifying a travelogue's theme location when there are multiple locations in a travelogue. [10, 12] apply a generative model to train location related local topic from travelogues, and extract locations' representative textual tags according to these local topics. Furthermore, these representative tags are used to retrieve related photos. Both representative tags and photos are clustered, ranked and, organized to give the user a better understanding about a specific location. In [11] Hao et al. not only generated locations' textual and visual summarizations as what they did in [10, 12], but also fully utilized the location's local topics trained from travelogues to perform the travel destination recommendation with respect to a user's query.

Local Dish Mining. The works which are most similar to us are [13, 14], which are dedicated to dish mining. [13] is focused on dish names extraction from restaurant reviews, and [14] pushes this work forward. Besides dish name extraction, [14] also tries to extract restaurant names from users' blogs and map them to a POI database, so that the extracted dish can be matched to restaurants in the POI database and can be deployed into a mobile map service. However, these works differ from us in the following (1). These works are focused on dish name extraction and restaurant name extraction, which are related to named entity extraction and recognition problem. But in our work, dish names are directly obtained from the local review websites, and our work is focused on the city's local specialty mining, which is related to ranking and recommendation problem. (2) The dishes extracted by [13, 14] are general dishes provided by

FIGURE 1: Example of local review websites. (a) Yelp, (b) Shenbian.

local restaurants which are more suitable for local residents, while dishes mined by our work are the city's local specialties, and that is of particular interest for travelers.

3. System Overview

This section first gives the annotations and formulates the local specialties mining problem, and then describes the overview of the algorithm.

3.1. Problem Formulation. Restaurant information often has similar structure in different local review applications. Figure 1 shows two typical local review applications: the left one is Yelp [1] and the right one is Baidu Shenbian [3]. Local mobile applications always associate business entities with locations, so the restaurant page is fixed to a city. A restaurant page has restaurant's name, user-generated rank, basic information, and the restaurant's featured dishes.

Each page in the local review website contains a ⟨city, restaurant, dishes⟩ hierarchical structure, so from restaurant pages of many cities, a hierarchical structure depicted in Figure 2 can be constructed.

The annotations of cities, restaurants, and dishes are listed in Table 1.

The local specialty mining problem is that: given a city c_i in C, rank the dishes in city $c_i \{d_1, d_2, \ldots, d_k, \ldots\}, d_k \in r_{ij}$ and $r_{ij} \in c_i$, so that dishes ranked higher are specialties in city c_i, which means these dishes are famous in city c_i, but seldom found in other cities.

3.2. System Architecture. Figure 3 illustrates the overview of the proposed method. Our local specialties mining and recommendation system consists of four steps: step 1, rank dish with structured local review data; step 2, rank dish with unstructured user-generated content; step 3, combine the ranking scores generated by steps 1 and 2; step 4, recommend local specialties and their associated restaurants, Q&A threads, and travelogues to a user. The local specialty mining algorithm will be elaborated in Section 4, and the recommendation service will be presented in Section 5.

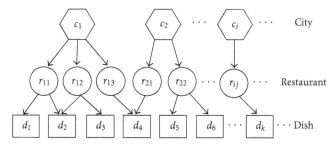

FIGURE 2: Hierarchical structure of local review data.

TABLE 1: Annotations.

Annotation	Meaning
$C = \{c_1, c_2, \ldots, c_N\}$	C: city collections. C_i: the ith city
$R_i = \{r_{i1}, r_{i2}, \ldots, r_{iM}\}$	R_i: restaurants in city C_i. r_{ij}: the jth restaurant in city C_i
$D = \{d_1, d_2, \ldots, d_k\}$	D: the dish collection. d_i: the ith dish name

4. Mining Local Specialties

This section elaborates the local specialty mining algorithm, which consists of 4 phases. (1) Filter dish to remove trivial dishes, noises and spams, and so forth. (2) Rank dish using local review data. (3) Calculate dish-city correlation using unstructured UGC. (4) Combine ranking scores generated by phases 2 and 3 to generate local specialties, and merge duplicates and rerank the top local specialties.

4.1. Dish Filtering. Since the dishes recommended in the restaurant page are often extracted from user's comments or added by restaurant owner, their quality cannot be assured. They must be filtered first during the dish mining process.

We consider a specialty's quality is low and must be discarded if it is in the two following cases.

(1) The specialty is trivial and not informative.

(2) The specialty is spam/noisy/meaningless.

We develop two simple rules to filter the specialty with low quality. For case 1, if the dish name often occurs in other dish name, then this dish name is not informative and can

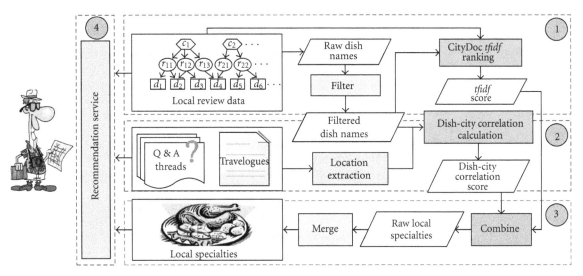

FIGURE 3: System overview.

be discarded. For example, *fried rice* often occurs in many other dish names, such as *Yangzhou fried rice*, *beef fried rice*, *egg fried rice*, and *shredded pork fried rice*, so the dish *fried rice* should be filtered out. For case 2, if the dish name is only recommended by one restaurant, then it should be discarded.

4.2. Dish Ranking Using Local Review Data.

As what can be seen from Figure 2, a restaurant can only recommend a dish once, but a dish can be recommended by more than one restaurant, thus a dish may be recommended several times in a city. Intuitively, if a dish is recommended many times by different restaurants in one city, but seldom recommended in other cities, then this dish might be the city's local specialty. So the question becomes how to find dishes that frequently appear in one city but seldom appear in other cities? And, how to analytically measure a dish's "appear in one city with high frequency but appear in other cities with low frequency"? To answer this question, the *tfidf* weighting is naturally brought into use.

The *tfidf* weighting (term frequency-inverse document frequency) algorithm [15] is often applied in text analysis and document retrieval task to select representative words for a document. A word will have a high *tfidf* weight if it matches the following two conditions: (1) the word has a high term frequency (*tf*) in the given document; (2) the word has a low document frequency (*df*) in the whole collection of documents, thus has a high inverse document frequency (*idf*). This exactly fits the local specialty mining problem, if we consider the city as a document, and the dishes as words. The *tf* can measure how frequently a dish is recommended in a city, while the *idf* measures how seldom the dish is recommended in other cities. So we adopt the *tfidf* weighting to rank dishes as follows.

For each city c_i, we concatenate the dishes recommended by restaurants in this city as a *city document*:

$$CityDoc(c_i) = \text{concatenate}(d_k), \quad \text{where } d_k \in r_{ij}, r_{ij} \in c_i. \tag{1}$$

If a dish is recommended several times by different restaurants in a city, then this dish will occur the same times in the city document. For example, city c_1 in Figure 2 has the city document in the following form:

$$CityDoc(c_1) = \{d_1, d_2, d_2, d_3, d_4\}. \tag{2}$$

After *CityDoc* is built for each city, *tfidf* weighting can be applied to rank dishes in the cities:

$$tfidf(c_i, d_k) = \frac{\#d_k}{|CityDoc(c_i)|} * \log\left(\frac{|C|}{\#c_j : d_k \in CityDoc(c_j)}\right). \tag{3}$$

In which $\# d_k$ stands for the times that dish d_k occurs in $CityDoc(c_i)$, $|CityDoc(c_i)|$ is the document length of $CityDoc(c_i)$, $|C|$ is the total city count, and $\#c_j$ is the amount of $CityDoc$ that contains dish d_k.

After the *tfidf* ranking, a dish d with higher *tfidf* (c,d) is more likely to be local specialty in city c.

4.3. Leverage Unstructured UGC.

Since cuisine hunting is often an important task for travelers, a traveler may wonder what is the local specialty in her travel destination when she is planning her trip. She may resort to community Q&A website for help, such as Yahoo! Answers [4] and Quora [16]. For example, she might ask "what dish I have to try when I travel to Beijing", and someone may answer "You should definitely try the *Beijing roast duck*". And after the trip, she might like to write travelogues to share her experience, including the local specialty she has enjoyed in the travel destination. In this way, the location "*Beijing*" and the dish name "*Beijing roast duck*" may cooccur many times in Q&A threads and travelogues.

So it is reasonable to exploit the information hidden in community Q&A websites and travelogues to help the local specialty mining task. A straightforward idea is to use the location and dish cooccurrence to measure the correlation of a dish and a location.

Due to the nature of social network applications, the question and answers tend to be short in community Q&A websites, therefore it might be easy to extract location from a community Q&A thread. But to identify a travelogue's associated location is a much harder task. The length of a travelogue is often long, and the description in a travelogue often contains many details. For example, a traveler may mention her starting location of her trip, locations along the trip, and the destination of the trip; furthermore she may compare the destination to some locations she has traveled before. As a result, a travelogue may mention multiple locations. So after locations are extracted from a travelogue, it is necessary but difficult to identify which location is the travel destination and is emphasized in the travelogue. In this paper, we follow the work in [9] to identify the location emphasized in a travelogue. In [9] locations are first extracted from the travelogues, and two types of features are calculated for these locations, textual features and geographical features. After that, to leverage the two independent types of features, a cotraining framework is adopted to build a classifier to identify a travelogue's emphasized location.

After locations are identified in Q&A threads and travelogues, the correlation between a dish and a city can be measured as

$$\mathrm{corr}(c, d) = \frac{co(c, d)}{\sum_{c \in C} co(c, d)}. \qquad (4)$$

In which $co(c, d)$ stands for the cooccurrence of the dish d and a city c in both Q&A website and travelogues, and C stands for the city collection.

The final ranking score for a dish to be a city's local specialty can be obtained by combining the *tfidf* weight from local review data and the correlation scores from user-generated content:

$$w(c, d) = \lambda * tf idf(c, d) + (1 - \lambda) * \mathrm{corr}(c, d). \qquad (5)$$

In which λ is a factor that controls the combination of structured local review data and unstructured UGC.

4.4. Merge Duplicate Dishes. Some dish may be referred to as alias or abbreviations in local review data's restaurants' featured dishes, Q&A threads, and travelogues. That might cause duplicate dishes in mined city specialties. For example, *Beijing roast duck* and *roast duck* refer to the same dish in Beijing, and they are all mined as Beijing's local specialties. It would be awkward and confusing if both of them are recommended to users, so we developed an algorithm to tackle this problem.

We observed that dish names often consist of 4 parts: ingredients, flavors, cooking methods, and other auxiliary words. We believe if the ingredients, flavor, and the cooking method are the same in different dish names, these dish names should refer to the same dish. Take the *Beijing roast duck* and *roast duck* as an example, the cooking method *roast* and the ingredient *duck* are the same in these two dish names, so these two dish names are considered to refer to the same

dish. The auxiliary word *Beijing* is ignored in the dish name matching process.

We crawled dish ingredients, flavors, and cooking methods from several cooking recipe websites such as [17], and we used these words as to segment dish names. If the ingredients, flavor, and the cooking method are the same in different dish names, these dish names are considered to refer to the same dish and should be merged. The dish name with highest weight $w(c, d)$ is chosen as the exemplar of the merged dish names, and merged dish names' weights are accumulated as the exemplar's weight. For example, if Beijing's ranked local specialties {(dish, w (Beijing, dish))} are {(*noodles with soybean paste, 0.18*), (*Beijing roast duck, 0.15*) (*fried pork tripe, 0.12*), and (*roast duck, 0.08*)}, then *Beijing roast duck* and *roast duck* will be merged and *Beijing roast duck* will be chosen as exemplar and their weights are accumulated. So the final ranked local specialties list will be {(*Beijing roast duck, 0.23*) (*noodles with soybean paste, 0.18*), (*fried pork tripe, 0.12*)}.

5. Recommendation Service

After local specialties have been mined for each city, we build a recommendation service, so that a traveler can easily find the city's local specialty and the associated restaurants, Q&A threads, and travelogues. That brings great convenience to travelers for the cuisine hunting and decision making. The recommendation service's user interface is given in Figure 4. When a user selects a city, the city's local specialty will be listed (Figure 4(a)). For each local specialty, the user can browse associated restaurants (Figure 4(b)), related Q&A threads (Figure 4(d)) and travelogues (Figure 4(c)).

A local specialty's associated restaurants are restaurants whose featured dishes contain the local specialty. We adopted HITS algorithm [18] with small modification to rank these restaurants considering both user-generated rank and the restaurant-dish relations. In the ranking algorithm, the restaurants are considered as *hubs* and the dishes are considered as *authorities*, and the *hub* scores of restaurants are initialized with restaurants' user-generated rank. The tradeoff between user-generated rank and restaurant-dish relations is controlled by iteration steps of *hubs* and *authorities* calculation. Convergence of iteration leads to a ranking result fully focused on restaurant-dish relation, and early stop in the iteration step can get a ranking result biased to user-generated rank. After the ranking procedure, a restaurant with a high *hub* score tends to have more popular dishes and a higher user-generated rank. This should be more preferred for a traveler.

Snippets of Q&A threads and travelogues will be presented to the user after a local specialty is specified. The local specialty's related Q&A threads and travelogues are first ranked by term frequency of the dish, and then the surrounding texts are extracted to form the snippets. These snippets serve as a great compensation for the restaurants list from local review application data. They can help the travelers a lot, because they are written by travelers and experienced users and contains more vivid and detailed information such

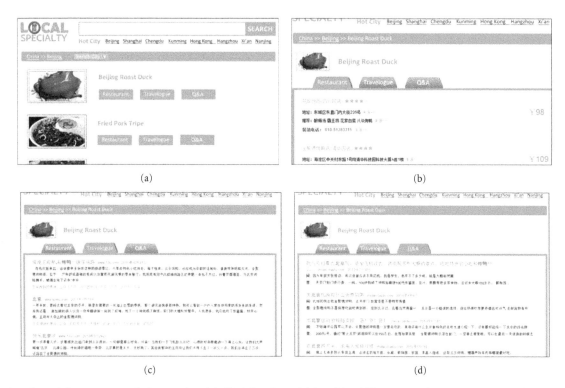

FIGURE 4: Local specialty recommendation service. (a) City's local specialties. (b) Dish's-associated restaurants. (c) Dish-associated travelogues. (d) Dish associated Q&A threads.

as how the dish tastes, which restaurant services the best dish, and how to get there.

This recommendation service has been integrated into the MSRA travel guide project: http://travel.msra.cn/.

6. Experiments

This section first describes the settings of experiments, and compares the proposed method to other three methods. The combination factor of local review data and unstructured UGC is also evaluated. The results are reported in details, followed by some discussions.

6.1. Data. We crawled 380965 restaurant pages from Baidu Shenbian, and extracted the ⟨city, restaurants, dishes⟩ hierarchical structure from them. Furthermore, we crawled 182706 location related community Q&A threads from popular Q&A websites such as Zhidao [19], Wenwen [20] and iAsk [21], and 324905 travelogues from travelogue sharing websites and such as Sina travel blog [22], Netease travel blog [23], and Lvping [24]. For the dish duplicates merging in Section 4.4, we crawled a dataset containing 1723 ingredients, 68 cooking methods, and 50 flavors from cooking recipe websites.

Figure 5 depicts the top 15 cities that have the most restaurants. The amount of restaurants in a city reveals the city's geographic scale and its economic development.

Figures 6 and 7 give the top 15 cities according to Q&A thread count and travelogue count. These counts reveal the cities' popularity of tourism.

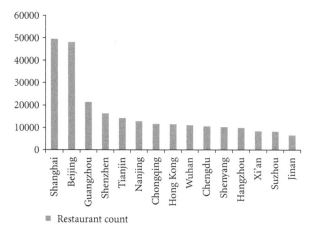

■ Restaurant count

FIGURE 5: Top 15 cities according to restaurant count.

6.2. Comparison Methods. In order to investigate the effectiveness of mining local specialty by leveraging both structured local review data and the unstructured user-generated content, we employ other three methods for comparison purpose. So there are total four methods which are evaluated in the experiments.

(i) *LocalReview_HITS*: This method utilizes the restaurant-dish relationship of local review data to rank restaurants and dishes in each city. It employs HITS algorithm [18] on the restaurant-dish graph by considering the restaurants as *hubs* and the dishes as

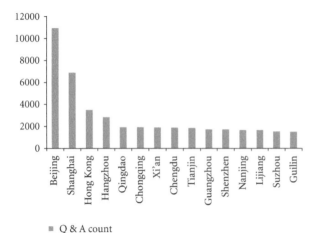

FIGURE 6: Top 15 cities according to Q&A count.

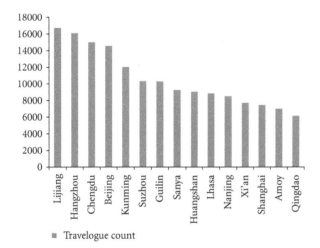

FIGURE 7: Top 15 cities according to travelogue count.

authorities, and the *hub* scores are initialized with restaurants user-generated rank. After the iterative score propagation is done, dishes with high *authority* scores are considered as the city's specialties. The basic assumption behind this algorithm is that a city's specialties are offered in large amount of restaurants in this city, especially the high-ranked ones, thus the specialties will have high *authority* scores. We refer to this method as *LocalReview_HITS*.

(ii) *LocalReview_tfidf*: This method groups all dishes provided by a city's restaurants as a document, and then *tfidf* weighting algorithm is applied on all city documents. Dishes with high *tfidf* weight are considered as a city's specialties. This method is elaborated in Section 4.2.

(iii) *Unstructured UGC*: In this method, the local review data is only used to build dish name dictionary to detect dish in unstructured user-generated content (UGC), that is, travelogues and Q&A threads. The correlation of dishes and cities are mined from unstructured UGC, and dishes having high correlation to a city are considered as the city's specialties. This method is discussed in Section 4.3.

(iv) *Combination*: This method is the local specialty mining algorithm proposed in this paper. It combines both the *tfidf* weight generated by *LocalReview_tfidf* and the city-dish correlation generated by *UnstructuredUGC*.

6.3. Combination Factor. The factor λ controls the tradeoff between the influences of two different data sources, that is, the structured local review data and unstructured UGC. We change the factor λ in a range from 0 to 1 with a step size of 0.1 and evaluate the local specialty mining performance with respect to λ. In this way, we can investigate how this factor affects the algorithm's performance and the contribution of two different data sources.

6.4. Evaluation. We select top 15 cities according to restaurant count, Q&A thread count, and travelogue count, respectively, and obtain a city set that contains 23 unique cities. They are Beijing, Shanghai, Hong Kong, Guangzhou, Shenzhen, Sanya, Chongqing, Lijiang, Hangzhou, Suzhou, Guilin, Nanjing, Xi'an, Shenyang, Jinan, Lhasa, Tianjin, Kunming, Huangshan, Chengdu, Qingdao, Wuhan, and Amoy. The evaluation of different local specialty mining algorithms is performed in these cities.

Since it is very difficult to find all the specialties in a city, even for human, the recall is hard to measure. So we only investigate the precision of mining algorithms here. Average precision [25], which is a widely used evaluation metric in information retrieval research community, is adopted to measure the effectiveness of different local specialty mining algorithms. The ground truth are manually labeled by people with domain knowledge.

6.5. Results and Discussions. Table 2 lists top 5 local specialties in some major cities which are generated by our proposed method. The Chinese dish names and their English translations are given, and the correct specialties are marked as italic.

Figure 8 shows the average precision of cities' top 5 dishes (AP@5) and top 10 dishes (AP@10) generated by different algorithms. λ is set as 0.4 in the *Combination* method. Table 3 shows the mean average precision over the 23 cities to demonstrate overall performance of different mining algorithms.

From Figure 8 and Table 3, we can tell that *LocalReview_HITS*'s performance is the worst, and *LocalReview_tfidf* works much better. This tells us that the assumption behind *LocalReview_HITS* is wrong, that is, local specialties are not provided by large amounts of local restaurants, which means a traveler cannot easily find local specialties just by browsing top restaurants in a local review website. This is especially the case in large cities such as Beijing, Shanghai, Guangzhou and Hangzhou. Because in these cities, the geographical scale is large, the economy is highly developed, and the residents are of various culture backgrounds, and these factors lead to

TABLE 2: Examples of mined cities' specialties. The italic dish names are the correct ones.

City	Top 5 specialties				
Beijing	*Beijing roast duck* (北京烤鸭)	*Noodles with soybean paste* (炸酱面)	*Fried pork tripe* (爆肚)	*Stewed liver* (炒肝)	*Fermented bean drink* (豆汁)
Shanghai	*Friedbun* (生煎)	Tripe (肚子)	Hamburger (汉堡)	*Nanxiang steamed small bun* (南翔小笼)	Apple (苹果)
Hong Kong	*Eggette* (鸡蛋仔)	*Dessert* (甜品)	*Wonton noodle* (云吞面)	*Fish ball* (鱼蛋)	Water convolvulus (通菜)
Hangzhou	*Shrimp with longjing tea leaves* (龙井虾仁)	*SongSao fish soup* (宋嫂鱼羹)	*West lake fish in vinegar gravy* (西湖醋鱼)	*Dongpo pork* (东坡肉)	*Pianerchuan noodle* (片儿川)
Suzhou	*Whitebait* (银鱼)	Lvyang Wonton (绿杨馄饨)	*Zhuangyuan Pork Knuckle* (状元蹄)	*fermented bean curd* (臭豆腐)	*shoe-shaped crispy cake* (袜底酥)
Nanjing	*Soup with duck flood and vermicelli* (鸭血粉丝汤)	*Chicken gravy dumpling* (鸡汁汤包)	Lion bridge (狮子桥)	*Boiled salted duck* (盐水鸭)	*Shredded bean curd* (干丝)
Xi'an	*Pita bread soaked in lamb soup* (羊肉泡馍)	*Chinese hamburger* (肉夹馍)	*Fried rice with pickled vegetable* (酸菜炒米)	*Cold rice noodle* (凉皮)	*Gravy dumpling* (汤包)
Tianjin	*Goubuli stuffed bun* (狗不理包子)	*Thin pancake with puffed fritter* (煎饼果子)	*Twist of dough* (麻花)	*Fried cake* (炸糕)	*Shredded mung bean pancake* (锅巴菜)
Kunming	*Puer tea* (普洱茶)	*Bridge rice noodles* (过桥米线)	*Chicken cooked with potato* (洋芋鸡)	*Yunnan rice cake* (粑粑)	*Yunnan cheese* (乳扇)
Amoy	*Ip's glutinous rice cake with sesame* (叶氏麻糍)	*Sweet herb jelly* (烧仙草)	*Sateysauce noodle* (沙茶面)	*Oyster omelet* (海蛎煎)	*Peanut soup* (花生汤)

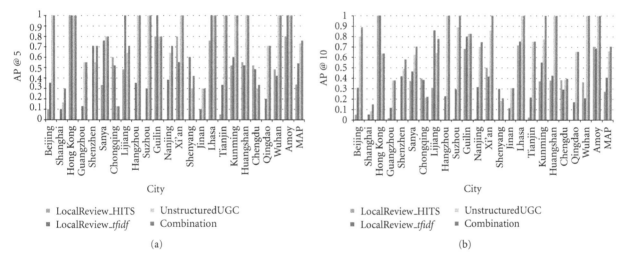

FIGURE 8: Average precision of top cities.

TABLE 3: Mean average precision of different algorithms.

MAP	*local reivew_hits*	*Local Review_tfidf*	Unstructured UGC	Combination
MAP@5	0.339	0.540	0.735	0.760
MAP@10	0.274	0.407	0.661	0.706

restaurants with enormous quantity and style. Algorithms leveraging unstructured user-generated content, that is, *UnstructuredUGC* and *Combination*, works much better than algorithm using only local review data. This result can be intuitively explained because the Q&A threads and travelogues reveal more information that is specifically related to travelers and tourism. The *Combination* method works best

in all evaluated algorithms, which proves the effectiveness of our proposed algorithm.

Figure 9 shows the performance changing of the proposed method with respect to the combination factor λ. The figure tells that (1) mining from unstructured UGC alone (λ is 0) can achieve a better performance than mining from the structured local review data alone (λ is 1), (2) when the contribution of local review data increases (a larger λ), the performance gets better, but when the local review data's contribution increases to a certain threshold (λ grows above 0.7), the performance degrades dramatically. That means the structured local review data and the unstructured UGC can mutually reinforce the mining performance, and the unstructured UGC plays a more important role in the proposed algorithm. The local review data alone is insufficient,

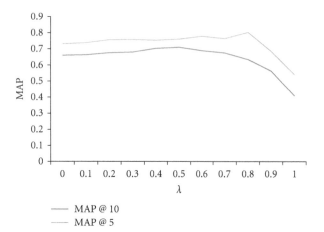

- —— MAP @ 10
- —— MAP @ 5

FIGURE 9: MAP w.r.t. combination factor λ.

but with the help of unstructured UGC, the performance can be boosted a lot.

7. Conclusion and Future Work

This paper proposes a mining algorithm to deal with the novel local specialty mining problem, which is of particular interest for travelers. The proposed algorithm leverages both structured data from local review websites and unstructured data from user-generated content from Q&A websites and travelogues. We first extract dish names from local review data to build a document for each city, and apply *tfidf* weighting algorithm on these documents to rank dishes. Dish-city correlations are calculated from unstructured UGC, and combined with the *tfidf* ranking score to discover local specialties, followed by duplicates removal. Finally a recommendation service is built to present local specialties to travelers, along with specialties'-associated restaurants, Q&A threads, and travelogues. Experiments on a large data set demonstrate the effectiveness of the proposed algorithm. The results show that, the proposed algorithm can achieve a good local specialty mining performance. And compared to using local review data alone, leveraging unstructured UGC can boost the mining performance a lot, especially in large cities.

In the future, we intend to continue this research in 2 directions. (1) Exploiting the hierarchical structure of the local review data more thoroughly, such as investigating the relation between restaurants and the relation between dishes. (2) To study the unstructured UGC in the semantic level to get a better insight of travel related information.

Acknowledgments

This work is supported by National Natural Science Foundation of China (Grant no. 60933013), National Science and Technology Major Project (Grant no. 2010ZX03004-003), and Fundamental Research Funds for the Central Universities (Grant no. WK2100230002). This work is performed at MSRA.

References

[1] Yelp, http://www.yelp.com/.

[2] Dianping, http://www.dianping.com/citylist.

[3] Baidu Shenbian, http://s.baidu.com/city.

[4] Yahoo! Answers, http://answers.yahoo.com/.

[5] Y. Gao, J. Tang, R. Hong, Q. Dai, T. S. Chua, and R. Jain, "W2Go: a travel guidance system by automatic landmark ranking," in *Proceedings of the 18th ACM International Conference on Multimedia ACM Multimedia*, pp. 123–132, October 2010.

[6] Yahoo! Travel, http://travel.yahoo.com/.

[7] R. Ji, X. Xie, H. Yao, and W. Y. Ma, "Mining city landmarks from blogs by graph modeling," in *Proceedings of the 17th ACM International Conference on Multimedia, MM'09, with Co-located Workshops and Symposiums*, pp. 105–114, October 2009.

[8] Windows Live Space, https://login.live.com/.

[9] M. Ye, R. Xiao, W. C. Lee, and X. Xie, "On theme location discovery for travelogue services," in *Proceedings of the 34th international ACM SIGIR conference on Research and development in Information*, pp. 465–474, 2011.

[10] Q. Hao, R. Cai, J. M. Yang et al., "TravelScope: standing on the shoulders of dedicated travelers," in *Proceedings of the 17th ACM International Conference on Multimedia, MM'09, with Co-located Workshops and Symposiums*, pp. 1021–1022, October 2009.

[11] Q. Hao, R. Cai, C. Wang et al., "Equip tourists with knowledge mined from travelogues," in *Proceedings of the 19th International World Wide Web Conference (WWW '10)*, pp. 401–410, April 2010.

[12] Q. Hao, R. Cai, X. J. Wang, J. M. Yang, Y. Pang, and L. Zhang, "Generating location overviews with images and tags by mining user-generated travelogues," in *Proceedings of the 17th ACM International Conference on Multimedia, MM'09, with Co-located Workshops and Symposiums*, pp. 801–804, October 2009.

[13] T. C. Peng and C. C. Shih, "Mining Chinese restaurant reviews for cuisine name extraction: an application to cuisine guide service," in *Proceedings of the International Conference on Information Engineering and Computer Science (ICIECS '09)*, pp. 1–4, December 2009.

[14] C. C. Shih, T. C. Peng, and W. S. Lai, "Mining the blogosphere to generate local cuisine hotspots for mobile map service," in *Proceedings of the 4th International Conference on Digital Information Management (ICDIM '09)*, pp. 151–158, November 2009.

[15] G. Salton, E. A. Fox, and H. Wu, "Extended Boolean information retrieval," *Communications of the ACM*, vol. 26, no. 11, pp. 1022–1036, 1983.

[16] Quora, http://www.quora.com/.

[17] Douguo, http://www.douguo.com/.

[18] J. M. Kleinberg, "Authoritative sources in a hyperlinked environment," *Journal of the ACM*, vol. 46, no. 5, pp. 604–632, 1999.

[19] Baidu Zhidao, http://zhidao.baidu.com/.

[20] Soso Wenwen, http://wenwen.soso.com/.

[21] Sina iAsk, http://iask.sina.com.cn/.

[22] Sina travel blog, http://blog.sina.com.cn/lm/travel/.

[23] Netease travel blog, http://blog.163.com/travel.html.

[24] Lvping, http://www.lvping.com/.

[25] C. D. Manning, P. Raghavan, and H. Schutze, *Introduction to Information Retrieval*, Cambridge University Press, Cambridge, UK, 2008.

Permissions

The contributors of this book come from diverse backgrounds, making this book a truly international effort. This book will bring forth new frontiers with its revolutionizing research information and detailed analysis of the nascent developments around the world.

We would like to thank all the contributing authors for lending their expertise to make the book truly unique. They have played a crucial role in the development of this book. Without their invaluable contributions this book wouldn't have been possible. They have made vital efforts to compile up to date information on the varied aspects of this subject to make this book a valuable addition to the collection of many professionals and students.

This book was conceptualized with the vision of imparting up-to-date information and advanced data in this field. To ensure the same, a matchless editorial board was set up. Every individual on the board went through rigorous rounds of assessment to prove their worth. After which they invested a large part of their time researching and compiling the most relevant data for our readers. Conferences and sessions were held from time to time between the editorial board and the contributing authors to present the data in the most comprehensible form. The editorial team has worked tirelessly to provide valuable and valid information to help people across the globe.

Every chapter published in this book has been scrutinized by our experts. Their significance has been extensively debated. The topics covered herein carry significant findings which will fuel the growth of the discipline. They may even be implemented as practical applications or may be referred to as a beginning point for another development. Chapters in this book were first published by Hindawi Publishing Corporation; hereby published with permission under the Creative Commons Attribution License or equivalent.

The editorial board has been involved in producing this book since its inception. They have spent rigorous hours researching and exploring the diverse topics which have resulted in the successful publishing of this book. They have passed on their knowledge of decades through this book. To expedite this challenging task, the publisher supported the team at every step. A small team of assistant editors was also appointed to further simplify the editing procedure and attain best results for the readers.

Our editorial team has been hand-picked from every corner of the world. Their multi-ethnicity adds dynamic inputs to the discussions which result in innovative outcomes. These outcomes are then further discussed with the researchers and contributors who give their valuable feedback and opinion regarding the same. The feedback is then collaborated with the researches and they are edited in a comprehensive manner to aid the understanding of the subject.

Apart from the editorial board, the designing team has also invested a significant amount of their time in understanding the subject and creating the most relevant covers. They scrutinized every image to scout for the most suitable representation of the subject and create an appropriate cover for the book.

The publishing team has been involved in this book since its early stages. They were actively engaged in every process, be it collecting the data, connecting with the contributors or procuring relevant information. The team has been an ardent support to the editorial, designing and production team. Their endless efforts to recruit the best for this project, has resulted in the accomplishment of this book. They are a veteran in the field of academics and their pool of knowledge is as vast as their experience in printing. Their expertise and guidance has proved useful at every step. Their uncompromising quality standards have made this book an exceptional effort. Their encouragement from time to time has been an inspiration for everyone.

The publisher and the editorial board hope that this book will prove to be a valuable piece of knowledge for researchers, students, practitioners and scholars across the globe.

List of Contributors

Basem Al-Madani, Anas Al-Roubaiey and Zubair A. Baig
Department of Computer Engineering, King Fahd University of Petroleum & Minerals, Eastern Province, Dhahran 31261, Saudi Arabia

Radu Boriga and Ana Cristina Dsscslescu
Faculty of Computer Science, Titu Maiorescu University, 040051 Bucharest, Romania

Adrian-Viorel Diaconu
IT & C Department, University of South-East Europe Lumina, 021187 Bucharest, Romania

Anna Lina Ruscelli and Gabriele Cecchetti
TeCIP Institute, Scuola Superiore Sant'Anna, 56124 Pisa, Italy

Markus Lanthaler
Institute for Information Systems and Computer Media, Graz University of Technology, 8010 Graz, Austria

Christian Gutl
Institute for Information Systems and Computer Media, Graz University of Technology, 8010 Graz, Austria
School of Information Systems, Curtin University of Technology, Perth WA 6102, Australia

Naif A. Haddad
Department of Conservation Science, Queen Rania Institute of Tourism and Heritage, The Hashemite University, Zarqa, Jordan

Jue-Sam Chou
Department of Information Management, Nanhua University, No. 55, Section 1, Nanhua Road, Dalin Township, Chiayi County 62249, Taiwan

Abderrahmane Elyousfi
Computer Science Department, National Engineering School of Applied Sciences, University Ibn Zohr, 80000 Agadir, Morocco

Xiao Chen
Jiangsu Key Laboratory of Meteorological Observation and Information Processing, Nanjing University of Information Science and Technology, Nanjing 210044, China
School of Electronic and Information Engineering, Nanjing University of Information Science and Technology, Nanjing 210044, China

Dongjue Gu
School of Electronic and Information Engineering, Nanjing University of Information Science and Technology, Nanjing 210044, China

Mukesh Saini and Mohan Kankanhalli
School of Computing, National University of Singapore, Singapore 117417

Pradeep K. Atrey
Department of Applied Computer Science, The University of Winnipeg, MB, Canada R3T 5V9

Sharad Mehrotra
Information and Computer Science Department, University of California, Irvine, CA 92697-3425, USA

Di Guo, Xiaofeng Du, Keshou Wu and Xuhui Chen
School of Computer and Information Engineering, Fujian Provincial University Key Laboratory of Internet of Things Application Technology, Xiamen University of Technology, Xiamen 361024, China

Xiaobo Qu
Department of Electronic Science, Xiamen University, Xiamen 361005, China

Mohammad Awrangjeb
Cooperative Research Centre for Spatial Information, Department of Infrastructure Engineering, University of Melbourne, VIC 3010, Australia

Markos Avlonitis and Konstantinos Chorianopoulos
Ionian University, 49100 Corfu, Greece

Sajid Nazir, Vladimir Stankovic and Ivan Andonovic
Department of Electronic and Electrical Engineering, University of Strathclyde, Glasgow G1 1XQ, UK

Dejan Vukobratovic
Department of Power, Electronics and Communication Engineering, University of Novi Sad, 21000 Novi Sad, Serbia

Deepayan Bhowmik and Charith Abhayaratne
Department of Electronic and Electrical Engineering, The University of Sheffield, Sheffield S1 3JD, UK

Kai Jiang and Nenghai Yu
MOE-Microsoft Key Laboratory of Multimedia Computing and Communication, University of Science and Technology of China, Anhui, Hefei 230027, China

Like Liu and Rong Xiao
Microsoft Research Asia, Tower 2, No. 5 Dan Ling Street, Haidian District, Beijing 100080, China

Printed in the USA
CPSIA information can be obtained
at www.ICGtesting.com
JSHW051443221024
72173JS00006B/1561

9 781632 401298